Institutions and
Social Mobilization

Institutions and Social Mobilization

The Chinese Education Movement
in Malaysia, 1951-2011

ANG MING CHEE

ISEAS

INSTITUTE OF SOUTHEAST ASIAN STUDIES
Singapore

First published in Singapore in 2014 by
ISEAS Publishing
Institute of Southeast Asian Studies
30 Heng Mui Keng Terrace, Pasir Panjang
Singapore 119614

E-mail: publish@iseas.edu.sg • Website: bookshop.iseas.edu.sg

ISEAS Library Cataloguing-in-Publication Data

Ang, Ming Chee.
    Institutions and social mobilization : the Chinese education movement in Malaysia, 1951–2011
    1. Malaixiya Hua xiao dong shi lian he hui zong hui.
    2. Malaixiya Hua xiao jiao shi hui zong hui.
    3. Chinese language—Government policy—Malaysia.
    4. Schools, Chinese—Government policy—Malaysia.
    5. Chinese—Education—Government policy—Malaysia.
    6. Social movements—Malaysia.
    7. Associations, institutions, etc.—Political aspects—Malaysia.
    I. Title.
    II. Title: Chinese education movement in Malaysia, 1951–2011.
LC201.7 M3A58   2014

ISBN 978-981-4459-98-3 (soft cover)
ISBN 978-981-4459-99-0 (E-book PDF)

Cover photo: The foundation stone that symbolizes the Chinese education movement is located at the movement headquarters in Kajang, Selangor. Photo taken by Ang Ming Chee.

Typeset by International Typesetters Pte Ltd
Printed in Singapore by Markono Print Media Pte Ltd

For papa and mama

CONTENTS

LIST OF TABLES, FIGURES, AND MAPS

Tables

Figures

ACKNOWLEDGEMENTS

This doctoral dissertation-turn-monograph project would not have been possible without the help of a lot of people. My utmost gratitude goes first to my doctoral supervisor, Jamie Seth Davidson, for his enduring support, which has helped me overcome many challenges during my candidacy. I also thank my thesis committee members, Hussin Mutalib, and Goh Beng Lan, as well as my examiner, Maznah Mohamad, for their valuable feedback.

Special appreciation goes to all interviewees and resource persons, many whom are not named in this book, but have selflessly shared their valuable opinions and experiences with me. I would like to credit the following institutions for their support: the National University of Singapore for providing most of the financial resources for my fieldwork in Malaysia; *Dongzong, Jiaozong*, Centre for Malaysian Chinese Studies, Lim Lian Geok Foundation Centre, *Kwangwahyitpoh, Sinchew Daily*, Penang Heritage Trust, National Library of Singapore, National Library of Malaysia, National Library of Taiwan, Universiti Sains Malaysia, and Penang Institute for allowing me to access their valuable collections; the National Chengchi University (Taiwan) and Lund University (Sweden) for hosting me while I was working on this book.

The revision process of the manuscript has been very challenging due to my limited language proficiency and lack of access to resources that are located in Malaysia. Therefore, I am hugely indebted to the endless efforts of Tey Li Li for proofreading and improving the manuscript's drafts, and Teo Sue Ann for her assistance in acquiring the much needed facts and resources. There are many individuals, who have not been named, but have helped me over the past seven years in completing this research. I thank them all.

Last but not least, I owe my achievements today to my beloved family: my parents and siblings in particular, who have been supportive and understanding during my long absence all these years. Their love has been the source of my motivation to continue pursuing my dreams and to be a better person.

Ming Chee
Lund, Sweden
28 February 2014

ABBREVIATION

BN	National Front coalition (*Barisan Nasional*)
DAP	Democratic Action Party
Dongjiaozong	Alliance of *Dongzong* and *Jiaozong* (董教总)
Dongzong	United Chinese School Committees' Association of Malaysia (马来西亚华校董事联合会总会)
Gerakan	Malaysian People's Movement Party (*Parti Gerakan Rakyat Malaysia*)
Jiaozong	United Chinese Schoolteachers' Association of Malaysia (马来西亚华校教师会总会)
MCA	Malaysian Chinese Association (马来西亚华人公会)
MCP	Malayan Communist Party
MPAJA	Malayan People's Anti-Japanese Army
NGO	Non-Governmental Organization
PAS	Pan-Malaysian Islamic Party (*Parti Islam Semalaysia*)
PR	People's Alliance (*Pakatan Rakyat*)
Suqiu Committee	Malaysian Chinese Organisations' Election Appeals Committee
UMNO	United Malays National Organisation (*Pertubuhan Kebangsaan Melayu Bersatu*)

1

INSTITUTIONS AND SOCIAL MOBILIZATION

The Chinese education movement in Malaysia is arguably one of the oldest nationwide social movements in Asia. It has ceaselessly engaged in non-violent contentious politics against a non-liberal democratic regime since 1951. Against all odds, the Chinese education movement has been able to overcome many on-going and changing constraints to persist in pursuing its agenda. This book seeks to answer the many puzzling questions that have led to its persistency and possibilities.

Over the years, the state has sought to constrain the Chinese education movement, its organizations, and its supporters through a range of restrictive regulations and discriminatory policies. Unlike liberal democratic regimes, the state in Malaysia has been dominated by a powerful executive branch, especially so during Mahathir Mohamad's tenure as the longest serving prime minister of the country (1981–2003). A weak system of checks and balances has enabled the National Front coalition (*Barisan Nasional*, BN) ruling regime, led by the United Malays National Organisation (*Pertubuhan Kebangsaan Melayu Bersatu*, UMNO), to weaken the rule of law, restrict media freedom, manipulate law enforcement, and exploit the distribution of state resources to political ends, amongst others.

The lack of recourse to democratic institutions, coupled with the imposition of state-directed restrictions, has yet to bring the Chinese education movement to its knees, however. Instead, this movement has adroitly adapted and established clientelistic relationships with ethnic

Chinese politicians within the ruling regime in exchange for benefits for the movement. While other social movements in Malaysia — such as the trade union movements or the Islamic movements — have either faded or been crushed, this tactic by the Chinese education movement has prevented it from facing a similar fate.[1] In return, politicians — mostly those associated with the Malaysian Chinese Association (马来西亚华人公会, MCA) or the Malaysian People's Movement Party (*Parti Gerakan Rakyat Malaysia*, Gerakan) — make opportunistic use of the collaboration to achieve political gains by acting as brokers between the ruling regime and the Chinese education movement.

Notably, the broader social movement literature — largely predicated on the experiences of stable, industrialized Western democratic states — has not paid sufficient attention to the survival of oppositional social movements in repressive states. Concomitantly, the literature has emphasized the important role of structural institutions, namely, resources, political opportunities, and identities. Problems and tensions arise, however, when these concepts are applied indiscriminately across cultures and state systems. The nature and practice of institutions within single-party-dominated or non-liberal democratic states (commonly found in developing countries) have a different, yet significant impact on the understanding of social movements. The frequent emergence of social movements as vehicles for channelling social — and sometimes political — grievances in non-liberal democratic states points to the urgent need to develop a better understanding of such phenomena empirically and theoretically.

This book argues that structural institutions within non-liberal democratic states are, in various degrees, significantly influenced by informal relationships — that is, those built on interpersonal networks and trust. Such informal relationships seem to have similar, if not greater, effects on state-social movement interactions than official and structural relations do. In other words, social movements in non-liberal democratic states develop parallel, at times overlapping, formal, and informal institutions to prolong their existence and increase their opportunities to effect change.

This chapter first surveys the background of the case study, proposes the research questions and makes four explanatory propositions. It then examines the mainstream social movement literature, identifies its gaps, and traces the rise of social movement studies in non-liberal democratic contexts. The theoretical framework correlates three main perspectives on the role of extra-institutional variables in the execution of structural institutions: (1) the intra-movement perspective focuses on the roles of social movement organizations and movement leaders in mobilizing movement activities within non-liberal democratic states, (2) the movement-state perspective concerns the dynamic interaction and the movement's actors through various movement repertoires, and (3) the inter-movement perspective explores the role of interpersonal bonds in forging and strengthening networks and alliances. Subsequently, this chapter presents the study's significance in the context of Malaysia's pluralistic society and non-liberal democracy. An elaboration of the research methodology, limitations of the research, and a general roadmap of the book concludes this introduction.

THE CHINESE EDUCATION MOVEMENT

As early as 1920, leading Chinese community leaders in the Straits Settlements of Penang and Malacca protested against the British colonial administration's efforts to exert order over Chinese vernacular schools in Malaya through the 1920 Registration of Schools Ordinance.[2] Loosely structured and lacking the capacity to respond uniformly to changing developments, pre-World War II resistance was confined to towns and districts. Although activists enjoyed the support of the local Chinese population, in particular the Chinese-speaking community, most attempts to oppose colonial policies ended poorly.[3] The British simply expelled these agitators. Not until after World War II did the movement coalesce into an organization-led entity.

The Chinese education movement formally began in 1951, led by a group of Chinese schoolteachers who precipitated a sense of crisis in the local Chinese society after the release of the *Report of the Committee on Malay Education* (Barnes Report). This report recommended all vernacular schools to be abolished and replaced by a single system of teaching primary schools using only English and Malay as mediums of instruction. The early years of the movement witnessed collaboration amongst three major Chinese associations of the time: The United Chinese Schoolteachers' Association of Malaysia (马来西亚华校教师会总会, *Jiaozong*), the United Chinese School Committees' Association of Malaysia (马来西亚华校董事联合会总会, *Dongzong*), and MCA.

They were drawn together under the framework of the Grand Three Associations of Chinese Education (三大机构华文教育中央委员会, Grand Three) and sought to defend the status of Chinese education during Malaya's rocky and uncertain transition from a colony to a new nation state.

However, the collaboration of the Grand Three began to break apart in 1960 when MCA President Lim Chong Eu (林苍佑) and his supporters — many of them sympathizers of Chinese education movements — left MCA over disagreements with the then Prime Minister Abdul Rahman (1957–70). When the new leadership of MCA dropped its uncritical support for the Chinese education movement, it marked a historical turning point for the movement, where *Dongzong* and *Jiaozong* began their long journey of resistance as *Dongjiaozong* (董教总).

The Chinese education movement has fluctuated along with the political developments in Malaysia. In 1965, the Chinese population in Malaysia suffered a dramatic drop from 42 per cent in 1963 to 25 per cent after Singapore departed from the Federation of Malaysia, putting the Chinese in the new state of Malaysia at a political disadvantage (Ongkili 1985, p. 154). Many Chinese communities began to relate the right to operate Chinese schools in a "Chinese way" to the preservation of their culture and to the security of their ethnic identity amid heavy-handed nation-building policies and Islamization by the ruling regime. It was during this time that *Dongjiaozong* made a name for itself nationally through its unsuccessful efforts to establish Malaysia's first independent Chinese university, Merdeka University (独立大学).

Today, outside of China and Taiwan, only Malaysia has a complete Chinese education system, and it is the only country in Southeast Asia that has managed to perpetuate the Chinese education system established during the colonial era. The Chinese education movement led by *Dongjiaozong* remains a legitimate organization in the eyes of the Chinese-speaking community in Malaysia. *Dongjiaozong* regularly conducts activities such as seminars, donation campaigns, and press conferences, and submits memorandums to the authorities to put forth the movement's demands. In the face of a repressive state, the movement has refrained from organizing extra-constitutional or violent-oriented activities to avoid confrontations with the state.

The movement manoeuvres within the country's limited democratic space to mobilize and maintain resistance through the networks of Chinese school communities at the local, state, and national levels. Thus far, it has continued to exercise its influence from within and beyond the state to promote the status of Chinese language and Chinese education in state policymaking. To develop a better understanding of the conditions that have induced the processes and persistence of such a movement, this book brings a social movement perspective into the analysis to illuminate the historical and cultural experiences of the struggles of the Chinese education movement beyond the mainstream, Western-centric social movement literature.

RESEARCH QUESTIONS AND PROPOSITIONS

The principal question this book seeks to answer is: How does a minority social movement persist in pushing its agenda despite facing on-going constraints imposed by a non-liberal democratic state?

The secondary questions of this book include:

(a) What are the factors that have motivated the movement's activists (and general supporters), and how have these factors changed over time?
(b) How do social movement organizations sustain a prolonged social movement?
(c) How have the interactions between the challengers and state authorities influenced the movement's trajectory, and how have these interactions changed over time?
(d) How has Malaysia, a non-liberal democratic state, constrained the movement? Why has the state yet to terminate the movement? Has it chosen not to do so, or have there been constraints placed on its repressive capacities?

To come to grips with these questions, the author suggests the following four propositions:

Proposition 1

Continuous threats and attempts by state authorities to dilute the identity of the ethnic minority have shaped a culture of resistance that has become a key source of motivation for the social movement.

Threats by the Malay-dominated regime to dilute the identity of the minority Chinese and to assimilate them into the Malay-dominated society have ironically created a powerful desire amongst the Chinese to preserve their cultural distinctiveness as a last-ditch effort to avoid being marginalized by the state (Means 1991). This desire is manifested as a culture of resistance against the state through the Chinese education movement (Anderson, B. 1991; and Scott 1976, p. 33). This study argues that the volume of threats of assimilation from the regime is positively related to the collective support received by the movement from the Chinese community. The threats have unwittingly helped to promote unity, strengthen solidarity, and overcome movement supporters' differences in dialect, political preference, social status, and economic class.[4]

Proposition 2

The combination of Western-style bureaucratization with a distinct Chinese characteristic has produced a hybrid social movement organization that acts as a sustainable platform to attend to the managerial and mobilization needs of the movement.

The Chinese education movement has managed to develop adequate strength to survive Malaysia's political hothouse by running a social movement organization that is formulated around loosely defined rules under its powerful leaders. The Constitution and regulated procedural system of the movement have transformed the traditional management operating style into a more result-oriented and responsive one. A bottom-up leader selection system has empowered and strengthened the traditional role of movement leaders who are vested with formal legitimacy to represent the movement in its interactions with the state. The social movement organization recruits individuals with a multitude of professional capabilities as full-time and salaried staff to maintain and execute the movement's activities, thus overcoming the free rider problems that commonly arise from the large and extensive grassroots support base of the movement.

Proposition 3

Movement activists sustain interactions with the non-liberal democratic state through interpersonal bonds, which have proven to be a more effective platform than structural institutions.

Structural institutions within non-liberal democracy are imposed in varied degrees according to the interpersonal relationship between the power-executer and power-receiver. Lacking a stable channel for collective bargaining, movement activists rely on interpersonal bonds and offstage influences to deliver their demands and interact with the state. The significance of relational institutions is, however, inversely related to the effectiveness of democratic institutions. Notably, over the course of its development, the Chinese education movement has grown increasingly dependent on both structural and relational institutions, although the latter tend to dominate.

Proposition 4

Malaysia's non-liberal democratic system has provided a limited but significant channel for political competition, which, in turn, has opened up opportunities for negotiation and thereby limited violent expression by state authorities and social movement activists alike.

Non-liberal democratic regimes may infuse state bureaucracy, mediate patronage, dispense clientelistic benefits and avail partial democratic procedures by limiting but not extinguishing civil liberties, and distorting but not excessively manipulating electoral procedures (Milne and Mauzy 1999, pp. 180–81; and Zakaria 1989). Therefore, although political contenders hardly have room to manoeuvre or curb politicking, and such electoral processes are often symbolically rather than politically significant, the voters' choice in selecting its government via elections remains an important political institution in non-liberal democratic states (Case 2004). States with a lower quality of democracy will need to acquire legitimacy by winning elections and therefore tend to utilize carrot-and-stick strategies — that is, compromise and collaboration versus pressure and threats — to win support from citizens. It is within this tightly contended political environment that social movement actors may manoeuvre by striking deals with politicians. For example, by providing necessary support to the ruling regime during elections, the Chinese education movement has been rewarded with favourable responses from the regime.

RESOURCES, OPPORTUNITIES, AND IDENTITIES

Contemporary social movement studies have their origins in the collective behavioural literature of the 1940s and 1950s that examined riots, crowds, and mass hysteria. These works considered the participants of these activities as irrational, dysfunctional, and abhorrent aberrations in the functioning of a modern social system.[5] In contrast to these studies that stressed the integration and equilibrium inherent in social systems, contemporary social movement studies pointed to conflicts and struggles as focal points of social systems.

Social movements are a series of sustained interactions and collective actions, contentious performances, displays, and campaigns by ordinary people outside established political institutions (Tarrow 1994; Thomas 2001; and Tilly 2004). These people share collective claims, common purposes, and solidarity to challenge authorities in order to change elements of the socioeconomic and political structure, or to change the distribution and exercise of power in society. Such collective actions are culturally oriented, socially conflictual, and based on the networks or movement areas of these individuals (Melucci 1985, pp. 793–99; and Touraine 1988, p. 68).

Social movements differ from political parties and interest groups. Political parties nominate candidates in elections and aim to win formal control of the state in order to implement its programmes, whereas interest groups and social movements do not principally engage in these activities. Social movements and interest groups overlap in terms of having the flexibility of being formally or informally organized to influence public policy in their areas of concern; some social movements may transform into interest groups when the need arises (Key 1964, pp. 9–10, 155; Thomas 2001, p. 5; and Truman 1951, pp. 33, 135–36). However, social movements cover broader issues, consist of heterogeneous membership, pursue transformational goals, engage in contentious interactions with the state, and have less access to political institutions than interest groups customarily do (Bashevkin 1996, pp. 134–59; Heinz et al. 1993; Kitschelt 2003; Smith, J. 2008, p. 109; and Walker 1991). Social movements, interest groups, and the state continuously and ineluctably influence each other. Movements influence state actors by setting agendas and suggesting new political strategies. The state, in return, influences movements by proactively employing overt, and occasionally covert, repression measures, as well as setting the rules for counter-movement activities (Goldstone 2003, p. 24).

Given that social movements involve collective behaviours and actions, how or why rational individuals act collectively in a sustained manner has puzzled scholars for a long time. Despite evident diversity in their processes and outcomes, social movements share commonalities and principles that make comparative research and generalizations possible (Coy 1978; Davis et al. 2005; della Porta and Caiani 2009; Edelman 2001; Escobar and Alvarez 1992; Klandermans 1993; Klandermans, Kriesi, and Tarrow 1988; Veltmeyer 2004; Zirakzadeh 1997; and Zurcher and Curtis 1973). Resistance entails costs and usually requires such stimuli as grievances and deprivation, although such stimuli do not axiomatically translate into movement activity (Zald 1992). Quite famously, Mancur Olson argued that "unless the number of individuals in a group is quite small, or unless there is coercion or some other special device to make individuals act in their common interest, rational, self-interested individuals will not act to achieve their common or group interests" (Olson 1965, p. 2). These free rider problems are especially common in large social movement groups.

Certain scholars have begun to recognize and emphasize the importance of resource mobilization in solving the problem of free riders and achieving movement success (Gamson 1975; Jenkins and Perrow 1977; Lipsky 1968; McCarthy, Smith, and Zald 1973; Snyder and Tilly 1972; Tilly 1978; and Wilson 1973, p. 131). Any given society possesses external resources (money, time, media, facilities, and material), as well as internal resources (members' capacity, commitments, and moral support), that can be put to use by movement leaders to coordinate, organize, mobilize, and ultimately, agitate (McCarthy and Zald 1977; Oliver and Marwell 1992; Olson 1965; and Tilly 1978). Mobilization is facilitated by the internal organization and structure of the collective, known as a social movement organization (Oberschall 1993, p. 56).

John McCarthy and Mayer Zald, two leading scholars in the resource mobilization school, placed special emphasis on the role of professional social movement organizations in solving collective action problems (McCarthy and Zald 1977). They defined a social movement organization as "a complex, or formal organization that identifies its goals with the preferences of a social movement or a counter-movement and attempts to implement these goals" (McCarthy and Zald 1977, p. 1217). Social movement activities may be organized by one or more social movement organizations. In some cases, the social movement organizations themselves constitute the movement; in others, the movement has no social movement organization. Nevertheless, the resource mobilization school tends to overstate the importance of external resources without explaining where and how these resources can be generated. It also fails to explain why social movements have not appeared in all countries where there are grievances and sufficient resources to mobilize people to act on their grievances.

The political opportunities school arose in response to the limitations of the resource mobilization approach. A principal proponent of this perspective, Doug McAdam, argued that political opportunities, a heightened sense of political efficacy, and the development of institutions, played a central role in shaping the civil rights movement in the United States, for example (McAdam 1982). The political process model places great emphasis on the structural constraints and opportunities that social movements face. These include political pluralism, internal fragmentation within political systems, receptivity of political systems to organized protests, as well as support and facilitation of political elites. McAdam asserted that the emergence of social movements was determined by expanding opportunities, indigenous organizational strength of the population, and cognitive liberation. The success of mobilization or politicization hinges on the opportunities afforded by the group in question (McAdam, Tarrow, and Tilly 1997; 2001). The opportunities present themselves when there is a shift in the institutional structure or the ideological disposition of those in power. Although this approach has been successful in justifying the growth and development of social movements based on grievances, material needs, and accumulation of resources, it cannot adequately explain how social movements based on ideas and grievances related to ways of life could arise.

The European-focused social movement literature sought to tackle this problem. These scholars argued that advanced industrialization had created structural possibilities for conflicts, especially with the widening of access to higher education and the en masse entry of women into the labour market (della Porta and Diani 1999). Individuals opposed the state's and market's intrusion into their social life and asserted their rights to determine their private identities and affective lives (Melucci 1980; 1985; 1989; 1996). These new social movements, such as preservation of the environment, human rights, as well as gay and lesbian rights, foregrounded quality of life issues (Offe 1985). The new social movement paradigm places importance on the actors and their abilities to capture the innovative characteristics of movements. The formation and creation of personal, collective, and public identities were defined by Alberto Melucci as "an interactive and shared definition produced by several interacting individuals who are concerned with the orientations of their actions, as well as the field of opportunities and constraints in which their actions take place" (Melucci 1989, p. 34).

This definition is supplemented by Joseph Gusfield, who saw that the members of the group "agreed upon definition of boundaries" and provided the basis that enabled shared beliefs, thus making collective action possible (Gusfield 1994, p. 15). This literature associated the formation and mobilization of movements based on the individualized, middle-class lifestyles and the diversity of social identity in post-industrial societies, especially in Western Europe. It went beyond the resource mobilization and political process schools that emphasized the availability of resources and political opportunities as key factors in giving rise to social movements. However, these three research agendas have been largely developed in the context of industrialized North American and Western European states with stable democratic regimes. The limitations of these camps are thrown into stark relief when their concepts and arguments are indiscriminately applied across cultures and state systems (Adams 2002, pp. 24–26; and Escobar and Alvarez 1992, pp. 317–19).

Social Movements in Non-Liberal Democratic States

Liberal regimes are able to perform because they are based on highly institutionalized rules and democratic procedures such as constitutions, elections, and courts that structure social interactions by constraining or enabling actors' behaviours (Campbell 2004, p. 1; Carey 2000, p. 735; Hodgson 2004, p. 424; Knight 1992, p. 2; and North 1990, pp. 1–4). Institutions within liberal democratic states invite comparison and evaluation, with emphasis on the reproduction and stability of social order. Nonetheless, societies' access to institutions varies according to local legal settings, institutional hierarchies, cultural orientations, and type of regimes (Scheingold 2004). Non-liberal democratic regimes, for example, tend to control institutional access tightly to strengthen their capacity in achieving economic, political, or social goals. Institutions are frequently arranged according to the styles and preferences of the power-holders, who consist of heterogeneous agents, each with divergent interests (DiMaggio and Powell 1983; Evans 1989; March and Olsen 1984; and Skocpol 1979; 1985, p. 9).

Non-liberal democratic states, either of the military or civilian type, do differ in the degree of legal and institutional legitimacy. Today, save for North Korea, most non-liberal democracies range from semi-democracies (those with mixed or hybrid characteristics) to those deemed more authoritarian (Helmke and Levitsky 2006, pp. 1–2; Jopple 1995, p. x; and Marsh 2006, p. 1). At the illiberal end, authoritarian regimes rule without accountability, enabling abusive state actors to enjoy absolute impunity (Linz 1975, p. 264; and Mainwaring 2003). According to Francisco Panizza, instrumental authoritarian regimes may be democratically elected but the regimes would not hesitate to defer democracy temporarily through coercive military rule during political turmoil, such as brutal repression of open demonstrations (Panizza 1995, p. 183). These regimes do not tolerate social activism, and tend to quell contention through hefty penalties.

Hybrid regimes can be both authoritative and competitive. Hybrid regimes have been categorized by scholars according to the proportion of authoritarian and democratic features (Levitsky and Way 2002). For starters, Andreas Schedler separated electoral democracies from electoral authoritarianism, with the former having free and fair elections that comply with minimal democratic norms, while such criteria are absent for the latter (Schedler 2002). Within electoral authoritarianism regimes, Larry Diamond distinguishes competitive authoritarian regimes from hegemonic electoral authoritarian regimes (Diamond 1999). The former are instituted via multi-party electoral competition and a significant parliamentary opposition, while these challenges and processes are politically closed in the latter (Diamond 2002; Levitsky and Way 2002; and Schedler 2002, pp. 37–38). There are also repressive yet responsive semi-democratic regimes, which respond to pressure and demands from society, but do so through co-optation, neutralization, and suppression to control social conflict (Crouch 1996, pp. 236–47).

Most hybrid regimes consist of some features of formal democratic institutions with tightly-contained liberalism, resulting in little real competition for power. Usually, hybrid regimes are controlled by a small number of individuals, rather than democratic institutions, and the rule of law (Ottaway 2003, pp. 4–5). Such manipulation of power sees some hybrid regimes intervene aggressively in the economy through skewed state policies, and use performance legitimacy to substitute procedural legitimacy. These hybrid regimes tend to manipulate state resources to establish political patronage with their supporters, or frequently abuse the law, resulting in poor representation of citizens' interests and low public confidence in state institutions (Diamond 1999; Forsyth 2001; Foweraker 1995, p. 2; Goodwin, Jasper, and Khattra 1999; Jones 1997; and Laothamatas 1997, p. 12).

Although such constraints have systematically weakened civil societies, avenues of social mobilization remain possible within these regimes as long as doing so does not challenge the state's political legitimacy (Case 1992; Gomez 1994; and Khoo 1997, p. 72). The emergence of an increasing number of hybrid states after the Cold War yielded a better understanding of the patterns and effects of these states on political systems, and of the influence of the domestic political environment on social movements (Armony and Schamis 2005; Carothers 2002, pp. 5–6; Diamond 2002; and Levitsky and Way 2002, pp. 51–52). Although political inequality is acutely felt by social movement actors in varied degrees, the need to fulfil one's internal motivations (such as self-expectations and conceptions, personal interests and political ideology) and external legitimacy (such as political structure and potential opposition) are elements that constrain the ability of institutions to achieve meaningful social change, making comparative analysis across states possible (Scheingold 2004).

Such a perspective was explored by Vincent Boudreau, who argued that the modes of people's resistance are shaped by the types, patterns, and degrees of repressive strategies imposed by authoritarian states (Boudreau 2004). Political opportunities — in particular, political openness — increase protests and anti-dictatorship pressure from democratization movements. Moreover, centralized and mediated movement organizational resources (such as formation of alliances) increase the capacity of resistance activities that may lead to successful contention against an authoritarian regime. Boudreau's study also demonstrated the state's ability to adapt its strategies in response to different patterns of contention, which may range from moderate to radical challenges.

Boudreau covered three different democracy movements in Southeast Asia. He showed how Ne Win's regime in Burma survived various challenges. The regime's intolerance of protest, its use of extreme means to weaken the oppositions' organizational capacities — which, amongst others, prevented alliances from forming amongst protest groups — resulted in a weak opposition that was easily crushed. In the Philippines, Boudreau highlighted how the coalition between politicians and the communist front survived initial repression and re-emerged as a strong

oppositional alliance; the latter played a key role in the toppling of
the Marcos regime. The uprising to bring down Soeharto's regime in
Indonesia was delayed until after the Asian financial crisis in the late
1990s, which formed the ripe moment that enabled a breakthrough in
collaboration amongst opposition groups.

Although social movements within non-liberal democratic states may
lack the capacity to effectively impose checks and balances on the state,
their appearances (and subsequent protests) place pressure on the state and
form the basis for political pluralism and structural change. Boudreau's
argument was illustrated by He Baogang using the 1989 democratic
movement in China (He 1996). Although the demonstrations at
Tiananmen Square (天安门广场) in 1989 were brutally crushed by the
communist regime, it had a positive impact on the subsequent liberalization
process in China. Pressure to bolster the Chinese Communist Party's
waning political legitimacy saw the party's political elites begin to adjust
their conceptions of legitimacy, implement economic reforms, and allow
the existence of populist and liberal notions of democracy proposed by the
democratic camp from within the party.

Similarly, Benedict Kerkvliet studied the seemingly unorganized
and non-confrontational manner in which Vietnamese peasants engaged
in undermining the system of collective farming dictated by the state
(Kerkvliet 2005). Consequently, the peasants forced the state into
replacing collective farming with peasant family farming in the 1980s. As
Kerkvliet convincingly argued, the character and power of "everyday
politics" had significant political implications to Vietnam's state policies.
Although the strong state had prevented the establishment of a broad
peasant social movement organization to conduct open protests, these
individualized forms of passive resistance successfully paralyzed the state's
farming policy. The centrality of peasants as a source of labour power
and its significance as the foundation of political support and national
unification prevented the authorities from using coercive methods to crush
peasant movements.

Somchai Phatharathananunth explored the struggles of small-scale
farmers' assembly of Isaan, a major grassroots movement comprising
farmers from the Northeastern region of Thailand, in their campaign to
protect the rights of the rural poor to participate in meaningful
democratization process since 1993 (Phatharathananunth 2006). The
movement provided a political channel for peasants who had been
marginalized in the Bangkok-based, elite-controlled electoral politics. The

state, in return, tried to control the increasingly powerful movement by co-opting key movement leaders and marginalizing the radical faction of the movement.

The differences in political ideology, experience of colonization, economic development, and social structure all have direct and powerful implications on the development and trajectories of social movements. Therefore, the analysis of social movements in non-liberal democratic states needs to pay special heed to cultural and historical contexts (Anderson, L. 1986; Callaghy 1988; Migdal 1988; Shevtsova and Eckert 2001, pp. 65–67; and Smith, A. 1986). This is what mainstream social movement literature — with its focus on structural conditions such as the availability of resources, political processes and opportunities, and the construction of identity — tends to lack. Moreover, power relationships between challengers and authorities are in a state of flux (and even more so in non-liberal than in liberal democratic states), ironically limiting the availability of opportunities on which social movements could capitalize. In light of this, activists rely less on formal institutions and more on unconventional methods to disseminate movement messages, mobilize support, and engage in contentious action.

In the social movement literature, the understanding of extra-institutional variables has been clumsily lumped into the categories of framing without much systematic analysis (Goodwin, Jasper, and Khattra 1999; McAdam, McCarthy, and Zald 1996; and McAdam, Tarrow, and Tilly 1997). Framing is a vital strategy for many movement activists in advanced Western states to instil a sense of injustice, shape collective identities, attract mass media coverage, garner bystanders' support, and demobilize antagonists (Benford 1993; Hunt and Benford 1994; McAdam 1996, pp. 340–41; Snow et al. 1986; Snow and Benford 1988, p. 198; 1992, p. 137; and Steinberg 1999, p. 737). The significance of framing and the distribution of its products (such as speeches, images, and writings) have different effects in the non-liberal democratic world. Limited access to media, higher risk of state suppression and a fragmented society divided along linguistic, ethnic, religious, and cultural lines make it distinctly challenging to create and sustain a universal frame that is equally appealing to all. Instead, cognitive understanding, community influences, moral missions, kinship links, and emotional attachments tend to matter more in the process of social mobilization in non-liberal democratic states. Therefore, it is necessary to take into consideration the humane, organic, dynamic, and interpersonal bonds in the execution of structural institutions. As will be discussed in the following section, the analysis of this book will be conducted at three levels: dynamics within the movement (intra-movement relations), dynamics between the movement and the state (movement and state relations), and dynamics between the movement and other movements (inter-movements relations).

Intra-Movement Relations

While studies on social movements focus on the logic of collective action, studies on social movement organizations expressly address the elements of agencies and institutions that harness collective action. Institutional elements such as regulations, strength of the organization, and financial and human resources set the criteria for defining a social movement organization. Social movement organizations are particularly important for reducing uncertainty through centralization of power, enhancing organizational effectiveness through collective decision-making procedures, mobilizing the grassroots to overcome external obstacles and constraints, as well as legitimatizing the selection of leaders to govern and consolidate the needs of social movements (Alberoni 1984, p. 171; Lounsbury and Kaghan 2001, pp. 25–51; North 1990, pp. 6, 37; and Oberschall 1993, p. 28).

Most social movement organizations are loosely organized, especially in the early phases, with institutionalization normally taking place following the height of mobilization (Kriesi, Koopmans, and Duyvendak 1995; and McCarthy and Zald 1977). Within many non-liberal democratic states, the execution of these institutions and the delivery of their functions are shaped and reshaped by temporal processes and political struggles. Unlike in liberal democratic states, social movement organizations in non-liberal democratic systems face higher risks of coercive suppression and encounter more constraints in terms of accessing resources and mobilizing support from the community. Such limitations force social movement organizations to adapt themselves frequently throughout their lifespan in response to pressures imposed on them.

The extent and sophistication of social movement organizations may vary throughout the process of achieving their objectives, but characteristically, there are divisions of labour and bureaucratic structures in social movement organizations. Formalization sees social movement organizations mature in terms of expansion in size and professionalization of staff. Appointed personnel serve as committee members while administrative officers are hired to fill a hierarchy of positions, each defined by a specific scope of authority and responsibilities (Wilson 1973, pp. 8, 164). Social movement organizations may also establish parallel institutions to confront and engage with state institutions more directly. For instance, movement leaders may deal with cabinet ministers, social movement organizations officers with various federal departmental officers, and state-level committees with state-level government officers, and so on (Oberschall 1993, p. 31).

As will be shown in Chapter 4, the social movement organizations that have sprouted from the Chinese education movement have also followed the path of increasing professionalization, and doing so with strong local influences, such as congregating school professionals to form a hierarchical bureaucracy and structure for the working committee to enable the constant flow of sustainable resources to the movement. Moreover, in a persistent yet amorphous existence straddling between loosely defined assemblies and institutionalized organizations, the movement has enabled democratically elected leaders with centralized authority to respond promptly and effectively to the rapidly changing landscape of contentious politics.

Once a social movement has transformed from a state of resistance into a state of persistence, goal transformation occurs as leaders begin to replace unattainable goals with those that are more pragmatic and relevant so that the movement can be sustained (Huntington 1968; Powell and DiMaggio 1991, pp. 381–99; and Thelen 1999; 2004, pp. 25–31). These changes allow social movements to endure, especially when opportunities for influence are minimal; however, they may also alienate supporters and draw normative commitment away from members (Andrews 2002, p. 108; and McAdam 1982, pp. 55–56). Because the decisions for such transformations and changes are made based on the movement leader's judgement, little justification or opportunities for bottom-up participation are provided. Such top-down, authoritative management styles can mimic the regimes that constrain the movement in the first place, and the movement depends on the capacity of good leaders to successfully execute such relational mechanisms.

What makes a capable leader is profusely subjective, and these individuals are rare. As will be examined in Chapter 5, the Chinese education movement suffered internal tensions at various occasions. Movement activists and supporters are divided in camps according to their preference of movement strategies, which may range from radical resistance to conservative persistence. In the case of the Chinese education movement, internal tensions became more complicated when each camp was supported by movement administrative officers who succeeded in the oligarchization of the movement — that is, concentrating power by manipulation of a hierarchical bureaucratic structure for personal desire and benefits (Wilkinson 1971, p. 108). As argued by Mayer Zald and Roberta Ash, the use of adversarial tactics increases with oligarchy (Zald and Ash 1966). An elaboration of the twists and turns of these contentions will contribute significantly to the literature on internal dynamics (and tensions) of social movement organizations, something that has been downplayed by contemporary social movement literature.

Movement and State Relations

Social movements within non-liberal democratic contexts are defined by the interests they represent and the ways such demands are carried out. Repertoires are relational products of contention between challengers and power holders that limit both the strategic choice of performances and the conceptual mapping of possibilities for action (Tilly 1995, p. 42). Charles Tilly argued that since the nineteenth century, repertoires of collective action in advanced Western countries had changed from being local, autonomous, and reactive to national, directed, and proactive due to the rise and formation of full-fledged nation states as dominant political organizations (Tilly 1986; 1995). Yet, such shifts are absent from, or only partially exist, in most non-liberal democratic states that lack experience in the building of democratic institutions. This is usually because these states have inherited these institutions from their colonial masters and often carry the burden of having to deal with a host of other more critical state-building problems, such as an underdeveloped economic sector and a polarized society.

Repertoires can come in the form of highly conventional actions such as lobbying and judicial action, or as passive opposition such as everyday resistance. The latter may better encapsulate the challenger-versus-state authority relations in non-liberal democratic states. Demonstrations may be common in many mature democracies, but their absence or infrequency in non-liberal democratic states cannot be taken as an absence of social movements. The state's control of law enforcement allows little space for manoeuvre or negotiation. Therefore, high intensity social protests, open political opposition, or any extra-constitutional mass groupings often face harsh, coercive repression. Movement leaders who (successfully or not) organize such contentious activities often face imprisonment and follow-up punishment from the regime.

Lacking institutional access and facing repression, resistance often occurs outside the political arena, and exists in a manner that is clandestine, small-scale, and constantly subjected to refrainment. The proliferation of everyday forms of peasant resistance observed by James Scott suggests that informal acts of resistance (such as foot-dragging, dissimulation, pilfering, or sabotage) involve no overt protest and require little or no coordination and organization (Scott 1987). These resistances concern largely immediate, *de facto* gains, and at the same time minimize the risks of any direct confrontation with the authorities. Scott's discourse, however, best applies to a small community with dense informal networks with historically deep subcultures of resistance.

This book proposes that social movement activists engage in active and dynamic collaboration, rather than passive resistance, with non-liberal democratic state regimes through brokers. Facing a regime that relies on interpersonal networks rather than on structured institutions has galvanized movement activists to seek informal yet potentially more promising channels such as brokerage to achieve their demands (Fukuyama 1995, pp. 7–9). Brokerage is a process in which intermediary actors facilitate transactions between other actors lacking access to or trust in one another. (Marsden 1982). Brokers connect and coordinate communication and interactions, improve access to material and state resources, and increase the success of promulgating changes between the movement and the regime (Foster 1961; North 1990, p. 37; Roy and Sidera 2006, p. 4; and Staggenborg 2002, p. 126). Brokers within a pluralistic society must be equipped with multi-linguistic ability and a good understanding of the sensitivities of traditional cultures. As will be discussed in Chapter 2, bilingual (English- and Chinese-proficient) Chinese politicians have created political advantages for themselves by assisting the inter-movement and state collaboration.

Inter-Movement Relations

The formation of inter-movement networks and alliances is a strategy to reduce competition over resources amongst social movements. Strong institutional bonds based on a shared identity provide opportunities for routine interaction and consequently reduces cleavages, develops trust, and promotes sharing of information and experiences (Bandy and Smith 2005, p. 4; Coleman 1990; Morrill 1995; Olson 1982; and Putnam 2000). Social movements establish both formal coalitions and informal collaboration with other movement organizations at local, national, and international levels, but social movements in non-liberal democratic states tend to rely on inter-leadership collaboration rather than inter-institutional coalition (Meyer and Tarrow 1998, p. 19). For one, not all social movements in such settings can afford to establish a formal organization. Moreover, agent-based alliance is easier to conduct — for instance, an underground meeting — and thus can remain under the regime's radar. Such agent-based networks rely primarily on the leaders' social reputation, professional commonalities, and political connections. Networks and alliances that are based on personal connections can be more reliable and enduring, especially in the face of oppression or co-optation by the state (Chwe 1999, pp. 128–56). A tight cadre of committed allies facilitates rapid and honest sharing of information.

Associational relationship can be dense, such as groups that share many similarities and a common identity, or weak, such as groups divided by ethnic, cultural, and linguistic differences. Sharing the same language, lifestyle, and experience of being exploited by the state and its policies, along with experiences of prior collaboration, helps to enhance collective bonds (Klandermans and Goslinga 1996; and Koopmans 2004, pp. 367–91). Because social movements in polarized societies tend to articulate their aims in terms of racialism or communalism rather than associational activities, opportunities for collaboration within the same ethnic, cultural, or linguistic groups are increased (Jennet and Stewart 1989).

Such prior collaboration is important for forming a strong associational alliance, which was the key to the success of the civil rights movement in the United States in the 1960s where black leaders and the non-black masses with similar religious backgrounds and experiences united for a common cause (McAdam 1982). Such an alliance may survive if members of the alliance can fulfil the components of a strong capital, which range from economic, cultural, and social to political resources (Bourdieu 1986; Diani 1997; and Purdue 2007, p. 224).

The lack of opportunities for collaboration between social movements may also result in a minimal level of trust across movement organizations, and delay the formation of a more unified and stronger alliance that would enhance the ability of the movement to overcome constraints imposed by a repressive state. It is only during times of frustration, such as the failure of intra-ethnic alliances or the co-optation of former allies by the regime, that such inter-movement collaboration may ripe. Operating in the often unpredictable environment of non-liberal democratic regimes, every step forward and every act of resistance is meaningful. By joining forces, allied movements increase their capacity to seize political opportunities and overcome constraints (Andrain and Apter 1995, p. 6; Boudreau 2002, p. 44; and Oberschall 1993, p. 31).

POLITICS AND SOCIAL MOBILIZATION IN MALAYSIA

Malaysia's BN regime, in particular during Mahathir Mohamad's era, has taken a relatively less authoritarian approach compared with its neighbours', such as General Ne Win's military regime in Burma, President Ferdinand Marcos' martial law regime in the Philippines, or Soeharto's New Order in Indonesia. Although Malaysia does claim some form of legitimacy through its domination of democratic institutions, it often waivers between authoritarianism and democracy, with notable variety and debate on the quality of its "brand" of democracy by scholars.[6]

During the 1950s and 1960s, the newly independent Malaya enjoyed a brief moment of democracy, with meaningful separation of power between the executive, legislative, and judiciary branches of government, and liberal political competition at the federal, state, and local elections (Ho, K.L. 1992a; LCHR 1990; Mohamed 1989a; 1989b; and Roger 1989, p. 158). The political arena during this time was dominated by the consociational collaboration between UMNO President Abdul Rahman, MCA President Tan Cheng Lock, and Malaysian Indian Congress President V.T. Sambathan Thevar under the framework of the Alliance coalition. The Alliance won the 1959 and 1961 General Election with a large majority (71 per cent of seats in 1959 and 86 per cent of seats in 1961) (Case 1996, pp. 1–2; Lijphart 1968, pp. 21–23; 1985, p. 6; 2008, p. 49).

Unfortunately, the political domination of Alliance was shaken by the formation of Federation of Malaysia in 1963. The rise of the opposition parties, escalating intra-party disputes within Alliance component parties, and the failure of the Alliance to compromise internally on critical issues (such as the installation of Chinese as an official language, and according

special privileges to ethnic Malays and citizenship rights to immigrants)
dealt a significant political blow to the Alliance. It secured only 42 per
cent of the total votes cast to win 51 per cent of parliamentary seats in
the 1969 General Election (Weiss 2006, pp. 76–80).

As a consequence, Abdul Rahman resigned and made way for
Abdul Razak to become the second prime minister of Malaysia in 1970.
To ensure continuous domination in Malaysia politics, Abdul Razak
broadened the Alliance and incorporated opposition parties, which included
Pan-Malaysian Islamic Party (*Parti Islam Semalaysia*, PAS), Gerakan, and
People's Progressive Party, to form BN.[7] The power of the executive
branch was expanded, which weakened the checks and balances amongst
government institutions, thus enabling BN, the ruling regime, to control
and manipulate state resources to strengthen its political domination.

Not until 1998 with the rise of Malaysia's reform (*reformasi*) movement
did a strong coalition of oppositions emerge to confront the BN ruling
regime. Although this opposition coalition failed to challenge BN's two-
thirds majority in parliament at the 1999 General Election, the formation
of the People's Justice Party (*Parti Keadilan Rakyat*) and the increasing
demands for democratic reforms by Malaysia's middle class laid important
foundations for political change.

After Mahathir Mohamad's retirement in 2003, the political system
gradually liberalized under the stewardship of his handpicked successor,
Prime Minister Abdullah Badawi (2004–08). Abdullah Badawi promised
to reconstitute an independent judiciary and reform the Anti-Corruption
Agency to counter the degenerative corrupt practices within UMNO
and across civil service agencies (Case 2005, p. 145). These promises
convinced Malaysian voters to support Abdullah Badawi's administration
and saw BN coalition win a landslide victory in the 2004 General
Election. However, as these political promises remain unfulfilled at
the end of Abdullah Badawi's first term as prime minister, Malaysians
became progressively impatient and disappointed with the administration's
inability to fulfil its campaign promises.

By 2008, for the first time after 1969, the opposition People's Alliance
(*Pakatan Rakyat*, PR) successfully overturned BN's two-thirds majority
in the parliament. It also won control of five state governments at the
country's twelfth General Election (Loh and Khoo 2002). Scholars and
pundits hailed these developments as the dawn of a true democracy,
especially when an increasing number of senior BN politicians admitted
there were deficits in the BN legitimacy that required political reforms

from within (Case 2010, pp. 113–14). While competing to remain as a significant player in the formal political arena, the BN regime also has to deal with demands from various social movements. One of the social movements whose interactions with the Malaysian government have produced significant yet puzzling outcomes is the Chinese education movement.

SOCIAL MOVEMENTS IN MALAYSIA

Social movements in Malaysia can generally be divided into two main types: inclusive and exclusive. The former is concerned with universal issues such as the environment, democratization, and human rights, while the latter is limited to ethnic- and religious-based concerns. Inclusive-based movements have often been studied by movement activists, who may also be academics and researchers at local and international universities, as part of the activities of civil societies or of the democratization process of Malaysia.[8] On the other hand, exclusive-based social movements have largely been under-studied in the English-speaking scholarly world of social movement studies for two main reasons: first, the activists of exclusive-based movements tend to be in professions that are non–research-related, such as schoolteachers and religious teachers. Second, and more importantly, linguistic limitation has restricted the accessibility of research works and resources of these movements, resulting in most of these important developments in a country's history being left undocumented and ignored.

The works on women's rights movements are mostly published by well-established women research centres at local universities in Malaysia and these works have been gaining considerable attention in the country over the years.[9] Amongst the most significant works on women's rights movements is that by Cecilia Ng, Maznah Mohamad, and Tan Beng Hui (Ng, Maznah, and Tan 2006). Ng and her associates studied the market forces that drove the politicization of feminism in Malaysia. They found that urban development and industrialization increased the number of women engaged in higher education and employment, thus strengthening their economic mobility and empowering them politically. Women's newly acquired economic and political positions enabled them to participate in democratization struggles.

The book by Ng and associates also highlighted the restrictions placed upon, and inherent limitations of the women's movement in Malaysia — in particular, conflicting interests within the multi-cultural and multi-religious milieu of the broader society. Like many other enduring movements, leaders of the women's movements have opted to collaborate with, instead of confront, the state, which has enabled prominent feminists to influence state policies from within the government, and thereby avoid incurring the state's wrath. The observations of Ng and her associates are important, for, as will be shown in this study, the Chinese education movement, to some extent, has also followed a similar repertoire.

Another noteworthy work on inclusive-based movements in Malaysia is that by Meredith Weiss and Saliha Hassan (Weiss and Saliha 2003). They provided insights into the sociological and economic circumstances that gave rise to the rapid growth of civil society in Malaysia in the 1980s. Booming in numbers in the 1980s, non-governmental organizations adopted strategies and tactics that ranged from antagonism to cooperation with the state in line with the state's ideology and interests. According to Weiss and Saliha, the state is particularly threatened by, and will react with harsh repression against, three types of movements: those that advocate Islamic fundamentalism, those that challenge the state's political foundation, and those that persist in the form of mass protests.

The Chinese education movement, the subject of this study, has steered clear of these three criteria in the course of its history. Unfortunately, because the contributors of Weiss and Hassan's edited volume are mostly practitioners and active movement entrepreneurs, the chapters, although richly detailed, failed to address wider social movement debates and issues. Moreover, by ignoring the exclusive-based movements, their works as a whole failed to consider a different kind of civil society envisioned by religious- or ethnic-based groups.

In *Protest and Possibilities*, Weiss took her analysis deeper to examine the conditions that prompted the formation of, and the factors that have constrained the sustainability of coalition capital between non-governmental organizations and opposition political parties (Weiss 2006). Illustrative of Weiss' proposition is the pro-Anwar opposition coalition formed to challenge BN's political hegemony in the 1999 General Election. Although the coalition fared poorly, it contributed to the country's democratization. Weiss argued that the gradual expansion of space for civil society activists to develop a non–communal-based movement and the opportunity to interact and cooperate with opposition parties helped to establish the coalitional capital — that is, mutual trust and understanding — necessary for groups to find a common cause and work in coalitions.

Weiss' two studies debated the formation and strengthening of coalitional capital necessary for mobilizing collective action amongst civil society agents. She concluded that the lack of a long-term strategy of resistance in the non-governmental organizations' coalition ultimately handcuffed the 1998 *reformasi* movement. The role of coalitional capital will be further explored in this study through the analysis of the Chinese community's networks and coalitions dating from the colonial era.

Exclusive-based movements on the other hand, as argued by Joshua Fishman using his multi-modal nations model, are predominantly discrete from their cultural, vernacular, lingual, and educational differences (Fishman 1969). Linguistic familiarity brings members of a common linguistic group together in spite of their different social backgrounds and economic classes. Path dependency from Malaysia's unique colonial experience, and inter-cultural compromises made during its nation-building process has shaped the fundamental differences amongst different linguistic groups; these differences are often determined by ethnicity. Scholars of these movements have explored the consequences of social grievances and the politics of collective behaviour, such as the Islamic religious movement, the religious and socio-economical struggles of the Indian minority, and the Chinese education movement.

The literature on the country's religious movements is dominated by Islamic scholars. Since the early 1970s, Arabic- and religious-educated groups such as *Jammat Tabligh* and the *Darul Arqam* have been spreading fundamentalist Islamic ideas at the grassroots (Mohamad 1981). The rise of the highly organized and well-financed Muslim Youth Movement of Malaysia (*Angkatan Belia Islam Malaysia*) led by Anwar Ibrahim in the late 1970s, in particular, captured the attention of scholars who wanted to explore the far-reaching political influence of the organization (Abdul F. 2000; Camroux 1996; Lee, L.M. 1988; and Mauzy and Milne 1983). This Islamic student movement questioned the gradual loss of religiosity and spiritual values amongst Muslim communities (and state actors) in the face of rapid urbanization and Westernization (Chandra 1987; and Shamsul 1994). To appeal for the reconstruction of Malay society, the Muslim Youth Movement of Malaysia formed a powerful coalition with PAS in the late 1970s.[10] However, the rise of the Muslim Youth Movement of Malaysia was quickly subdued after its key leaders (such as Anwar Ibrahim) were co-opted into the BN ruling regime (Kessler 1980;

Lee, L.M. 1990; Lyon 1979; Mauzy and Milne 1983, p. 634; Maznah 2009; and Means 1978).

Norani Othman detailed the strategies adopted by the Sisters-in-Islam movement — comprising largely middle-class professional Muslim women — in negotiating for equal rights in the legal, political, economic, and social arenas for Muslim women (Norani 2005). The Sisters-in-Islam is a civil society group that professes greater religious expressions and demands for greater gender equality in Malaysia's male-dominated Islamic society. Tensions between the movement on the one hand, and the male-dominated PAS (which advocates an Islamic state) and UMNO (which has implemented a series of Islamization programmes since the 1980s within a secular nationalist vision) on the other hand, continue to this day (Wazir 1992).

Studies of the Indian community's movements have predominantly focused on religious or socio-economical perspectives. Andrew Willford studied the contrast between Hindu ecumenical movements and the Tamil identity (Willford 2006); Ravindra K. Jain compiled the sociological and economical challenges faced by Indian plantation workers (Jain 2009); Farish Noor researched the rise of Hindu Rights Action Force — a coalition of thirty Hindu- and Tamil-based non-governmental organizations in 2006 — that generated a new wave of collective action to protect the minority community (Farish 2008). In spite of the diversity of local studies on the Indian community, the quantity of the literature does not do justice to the magnitude of grievances suffered by the Indian community in Malaysia over the years.

Not surprisingly, the bulk of social movement research related to the Chinese community has revolved around the Chinese education movement. These studies will be explored in detail in the following section.

STUDIES ON THE CHINESE EDUCATION MOVEMENT

Studies on the Chinese education movement can be categorized into three types: in-house publications by *Dongjiaozong* and affiliated organizations form the first, and independent authors and academic writers form the second and third types, respectively. *Dongjiaozong* has published prolifically on themes surrounding the various campaigns it conducted. These include its collections on selected issues of the Chinese education movement, historical descriptions of the movement, essays on its movement leader, Lim Lian Geok (林连玉), and others (UCSCAM 2001a; 2003a;

2004*a*, 2004*b*; 2004*c*; Lee, P.K. 2005; and Lew and Loot 1997). Amongst these in-house publications, the works of a prominent historian of Malaysian Chinese, Tay Lian Soo (郑良树), are notable (Tay 1998*a*; 1998*b*; 1998*c*; 1999; 2001; 2003; 2005). He compiled some of the most complete encyclopaedic references on the movement from the perspective of the Chinese community. Employing various vernacular sources such as school magazines and the vernacular presses, Tay's historical studies covered 600 years of the development of Chinese education, with detailed descriptions of the roles played by local actors at the school and community levels. Although Tay's works are largely limited to West Malaysia, they are significant records on the transition of the Chinese education movement from before, during, and after the colonial period.

One of the few in-house publications that examined intra-movement dynamics of the Chinese education movement was *The United Chinese Schoolteachers' Association of Malaysia and Its Activists* (华校教总及其人物) written by Lew Bon Hoi (廖文辉) (Lew 2006). The book surveyed the contributions by *Jiaozong* and movement leaders in the field of education, politics, and culture from 1951 to 2005. The first half of the book revealed the activities conducted by *Jiaozong* in promoting Chinese culture and its involvement in domestic politics. Lew also detailed the relationship between *Jiaozong* and *Dongzong* as partners in the movement. The second half of the book focused on the contributions of former *Jiaozong* leaders. Lew concluded that *Jiaozong* had played a significant role in safeguarding Chinese education in Malaysia, despite having failed to promote and secure benefits for Chinese schoolteachers as suggested in *Jiaozong*'s constitution. However, Lew's analysis overstated *Jiaozong*'s achievements during the 1950s and 1960s, and overlooked the factors that led to its weakening afterwards. Without analysis of the latter, there remains a lack of an understanding of the internal problems that plagued *Jiaozong* and the strategies it employed to overcome these challenges.

The second type of publications on the education movement comprises works written by independent authors. These works revealed another side of the movement, giving accounts from bottom-up perspectives, and discussing critical and sensitive issues regarding the movement. For example, long-serving Chinese educators, Wang Siow Nan (王秀南), Liu Bo Kui (刘伯奎), and Huang Zhao Fa (黄招发) published their experiences and personal observations derived from running the Chinese schools — the most important and autonomous institutions of the Chinese education movement (Huang, Z.F. 2004; Liu 1986; and Wang 1970). There are also independent writers such as Lin Wu Cong (林武聪) et al., who disclosed secrets related to the controversy over the alleged corruption amongst principals of Chinese primary schools (华文小学) in Malaysia (Lin, W.C. et al. 2006). Other independent writers who also wrote about the movement included Tan Ai Mei (陈爱梅), who discussed the embedded dilemmas faced by the Malaysian Chinese schools education system, and Kua Kia Soong (柯嘉逊), who revealed his side of the story regarding the 2008 New Era College (新纪元学院) controversy that led to his resignation and that of the college's senior staff (Kua 2009; Tan, A.M. 2006).

The third type of writings on the Chinese education movement consists of academic publications, which can be categorized predominantly into historical, institutional and political approaches. Notably, Victor Purcell's documentation provided an important historical sketch of the early Chinese immigrants' political and sociological situation in Malaya from an English official's perspective (Purcell 1948). According to Purcell, Chinese immigrants viewed themselves as an exclusive race, and their desire to preserve their Chinese identity became the key motivation for the establishment of Chinese schools as educational and sociological institutions. Purcell, in another work, *Malaya: Communist or Free*, gave a chronological account of the political and social developments in post-war Malaya (Purcell 1954). He analysed the communist aggression in Malaya and its impact on Chinese school communities in particular. The threats of communism (whose ideology was supported predominantly by the Chinese community) and Chinese nationalism towards China became the basis for a series of public policies imposed by Malayan state authorities to control local Chinese schools. This marked the beginning of the Chinese education movement.

Another frequently cited work, *The Politics of Chinese Education in Malaya, 1945–1961*, authored by Tan Liok Ee, provided fundamental analysis on the emergence, challenges, controversies, and dilemmas of the movement from 1945 to 1961 (Tan, L.E. 1997). Adopting a chronological approach, Tan's study categorized the movement's trajectories into three periods: the reaction of activists towards the 1951 Barnes Report, the collaboration of Malaya's Alliance regime with the Chinese education movement leaders, and the failure of the *Jiaozong-Dongzong*-MCA alliance. Tan's work confirmed that the Chinese education movement in Malaysia had developed into a social movement. Not only did she show that the movement was a heterogeneous entity, she also showed the dynamic interactions between the state and the social movement across various political trajectories.

Drawing on Tan's and Purcell's work, Chapter 2 of this study broadens the analysis of the movement in its early stages by discussing issues such as the influences of the anti-communist movement, the role of Chinese elites and the impact of the New Economic Policy. There are also scholars, such as Zainal Abidin Ahmad, who asserted that since the ethnic responses to education policies seemed to enhance the objectives of certain interest groups, educational reform efforts tended to be functionally disintegrative (Zainal 1980). However, most scholars who examined the impact of such policies using the Chinese education movement as their case study tended to disagree with Zainal's position. These scholars were mostly fixated with the idea that manipulative institutional policies were covert forms of ethnic discrimination.

Utilizing the development of Chinese schools in Malaysia from 1956 to 2000 as an example, Sia Keng Yek argued that the fears and resistance of the Chinese community towards the Ministry of Education of Malaysia were key factors in sustaining the movement (Sia 2005). Sia thematically analysed the physical development, management, and curriculums of these schools to demonstrate the movement's resistance. Similarly, Tan Yao Sua maintained that such manipulative state institutions exacerbated the conflict of interests between the Malay majority and the Chinese minority (Tan, Y.S. 2005). He adopted the concept of identity and framing from the social movement literature to analyse the role of *Dongjiaozong* as a social movement organization in the Chinese education movement.

Many authors have studied the responses of independent Chinese secondary schools (华文独立中学) in Malaysia towards the government's nationalization policies. Huang Guan Qin (黄冠钦) and Ku Hung Ting (古鸿廷) both studied the resistance of these schools against incorporation into the national system under the 1961 Education Act (Huang, G.Q. 1984; and Ku 2003). With Huang providing perspectives from West Malaysia and Ku from Sarawak in East Malaysia, the autonomy of Chinese school committees in school policymaking was credited as the main factor behind the success of Chinese schools in resisting the conversion. On the other hand, Tang Tze Ying (陈子鹦) argued that power relationships between Chinese schools committee members and state actors influenced the reactions of Chinese schools towards the 1961 education reforms (Tang 2004). School committee members who had a close relationship with state agencies (Chinese politicians from MCA in particular) more readily accepted the government's call to include Chinese secondary schools in the converted system. In fact, the diverse outcomes of these studies reveal the reality of the Chinese education movement: the movement is divided between those supporting and those contesting the conversion. The division, as one of the causes behind the prolonged struggle of the movement, will be further explored and discussed in Chapter 5.

The struggles of the movement were also analysed through political approaches, as demonstrated in Lee Leong Sze (利亮时) and Cheong Yuen Keong (Cheong 2007; and Lee, L.S. 1999). Both studied the dilemmas of Chinese political parties within the BN ruling regime and their reactions towards the Chinese community's demands, such as demands for better protection of the interests of Chinese vernacular schools and better access of Chinese minorities to state resources. Both agreed that vernacular educational issues had been politicized to sustain the political interests of the Chinese political parties. Lee concluded that the politicization of vernacular educational issues widened the gap amongst ethnic groups, which was one of the escalating factors that led to the 1969 riots.

However, Cheong, who continued his observations into the post-1969 era, concluded that both MCA and Gerakan acted as intermediate agents, especially during general elections. Not only have their roles enabled parties to broker a compromise between the needs of the BN ruling regime and the Chinese education movement, but also their roles were the critical factor behind the survival of both Chinese political parties. Such dynamic interactions between the Chinese political parties and the movement, and the political opportunities arising from such interactions, will be further elaborated in Chapter 4.

To date, few studies have looked into the role of the social movement organization in the Chinese education movement's struggles. An exception is Teoh Ai Ling, who examined the institutional structure and functions of *Dongzong* (Teoh 1999). Her work provided rich descriptions of the functions and roles of each department within *Dongzong* and clearly explained the structural relationships amongst these departments. Nevertheless, her study fell short of analysing the competition and contentious politics amongst the departments. Admittedly, much light has been shed on the Chinese education movement, especially on its reactions and resistance towards unjust policies. Yet, almost all studies have treated the movement as a homogenous entity.

In actuality, the movement's entities are stratified and factionalized. Additionally, most of the literature has taken for granted the resources (financial and human resources alike) that are needed to maintain and sustain the movement. In the current study, the author explores the intra- and inter-relationships amongst movement actors, comparing the various dilemmas faced by *Dongzong* and *Jiaozong*, the changing relationship between the movement and the state, as well as the transformations of the collaborative relationships between the movement and the Chinese guilds and associations (华人社团).

This study is the first to cover the movement in its entirety from 1951 to 2011. The analysis of the movement in the post-1998 period is particularly important, as there is a vacuum in the existing literature in the analysis of the logic and impact of the movement's shift from open contention to low-profile resistance. Information gathered during fieldwork, especially that related to the little known underground negotiations between movement activists and state agencies, is a theoretical and empirical attempt to broaden our understanding of the scope and depth of the movement.

RESEARCH METHODOLOGY

The author collected the primary data for this study in Malaysia over the course of eleven months.[11] A major component of the fieldwork was conducting interviews. The author conducted seventy-four in-depth, open-ended, and semi-structured elite interviews. Almost all of the interviews were conducted in Chinese (华文), with about 20 per cent conducted in a mix of local dialects such as Hokkien (福建话) and Cantonese (广东话). The choice of conducting the interviews in the interviewees' vernacular languages was precipitated by the consideration that doing so would enable interviewees to relate to the author and share their thoughts with greater ease. Confidentiality of identity was assured to all interviewees at the beginning and reiterated at the end of every interview. The length of each interview was restricted to an average of one hour to optimize concentration for both the author and the interviewees.[12]

The informants can be divided into the following clusters (including both current and retired categories): local-, state-, and central-level movement leaders; movement executive officers; schoolteachers, school principals, and school committees; and lastly, other influential Chinese community leaders outside the framework of *Dongjiaozong*, including commercial, political, societal, and educational leaders, amongst others. No state or federal government officials agreed to be interviewed. Thus, the author had to operate with caution, such as not to mention sensitive keywords, or any anti-government sentiments, when dealing with various state agencies. The author also kept a low profile while conducting fieldwork to avoid unnecessary scrutiny. The interviews were mostly conducted at the interviewees' office, or at a secure location. Some interviewees offered conservative views and were less candid at the beginning of the interview, but most began to shed light on the internal dynamics of the movement's structures, functions, goals, and framing strategies of issues as the interview progressed. The author strove to corroborate all information with data from other sources. Follow-up interviews and countercheck interviews were conducted, especially with those who played critical roles in various decision-making processes.

Primary sources included archival documents, letters, and annual working reports of *Dongzong*, *Jiaozong*, Lim Lian Geok Cultural Development Centre (林连玉基金会), and *Dongjiaozong* Higher Learning Centre (董教总教育中心). Other vernacular sources such as school magazines provided insights about the schools' organization, funding, and activities. The author also explored collections of theses, newspaper clippings, and reference books in various languages to balance diverse perspectives. Multiple visits were made to the offices of the Chinese printed media of *Sinchew Daily* (星洲日报), *Kwongwahyitpoh* (光华日报), and the Centre for Malaysian Chinese Studies (华社研究中心) to access their collections of newspaper clippings.

SCOPES AND LIMITATIONS

The struggle against time had been paramount. Spending a total of only eleven months in the field forced the author to compromise and conduct fieldwork only in West Malaysia. Although the Chinese population in Sabah and Sarawak of East Malaysia constitute about 14 per cent of the total Chinese population of Malaysia, Chinese schools in these states have developed in different historical settings, which make generalizations from a study based on these two populations difficult (DSGM 2011).

To overcome this limitation, this study looks at the shared grievances of Chinese schools in West Malaysia across geographical boundaries. Although the establishment and set-up of Sabah's and Sarawak's state-level Chinese schools associations varied from those in the Peninsula, and they have yet to play a leading role in the movement, Chinese school communities of Sabah and Sarawak are represented within the Chinese education movement led by *Dongjiaozong*. More importantly, Chinese schools across Malaysia faced similar discrimination by the education laws, and shared the constraints in resources and other dilemmas (Huang, Z.F. 2004; and Liu 1986).

The second limitation pertains to the qualitative approach employed in this study. The author is aware of the methodological imperfections and domination of the qualitative approach in the study of the Chinese education movement in Malaysia and of social movement studies in general. However, given the exploratory nature of this study, the approach permitted intensive examination of the selected topic when time and resources available were limited. Lijphart's longitudinal (cross-historical) extension helped to minimize the conceptual and analytical weaknesses of having more variables than cases (Lijphart 1971, p. 686). Moreover, the process of making observations in an empirical case study allowed the author to trace causal processes and highlight the richness of their interactions, thus enhancing the magnitude, depth, and validity of this study's findings.

This research includes many observations on human behaviour, and, unlike the precision of natural science, the ability to observe accurately the attributes of people is rather limited. Interview effects and sensitizing of interviewees to the topics in the survey process (the participants of research might guess the rationale of the study and thus adjust their behaviour or opinions accordingly) might have reduced the internal validity of this study. Therefore, follow-up interviews and countercheck interviews were conducted to reduce these effects.

Last but not least, the author would like to excuse herself from acknowledging the various social and professional titles commonly used in Malaysia, as she seeks to treat all individuals as equals regardless of their background. As most of the primary and secondary data were in Chinese and some in Malay, the translated words followed by their original characters will be included on first mention. *Hanyupinyin* (汉语拼音) will be used to transliterate Chinese words if official translation is not available. Unless otherwise mentioned, all translations from the written and verbal sources used in this book are by the author. For details, readers can refer to the glossary of non-English text and list of abbreviations in this book.

ROADMAP OF THE BOOK

This book consists of six chapters. They are arranged thematically to illustrate the relationships of various institutions with social mobilization. Chapter 2 draws the readers' attention to the nation-building process and the rise of the Chinese education movement in Malaya. The chapter seeks to reveal many important, yet under-explored developments that took place from the post-World War II period to 1974 — the year Malaysia normalized its diplomatic relations with the People's Republic of China. The main players of the Chinese education movement, *Dongzong* and *Jiaozong*, were established during the nation formation stage, and played significant roles in securing Chinese citizenship rights and the survival of vernacular schools in Malaysia. Elites — especially those from political parties and business groups — became important agents who initiated collaboration and brokered compromises between the state and the social movement until the new elites brought about the collapse of this relational institution when they discontinued their intimate collaboration.

The subsequent three chapters examine the design of the structural institutions and the adaptations made by various relational institutions in the face of state-imposed challenges. Chapter 3 analyses the elements of the lowest but most autonomous and fundamental units in the movement's hierarchy, such as the school committees and schoolteachers of Chinese schools. These include three types of Chinese schools, namely, Chinese primary schools, independent Chinese secondary schools, and converted Chinese secondary schools (国民型华文中学). These schools experienced continual marginalization as a result of the government's educational policies — especially in funding allocation — despite the fact that Chinese schools (with the exception of independent Chinese secondary schools) had already been incorporated into the national educational system. The chapter then analyses the role, formation, and collaboration of associational capitals of state-level Chinese school committees and Chinese schoolteachers' associations. The chapter ends with an exploration of the inter- and intra-organizational transformations in *Dongzong* and *Jiaozong*, and evaluates the changing roles and challenges faced by the central-level leadership.

The analysis of any social movement organization will not be complete without an analysis of domestic contentious politics. Chapter 4 explores such interactions, particularly that of social movement leaders exploiting political opportunities through the state's electoral institutions. Many new repertoires have grown out of desperation during the process, and have resulted from changing relationships and formation of alliances between the movement and Chinese guilds and associations. The chapter also presents the emergence of various campaigns such as the Alliance of Three campaign (三结合) in 1982, the Alliance of Fifteen Leading Chinese Guilds and Associations (全国十五华团领导机构) since 1983, the promotion of the dual coalition system (两线制) since 1986, the national Chinese primary schools sit-in protest in 1987, joining of the opposition parties in 1990, and chairing of the Malaysian Chinese Organisations' Election Appeals Committee (马来西亚华人社团大选诉求委员会, *Suqiu* Committee) in 1999. The chapter also shows how the authorities deployed carrot-and-stick measures to co-opt and suppress the movement, although these efforts have failed to terminate the movement altogether.

Chapter 5 extends the scope of research into the functions of two nationwide working committees of the Chinese education movement, namely, the Malaysian Independent Chinese Secondary Schools Working Committee (董教总全国发展华文独立中学工作委员会) and the *Dongjiaozong* Chinese Primary Schools Working Committee (董教总全国发展华小工作委员会). The chapter reveals the working relationship between movement activists at the central level and the movement's local level supporters. The chapter also focuses on resource accumulation and mobilizational mechanisms of the movement, and the role of the professional secretariats in the process. The chapter ends by addressing the controversy surrounding the formation and maintenance of the *Dongjiaozong* Higher Learning Centre and the New Era College, highlighted by tensions within the movement.

In Chapter 6, the aforementioned themes are drawn together to examine the impact of institutions on social mobilization in the Chinese education movement, and to better understand various processes, stages, and structures of the social movement organizations. It is hoped that by analysing the general incompatibilities found in the Chinese education movement, this research would jumpstart the discussion about their resolution and trends, so as to acquire a better understanding of social movement organizations in the future.

Notes

1. On the trade union movements, see Jomo and Todd (1994); Ramasamy and Rowley (2008); Stenson (1970); and Wong, L. (1993). On Islamic related movements, see Hussin (1993); Jesudason (1996, p. 156); Lee, C.H. (2010); and Sheila (1999, p. 97).
2. The Federal Council of the Federated Malay States passed a similar law on 20 November 1920. Under this enactment, all schoolteachers and school committees had to register with the Department of Education and comply with various regulations. Many believe that the regulation was imposed due to the increase in Chinese nationalism and anti-imperial sentiments in Chinese schools strongly influenced by the 1919 May Fourth Movement in China. From 1925 to 1928, 315 Chinese schools' registrations were revoked for failure to comply with curriculum, administration and management, or sanitary standards. For more, see UCSCAM (1992*b*, pp. 76–77; 2004*b*, p. 183).
3. The Chinese population in the Federation of Malaya in 1921 was 1,174,777 or about 35 per cent of the total population. See Vlieland (1932, p. 36).
4. There are five major dialect groups within the Chinese community in Malaysia, namely, Hokkien, Cantonese, Hakka (客家), Teochew (潮州), and Hainanese (海南).
5. On European tradition, see de Tarde (1969); and Durkheim (1938). On American tradition, see Blumer (1939); Park (1955); Parsons (1937); and Smelser (1963).
6. Case (1992) introduced Malaysia as a semi-democracy; Chandra (1989*a*) used fettered democracy; Crouch (1992; 1993) described it as a modified democracy; Weiss (2006) refers to it as illiberal democracy; and Zakaria (1989) referred it as quasi-democracy.
7. Democratic Action Party, *Partai Rakyat*, and Social Justice Party of Malaysia refused to join BN. See DAP (1991).
8. On civil societies related studies, see Hilton (2009); Johan (2001); and S.M. (1986). On democratization process related studies, see Loh (2009), Tan, L.O. (2010); and Tan, J.E. and Zawawi (2008).
9. Other books that look into the women's movements in Malaysia are Lai, S.Y. (2004); Makmor (2006); Ng, C.S. (2010*a*; 2010*b*); Tan, B.H. and Ng (2001); and Wazir (1992).
10. PAS has been the main Islamic opposition party in Malaysia. It joined BN coalition and became part of the ruling regime from 1973 to 1977. However, conflicting political interests with the UMNO-led federal government in

early 1977 over the control of Kelantan state government eventually forced PAS to leave BN in December 1977. For more, see Mauzy (1983*a*, pp. 84, 112–14); and Milne (1976, pp. 186–92).

11. Fieldworks were conducted from February to March 2008; December 2008 to February 2009; November 2009 to March 2010; and July 2010. The first two trips of the fieldwork were partially financed by the National University of Singapore, while the rest were self-sponsored.

12. Many of the interviewees had witnessed important changes in the movement and Malaysia's transition from a colony to a developing country. Almost all the activists interviewed for this research had encountered state discrimination (for example, being detained under the Internal Security Act), and these experiences have motivated them to participate in the movement. Despite having operated in various factions, the interviewees were — and some remain to this day — well-connected with one another. They regularly share updates and information regarding the movement through small talk.

2

NATION BUILDING
AND FORMATION OF
SOCIAL MOVEMENT

INTRODUCTION

The development of the Chinese education movement in Malaysia parallels Malaysia's domestic politics after the British colonial era. The decolonization of the Malaya Peninsula in the post-World War II years redefined the balance of power, especially amongst the English-educated ethnic leaders. Although these elites dominated official state decision-making mechanisms, Malaya (renamed as Malaysia after the Peninsula merged with Singapore, Sabah, and Sarawak to form the new federation in 1963) was vulnerable during its infancy and therefore allowed space for negotiation with the influential vernacular-speaking ethnic elites. This chapter gives special attention to the role of Chinese elites in raising political awareness and creating a series of social movements amongst Malaya's Chinese communities through three main platforms: Chinese political parties, Chinese guilds and associations, as well as Chinese schoolteachers and Chinese school committees associations.

The chapter first explores the formation of political parties such as UMNO and MCA, and the significance of the Alliance coalition in making a peaceful demand for state independence from the British. To strengthen intra-Chinese collaboration, MCA established the Grand Three Associations of Chinese Education in collaboration with *Dongzong* and *Jiaozong* in 1952. The Grand Three was successful in bridging the state and the Chinese education movement actors until it started crumbling in 1960, when its pro-vernacular education leaders left MCA. From then on, the Chinese education movement began to nurture stronger bonds with Chinese guilds and associations, which laid the foundation for the movement's trajectories from the 1970s to the 1990s.

The efforts of nation building by the Malay-dominated state unavoidably posited threats that would dilute the vernacular identities of the non-Malay communities, especially after the departure of Singapore from the Federation of Malaysia in 1965. The Chinese' resistance against the state's assimilation attempts is best demonstrated in their overwhelming support of *Dongjiaozong's* Merdeka University campaign in 1967. The chapter ends with a discussion on the impact of the implementation of the New Economic Policy in 1971, and the political consequences of normalization of diplomatic relations between Malaysia and the People's Republic of China in 1974.

IMPACT OF COMMUNIST THREATS

Prior to World War II, massive migration had resulted in the number of Chinese and Indian immigrants outnumbering the Malays in the Peninsula, making it possible for immigrants to challenge the status quo of the native majority.[1] The British's policy and practice of divide and rule polarized the colony's social structure and led to a discernible economic division along ethnic lines that resulted in heightened tensions, fuelling local nationalist movements that were ethnically oriented (Abraham 1997). The situation worsened during World War II, when the Malayan Communist Party (MCP) and the Malayan People's Anti-Japanese Army (MPAJA) emerged as the backbones of resistance against the Japanese occupation of Malaya. MCP in particular emerged as a formidable political force after the defeat of Japan and briefly ruled Malaya from March to August 1945, before British authority was re-established.[2]

Aided by a power vacuum, the MPAJA killed some 2,500 Japanese collaborators (mostly Malays), abolished the sultanates, and attempted to make Malaya part of China (Horowitz 1985, p. 398). The Red Bands of the Holy War (*Sabillah*) was formed by Malays to combat the MPAJA. The intensity of this communal violence sealed in the minds of many Malays a negative stereotype of Chinese as communists and as a threat to Islam, the sultanates, and the Malay community (Lomperis 1996,

p. 204). When the British retook control of Malaya after the war, the Malayan Union government was introduced in April 1946 as a unified and more cost-effective government structure. It was also conceived as a form of preparation for the possibility of self-rule and independence. The scheme offered full citizenship rights to Chinese and Indians born in Malaya, and dissolved the sultanates into one secular union.[3]

The imposition of the scheme shocked the Malay community and led to the emergence of the first Malay nationalist party, UMNO, founded in May 1946, to oppose the Malayan Union. Due to strong protest and pressure from Malay aristocrats and former Malayan governors in London, the Malayan Union was dismantled and replaced by the Federation of Malaya, which reinstated the traditional prerogatives of the sultans and restored special positions to the Malays as "sons of the earth" (*bumiputera*) in February 1948.[4] It also tightened the qualification for federal citizenship by disqualifying over three quarters of the Chinese population.[5]

Facing increasing political uncertainties and discrimination against their rights to Malayan citizenship, disparate ethnic Chinese, although initially divided by their clans, dialects, social statuses, political views and economic identities, were given the impetus to unite again, in particular after the painful experience of the massacres during the Japanese occupation.[6] Chin Peng (陈平) became the MCP's secretary general in 1947 after the party's predecessor, Lai Tek, absconded with the party's funds in March 1947 (Fujio 1995, pp. 37–58; and Ramakrishna 2002, p. 32). In a bid to empower the weakening party, Chin emulated the successful model of Mao's revolutionary movement in China and launched an armed guerrilla rebellion under the Malayan Races Liberation Army, which prompted the British to declare a State of Emergency in June 1948 (Clutterbuck 1966, pp. 22–24; Heng 1988, p. 50; Keylor 2003, p. 51; Lee, K.H. 1998, pp. 31–32; Lomperis 1996, p. 204; and Pye 1957, p. 7). The Emergency also gave the British and their Malay successors justification to mobilize a significant amount of resources in their war against communism.[7]

As members of the MCP were largely ethnic Chinese, and many Chinese schools were used as centres of the Chinese Communist Party's propaganda, the British stereotyped the Chinese in Malaya as communist supporters, or as fence sitters in the anti-communist campaign (Chew 1975; Freedman 2000, p. 55; and Heng 1988, p. 251). For example, the British believed that the many Chinese squatters who hid in the jungles during World War II had either provided supplies to the MCP, or had been recruited as new party members (Chai 1977, p. 10; and Lee, K.H. 1998, pp. 31–32). The new high commissioner in 1952, General Gerald Templer, launched the Briggs Plan and forcibly resettled almost 570,000 Chinese squatters into hundreds of new villages.[8]

The effort, albeit controversial and authoritative in its implementation, did in the end help to control and contain the communist rebellion (Sandhu 1964). According to Ramakrishna, "the rural Chinese were the target of government's emergency measures: in particular individual detention and deportation, communal fines and curfews" (Ramakrishna 2001, p. 82). In total, 30,000 communist activists were jailed, and another 15,000 were deported to China, for many of them were school principals and schoolteachers recruited from China by the Chinese schools in Malaya (Lomperis 1996, p. 204).

With the establishment of the People's Republic of China in 1949, most overseas Chinese communities harboured fears that the new communist state might confiscate their properties and businesses, and were therefore reluctant to express their loyalty to the new Chinese government. This included the Chinese in Malaya, who were beginning to think of Malaya as their only hope for a permanent homeland (Heng 1988, p. 251). In an attempt to alleviate the Chinese community's dilemma, Tan Cheng Lock (陈祯禄) formed MCA in February 1949.[9] MCA sought to provide relief and welfare assistance to Chinese villagers displaced by the Briggs Plan, redirect Chinese support away from the communists, and provide an image of loyalty of the Chinese in the midst of suspicions aroused by the emergency decree against the Chinese community in general (Roff 1965, pp. 42–43).

MCA leaders were dominated by Straits-born, English-educated, ethnic Chinese elites who enjoyed linguistic advantages and were generally well accepted by both British and UMNO leaders. They incorporated wings of Chinese-educated, *Kuomintang-* (国民党) inclined leaders, established trust, and, through networking with various Chinese associations, successfully expanded MCA membership from about 3,000 in 1949 to about 250,000 in 1953.[10] In return for the strong support from Chinese-speaking communities, MCA began to take on a more comprehensive role, such as lobbying for more liberal requirements in acquiring citizenship rights for Chinese immigrants, protecting the status of Chinese education and preserving the Chinese identity in the Independence Constitution (Chan 1965; and Heng 1983).

Strong support from the British enabled MCA to outplay the MCP and the Chinese consulates in Malaya as the most effective legitimate Malayan-oriented organization in successfully creating a consciousness of Malayan identity within the local Chinese community (Hara 1997, p. 99). By 1952, the Alliance coalition was established between UMNO and MCA during the Kuala Lumpur municipal election, and with the Malaysian Indian Congress in 1954.[11] This marked the beginning of Malaya's national politics, characterized by compromising tactics and consociational collaboration that resulted in a series of unintended consequences over time.

VERNACULAR STATUS WITHIN THE UNIFIED EDUCATION SYSTEM

Post-war and pre-independence Malaya was a fragile plural society that lacked social integration and capital for nation building (Furnivall 1948). The colonial government's lack of interest in unifying the educational system in the Federation of Malaya had resulted in the "absence of a consistent educational policy with definite aims and objectives" (Yeok 1982, p. 37). The formation of the British-administered Central Advisory Committee on Education came as late as in 1949, with the aim of preparing an integrative and nationally-focused educational system for Malaya.[12]

There were four main types of school systems in Malaya at that time: English, Chinese, Malay, and Tamil. Each system was different in terms of its sponsorship base, cultural orientation, and medium of instruction, and they co-existed to fulfil the needs of Malaya's diverse ethnic groups.[13] Harbouring an optimistic faith in the value of education as a primary instrument in nation building, the British perceived that an integrated national identity could be achieved by imposing a standardized educational system with a common medium of instruction. Three committees were commissioned between 1950 and 1951 to investigate and explore the most suitable educational system for Malaya (Chai 1977, p. 1).

The Special Committee by the Central Advisory Committee on Education, chaired by M.J. Hogan and consisted of eleven members, of which two were ethnic Chinese, proposed that English be used as the common medium of instruction in all schools in the colony (FM 1952c). The suggestion was rejected by the Federal Legislative Council due to overwhelming opposition from the Malay community, which saw the proposal as undermining the primacy of the Malay language.

The second committee, led by L.J. Barnes and consisted of five Europeans and nine Malays, "advocated a system of National Schools in which the medium of instruction would be either Malay or English" (FM 1951b; Mason 1954, p. 31; and Purcell 1954, p. 154). The Barnes Report recommended "the end of separate vernacular schools for the several racial communities, and their replacement by a single type of primary school common to all" (FM 1951b, p. 75). The Chinese community reacted to the Barnes Report with uproar and rebuttal.[14] The report also received little support from the Malays, who were concerned about the subordination of the Malay language and the existing educational system to the English system (Ingham and Simmons 1987, p. 206).

Concurrently, the third committee, led by William Fenn and Wu Teh Yao (吳德耀) also released its report, *Chinese Schools and the Education of Chinese Malayans* (Fenn-Wu Report), soon after (FM 1951a). This report proposed that Chinese-medium schools be integrated into the national education system, but these schools should not be eliminated until the Chinese themselves decided that such schools were not needed. In addition to the use of Chinese as the main medium of instruction in these schools, Chinese students would also study both English and Malay. It was during the various group conferences and individual interviews conducted by Fenn and Wu between February and April 1951 that the Chinese education movement leaders and supporters were alerted to the implications of the recommendations by the Barnes Committee (Purcell 1954, p. 156; and Tan, L.E. 1985).

The great disparity between the Barnes and Fenn-Wu reports forced the Central Advisory Committee on Education to review the suggestions from both reports and led to the *Report on the Barnes Report on Malay Education and the Fenn-Wu Report on Chinese Education*, which, in essence, endorsed Barnes' proposals (FM 1951c). The Chinese-speaking community generally felt that all three reports (Barnes, Fenn-Wu, and the Report on Barnes and Fenn-Wu) had failed to provide sufficient protection for Chinese education.[15] Fears amplified amongst the Chinese over the potential closure of all 1,319 Chinese schools in Malaya. Chinese guilds and associations nationwide held conferences at the state level and drafted memorandums to protest against these reports.[16] Continuous debates over the most appropriate educational system for the

Chinese communities led to the formation of the first formal Chinese education association, *Jiaozong*, which later became the institution that provided chief leadership in subsequent Chinese civic movements in Malaya.

In December 1950, Malacca Chinese Schoolteachers' Association (马六甲华校教师公会) Chairman Sim Mow Yu urged that "a national organization should convene as soon as possible to enhance the efficiency of Chinese education and improve the status of Malaya's Chinese schoolteachers".[17] Despite the growing number of Chinese schoolteachers' associations (华人教师公会) and the rapid expansion of its membership, Sim's proposal was turned down because most of these associations preferred to function as welfare associations rather than as pressure groups.[18] The proposal to form a unified Chinese schoolteachers' association was turned down in 1950, but events took a dramatic turn after the Barnes Report was made public. In July 1951, the Negeri Sembilan Chinese Schoolteachers' Association (森美兰华校教师公会) proposed to hold a National Convention of Chinese Schoolteachers' Associations in Malaya (全马教师公会代表大会) to consolidate the power of schoolteachers.

As the Barnes Report would dictate the future of Chinese schools and the career of Chinese schoolteachers, the national convention received tremendous support from associations nationwide. The two-day conference held from 24 to 25 August 1951 in the Selangor Hokkien Association (雪兰莪福建会馆) saw participation from representatives of Chinese schoolteachers' associations from local and state levels. Collectively, the participants voiced their rejection of the Barnes Report and drafted a memorandum to the Central Advisory Committee on Education to demand the incorporation of Chinese schools into the national education system.

On 25 December 1951, *Jiaozong* was formally inaugurated at the Second Conference of the Pan-Malayan Chinese Schoolteachers' Association (全马教师公会第二次代表大会). *Jiaozong*'s main objectives were to improve the standard of Chinese education, promote Chinese culture within Malaya, safeguard schoolteachers' status, and improve schoolteachers' welfare (UCSTAM 1952*a*). At the first General Meeting of Member Associations, Penang Chinese Schoolteachers' Association (槟城华校教师会) was selected as the presidential association, and its chairman, David Chen (陈充恩), became the first *Jiaozong* chairman.[19]

Despite *Jiaozong*'s efforts to lobby for support from the Central Advisory Committee on Education and MCA representatives in the Legislative Council's Education Special Committee, the 1952 Education Ordinance was drafted based on the Barnes Report.[20] Chinese educationalists from *Jiaozong* and community leaders who sat on Chinese school committees were generally displeased with MCA's councillors for neither speaking up for, nor voting against the ordinance when it was unanimously passed by the Federal Legislative Council in November 1952.

THE GRAND THREE

Although social movement and the state authorities may have conflicting interests, the nature of the Alliance coalition enabled the movement to pursue its goal through brokerage via MCA, the sole Chinese political party within the coalition. This brokerage was the key factor to the movement's survival in its early phase, and has been so in the ensuing development of non-violent interactions between the state and the social movement.

It was through the efforts and intervention of Wen Tien Kuang (温典光),[21] an active senior MCA member and an influential member of United Chinese School Committees' Association of Selangor and Kuala Lumpur (雪兰莪暨吉隆坡联邦直辖区华校董事会联合会), that the Joint Conference of Chinese School Committees and Schoolteachers' Representatives in Federation of Malaya with MCA Representatives (联合邦华校董教代表及马华公会代表联席会议) was made possible at the Selangor Chinese Assembly Hall (雪兰莪中华大会堂) in November 1952. By making MCA the sponsor of the conference, MCA President Tan Cheng Lock was given the opportunity to affirm the MCA's position in supporting the joint efforts of Chinese educational organizations in opposing the Barnes Report, thus strengthening MCA's political influence and collaboration with *Jiaozong*.

The conference provided a platform for representatives of various Chinese communities to affirm the collaborative framework of the Grand Three. Persuaded by MCA, the conference representatives entrusted the Chinese Education Central Committee (the working committee for the Grand Three) to act as an MCA subordinate. It was hoped that by associating the Grand Three with a political party, the Grand Three could become an asset for Chinese educationalists in their dealings with the government. In return, four Chinese educationalist representatives (two schoolteachers and two school committee members) would work side-by-side three MCA representatives in the central committee.

The Second Joint Conference of Chinese School Committees and Schoolteachers' Representatives in Federation of Malaya with MCA Representatives (联合邦华校董教代表及马华公会代表第二次联席会议) was held in April 1953 to inaugurate the Grand Three and its constitution. The charismatic Tan Cheng Lock delivered a stirring speech to the Chinese education communities at the conference that won him respect and recognition in the Chinese community and movement community alike. Amongst the most important contents from Tan's speech was as follows:

> ... if you are not interested in politics, the practice of politics will not be uninterested in you. You must either pull your weight with the rest in the political sphere or you will certainly and compulsorily be pulled, whether you like it or not. That is politics, though you may care nothing for politics... Now you say, perhaps another president of the MCA may be antagonistic to the spread, development, and growth of Chinese education in this country. To me, such a situation is unthinkable and impossible because the constitution of the MCA is such that it must protect the interest of the Chinese not only politically but economically, culturally, educationally and in every other respect because if the Chinese don't know Chinese [language], they cannot be Chinese. They cannot be Chinese if they do not practise Chinese customs and traditions; and if they are not Chinese, they cannot be Malays or English or Indians. They will be described as pariahs (UCSTAM 1952*b*).

Subsequently, Tan was selected to head the Chinese Education Central Committee. Through his role as head of the Chinese Education Central Committee and through MCA's political influence, he played a bridging role between Chinese educationalists and the Alliance government during his tenure, enabling the Chinese Education Central Committee to become the highest authority and the leading vehicle of the Chinese education movement throughout the 1950s (Tan, L.E. 1988, p. 49). On 22 August 1954, the second primary component of the Chinese schools, *Dongzong*, was established. It was a national body that sought to unify, strengthen, and represent the interests of Chinese school committees in response to the government's education policy (UCSCAM 2004*a*, p. 42). Unlike *Jiaozong*'s membership, which was divided into the local, county, and state level, *Dongzong's* membership comprised only state-level Chinese school committees' associations (董事联合会). For the list of *Dongzong's* members, see Appendix 2.

Despite fears and worries within the Chinese communities about the threats posed by the 1952 Education Ordinance, in actuality, this Ordinance could not be fully implemented. Financial constraints posed by the war on communism affected the budget originally allocated to build new national schools and to train new schoolteachers. The sharp increase in the country's student population from the post-war baby boom also pressured the government to utilize the existing infrastructure of schools, in particular Chinese schools, to meet the rocketing needs (Tan, L.E. 1997, p. 283). Additionally, the government was reluctant to take harsh measures against Chinese schools, as closing them would further alienate the Chinese and provide an opportunity for communists to recruit them.

By November 1953, a special committee headed by Education Minister E.E.C. Thuraisinghamhad had been appointed to identify means to implement the 1952 Education Ordinance.[22] The special committee released the *Report of the Special Commission Appointed by the High Commissioner in Council to Consider Ways and Means of Implementing the Policy Outlined in the Education Ordinance* (1954 White Paper on Education Policy) in 1954, and reaffirmed the government's support to make English the main medium of teaching in all schools.[23] A common curriculum would be introduced, and Malay would be taught as a subject. To overcome the financial constraints in building new national schools, features typical of English schools, such as more time in the teaching of English as a subject, and teaching mathematics and science in English, were recommended to be introduced in all vernacular schools. Above all, the report also proposed that its ultimate aim would be to gradually replace all mother tongues with English in all schools.

The 1954 White Paper on Education Policy was seen by Chinese educationalists as a scheme by the government to eliminate Chinese schools in the country. The Chinese Education Central Committee expressed its opposition through the Memorandum Submitted by the United Chinese Schoolteachers' Association of Malaya in Opposition of the Conversion of Vernacular Schools into National Schools (教总反对改方言学校为国民学校宣言). The memorandum was submitted to the high commissioner in March 1954.[24] The committee also released statements through Chinese media, conducted large-scale signature campaigns, and mobilized a nationwide boycott against the instalment of features of English schools in Chinese schools.[25] By late 1953, Malay educationalists were also opposed to the domination of English as a medium of instruction in Malay schools. In January 1955, chief minister of the Federation of Malaya, Abdul Rahman, finally pronounced the 1954 Education White Paper policy dead.

By September 1955, a fifteen-member Legislative Council Committee on Education, chaired by Education Minister Abdul Razak Hussein, had been formed to review Malaya's educational system. The *Report of the Education Committee* (Razak Report), released in April 1956, was a rare official document that favoured the interests of non-*bumiputera*. Its conception was credited to MCA representatives who sat in the education committee headed by Abdul Razak, and comprised members such as Lim Chong Eu, Goh Chee Yan (吴志渊), Too Joon Hing (朱运兴), Leung Cheung Ling (梁长龄), and Lee Thean Hin (李天兴), who had established an intimate working relationship with *Jiaozong*.

During the drafting of the Razak Report, MCA and *Jiaozong* exchanged information and conducted closed-door discussions to find solutions that would benefit the future of Chinese education (Lim, L.G. 1990, p. 145). Bilingual activists such as Wen Tien Kuang, Yan Yuan Zhang (严元章), Sha Yun Yeo (沙渊如), and Ding Pin Song (丁品松) translated the education memorandum drafted by *Jiaozong* from Chinese to English and shared it with MCA.[26] The document was later presented by MCA representatives to the Razak Committee. Working collaboratively, the Grand Three had a definite influence on the Razak Report, resulting in the integration of the vernacular schools (Chinese, Tamil, and English primary schools) into the national educational system as "national-type" primary schools (国民型小学). All schools (national and national-type) would adopt a common syllabus, and their students would be allowed to sit for common public examinations. In addition, teaching of Malay and English would be compulsory, but vernacular languages would be used as the main mediums of instruction in national-type schools.

The incorporation of vernacular schools into the national education system would allow vernacular schools to receive financial support and, most importantly, official recognition from the government, while being administered by their respective management committees (Heng 1988, p. 255). These compromises by the government were, to some degree, financially motivated. At the dawn of independence, the Malayan government was young and faced demanding tasks in nation-building.

The urgency of tackling nation-building issues such as strengthening national security, urban development, and poverty reduction was given priority over that concerning the vernacular schools. Moreover, the government had been operating short on funds and manpower; thus, sustaining these schools with support from their respective communities was seen as the most rational option during this period for both the government and its people.[27]

After approving the Razak Report in May 1956, the government conducted a nationwide survey, the Torch Movement (火炬运动), to register school-aged children who intended to enrol during the August school holidays in 1956. English schools had begun registering students since June that year, two months before the Chinese schools were informed by the Ministry of Education about the survey. Realizing the importance of the Torch Movement, *Jiaozong* alarmed Chinese schools nationwide and mobilized its members to conduct door-to-door visits to seek new students. Chinese schoolteachers conducted family visits to remind parents to register and enrol their children into Chinese schools, and Chinese school students were mobilized to inform their friends and relatives about the importance of the survey (UCSCAM 1992*a*; and YCSHEC 2008, p. 263).

With the help and intervention of the Chinese Education Central Committee, the Ministry of Education finally agreed to allow MCA branches, state-level Chinese assembly halls (华人大会堂) and more Chinese schools to operate as student registration facilities.[28] Through wide publicity by local Chinese newspapers and collective efforts of Chinese educationalists, Chinese schools successfully obtained a stable enrolment rate and legitimated the continued existence of vernacular schools in Malaya (UCSCAM 1992*a*, p. 79).

FORMATION OF A NEW NATION

The political backdrop in Malaya in the late 1950s was one of passionate anticipation in becoming an independent state. The first Independence Mission led by Abdul Rahman in 1954 had failed due to the British's reluctance to grant Malaya independence unless there was evidence that the party that took over government had the support of the majority of the people in the colony.[29] After a series of political bargains, the Alliance successfully persuaded the British to hold Malaya's first Federal Election in 1955 in preparation for the country's independent rule.[30]

Under tremendous amount of pressure to win this election, the Alliance coalition tried to garner support to defeat its main political opponent, the Independence of Malaya Party, led by veteran Malay politician, Onn Jaafar.[31]

In a move to solidify support from the Chinese, Abdul Rahman agreed to meet leaders of the Chinese Education Central Committee in January 1955 at a secret meeting initiated by Tan Cheng Lock in Tan's private residence in Malacca. At this meeting, Abdul Rahman endorsed that "it would not be the Alliance's policy to destroy the schools, language and culture of any race".[32] The Alliance's representatives agreed to *Jiaozong's* demands to remove provisions in the Education Ordinance that threatened the existence of Chinese schools and promised to consider providing a two million straits dollar subsidy to Chinese schools in Malaya. However, both UMNO and MCA rejected the demand from *Jiaozong* to include Chinese as the second official language in their election manifesto at this meeting (UCSTAM 1975, p. 26).

Persuaded by Tan Cheng Lock, *Dongzong* and *Jiaozong* representatives softened their stand and agreed to postpone the issue until after the election. From the perspective of *Dongzong* and *Jiaozong*, they only agreed to temporarily cast the issue aside for the 1955 General Election. Nevertheless, it was perceived by UMNO and MCA that the Chinese educationalists had agreed to drop the petition in exchange for citizenship for the Chinese and inclusion of the Chinese vernacular system into the national education system.

With support from the Chinese Education Central Committee and majority of Malays, the Alliance coalition won a landslide victory at the 1955 General Election, taking fifty-one out of fifty-two elected seats in the Federal Legislative Council. The first self-government was formed on 2 August 1955, with Abdul Rahman as the territory's chief minister. He was given the mandate to form a new Malayan government and later successfully persuaded the British to grant Malaya independence during the London Talks in January 1956.[33]

By June that year, the Independent Constitutional Survey Commission headed by William Reid arrived in Malaya to assess views and formulate a new Constitution for Malaya (Abdul R. 1984, p. 180). The Alliance government submitted a memorandum representing official views of the self-rule government to the Commission in August 1956. Realizing this opportunity, the influential Federation of Malaya Chinese Guilds Association (马来亚华人行业社团总会) submitted an independent memorandum in April 1956 and pressed for the Chinese cause in the drafting of the Independence Constitution.[34]

The Memorandum to Acquire for Citizenship by Representatives of Chinese Associations and Guilds in The Federation of Malaya (马来亚联合邦华人社团代表争取公民权宣言), which was drafted without the support of MCA, demanded *jus soli*-based citizenship and equal rights and responsibilities for all, regardless of ethnicity. It also called for waiver of the Malay proficiency test in granting citizenship rights to foreigners who have lived in Malaya for five or more years.[35] Above all, this memorandum suggested that Malay, Chinese, and Tamil should all be the official languages of Malaya. The Chinese groups' timely demands were rewarded: the *Report of the Federation of Malaya Constitutional Commission 1957* drafted by the Reid Commission included some of the suggestions proposed in the memorandum (CC 1957).

Malaya gained independence on 31 August 1957, with Abdul Rahman as its first prime minister. However, social and political stability — especially that tied to ethnic relations — in the new Malaya remained fragile. It was in the crucible of early independence politics and struggles over the definition of citizenship that the Chinese education movement in Malaya was given the impetus to come into being. Ethnic Chinese activists had accelerated their appeal on the drafting of the Independence Constitution in anticipation of further marginalization of the Chinese in Malaya. However, most working-class Chinese had been focusing their wholehearted efforts on securing their livelihoods and rebuilding homes. Therefore, the concept of Malaya as an independent nation and the importance of citizenship rights were relatively new and did not appeal to many of them.[36]

In an effort to increase political awareness amongst the Chinese, the most significant pillars of Chinese communities at that time — MCA, Federation of Malaya Chinese Guilds Association, *Dongzong*, and *Jiaozong* — jointly mobilized a nationwide Chinese citizenship registration movement between 1957 and 1958 (FM 1957*b*). The campaign was a success: by 1959 about 50,000 qualified Chinese residents in Malaya had successfully secured Malayan citizenship (K.J. Ratnam 1965, p. 84).

Other than citizenship, other difficult issues faced by the ethnic Chinese community in Malaya were the problems of overage students and the medium of the state examination conducted at the end of secondary education. Poverty, lack of initiative amongst illiterate parents to ensure their children received formal education, and school closure during the

Japanese occupation were the key factors that contributed to many overage students still residing in Chinese schools. These students, who tended to be influenced by left-wing political ideology, were perceived by the authorities as troublemakers and threats to their schools and younger classmates.

Therefore, soon after the Razak Report was announced, government officials at the state level began to disqualify overage students from continuing their education in Chinese secondary schools despite on-going negotiations between the Grand Three and the Education Minister Abdul Razak. Feeling frustrated and victimized by the Razak Report, a nationwide strike by Chinese students first sparked off in Penang on 14 November 1957 and spread like wildfire to some twenty Chinese secondary schools across the country (Lim, L.G. 1988, pp. 208–21). Students from the largest of these schools in Penang, namely, Chung Ling High School (钟灵中学), Han Chiang High School (韩江中学), and Chung Hwa Confucian High School (孔圣庙中华中学), marched on the streets and assembled at Penang Chinese Girls' High School (槟华女中).

The following accounts are statements by a student activist who participated in the strike:

> The [Penang Chinese Girls'] school field was full of students — about 2,000 boys from Chung Ling, Han Chiang, and Chung Hwa. Many were overage students and their sympathizers who were angry at the new policy. The demonstration ended chaotically when anti-riots police started firing tear gas at those of us who had just entered the school assembly hall. I ran home and learnt later that some ten students were injured. My school was closed for one week. I faced disciplinary action when the school reopened, and I was warned that I would be expelled from school if I participated in any future strike activities again.[37]

Simultaneously in Kuala Lumpur, students from Confucian Secondary School (尊孔中学), Kuen Cheng High School (坤成中学), and Tsun Jin High School (循人中学) also organized peaceful gatherings at their schools. Prompt intervention by *Jiaozong* leaders and Chinese educationalists reassured the students and persuaded them to abandon the strikes.[38] However, strikes continued in most parts of Perak and Johore (UCSTAM 1976, pp. 24–26). Facing increasing pressure from the Chinese community and having witnessed the manifested capacity of the students' strike, the government finally agreed to compromise. It agreed to continue the grant-in-aid for most Chinese secondary schools, include Chinese as one of the language medium of the national examinations, and end the forceful expulsion of overage students (Lim, L.G. 1988, pp. 218–21).

BEYOND CHALLENGES

Tension within the Alliance coalition surfaced after Lim Chong Eu defeated Tan Cheng Lock to become MCA's second party president in March 1958. The new MCA leadership was not endorsed by Abdul Rahman, who indicated his displeasure in his memoirs:

> A new group of young MCA leaders took over the party from Tan Cheng Lock; and with that they also introduced a new MCA policy, which was to acquire more rights for the Chinese, and to end — what they imputed — UMNO control of the Alliance and the country, and to make Chinese language one of the official languages of the country (Abdul R. 1986a, p. 70).

The relationship between Lim Chong Eu and Abdul Rahman continued to worsen when Lim Chong Eu led MCA's reform faction to support the demand to acquire official status for Chinese language during the 1958 National Convention on Expansion of Chinese Education (全马华文教育扩大会议).[39] Their demand was further consolidated in the Memorandum of Demands on Chinese Education by Chinese Citizens in the Federation (本邦华人对教育总要求) at the Grand Three Associations of Chinese Education's National Convention of Chinese Education in Malaya (三大机构华文教育中央委员会全国华文教育大会) in 1959 (GTACE 1960).

By July 1959, the deteriorating relationship between Lim Chong Eu and Abdul Rahman reached a boiling point when a letter written by Lim to Abdul Rahman was cited by the press. The "Alliance Crisis", as it was dubbed by the press, came to be seen as an issue of "Chinese versus Malays" because of the highly controversial contents of the letter. The demands stated in this letter included a pledge to petition for vernacular schools to hold examinations in their own mediums of instruction and for the government to recognize these examinations as equivalent to national certificates, and objection to the requirement that all MCA candidates for competing in the elections had to be personally approved by the Alliance chairman (Abdul R. 1986a; and Ho, K.C. 1984, p. 12).

Above all, Lim also demanded forty parliamentary seats to be allocated to MCA in the coming general election.

Lim's efforts to secure political equality for MCA within the Alliance halted when MCA lost thirty out of thirty-two contested seats during the first post-independence general election held on 19 August 1959. After failing to secure unanimous support from MCA's Central Committee, Lim and his reform faction withdrew from MCA in December 1960. At the MCA Extraordinary General Meeting held on 10 November 1961, MCA appointed a more submissive Tan Siew Sin (陈修信) to head the new MCA party, and declared its support to UMNO.[40] This also marked Abdul Rahman's resumption of full control of the Alliance collaboration (Abdul R. 1986a, p. 70; and Daniel 1995, p. 36).

The departure of many sympathizers of the Chinese education movement out of MCA dealt a serious blow to the Chinese education movement, for MCA had been a powerful benefactor of the political negotiation in the collaboration amongst the Grand Three. The newly installed MCA leaders were unable to build a trusting relationship with the Chinese education movement activists, resulting in the fading and eventual termination of MCA's unconditional support for the Chinese education movement. Leaders of the movement were thus forced to establish closer alliances and rely heavily on Chinese guilds and associations for support in their battle to preserve Chinese education in Malaya. Chinese leaders from the Federation of Malaya Chinese Guilds Association, with their strong networks and robust financial resources, quickly took over the role of MCA (Yeok 1982, p. 118). The political change of tide eventually saw the Federation of Malaya Chinese Guilds Association, *Dongzong*, and *Jiaozong* become the most articulate social mobilization vehicles of the Chinese community in the 1960s.

The Chinese education movement faced further challenges in the 1960s with the publication of the *Report of the Education Review Committee* (Rahman Talib Report) in August 1960 (FM 1960). The Rahman Talib Report proposed taking a more aggressive approach to strengthen the role of Malay language as the main medium of instruction in all schools in Malaya. The report invoked Article 21 (No. 2), which empowered the Minister of Education to convert any national-type primary school into a national primary school at its discretion. A similar clause was included in the Razak Report; however, it had been removed from the 1957 Education Ordinance after heavy lobbying by MCA (FM 1957a). This clause had been perceived by Chinese educationalists as an attempt to abolish the vernacular schools from the national education system. Their fears were rekindled with the setting of a definitive timetable to phase out English medium schools and convert government-aided Chinese secondary schools into Malay-medium schools. In addition, all national public examinations would be conducted in one of the official languages, that is, either English or Malay.

Threatened by these measures, *Jiaozong*'s Chairman, Lim Lian Geok, led *Jiaozong* in mobilizing the Chinese community to reject the Rahman Talib Report. He also accused the Ministry of Education for violating the Constitution, infringing the Alliance's election manifesto, destroying the spirit of the Razak Report and ultimately, attempting to abolish Chinese schools in Malaya.[41] However, Lim failed to stop the implementation of the Rahman Talib Report, which was enacted as the Education Act in 1961. One of the most significant impacts of the new Education Act was the termination of the partially government-aided schools system by 1 January 1962. The act would accord funding only to schools that converted to national-type secondary schools, which would use English and Malay as mediums of instruction and examination.[42] This forced Chinese secondary schools to choose between converting to the use of English and Malay as mediums of instruction and becoming financially independent as a private school.

In total, at least fifty-three Chinese secondary schools nationwide accepted the government's terms of conversion and were transformed into the national-type system in 1961. Most schools accepted the conversion offer due to the reality of financial constraints that had been plaguing most Chinese schools in Malaya. In addition, the Alliance regime launched an impactful pro-conversion campaign, culminating in the successful conversion of Penang Chung Ling High School. Chung Ling High School was the first Chinese secondary school to accept the government's special allowances and was able to reduce its school fees and offer better salaries for its schoolteachers after receiving financial aid from the government (Tan, K.H. 2007, p. 175; and Tan, L.E. 1997, p. 223). In addition, state-level education departments also held informal meetings with Chinese secondary schools' committees to persuade them to convert to the national-type system (Huang, X.J. 2002, p. 44). More importantly, the Ministry of Education also provided special permission for converted Chinese schools to establish affiliated independent schools, which used Chinese as their medium of instruction. The permission was granted to appease angry Chinese communities and protect the social interests of the school committees that had acceded to the conversion.[43]

Not surprisingly, the decision of these Chinese schools to accept the offer of conversion sparked off a wave of protests from students, parents, and the public alike. However, it was the decision of the Ministry of Home Affairs on 12 August 1961 to strip Lim Lian Geok's teaching permit and, soon after, revoke his citizenship under the pretext of "disloyal and disaffected towards the Federation of Malaya" (Lim, L.G. 1989, pp. 11–12) that became the pivotal point in the conversion of Chinese schools. Extreme retaliation by the government had been rare, and therefore the measures taken against Lim sent a message strong enough to strike fear in dissidents.

The self-censorship that constrained the reactions of the Chinese community was best exemplified by the reaction of *Jiaozong*'s central level leaders after the incident.[44] On 3 September 1961, at the request of Lim, *Jiaozong* held an emergency meeting to discuss the position of the next chairman. However, none of the attendees was willing to take on the politically precarious position. The burden fell on Huang Yun Yue (黄润岳) — who had not held any senior position within *Jiaozong* and was a mere editor of *Jiaozong*'s in-house publication, *Teachers' Journal* (教师杂志) at that time — as the acting chairman. *Jiaozong*'s Advisor Yan Yuan Zhang, who was then based in Singapore, strongly criticized the Malayan government at the meeting:

> Lim Lian Geok, as the chairman of *Jiaozong*, has the responsibility to criticize unfair education policies, and is merely exercising his right to free speech under a democratic constitution. If this right is taken away, it signifies either the death of democracy, or that the government is against the Constitution (Lim, L.G. 1989, p. 44).

In the end, Yan Yuan Zhang paid a high price for his speech: he was forbidden by law from entering Malaya indefinitely. With two *Jiaozong* leaders' dissidence countered by draconian measures from the government, the rest of the *Jiaozong* activists were cowed into silence.[45] During this crisis, only sixteen Chinese schools chose to forsake government subsidies and continue using Chinese as their medium of instruction. These schools were later referred to as independent Chinese secondary schools.[46] The converted Chinese schools used English as their medium of instruction until the 1970s, when Malay was made the sole medium of teaching in all national schools. The switch in the medium of teaching from Chinese to English and ultimately Malay was perceived by many as a betrayal and trap set by the ruling regime. This perception persists to this day, as Chinese educationalists continue to frown upon Chung Ling High School's principal, Wang Yoon Nien (汪永年), and executive director of the school committee, Ong Keng Seng (王景成), as chief betrayers of the Chinese community.[47]

NEW MALAYSIA AND MERDEKA UNIVERSITY

Malaya merged with the British colonies of Sarawak, Sabah, and Singapore to form an enlarged Federation of Malaysia on 16 September 1963. However, the formation of Malaysia was not welcomed by its larger and more imposing neighbours. Indonesian President Sukarno voiced threats to crush Malaysia, which was deemed by him as a neo-colonial puppet state of the British, and declared a policy of confrontation in January 1963 (Mackie 1974). It was a tense moment for the new Malaysian state, as armed conflict loomed in the region, especially after the Philippines President Macapagal had staked his claim on Sabah.[48]

Domestically, Singapore People's Action Party leader, Lee Kuan Yew, provoked a debate on a "Malaysian Malaysia", whereby equality before the law predicated on citizenship and no one community would enjoy special privileges. Lee's ideology tapped into the brewing resentment against the Malays' political domination of the new state (Cheah 2002, pp. 54–55; and Rudner 1970, p. 3). Lee also requested for partnership amongst members of the Alliance (Heng 1988, p. 254). Following the outbreak of ethnic riots between Chinese and Malays in Singapore in 1964, Singapore was asked to leave the federation in August 1965 by Prime Minister Abdul Rahman due to fears that the assertive Chinese minority would undermine the stability of the federation (Keylor 2003, p. 252; and Lee, K.H. 1998, p. 35).

With Singapore's departure, the proportion of the Chinese population in Malaysia dropped dramatically from 42 per cent to 25 per cent by the end of 1965 (Ongkili 1985, p. 154). It was a significant political disadvantage for the Chinese in Malaysia. In an effort to boost the political spirits of the ethnic Chinese in Malaysia, the Convention of Chinese Guilds and Associations Against the Invasion of Rights (华团反侵略大会) was held in June 1965, hosted by Selangor Chinese Assembly Hall. More than 280 representatives of Chinese guilds and associations nationwide attended the assembly to demand that Chinese be installed as an official language of Malaysia.

The Convention chairperson, Lee Hau Shik (李孝式), persuaded participants of the National Convention to entrust their appeal to MCA and wait for an appropriate moment to seek legitimacy for their mother tongue. Unfortunately, the participants discovered in August 1965 that their trust had been misplaced: in the midst of widespread objections from the Chinese community, the MCA Central Working Committee (马华中央工作委员会) opted to endorse the decision of the Alliance coalition not to support the demand for Chinese to be installed as an official language.

In response, *Dongzong* and *Jiaozong* joined the Federation of Malaya Chinese Guilds Association in drafting the Memorandum to the Prime Minister for a Rightful Place of the Chinese Language (为争取华文地位向首相东姑阿都拉曼呈送备忘录). It was submitted to the Prime Minister in November 1965 after the organizers had successfully obtained more than 2,000 signatures as a collective act of support from Chinese guilds and associations nationwide (PWCRCAGM 1965).

Somewhat surprisingly, MCA's Youth Division leader, Sim Mow Yu, did back the demand. Sim was a schoolteacher in Malacca, but also a very powerful political leader amongst the MCA youth community. He founded the MCA Youth Division, and was elected as chairman in February 1966. However, he volunteered to let Lee San Choon (李三春) assume the position of chairman while he opted to be a vice chairman. He explained his reason for doing so in an interview for this study:

> San Choon had a better working relationship with MCA's party president, while I could work closely with the Chinese pressure groups. This would ideally reap the greatest benefits for the Chinese community, especially with regard to our petition for Chinese language become one of the official languages of the country.[49]

Nonetheless, Sim's hope of forming a "San Choon and Mow Yu dream team" was dashed in October 1966 when Sim was expelled from MCA. Sim's insistent demands to instate Chinese as an official language were also not well received by MCA's leaders, and Sim was expelled for purportedly breaching the rules of MCA and the Alliance. Members of many MCA Youth Division branches demonstrated their great displeasure over Sim's expulsion in boycotts and freezing of activities; some supporters even quit the party in displeasure over the decision of the central committee. The magnitude of the protests, which lasted for about two years, almost paralyzed MCA. The expulsion motivated Sim to transform himself from a mainstream political actor into a wholehearted *Jiaozong* activist.

Sim, together with fellow Chinese educationalists, participated actively in the Chinese Education Working Committee (华教工作委员会) — a reformed collaborative body established in 1966 between *Dongzong* and *Jiaozong* — after the failure of the Grand Three. The momentum of active political activities within the Chinese communities reached its height in 1967 in response to the restrictions by the Ministry of Education requiring all students to obtain either a Cambridge School Certification or the Malaysian Certification of Education before they could leave the country for further studies abroad. This regulation hit hard particularly the non-converted Chinese secondary school graduates who had obtained only a Chinese secondary school certificate. Thus, limited enrollment opportunities at local universities forced many Chinese school graduates to continue their studies at overseas universities, or quit school altogether (Chian 1994, p. 60).

Calls for an independent Chinese university started to grow after the government refused to include Chinese as an official language under the 1966 National Language Bill (GM 1963). In an attempt to resolve the impasse, *Dongzong* and *Jiaozong* suggested the formation of Merdeka University, and the suggestion was met with overwhelming positive response from the Chinese community nationwide.[50] During the opening speech at the Merdeka University Founders' Assembly (马来亚独立大学发起人大会) held at Selangor Chinese Assembly Hall in April 1968, the chairman of the founding committee, who was also *Dongzong* chairman, Ye Hong En (叶鸿恩), summoned support from his fellow countrymen with the following call:[51]

> The founding of Merdeka University has a significant meaning for the Chinese community here, and the university has a long road ahead of it. Although we will face many challenges, we shall possess the determination and courage to surmount all difficulties, and we shall not be daunted by repeated setbacks (UCSTAM 1968).

In this Assembly, a Merdeka University Formation Working Committee (马来西亚独立大学筹备工作委员会) was formed to establish a non-profit

Merdeka University (Limited) Company (独立大学有限公司). Merdeka University received overwhelming support from the Chinese community, as well as from MCA's Youth Division and Women Wing (MUB 1978*b*, p. 75). The strength of its support base was apparent in the various fundraising campaigns held by Merdeka University in 1968, which successfully collected about two million straits dollars by May 1969 (NUAAM et al. 1982, pp. 84–85; Zeng et al. 1993, pp. 149–51; and Zhuan 2004, p. 242). More significantly, *Dongjiaozong*, as an entity that represents the collaboration between *Dongzong* and *Jiaozong*, was popularized during the Merdeka University movement, and has since been widely recognized by the Chinese communities in the country as the defenders of Chinese education.

Despite overwhelming support from the rank and file of MCA, the formation of Merdeka University did not meet with the blessings of MCA's central leaders (DNICSSDWC 1993, p. 21; and MUB 1978*b*, p. 86). MCA President Tan Siew Sin criticized the formation of Merdeka University as being "politically motivated" and that "it would have been easier for 'hell to freeze' than for Merdeka University to be established in this country".[52] As a counter response, MCA proposed the expansion of the University of Malaya's Department of Chinese Studies into a full faculty and set up the Tunku Abdul Rahman College (拉曼学院) as palatable alternatives.[53] Still, flagging political strength and mounting pressure from MCA members forced MCA to finally back down and agree to work with Merdeka University Company. The registration of Merdeka University Company was approved by the government as a non-profit corporation under the Companies Act on 8 May 1969 — two days before the 1969 General Election. This, however, did not save the Alliance coalition from losing two-thirds of the parliamentary majority in the elections held on 12 May 1969, resulting in MCA leaders declaring that the party would pull out from the cabinet.

At the same time, opposition parties, mostly non-Malays who won the polls, celebrated their victory in organized demonstrations. The demonstrations only served to deepen the fear and mistrust amongst the Malays over the Chinese's growing influence and power in the country. The immediate eruption of ethnic riots on 13 May 1969, involving ethnic Malays and Chinese communities, resulted in hundreds of deaths.[54] As a consequence of the ethnic riots, the formation of Merdeka University was stalled after the subsequent declaration of a State of Emergency, with

Merdeka University Company's financial assets frozen by the government (Zhen 2006, p. 84).

Prime Minister Abdul Rahman resigned and paved the way for Abdul Razak as the second prime minister of Malaysia in September 1970. Abdul Razak led the National Operation Council in governing the state with an Emergency Decree for the next twenty-one months. Abdul Razak's regime sought to restructure state and society relations in Malaysia, and the centrepiece of this overhaul, the New Economic Policy, was introduced in 1971. Aimed at restructuring state and society, the main approach of the New Economic Policy was to:

> ... eradicate poverty, by raising income levels and increasing employment opportunities for all Malaysians, irrespective of race. It also aimed at accelerating the process of restructuring the Malaysian society to correct economic imbalance, so as to reduce and eventually eliminate the identification of race with economic function (cited from GM 1971e, p. 2).

The first decade of the New Economic Policy saw state-led *bumiputera* capitalist development rocketing. Civil servants' wages were increased and an official Islamization programme was promoted to nudge Muslims on the path to capitalism in Malaysia.[55] As discussed in Chapter 1, Alliance coalition was broadened after the 1969 riots by co-opted PAS, Gerakan, and People's Progressive Party to form BN.[56] The expanding ranks of the ruling coalition enhanced UMNO's political domination and procured more power in the hands of Malays; it also weakened the status of MCA as the sole representative of the Chinese population in the government.

MCA launched a series of nationwide Chinese Solidarity Conventions (全国华人团结大会) after the end of the Emergency Decree in 1971 to garner support from the Chinese community in an attempt to rebound from its declining political status (Loh 1982). Leaders and communities assembled at the Seminar of National Chinese Leaders in Malaya (全马华人领袖座谈会) in February 1971 to discuss the issues and challenges of unity amongst the Chinese. Sim Mow Yu, who remained influential and popular at the grassroots level despite having been expelled from MCA, was invited to be the keynote speaker.[57] The Chinese Solidarity Conventions continued in Perak, Negeri Sembilan, and Penang.[58] Despite overwhelming participation from the community in the

National Chinese Alliance Movement, the movement neither reformed MCA nor improved the political status of the Chinese by means of securing the status of Chinese language and culture in Malaysia (Lee, K.H. 1998, pp. 39–40; and Lew and Loot 1997). The movement ended dramatically when Sim and Gu Hsing Kuang (顾兴光) were arrested in April 1971 under the Sedition Act.[59]

Later in December 1971, *Dongzong*, *Jiaozong*, and the Chinese Education Central Committee jointly organized the National Convention of Chinese School Committees and Schoolteachers (全国华校董教大会) to discuss strategies to persuade the government to allow Chinese schools to retain their traditional features. Despite this being the largest gathering of Chinese educationalists with more than a thousand attendees, including representatives from Sarawak, the weakened MCA failed to achieve any breakthrough in negotiations with the government on this issue.

The Chinese education movement suffered more setbacks in 1974 with the normalization of diplomatic relations between Malaysia and the People's Republic of China. Not only did this diplomatic move signify the end of China's state-level support to the MCP, but it also confirmed both governments' recognition of the principle of *jus soli*, rejection of dual nationality, and recognition of Malaysian Chinese as legitimate citizens of Malaysia.[60] The recognition and acknowledgement Abdul Razak and his administration gave to China rewarded him with favourable support from the Chinese community, leading to his landslide victory in the 1974 General Election (Loh, Phang, and Saravanamuthu 1981, pp. 27–33).

CONCLUSION

Anti-communist sentiments arising from the Cold War controversies of the 1960s and 1970s generally targeted Chinese as supporters of communists in Malaya, especially those who fought against the Japanese under the MCP-led MPAJA in World War II. The Chinese education movement arose in the process of the British's efforts to fight communism in Malaya and the rise of nationalism amongst Malayan Chinese prior to Malaya's independence in 1957.

The Grand Three coalition in the 1950s marked the birth of the movement in Malaya's nation-building process. Although state and movement actors did not share many of the same principles, their interpersonal and inter-institutional working experiences had built gradually upon a foundation of trust to become the key factors for the widespread support the Alliance coalition garnered from vernacular communities for the 1955 Malacca Meeting. Nevertheless, the "honeymoon" of the political marriage was brief. When elites in the top echelon were changed, pro-vernacular MCA leader, Lim Chong Eu, and his reformist wings did not have the blessings of Alliance Chairman, Abdul Rahman. When Tan Siew Sin came into power through the help of the Alliance regime's old guards, the Chinese education movement was forced to turn to the support from Chinese guilds and associations.

This shift in support base expanded the magnitude of the movement to include intellectuals, financially-established Chinese entrepreneurs, as well as the Chinese speaking community that harboured similar grievances. The Chinese education movement transformed from a claim by a small organization over educational issues into a full-blown campaign to secure citizenship rights for the Chinese in Malaya, along with demands for installing the Chinese's vernacular language as an official language and forming a more comprehensive and inclusive national education system.

While the implementation of the New Economic Policy, National Educational Policy, and other pro-Malay affirmative actions fostered the growth of political patronage in the Malay middle class, yet it also further polarized the dichotomy between Malays and non-Malays in the country (GM 1971*a*). Ironically, ethnic exploitation, inequitable distribution of national wealth and deliberate marginalization of the non-*bumiputera* would become the key factors that united the Chinese in the Chinese education movement. The events presented in this chapter form the backdrop for the establishment of various institutions in the social movement in its later stages.

Although Malaysia has grown from a new state in the 1950s into a successful developing country by the 2010s, yet the Chinese education movement, with its claim on constitutional discrimination, has left an ugly scar on the country's facade of political progress. The reminder by Donald MacGillivray to *Jiaozong* leaders in November 1952 remains eternal: "… lacking the status as an official language in Malaya, Chinese [language] and Chinese schools will never be recognized within the Malaysian education system".[61]

Notes

1. According to Silcock and Aziz (1953, p. 279), Malays are territorially allegiant to sultans, culturally to Islam. By 1951, the non-Malays comprised about 50 per cent of the total population in Malaya. Amongst them, 62 per cent Chinese and 50 per cent Indians were locally born. See FM (1952*b*, p. 2).

2. The MCP was formed in 1930, crushed by the British government in 1955, with remnants of the party continuing military resistance against the Malaya federal government along the Thai-Malaya border until the 1989 peace treaty. The MPAJA was a political association controlled by the MCP, and was once equipped by the British. It grew from 200 in 1942 into a force of 10,000 by 1945. For more, see Purcell (1967, pp. 258–62); Pye (1957, p. 8); Ramakrishna (2002); and Springhall (2000, p. 50).

3. The British ruled Malaya through direct and indirect governments. The *entrepot* trade centres of Penang, Malacca, and Singapore had non-Malay majorities, which were ruled directly as crown colonies. Malay states with significant commercial activities (tin mines and rubber plantations) — Perak, Selangor, Negeri Sembilan, and Pahang — were set up as Federated Malaya States. Those states lacking in such activities — Perlis, Kedah, Kelantan, Terengganu, and Johore — were ruled as Unfederated Malaya States. See Cheah (1983, pp. 441–46); and von Vorys (1975, pp. 22, 142).

4. *Bumiputera* refers to two groups of people: the ethnic Malay who habitually speaks Malay, professes Islam, and conforms to traditional Malay customs (*adat*), and the indigenous occupant of the Malay archipelago. For more, see Chai (1977, p. 7).

5. Only 350,000 (11 per cent) Chinese and 225,000 (7 per cent) Indians were eligible to become citizens of Federation of Malaya under the "operation of law" condition in February 1948. Ibid., p. 8.

6. Japanese military began the *Kakyo Shukusei* (purge through purification) — operation wartime massacres on ethnic Chinese — from December 1941 to April 1942, and continued in other forms until August 1945. The number of victims reached as high as 50,000 in Singapore and 40,000 in Malaya. For more, see Cheah (1983, p. 23); Hirofumi (2008); and Peattie (1996, pp. 230–31).

7. The lengthy guerrilla war (1948–60) cost the British and the Malayan government about 850 million straits dollar. About 11,048 people were killed (6,710 guerrillas, 1,865 security forces and 2,473 civilians). For more, see O'Balance (1966, p. 177); Pye (1957, p. 15); and Stockwell (1999, p. 486).

8. General Templer arrived in Malaya in February 1952 to replace Henry Gurney who died in a terrorist ambush in late 1951. Templer was both high commissioner and military director of operations, and had full authority to

wage counter-communist insurgency operations, using policing, intelligence and psychological warfare. For more, see Abdul R. (1986a, p. 35); and Ramakrishna (2001).

9. Tan was Straits-born, English-educated and a nominated member of the Malacca Municipal Council and Straits Settlements Legislative Council, and known to British's highest officials, such as Malcolm MacDonald and Henry Gurney. For more, see Heng (1988, pp. 67, 251); and Tan, L.E. (1988, pp. 50–51).

10. These leaders included Sim Mow Yu, Leong Yew Koh (梁宇皋), and Lee Hau Shik. For more, see Heng (1983, pp. 291–309); Lee, K.H. (1998, p. 31); and Lomperis (1996, p. 212).

11. Malaysian Indian Congress was established since 1946 to support India's independence from British. After India had gained its independence, it started to support the independence of Malaya. For more, see Abdul R. (1986a, p. 35); and Lomperis (1996, p. 207).

12. In 1946, the Malayan Union Council Paper (No. 53) marked the first official education reform plan by the British. The plan proposed English as the compulsory subject for all vernacular schools but it vanished with the rejection of the Malayan Union in 1949. For more, see MU (1947).

13. English and Malay schools received full support and control from the government. As Tamil schools were mostly located in rural areas and functioned independently like the Chinese schools, they faced more challenges to sustain the financial resources necessary to maintain the schools' operation.

14. The day after Barnes Report was published in the newspapers, domestic Chinese press filled their pages with articles attacking and accusing the Barnes Report of intention to abolish the Chinese schools and subsequently to destroy the Chinese culture. For more, see China Press, 12 June 1951; and Nanyangshangpao, 13 June 1951.

15. Kinkwok Daily News, 12 July 1951; Nanyangshangpao, 9 July and 19 July 1951; and Sinchew Daily, 8 July and 10 July 1951.

16. Anti-Barnes Report gatherings were also conducted in Selangor (19 July 1951) and Johore (9 August 1951). For the debates, see China Press, 12 June 1951; Kinkwok Daily News, 12 July 1951; Nanyangshangpao, 13 June, 9 July, and 19 July 1951; and Sinchew Daily, 8 July and 10 July 1951.

17. Sim Mow Yu (founder of the Malacca MCA Youth, former Jiaozong chairman), interview by the author, Malacca, 26 March 2008.

18. Ibid.

19. The presidential association (主席区) was a system practised by Jiaozong from 1951 to 1954, whereby one of the member associations would be selected and be responsible for all office-bearer positions (chairman, general secretary, and treasurer). The role of the presidential association was further consolidated

in 1954 to allow the same Chinese schoolteachers' association to hold the committee position without term limits. This change allowed capable leaders to stabilize the organization in the fragile early phase of *Jiaozong*. After more Chinese schoolteachers' associations were established and potential leaders promoted from across Malaya, *Jiaozong*'s Constitution was amended in 1954 to enable the selection of the executive committee on a personal basis. For more, see UCSTAM (1976, p. 2). For the list of *Jiaozong*'s members, see Appendix 1.

20. The special committee was appointed on 20 September 1951 to make recommendations for various Education Reports and draft the 1952 Education Ordinance. Chong Khoon Lin (张崑灵) and Leung Cheung Ling were in the Central Advisory Committee; Lee Hau Shik and Leung Cheung Ling were in the Special Committee. For more, see CACE (1951).

21. Graduated from Columbia University in the United States, Wen Tien Kuang (温典光) had been the Chinese-English translator of MCA during the 1950s, responsible for almost all documents between *Jiaozong* and *Dongzong* with MCA. He was the Selangor Chinese School Committee Association general secretary (1956–59), deputy chairman (1960–64), Chinese Education Central Committee secretary, and the middleman between Lim Lian Geok and Tan Cheng Lock. The Selangor Chinese Assembly Hall was renamed as Kuala Lumpur and Selangor Chinese Assembly Hall (吉隆坡暨雪兰莪中华大会堂) in 2006 to legitimize and strengthen the power of representation of this organization on behalf of Chinese communities at Selangor and Kuala Lumpur regions.

22. MCA was represented by Lee Chang Jing (李长景) and Yong Xu Ling (杨旭龄).

23. For the report, see FM (1954). For the implementation suggestions of this report, see FLC (1954).

24. The memorandum claimed that schooling through the "mother tongue" was a basic means of preserving one's culture. The memorandum also clarified, for the first time, the Chinese's demand to affirm Chinese language as an official language. It warned that Chinese and Tamils should be won over — not forced — to become Malayans. For more, see UCSCAM et al. (2009); and UCSTAM (1954; 1983*a*; 1987*b*).

25. Protest at the state-level spread like wild fire, especially in November 1954. Open contention was manifested in the local Chinese communities in Perak (2 and 8 November), Batu Pahat (4 November), Johore (6 November), Perlis (11 November), and Penang (13 November). See *Nanyangshangpao*, 20 October and 23 October 1954; 10 November and 15 November 1954; and *Sinchew Daily*, 31 October and 9 November 1954.

26. Yan Yuan Zhang (1909–96) acquired his Doctorate in Education from London University in 1951. He was well respected amongst the Chinese

scholarly community and leading Chinese education activists in Malaya during the 1950s. He was deported from Malaysia in 1962, but continued his involvement in the movement from Singapore as the head of department of education at Nanyang University (1960–65).

27.   The Razak Report's second recommendation was to use either English or Malay as the medium of public examinations (Lower School Certificate and Federation of Malaya Certificate of Education). A minimum requirement of "pass" in Malay was required for the award of these certificates. The exclusion of Chinese as a medium in public examinations was seen by Chinese educationalists as a threat to the existence of Chinese secondary schools and to the preservation of Chinese language and culture. For more, see FM (1956*b*, p. 1).

28.   Only twenty registration centres were located at Chinese schools amongst the total 133 registration centres in Selangor, despite there being more Chinese schools than Malay or English schools. See Tay (2001, pp. 375–80).

29.   The first Independence Mission was led by Abdul Rahman and the delegation consisted of Abdul Razak and Tan Tiong Hai (陈东海). For more, see Abdul R. (1986*b*, pp. 213–16).

30.   The Alliance coalition threatens to withdraw its members from all towns, municipals, and legislative councils if the British refused to accept their suggestion to hold the state and federal elections in 1955. For more, see Abdul R. (1983, pp. 33–38, 94–100).

31.   Abdul Rahman and Alliance coalition representatives conducted negotiations with the MCP's representative, Chin Peng, in the Baling Talk on 28 December 1955. For more, see Abdul R. (1986*a*, pp. 63–68); Chin, P. (2003, p. 328); and FM (1956*a*).

32.   Conducted at Tan Cheng Lock's private residence in Malacca, the meeting was attended by twenty-one representatives from UMNO, MCA, *Jiaozong*, and *Dongzong*. See UCSTAM (1975, p. 26).

33.   The London Talks were led by Abdul Rahman, joint by Abdul Razak, Lee Hau Shik, and Tan Tiong Hai. For details on the independent process, see Abdul R. (1977, p. 25; 1984, pp. 138–46; 1986*b*, pp. 213–16).

34.   Known as the Federation of Malaysia Chinese Guilds Association after 1963, this federation was officially registered in 1955 and was one of the leading pressure group in the Chinese citizenships, language, and education movement during the pre-independence era. It consisted of a wide network of registered Chinese guilds and associations in the Federation of Malaya.

35.   The conference was in collaboration with Selangor Chinese Assembly Hall, Ipoh Chinese Assembly Hall, and *Jiaozong*. It was participated by 1,094 Chinese organizations. Lim Lian Geok, Lau Pak Kuan (刘伯群), and three other members were selected as representatives to London to put forth their

appeal at last resort if the negotiations with Lord Reid failed. For details of the memorandum, see FMCGA (1956).

36. By 1954, despite two years after the liberalization of citizenship requirements, the non-citizen proportion of the Chinese population remained as high as 50 per cent. See Heng (1988, p. 83); and Lomperis (1996, p. 210).

37. Huang J.J. (pseudonym, one of the students who participated in the Penang school strike in 1957), interview by the author, Penang, 17 January 2009.

38. Liu Huai Gu (刘怀谷), Yang Ya Ling (杨雅灵), Chong Min Chang (钟敏章), Lim Lian Geok, Cheng Ji Mou (陈济谋), and Wen Tien Kuang have played important roles in calming the students.

39. *Sinchew Daily*, 23 September 1958.

40. Tan Siew Sin served as MCA president from 1961 to 1974 and was minister of finance and minister of commerce and industry, both are powerful positions, from 1957 to 1974.

41. Lim Lian Geok (1901–85) played a key role in the Chinese education movement during the 1960s. Born in Fujian province (福建省) of China and migrated to Malaya in 1927, he taught at Confucian Private Secondary School from 1934 until 1961, and was *Jiaozong* chairman from 1953 to 1961. For more, see Lim, L.G. (1960, p. 3).

42. Once converted, the medium of instruction in a Chinese school would no longer be Chinese, except for Chinese language and literature. For details, see Heng (1988, p. 255); and Yeok (1982, pp. 120–21).

43. Sim Mow Yu, interview by the author, Malacca, 26 March 2008.

44. Expression of support from Kuala Lumpur Chinese Teachers' Association came as late as 23 August. Three days later, Sim Mow Yu, who had just concluded his visit in Indonesia, attempted to persuade Tan Siew Sin to retract the decision, but failed.

45. Parliament opposition leader, People's Progressive Party Chairman S. Seenivasagam, challenged Abdul Rahman to revoke his (Seenivasagam) citizenship too, at the 20 October parliamentary debate. Lim Lian Geok fought against the revocation for three years through judiciary prosecutions but was ultimately not vindicated at the Court of Appeals. Lim secluded himself from the society since, and spent the rest of his life writing memoirs.

46. For the list of Chinese secondary schools which refused the conversion, see Appendix 3.

47. Loot Ting Yee (陆庭瑜) (former vice chairman of *Jiaozong*), interview by the author, Kuala Lumpur, 24 March 2008.

48. The confrontation ended after Soeharto assumed power in March 1966. Indonesia eventually accepted Malaysia as an independent country during the Peace Talks in Bangkok on May 1966. For details on the confrontation, see Abdul R. (1986*a*, pp. 77, 81); Mackie (1974, pp. 318–22); and Milne (1964).

49. Sim Mow Yu, interview by the author, 26 March 2008.

50. The Federation of Malaya Chinese Senior Normal Graduate Teachers' Union (高师职总) proposed the establishment of a Chinese university in Malaysia, mimicking the format of Nanyang University (南洋大学) in Singapore on 7 December 1967. The proposal was accepted by the *Jiaozong* annual representative assembly the next day and engaged *Dongzong's* involvement. Other names proposed for the university included Harmony and Union University (协和大学), Cheng Ho University (郑和大学), Kuala Lumpur University (吉隆坡大学), Tan Cheng Lock University (陈祯禄大学), and Tunku Abdul Rahman University (拉曼大学). It was eventually named Merdeka University to commemorate Malaya's independence. For details of the naming process, see *Sinchew Daily*, 25 February 1968; and UCSTAM (1968, pp. 18–28).

51. Ye Hong En was the founder of Perak United State-Level Chinese School Teachers' Association (吡叻州华校教师会联合会) and played a significant role in supporting *Jiaozong's* formation in 1961. He was an active leader in Selangor Chinese School Committees' Association from 1958 to 1978.

52. Chinese educationalists and the Chinese-speaking community perceived the comments as an ultimate act of betrayal of ethnic Chinese by English-educated Tan Siew Sin. For Tan's comments, see *Malay Mail*, 17 April 1969.

53. *China Press*, 15 July 1968.

54. No precise fatality figures were made public until today. Casualties' counts by the police reported 196 dead, 439 wounded, and 9,183 detained. For details of the riot, see NOC (1969, pp. 89–92).

55. By 1970, Malays owned only 2 per cent of the share capital, 22 per cent by Chinese, 1 per cent by Indians, and 60 per cent by foreigners. The New Economic Policy aimed to ensure 30 per cent shares for Malays in the country's corporate interests by 1990. The second phase of the New Economic Policy saw Mahathir introduced a greater sense of Malay nationalism in the national economy by "UMNO-nizing" ownership of European corporations, and through the "Look East" industrialization model. For details on the policy, see Chin, B.N. (2000, pp. 1043–44); GM (1971c); Means (1991, pp. 19–53); and Torii (2003).

56. Democratic Action Party, *Partai Rakyat*, and Social Justice Party of Malaysia refused to join BN.

57. Sim mentioned in the interview that he was persuaded by Tan Siew Sin and other senior MCA party leaders to be the speaker of the seminar for the sake of the Chinese. Sim Mow Yu, interview by the author, Malacca, 26 March 2008.

58. *Tongbao*, 9 February 1971.

59. They were prosecuted for giving stirring speeches in Ipoh on 29 April;
     however, Malaysian authorities dropped the case on 27 October 1972, and
     proposed Sim to take on a senator position; however, the invitation was
     declined. Sim Mow Yu, interview by the author, Malacca, 26 March 2008.
60. Although China promised the end of state-level support towards the
     MCP, the party level ties (Chinese Communist Party-MCP) continued until
     the dissolution of the MCP in 1989. For more, see Chin, P. (2003).
61. *Jiaozong*'s representatives had a closed door meeting with the Deputy
     High Commissioner of the Federation, Donald MacGillivray in November
     1952 to discuss the problems faced by Chinese schools. During this
     meeting, *Jiaozong* leaders were informed that as Chinese language was not
     Malaya's official language, therefore it could not be used as a medium of
     instruction in schools; nor would Chinese schools be recognized within
     the Malayan education system. Aware of the importance of gaining official
     recognition, *Jiaozong* began to demand for Chinese as an official language
     in Malaya since then. For details of this meeting, see Lim, L.G. (1965;
     1988); Tay (2001, pp. 251–53); and UCSTAM (1987*a*, p. 515).

3

CHALLENGES AND ADAPTATIONS

INTRODUCTION

Chapter 2 detailed the formation of the Chinese education movement, its trajectories and the external challenges faced during the early stages of the movement during Malaya's transition from a colony to an independent state. The chapter demonstrated the significant role that Chinese elites' personal social capital played in determining the social movement's trajectories. The movement gained momentum in the 1950s through the collaboration amongst MCA, *Dongzong*, and *Jiaozong* under the framework of the Grand Three Associations of Chinese Education. The collaboration proved its value in defending the interests of Chinese schoolteachers and Chinese school committee communities when Chinese schools were incorporated into the national education system under the 1957 Education Ordinance. Unfortunately, the collaboration fell apart when MCA's leadership was reshuffled, placing the survival of Chinese schools under threat as the state's assimilative policies of the 1960s and 1970s took hold.

Due to the difficulty of penetrating the movement's stronghold at the central level, the state began to impose a series of limitations and soft coercive approaches by manipulating state agencies, such as Ministry of Education, to weaken the movement at the local level. This divide-and-attack strategy significantly limited the capacities of the movement agencies, hitting the movement's local-central associational linkages particularly hard. This chapter argues that the state, through manipulating state institutional mechanisms such as education policies and distribution of financial resources, managed to weaken the movement without using force. This strategy enabled the state to suppress the movement, and at the same time, secure the political interests of the non-liberal democratic government to stay in power. Such an environment forced the social movement to learn, adapt, and withstand challenges, which became the key factor to its survival.

In order to examine each of these challenges in detail, this chapter is divided into four sections. The first section presents the challenges faced by Chinese school committees when their traditional role as caretakers of Chinese schools were severely threatened and weakened by state-imposed structural constraints through educational policies and distribution of state resources. These constraints altered the character, structure, and capabilities of these local agencies, resulting in changes to their involvement in the Chinese education movement.

The second section describes a critical turning point for Chinese schools in the 1970s when English-medium primary schools were phased out by the state. Similar to the Chinese and Tamil vernacular schools, English-medium primary schools (many of them formally Christian mission schools) were incorporated into the national education system as "national-type" primary schools. Although these schools could retain their original English name, they could no longer enjoy the privilege of teaching only in the English language. Phasing out of the English-medium schools resulted in a spike in student enrolment in Chinese schools, which in turn caused a revival in the role of Chinese school committees.

Competition to enrol in already overcrowded urban Chinese schools saw the development of a patronage relationship between Chinese parents and school committees, which have the power to recommend candidates for enrolment into popular schools. Opaque policies in the allocation of state grants to these vernacular schools also stimulated the participation of urban middle-class parents in the schools' fundraising campaigns. Efforts to overcome state constraints saw some school committees seek political intervention from MCA to obtain special funding allocation or facilitate the relocation of the school to a more populated neighbourhood to boost enrolment. Although the phasing out of English-medium schools provided justification for keeping Chinese school committees, it did not solve the fundamental problems faced by Chinese schoolteachers.

The third section of this chapter takes on this issue. Chinese schoolteachers, as civil servants, felt uneasy about their participation in anti-government activities. This resulted in the lack of a broad support base in most Chinese schoolteachers' associations. Facing the lack of resources and new leadership, most of these associations were forced to operate under the patronage of school principals, thus weakening the central institution of *Jiaozong* considerably.

The chapter's final section evaluates the impacts of the state's efforts to co-opt the movement during the 1990s. During this period, politically ambitious individuals tried to seek positions in various Chinese education associations, especially at the state-level alliance of Chinese school committees' association, as a stepping stone for their political career. These individuals gradually made their way into the national organizations of the movement, but held the integrity and independence of the Chinese education movement hostage in various accounts after they had been co-opted by the state. The implementation of the controversial 1996 Education Act also presented new challenges to the role of school committees and the overall sustainability of the movement. All these technical challenges and changes experienced by local level agents have a domino effect on the movement's overall capacity and ability to mobilize support from movement members and the Chinese community at large. The chapter ends with an evaluation of the consequences of changes to the relationship between *Dongzong* and *Jiaozong* at the national level.

CONTROL AND CONSTRAINTS ON CHINESE SCHOOLS

All Chinese primary schools in Malaya were incorporated into the national education system under the 1957 Education Ordinance, followed by a mass conversion of Chinese secondary schools into the national system under the 1961 Education Act. Only sixteen Chinese secondary schools refused the conversion in the 1960s and became the last independent standing institutions of the Chinese education movement as independent Chinese secondary schools. This also meant that about three quarters of the Chinese schools in Malaysia became entitled to receive financial support from the state, and therefore, were constrained by the national education acts to participate in the movement.

To begin with, the status of school committee was degraded from "owner" of the school into "a trustee institution" under the 1961 Education Act.[1] As a consequence, the school committee no longer enjoyed its powerful role of being the sole decision-maker of Chinese schools during the colonial era, nor could it continue to enjoy unquestioned power to relocate or transfer the school's property without the consent and authorization of school sponsors and the Ministry of Education. In its attempt to persuade Chinese schools to be incorporated into the national education system as its larger social control strategy, the state agreed to provide substantial financial support to these schools.

However, the actual implementation and distribution of state resources were skewed. The state's efforts to promote Malay-medium national schools had resulted in limited opportunities for Chinese and Tamil schools to access state resources. Moreover, vernacular schools built on non-government-owned premises were categorized as "partially-assisted schools", and therefore only entitled to state subsidies for executive expenses and schoolteachers' salaries.[2] By 2008, a total of 68 per cent or 879 Chinese schools in Malaysia had been categorized as partially-assisted schools (MCACEB 2008). Not only did these schools receive less entitlement for state resources as a rule, in practice, they were also allocated insufficient resources for development.

As illustrated in Table 3.1, a comparison of funds allocated under the Malaysia Plan from 1972 until 2010 demonstrated that national schools received most of the allocated budget. Chinese and Tamil primary schools received considerably less funds in proportion to the student distribution ratio in the Malaysia Plan during the same period.

As education is an expensive investment, the lack of financial support from the government seriously weakened the development of Chinese schools and other vernacular education institutions in the country alike. Many of these schools had been built during the colonial era and their wooden and zinc roofed facilities had been left unrepaired. As a result, many of the school facilities were infested with termites. In order to meet the costs of maintenance and improvement works, Chinese schools had been depending on financial sources derived from renting out the school canteen and profits from the school cooperative shops to survive.

Nevertheless, the imposition of a tenure of three years for each term on all school committee members under the 1957 Education Ordinance resulted in frequent turnover of school committee members, thus reducing the opportunity for junior members of school committees to learn from their senior partners, and weakening the line-up of school committees. Due to the lack of written documents that defined the rights of school committees, inexperienced school committees lacked the knowledge and skills to subsist abusive decisions from the state agencies. Hence, if Chinese school committees were unable to defend their affirmative rights to administrate such incomes, not only was the sustainability of the respective Chinese schools at risk, but the impact reverberated throughout the Chinese education movement and threatened the overall survival of the movement.

TABLE 3.1
Public Funding for Primary Schools under Malaysia Plans
(1972–2010)

	National Schools	Chinese Schools	Tamil Schools
Allocated Public Funding (1972–78)	237,118,327 (91 per cent)	18,097,380 (7 per cent)	5,892,660 (2 per cent)
Number of Students in 1970	1,046,513 (67 per cent)	439,681 (28 per cent)	79,278 (5 per cent)
Ideal distribution	174,550,943	73,319,229	1,323,819
Sixth Malaysia Plan (1991–95)	1,133,076,000 (90 per cent)	102,726,000 (8 per cent)	27,042,000 (2 per cent)
Number of Students in 1991	1,845,400 (73 per cent)	583,218 (23 per cent)	99,876 (4 per cent)
Ideal distribution	921,623,551	291,338,111	49,882,338

TABLE 3.1 (Cont'd)

	National Schools	Chinese Schools	Tamil Schools
Seventh Malaysia Plan (1996–2000)	1,027,167,000 (97 per cent)	25,970,000 (2 per cent)	10,902,000 (1 per cent)
Number of Students in 1996	2,128,227 (75 per cent)	595,451 (21 per cent)	102,679 (4 per cent)
Ideal distribution	801,221,367	224,193,017	38,624,616
Eighth Malaysia Plan (2001–05)	4,708,800,000 (96 per cent)	133,600,000 (3 per cent)	57,600,000 (1 per cent)
Number of Students in 2001	2,209,736 (76 per cent)	616,402 (21 per cent)	88,810 (3 per cent)
Ideal distribution	3,714,690,000	1,035,860,000	149,450,000
Ninth Malaysia Plan (2006–10)	4,598,120,000 (95 per cent)	174,340,000 (4 per cent)	54,840,000 (1 per cent)
Number of Students in 2006	2,298,808 (76 per cent)	636,124 (21 per cent)	100,142 (3 per cent)
Ideal distribution	3,663,838,480	1,013,854,230	159,606,290

Notes: Data for the Tenth Malaysia Plan (2010–15) was not made public by the government. The currency unit used is ringgit.

Sources: GM (1971c; 1976; 1981b; 1986; 1991; 1995; 2001; 2006b); MEM (1986a); UCSCAM (2007, p. 156).

To further reduce the power of any school committee, the 1957 Education Ordinance also regulated the selection of school committee members, and required three to six representatives from each of the following clusters to form a school committee: school sponsors, alumni, parents of current pupils, school trustees and representatives appointed by the Ministry of Education. The inclusion of representatives appointed by the Ministry of Education as a key condition for continuation of government subsidies, in particular, was part of the state's efforts to control the authority of school committees. Other than financial and structural constraints, the state had also halted the formation of new vernacular schools since the independence of Malaya in 1957. All the slots for schools in the new housing areas were exclusively reserved for Malay-medium national schools, resulting in a significant decrease in the number of vernacular schools (Chinese and Tamil schools) since the 1970s.

As illustrated in Figures 3.1 and 3.2, the number of national schools rose from 4,277 in 1970 to 5,848 in 2011, a sharp increase of 36 per cent or 1,571 schools. Correspondingly, the number of students in

FIGURE 3.1

Distribution of Primary Schools in Malaysia

(1970–2011)

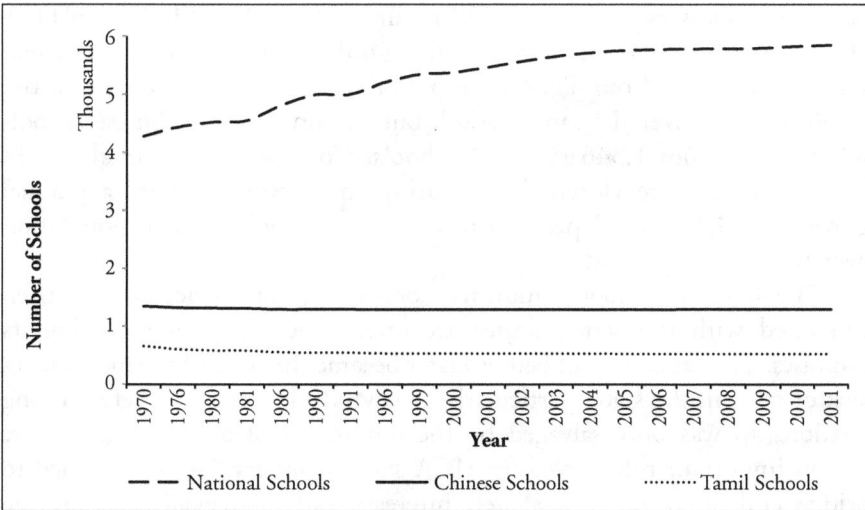

Source: Compiled by the author with data provided by *Jiaozong* and data extracted from MEM (1978; 1986b; 1990; 1991; 2007; 2011).

FIGURE 3.2

Distribution of Primary School Students in Malaysia

(1970–2011)

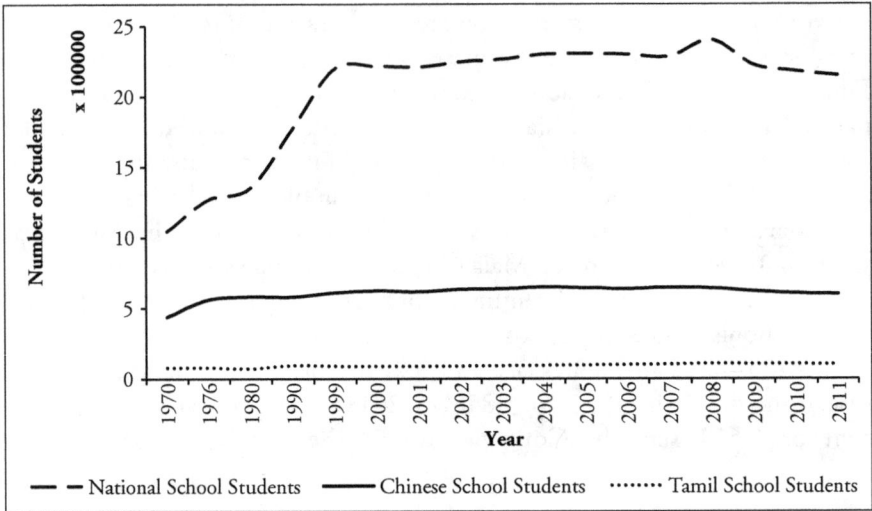

Source: Compiled by the author with data provided by *Jiaozong* and data extracted from MEM (1978; 1986*b*; 1990; 1991; 2007; 2011).

national schools grew from 1,046,513 in 1970 to 2,150,139 in 2011, a 105 per cent increase. In contrast, although the number of Chinese school students increased from 439,681 to 598,488 students, equivalent to a rise of 36 per cent over the same period, but the number of Chinese schools was reduced from 1,346 to 1,291 schools. Comparatively, a total of 134 Tamil schools were closed down during this period, despite a gradual growth of 23,364 or 29 per cent of the Tamil schools' student population over time.

The Chinese school committee community, in particular, had been frustrated with the state's unjust treatment and delay in executing its promises. The experience of betrayal later became the basis of the movement's lack of trust in the state, particularly in UMNO leaders. The deteriorating relationship was only salvaged by the outgrowth of a brokerage culture — an important role played by MCA state members — that helped to bridge collaboration, link shared interests and, above all, prevent the escalation of any violent confrontations, which will be elaborated in the next chapter.

THE TURNING POINT

The state's educational policies and its control of resources have successfully contained the development of vernacular schools to this day. However, one of these state strategies was a crucial turning point for the Chinese education movement. After the 1967 National Language Bill was passed to secure Malay language as the country's sole national language, Malay formally replaced English as the medium of instruction in all primary one classes in English-medium schools; the higher levels followed suit thereafter (GM 1971*b*). By 1986, English schools in the country had been completely eliminated.

Phasing out of English schools had a strong impact on the Chinese education movement, especially in the 1980s. It confirmed the concerns raised by *Dongjiaozong* since the 1950s that the same fate awaited the Chinese schools, and proved to be a timely wake-up call for fence-sitting Chinese communities to defend the future of Chinese primary schools. Beyond being a place to learn the Chinese language, Chinese schools had also become a symbolic institution that secured the Chinese's ethnic identity and that presented the Chinese's resistance against the continuous denial of their rights by the Malay-dominated state. Hence, in hindsight it is ironic for the government unwittingly did the Chinese primary schools a favour by eliminating all English schools — the then leading and most popular primary educational institution — and converting the English schools into Malay-medium national schools.

Chinese parents who used to favour competence in English were reluctant to place their children in national schools, so they began to send their children to the second best option available, which were Chinese schools. Compared with national schools and Tamil schools, Chinese schools were more competitive academically (especially for mastering mathematics and science), and well reputed for strict discipline. Chinese schools also offered the benefit of trilingual education (Chinese, English, and Malay).[3] Hence, Chinese schools began to see a boost in student enrolment in the 1970s. Recognition of the quality of Chinese schools even went beyond ethnic boundaries. Over time, many non-ethnic Chinese parents, including Malays, began enrolling their children in Chinese schools.

As elaborated in Figure 3.3, the number of non-Chinese students enrolled in Chinese primary schools rose from 17,309 students (about 3 per cent) in 1989 to 65,000 students (about 10 per cent) in 1999. As a consequence of their popularity and the state's refusal to build new Chinese schools, almost all Chinese schools located in heavily Chinese-populated neighbourhoods

FIGURE 3.3

Distribution of Students by Ethnicity in Chinese Primary Schools
(1989–99)

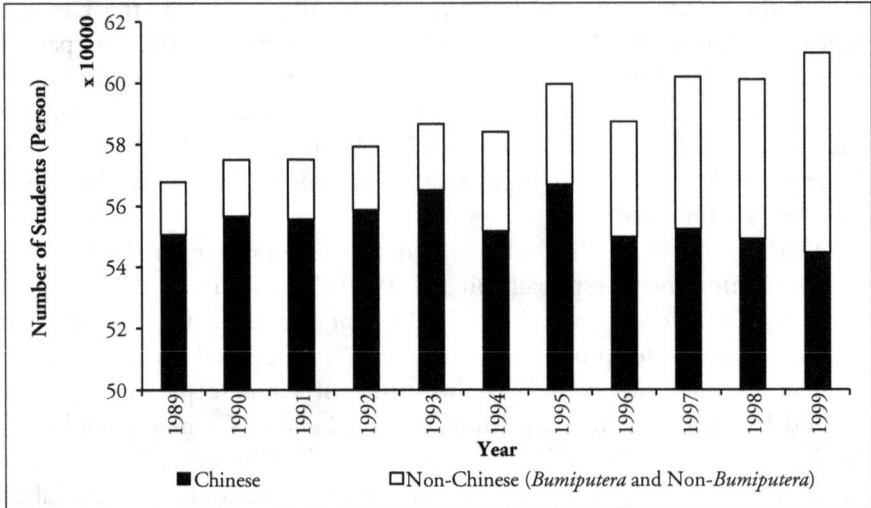

Note: Data for non-Chinese category was not made public by the government after year 1999.
Source: Compiled by the author with data provided by *Jiaozong* and data extracted from MEM (1990; 1991).

were overcrowded. The situation forced Chinese school committees to raise funds from the public to expand the schools' infrastructure. The fundraising activities, in turn, led to a revival of the role of these school committees as an important mechanism and key benefactor of Chinese schools.

Generally, the school committees of Chinese schools in Malaysia were managed by the main office-bearers, namely, the chairman (董事长), general secretary (总务), and treasurer (财政). The chairman played the most important role in safeguarding the school's interests and generating money for the school. According to Quek Suan Hiang (郭全强), a former *Dongzong* chairman (1993–2005) and school committee chairman of Kluang Chong Hwa High School (居銮中华中学) from 1987 to 2006,

A successful chairman might not be the richest, or the most generous donor, but he has to be the one who can and is willing to assume the role of a noble 'beggar'. He must have the audacity and persistence to seek donations from the local communities. To establish a successful fundraising campaign, the chairman must plan strategically. One can start the momentum for fundraising by first donating a sum of money, and then mobilize a few individuals to contribute impressive amounts of donations, the more the merrier. This will keep the ball rolling and generate waves of donations from the rest of the communities.[4]

To raise funds, school committees also organized events such as temporary amusement parks, stage performances, and fundraising dinners in the school compound. Members of the schools, including schoolteachers and students, were often mobilized for the preparation and execution of these events. Teachers and students multitasked to manage logistics, decorate the venue, create and circulate publicity materials, prepare various entertainment and performances, and so on. School committee members rode on their personal connection to invite influential figures, such as famous entertainers, successful businessmen and important politicians to grace these events and attract more community participation. To this day, these events remain as significant platforms for engaging and enhancing the bonds between schools and the communities. The success of these events also reflects the reputation and popularity of a school and its school committee.[5]

Chinese schools also generated incomes through the school sponsorship system. Although the 1957 Education Ordinance had limited the size of school committees to a maximum of fifteen members in each committee, their numbers in Chinese schools sometimes reached a hundred in reality. Considered as the schools' sponsors, these committee members contributed cash donations to the school, and were entitled to recommend an allocated number of new students to be enrolled into the school. This sponsor-recommended enrolment system was prevalent in overpopulated Chinese schools, where enrolment was exceedingly competitive, and gradually became the best means of securing enrolment for new students. The donor-beneficiary relationship helped to solidify committee members' social status and strengthen their networks with the local community.

While the sponsorship system motivated businessmen to involve and invest themselves as members of Chinese school committees, incomes from the system had also been especially crucial for the survival of the schools. As mentioned earlier, partially-assisted schools were not entitled to full state subsidies: the state paid only the teachers' salaries and benefits, but did not finance water and electricity bills. Therefore, all the Chinese schools, whatever the size of their coffers, were constantly under pressure to be creative in operating within a limited budget. According to a retired schoolteacher, Huang:

> Although we were one of the biggest schools in Penang, we often picked up used chairs and tables from the national schools to replace broken facilities in our schools. [The national schools] needed to discard them anyway, and principals of the national schools did not mind that we took them because they also knew that Chinese schools were receiving much less funding from the government than them. The national schools received funds for new tables and chairs every two to three years, but we [Chinese schools] had been using the same set of tables and chairs for decades. By recycling these valuable resources, we could save a lot of money. This also minimized the financial burden on our school committee.[6]

The above interview was reflective of the general phenomenon at the grassroots level. Although the Chinese education movement involved contentious interactions between Chinese educationalists and the UMNO-dominated state, relations at the local level could be perceived as harmonious and peaceful. Members of school communities at the national schools (dominated by ethnic Malay) and Chinese schools generally knew each other in their private capacity, and enjoyed good interpersonal relationships. Although they did not and would not interfere with each other schools' business, requests to share used and unwanted resources as mentioned above, were common and often seen as a win-win situation for both parties: the Chinese schools could have new resources, while the national schools could dispose these resources at ease.

Other than facing the problem of scarcity of resources, many schools located in smaller towns had also been facing the crippling problem of diminishing community population (UCSTAM 2007*a*; 2007*b*). Contrary to the overpopulated schools in the cities, schools located in deserted town had been facing the problems of shrinking student enrolment and, ultimately, the threat of closure. To overcome these problems, some Chinese school committee who were also MCA members began to seek assistance from MCA central leaders to relocate these schools. Playing the role of broker and facilitating negotiation between the Chinese schools and the Ministry of Education, these politicians manipulated the mechanism to gain political leverage. Although the approval rate for school relocation under such approach was very low, it was one of the approaches that worked in particular during the 1980s and 1990s.

By 2008, a total of forty-two out of seventy-five Chinese primary schools had received approval for relocation prior to a general election — a timely and strategic political move for MCA to gain support from Chinese voters (Dongjiaozong 2010). The political influence of the MCA members was seen not only in the relocation of Chinese schools but also in the way pro-BN agents began to intrude on the Chinese education movement at the state and central levels in the early 1990s, which will be elaborated at the later section of this chapter.

TAMING OF SCHOOLTEACHERS

While Chinese school committees had survived the various challenges to their continued existence and importance to Chinese schools by redefining their roles, Chinese schoolteachers had not fared as well. As leading partners of the Chinese education movement in the 1950s, Chinese schoolteachers were the most outspoken critics of the state then. In order to constrain the movement, the state sought to tame these schoolteachers via a series of tough approaches.

First, the state removed their leaders. This included the revocation of *Jiaozong* Chairman Lim Lian Geok's citizenship and expulsion of *Jiaozong* Advisor Yan Yuan Zhang from Malaysia in 1961, followed by the dismissal of the then newly elected *Jiaozong* Chairman Sim Mow Yu from MCA in 1966. Upon removal of the influential leaders of the Chinese education movement, the state exploited the unstable political situation during the Indonesia Confrontation (1963–66) to instil White Terror. The state police, for example, detained suspicious individuals, leftists, and social activists by force and without trial under the Internal Security Act. Sim Mow Yu, for example, was regularly observed by secret police during his early days as *Jiaozong* chairman. Although there were no serious threats to his life and freedom until he was detained under the Internal Security Act during the Weeding Operation (*Operasi Lalang*) in 1987, the fear of being targeted and the risk of being detained effectively discouraged the rise of new leaders to take over *Jiaozong's* premiership. According to Sim, in his review of his years as *Jiaozong* chairman,

> One would become famous for being a *Jiaozong* chairman. It was a highly respected position [amongst the Chinese community], but you also posited yourself at the forefront of the battle. Everything you did must be accountable to the community. At the same time, you were also risking your safety, your official ranking [as a schoolteacher], and

your retirement pension. If the government targeted you, you might
end up like Lim Lian Geok, whose citizenship was revoked and teaching
permit stripped by the government.[7]

Next, the state exerted control over schoolteachers by incorporating them
into the civil servants system. Unlike in the colonial era when the salaries
of Chinese schoolteachers had been paid by the school committee, the
state financed the salaries and benefits of all schoolteachers in the national
and national-type schools. Thus, the state also enjoyed absolute power
to appoint, dismiss, or regulate the posting location and ranking of a
schoolteacher. Via the 1961 Education Act, the state had also been controlling
schoolteachers' training institutions, registration of their teaching permits
and distribution of salaries and pensions. Specifically, Part VI, Article 78
empowered the Registrar of Teachers to refuse to register (and deregister)
a person if the former had reason to suspect that a teacher was likely to
promote unlawful activities in the school or would harm the interests of
the Federation, the public or pupils.

In 1962, the state successfully created a rift within *Jiaozong* by
manipulating schoolteachers' salary scheme to reduce the latter's capacity
to fight back. *Jiaozong* was accused of sacrificing the interests of senior normal
graduate schoolteachers (华文高级师范毕业教师) in their negotiations
with the Ministry of Education over the terms of salaries for the Chinese
schoolteachers. Senior normal graduate schoolteachers had been the pioneers
who received formal training from the newly established teachers' training
college in Malaya between 1948 and 1957. About 2,000 of them enjoyed a
special salary allocation from the British government for their qualification.
Therefore, these teachers were angry when the special allocation was cancelled
in 1962.[8] The dispute proved to be a lose-lose situation for the Chinese
education movement as many of these schoolteachers began to shun *Jiaozong*-
related activities. The disputes consequently led to the first major divisions
within the Chinese schoolteachers' community when the Malaya Chinese
Senior Normal Graduate Teachers Union (马来亚联合邦华文高级师范)
was established later that year.

To make matters worse, the National Union of the Teaching Profession
(*Kesatuan Perkhidmatan Perguruan Kebangsaan Malaysia*) was formed
in 1974 to serve as the public service union for all schoolteachers. Unlike
Jiaozong, which was open to Chinese schoolteachers only, the national
union offered automatic membership to all graduates from the Ministry
of Education's schoolteachers' training programme regardless of rank,
qualification, ethnicity, religion, training or political affiliation. Moreover,

the National Union of the Teaching Profession was the only official schoolteachers' union recognized by the Ministry of Education. It provided important information on salary schemes, group insurance, welfare, and legal assistance. Operating under the auspices of the Ministry of Education enabled the National Union of the Teaching Profession to be more efficient in protecting and improving the welfare of the teaching profession.

Another strategy used by the government to limit schoolteachers' participation in the Chinese education movement was to prohibit the import of Chinese schoolteachers from China in 1948 and to gradually replace these imported schoolteachers with locally-born counterparts. Unlike the Chinese-imported schoolteachers who were monolingual and mostly not fully integrated into the local community, locally-born Chinese schoolteachers were multilingual and able to adapt quickly to the society and to the changes in the national education system. Therefore, the new generation of locally-born schoolteachers no longer saw *Jiaozong* or the Chinese schoolteachers' association as their sole sanctuary. Slowly but surely, the National Union of the Teaching Profession became the more appealing teachers' union to schoolteachers all over the country.

Lastly, the state's determination to send a clear message about its authority to the supporters of the Chinese education movement was demonstrated in the fate of the outspoken *Jiaozong* Vice Chairman, Loot Ting Yee. In an attempt to reduce Loot's participation in *Jiaozong*'s activities, the Minister of Education transferred Loot from Kuala Lumpur to the coastal state of Terengganu in 1981. In protest, Loot resisted the transfer and sued the Ministry of Education. After he suffered an inevitable loss with the lawsuit, the Ministry of Education revoked his teaching permit two years prior to his retirement, effectively stripping him of all of his pension benefits.[9]

In all, these carrot-and-stick strategies effectively dampened morale and depressed the capability of Chinese schoolteachers to function as core agents for *Jiaozong* in the Chinese education movement. Many schoolteachers began to refrain from engaging in open criticisms of the government. Schoolteachers from independent Chinese secondary schools were similarly inactive in the Chinese schoolteachers' association due to their heavy workload, which included fundraising activities, even though they did not face similar constraints under the government civil servant regulations as their counterparts in national-type schools. After the departure (due to old age or death) of the older and more enthusiastic generation of Chinese schoolteachers in the 1980s, the younger generation lacked either the interest or motivation to be actively involved in the Chinese schoolteachers' association.

As elaborated in Figure 3.4, the membership trends of the Chinese schoolteachers' associations developed in five directions between 1982 and 2011. Of the forty associations observed, two associations (5 per cent) showed a reduction in membership; fifteen associations (37 per cent) showed a slow climb; nine associations (22 per cent) had moderate growth; seven associations (18 per cent) showed a steady expansion; and seven associations (18 per cent) proliferated.

Demographical changes, recruitment campaigns, and regular updates to existing membership lists were some of the factors that contributed to the trends shown in Figure 3.4. Although the overall membership of

FIGURE 3.4

Changes in Membership of the Chinese Schoolteachers' Associations

(1982–2011)

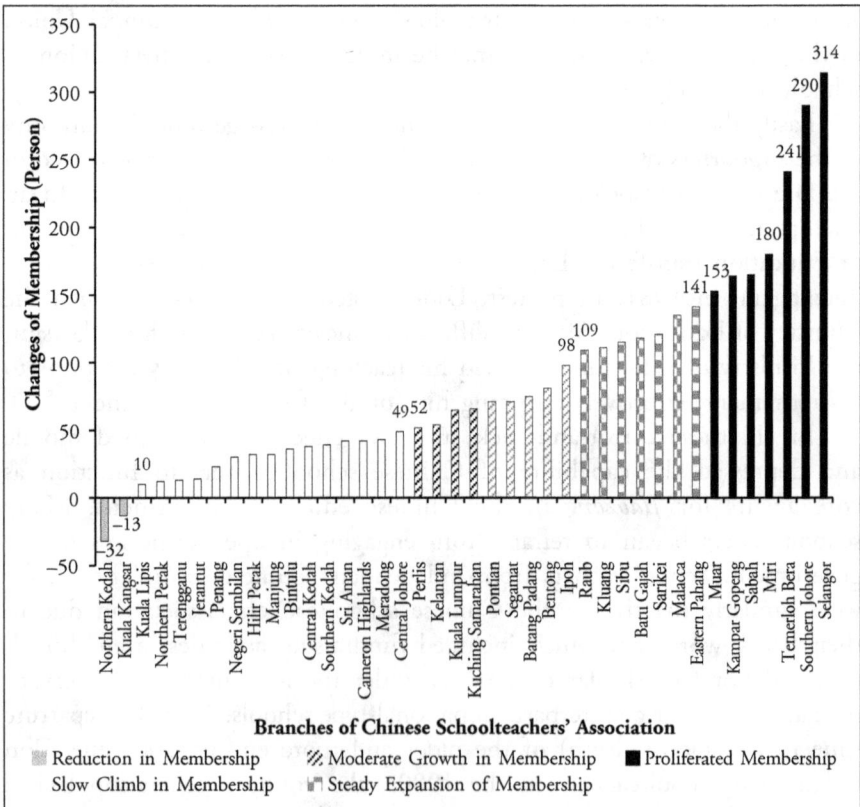

Source: Compiled by the author with data extracted from UCSTAM (1987*a*; 1988–2006; 2007*c*; 2008*b*; 2009–12).

the Chinese schoolteachers' associations continued to climb, the associations failed to cultivate new leaders sufficiently capable of taking over the premiership. Facing these challenges, many Chinese schoolteachers' associations had to be presided over by principals of Chinese primary schools who could and did use their schools as bases for the associations' secretariats and the schools' resources to support the association's activities.[10]

The weakened local institutions also caused a more severe problem with leadership at the central level of the Chinese education movement. Due to the lack of suitable new leadership, Sim Mow Yu served as *Jiaozong* chairman for a record length of twenty-nine years (1965–94). Although the longevity of his tenure brought stability to the movement, it also highlighted the reality of the brain drain of a once-influential social force. Sim's multiple attempts at resigning from his post were repeatedly rejected by the movement's supporters. One of the main reasons was that Sim's preferred successor was Loot Ting Yee, who had served as *Jiaozong* vice chairman since 1965. Nevertheless, Loot's fiery resistance style worried the Chinese schoolteachers community. It was as late as in 1994, when Sim reached eighty-one years old, that his resignation was finally accepted. Although Loot was Sim's chosen successor and was the last schoolteacher left standing in *Jiaozong*'s central committee at the time, Loot was defeated by the soft-spoken, nondescript MCA member, Ong Kow Ee (王超群), in the 1994 chairman election.[11] In one of his press statements as the new *Jiaozong* Chairman, Ong remarked,

> We do not need to strongly disagree or become emotional to reach our objectives. This approach may be dysfunctional sometimes and does not allow you to reach your objectives... We should try to communicate directly with officials from Ministry of Education. We can also go through MCA or Gerakan to get funding for the [Chinese] schools.[12]

At the time of writing, Ong was still *Jiaozong*'s chairman. His era marked a clear preference by the *Jiaozong* central committee for a softer, more collaborative approach in its dealings with the state. For *Jiaozong* and its central-level leaders, this might be their only available option, given such challenges as the gradual loss of importance of the Chinese schoolteachers' association and the lack of support from most of the Chinese schoolteachers.

THE TROJAN HORSE

While *Jiaozong* was troubled with the above-mentioned challenges, *Dongzong* was also embroiled in internal partisan politicking by opportunists during the 1990s. Unlike the majority of the school committee members who, although were politically affiliated, but still managed to exercise self-restraint and place communal interest above personal political gains, ill-initiated political opportunists made use of their position as school committees members to control state-level Chinese school committees' associations, with the ultimate aim of taking over *Dongzong* and controlling the Chinese education movement.

The scenario then is best exemplified by the controversial Negeri Sembilan Chinese School Committees Council (森美兰华校董事会联合会)'s election in 1994. Negeri Sembilan MCA Deputy President and Negeri Sembilan Chinese Assembly Hall (森美兰中华大会堂) Chairman Hoo Huo Shan (胡火山) openly challenged the three-time Negeri Sembilan Chinese School Committees Council's Chairman and *Dongzong* Vice Chairman Chin Choong Sang (陈松生).[13] Many believed Hoo's candidacy echoed the call of MCA leaders in Selangor to reform *Dongjiaozong* from within. In the end, although 70 per cent of the 148 representatives who voted for the new committees at the General Assembly were MCA members, Hoo gained only 61 votes.[14] All the other candidates in Hoo's faction lost the election, an unequivocal indication that these representatives preferred to keep partisan politics out of the council.[15]

In order to strengthen its internal institutions, *Dongzong* imposed a series of awareness campaigns and reform strategies. At the primary school level, the *Sample of Working Guidelines for Malaysia Chinese Primary School Committee* (马来西亚华文小学董事会工作手册样本) was published in 1998, while the *Handbook for Chinese Education Workers* (华教工作者手册) and the Chinese translation of the 1961 Education Act were reprinted (Dongjiaozong 1989; 1998). These publications provided detailed information on the rights and duties of Chinese school committees, and were widely distributed to the Chinese school committee communities through the network of state-level associations. Such efforts provided accurate and updated information to the school committees communities; it was also the first systematic reform operation introduced by *Dongzong* to modernize the operations of Chinese school committees nationwide (UCSCAM 1991, p. 29).

Dongzong also engaged in nationwide activities to strengthen relations and foster closer bonds amongst independent Chinese secondary schools' communities. Each year, state-level Chinese school committees' associations took turns to organize various sports- and games-related events for the students of independent Chinese secondary schools. Although these activities focused more on students' participation, the event organizers (school committees and schoolteachers) also rode on the hosting opportunities to improve interpersonal bonds and strengthen collective solidarity with peers from other states.

On top of this, *Dongzong* also tried to mend old wounds by promoting collaboration with school communities from converted Chinese secondary schools. In reality, after the mass conversion exercise in 1961, the converted and independent factions were strongly prejudiced against one another.[16] In order to promote dialogue, *Dongjiaozong* initiated the first National Seminar for Converted Chinese Secondary Schools School Committees (全国国民型中学董事交流会) in 1997, and subsequently established the *Dongjiaozong* Converted Chinese Secondary Schools Working Committee (董教总全国国民型中学工作委员会) in 1998. However, fundamental differences in perspectives and approaches in the management of Chinese schools led to the premature dismissal of the working committee in 2001 shortly after its first term (UCSTAM 1997, p. 9). Many conservative Chinese educationalists refused to consider the converted cluster as part of the movement. As explained by former *Jiaozong* Vice Chairman Yeoh Ban Eng (杨万荣),

> The converted cluster abandoned the privilege of other Chinese schools when it accepted the conversion in 1961. One must comply with three principles to qualify as a Chinese school: the usage of Chinese in teaching all subjects except Malay and English language, management by the school committee, and the usage of Chinese as the main administrative language in the school. Schools from the converted cluster only taught Chinese language subject in Chinese, and they no longer used Chinese as the main administrative language. Therefore, they were not a real Chinese school.[17]

The converted cluster also refused to bow to *Dongjiaozong*'s pressure and maintained firmly that the converted schools system was a more pragmatic and sustainable approach for the continuity of Chinese education in Malaysia.[18] Divisions between these two clusters escalated in October 2003 when the

TABLE 3.2
Characteristics of a Chinese School

Defined by *Dongjiaozong*
- The school committee is the highest authority of the school.
- School uses Chinese as the main medium of teaching.
- Textbooks should be mostly written in Chinese.
- Administrative language in the school should be in Chinese.

Defined by Converted Chinese School Principals' Association
- School has a Chinese name.
- Chinese school song and school motto.
- Rules and regulations for students spelt out in Chinese.
- School committee plays an important role in school activities.
- School alumni who identify themselves as "Chinese school graduates".
- Chinese-qualified teachers hold senior positions in the school.
- A school principal who speaks in Chinese during school assemblies.
- Majority of students come from Chinese primary schools.
- Chinese as a compulsory subject for all students.
- Students use Chinese as the default language of communication.
- Active Chinese cultural co-curriculum activities, such as Chinese Association, Chinese Chess Association, amongst others.

Source: Compiled by the author with data extracted from MPSSMCM (2006, pp. 8–11) and Yeoh Ban Eng, interview by the author, Penang, 7 January 2009.

Converted Chinese School Principals' Association (国民型中学校长理事会), a united front of all converted Chinese secondary schools established since 1994, suggested to change the name of all converted Chinese secondary schools into "Chinese secondary schools" (华文中学) (MPSSMCM 2006, p. 8).

Technically, the converted cluster shared various characteristics of a Chinese school and should qualify as a Chinese school within *Dongjiaozong*'s context (see Table 3.2). However, these suggestions and arguments were resoundingly rejected by *Dongjiaozong*, which perceived the whole name-changing campaign as a move to challenge the hegemony of independent Chinese secondary schools.[19] At the time of writing, these two factions remained disparate in their management and definition of Chinese schools. Their amicableness had been maintained by minimizing interfering and contradicting each other. Maintaining distance was one of the key factors that led to the prolonged persistence of the Chinese education movement. Although both factions shared a common interest to protect and maintain the identity of Chinese schools, pride had prevented them from forming a more powerful collective representation of *Dongjiaozong*. Hurdles needed to be bridged, prior misunderstandings and blame had to be forgiven and forgotten, before any future collaboration could be achieved.

One of the greatest challenges faced by the Chinese education movement had been the division between school principals who supported *Dongjiaozong* and those who were inclined towards the Ministry of Education. The divisions were best observed during the 1998 incident, when Selangor State Education Department demanded all Chinese school principals to take over authority from their school committees and assume full responsibility for the tender process of school canteens and bookshops. The education department also demanded school principals to include all proceeds from both tender activities in the schools' financial accounts and not those of the school committees.[20]

This new regulation not only ended the last vestiges of management authority of Chinese school committees in Chinese schools, it also removed a significant source of income for Chinese schools. Even though the policy was implemented in Selangor state, the potential threat of similar policies being implemented nationwide could not be underestimated. Aware of the potential consequences, many Chinese school principals who implemented the orders of the Selangor State Education Department tried to uphold the traditional status of school committees and establish the new operating culture of the school committees at the same time. However, there were a few who did not.

School principals were, to some extent, under pressure to fulfil their duty to preserve the identity of Chinese schools by resisting the education department's decisions. School principals who had sided with the authorities faced severe criticisms from the school committee and Chinese community at large. Continuous pressure from the United Chinese School Committees' Association of Selangor and Kuala Lumpur, as well as from *Dongzong*, forced Deputy Education Minister Fong Chan Onn (冯镇安) to intervene. Fong later explained that there was a misunderstanding and the regulation would be implemented in all schools in the country with the exception of Chinese primary schools.[21]

Six years later, the "takeover exercise" returned to threaten the existence of the Chinese school committees — this time by the Penang State

Education Department in September 2004.[22] Chinese school committees in Penang promptly utilized their powerful social and political influence to resist this decision. The protest reverberated throughout the umbrella organizations of Penang and Province Wellesley United Chinese School Management Association (槟威华校董事会联合会). The protesters demanded intervention by the ethnic Chinese-dominated Gerakan-led Penang state government and its Chief Minister Koh Tsu Koon (许子根) to halt the takeover exercise.[23] The confrontation was quickly resolved by the then Education Minister Hishamuddin Hussein, who explained that the rights of Chinese school committees on the disputed issues should be honoured, and stressed that Chinese schools were excluded from the new regulation.[24] It was believed that the new Education Minister Hishamuddin Hussein who had just been appointed to his position in March 2004 saw no gain in making more enemies out of these influential and potentially beneficial Chinese school committees in Penang.

Although most Chinese school committees had their traditional roles and power restored by 2005, the controversy continued at Kuala Lumpur Chen Moh Chinese Primary School (吉隆坡精武华文小学). The bookshop of Chen Moh Primary School, which was managed by Pustaka Matu Company, had received its tender from School Principal Ye Xia Guang (叶夏光) who executed the order of the state education department. When the order was later recalled and cancelled, Pustaka refused to withdraw from the school. With the intention of getting Pustaka to withdraw on its own accord, Chen Moh Primary School's school committee opened another bookshop in the school premises that offered more competitive prices for its items. Facing competition from the bookshop opened by the school committee, Pustaka demanded that Principal Ye remove the "unauthorized store".[25] The conflict peaked in November 2005 when Chen Moh Primary School's School Committee Chairman Wang Guo Feng (王国丰) pointed to evidence suggesting that corruption might have been involved: Ye had failed to explain the whereabouts of four cheques (total sum of 20,000 ringgit) issued by Pustaka for the development project of Chen Moh Primary School development project (Lim, H.S. 2005). Furthermore, it was revealed that the two other companies that had supposedly competed with Pustaka for the tender of the school bookshop were in fact phantom companies (Lim, H.S. 2006c).

Wang and the school committee successfully pressured the Selangor State Education Department to transfer Principal Ye to another primary school in January 2006. Ye was the third school principal to be transferred out of the school since May 2003 after Wang took over chairmanship of the school committee.[26] In defence of his fellow school principals, Kang Siew Khoon (江秀坤), who was chairman of the National Union of Heads of Schools (全国校长职工会) from 2004 to 2006, blamed the frequent change of school principals in Chen Moh as a consequence of *Dongzong's* call for school committees to seize the tender rights of the canteen and bookshop back from the Ministry of Education, which had put Chinese primary schools principals in an exceedingly difficult position (Lim, H.S. 2006*a*).

Kang's comment infuriated Chinese educationalists, especially school committee members. Many were angrier with Kang for brushing aside a more serious issue: corruption committed by a school principal — for the evidence, if proven to be true, suggested that Ye had been receiving bribes through tenders and pocketing the earnings from the sales of school magazines and extra school tuition classes (Lim, H.S. 2006*b*). Soon, private grouses erupted into a national debate when Malaysia's cable media Astro Asian Entertainment Channel's weekly Chinese forum programme aired a four-episode coverage on the issue of "(Corrupt) Business Opportunities in Chinese Primary Schools" (华小处处商机) in February 2006.[27] Facing increasing attacks and accusations of corruption, the National Union of Heads of Schools Deputy Chairman Yang Qing Liang (杨清亮) publicly reiterated that "*Dongzong* should stop oppressing school principals and deliberately making things difficult for school principals on the issue of the rental rights of school canteens".[28]

In defence, *Dongzong* Chairman Yap Sin Tian (叶新田) released a stinging press statement, which was splashed across the headlines of *Nanyangshangpao* (南洋商报) — one of the largest Chinese newspaper in Malaysia at the time — entitled "Enmity between *Dongzong* and the National Union of Heads of Schools" (董总校长职工会交恶). In this statement, Yap said,

> To those individuals or organizations that have accommodated the state's attempts to erode the legitimate rights of Chinese schools by undermining the sovereignty of the school committee for whatever reason — consciously or voluntarily — I would like to warn and advise them to stop acting like the paws of the tiger and stop assisting the enemy in violating the general interests of the Chinese community, or you will be cast aside by the Chinese community (UCSCAM 2006*b*).

Badmouthing from both sides continued until Kang was replaced by the more soft-spoken Pang Chong Leong (彭忠良), thus narrowly averting the destruction of the relationship between National Union of Heads of Schools and *Dongzong* (Kok 2006). This incident reflected fundamental problems of the Chinese education movement. Throughout the period during which this controversy unfolded, *Jiaozong* sat on the fence on the issue of corrupt school principals because many of *Jiaozong* supporters were also members of the National Union of Heads of Schools. Moreover, the weakened *Jiaozong* leaders were neither able to constrain nor persuade some of the Chinese school principals from taking an antagonistic stand against the school committees, or to stop them from damaging the interests of Chinese schools.

In the face of these disputes, *Dongzong* launched a working committee in March 2006 to compile the *Management Handbook for Chinese Primary Schools* (华小管理机制指南) and organize the Awareness Campaign for Chinese Primary Schools' School Committees (华小董事觉醒运动) (Dongjiaozong 2006). The handbook was a set of guidelines, jointly compiled by representatives from school principals, school committees, and parents, which aimed to enhance awareness within the school community about their roles, rights, and responsibilities in the management of Chinese schools. The awareness campaign encouraged school committees to register with the Ministry of Education and acquire the certificate of registration requested of schools under Section 88 of the 1996 Educational Act.[29]

Disappointingly, the impact of the handbook and the awareness campaign was relatively poor. Although the handbook detailed basic information on the do's and don'ts, it lacked the legislative machinery and judiciary power to take action — for instance, to conduct investigations and take disciplinary action against those alleged for wrongdoing — should one fail to comply with the guidelines. More critically, the awareness campaign failed to convince Chinese school committees of why they must bow down and comply with the new regulations of the Ministry of Education.

Many Chinese school committees felt that the government should regard and appreciate their contribution as partners who have been providing the necessary infrastructure for schools run by the Ministry of Education.[30] On top of that, Chinese school committees also remained very critical of *Dongzong's* failure to prevent the implementation of the 1996 Education Act in the first place. By 2009, the awareness campaign had been terminated and replaced by the Campaign to Strengthen the Role of School Committees in Chinese Primary Schools (强化华小董事会运动).[31]

Throughout the entire awareness campaign, *Jiaozong*'s participation remained limited. Other than attendance at formal events and meetings, its contribution to these awareness campaigns was minimal, not to mention its passivity also in mobilizing support and participation from Chinese school principals communities. It was clear that the two "siblings" of the Chinese education movement were moving in different directions. In a press statement in October 2006, *Dongzong* explained that,

> [*Dongzong* and *Jiaozong*] have built a strong consensus and mutual understanding with regard to the larger direction of the movement. However, being two independent organizations, having different strategies and approaches in certain issues should be considered as normal (UCSCAM 2006c).

Despite *Dongzong*'s official pronouncement of unity, a comparison of the collective strength of the movement over time shows that both organizations had weakened significantly since the 1960s as a result of the structural constraints imposed by the state. The fact remains that the movement's top office-bearers in the central institutions of *Dongzong* and *Jiaozong* can only represent the interests of the respective groups with support from the larger community of Chinese school committees and schoolteachers. The weakening of the Chinese schoolteachers' associations at the local level not only affected the negotiation power of *Jiaozong*'s top office-bearers in their interactions with the state, but it also prohibited the central institutions from justifying their authority in representing the collective interests of the group and burdened its movement partner, *Dongzong*, with the brunt of the operational and execution work for both organizations. A weakened limb had thus made it more difficult for the Chinese education movement to achieve its aim of securing fair and just treatment for Chinese schools in Malaysia.

CONCLUSION

By exploring the challenges faced by various levels of the movement's institutions and agencies, this chapter has covered three key issues that have been overlooked by the social movement literature. First, the non-liberal democratic state is a dynamic, complex — yet creative — entity. The state has proven its creativity in manipulating its legitimate power to constrain and suppress social movements through various soft-coercive approaches, exemplified by its education acts and the distribution of resources for education. Through these approaches, the state avoided taking extreme measures to contain and weaken the movement's local supporters, in particular, schoolteachers and school committee communities. However, due to the existence of many grey areas in the legitimacy of these decisions, they were overridden easily by more superior officers, such as the Education Minister of his deputy. Such flexibility thus provided opportunities for Chinese education activists to overcome the constraints imposed by the education acts and limited resources through interpersonal mediation, negotiation, and persuasion.

The second finding presented in this chapter is the presence of internal factions that hampered the movement. The incorporation of Chinese primary schools and two-thirds of Chinese secondary schools into the national system significantly limited the capacity and flexibility in participating in movement activities of local movement members. *Jiaozong* suffered a massive drain in human and financial resources after Chinese schoolteachers became civil servants. As employees of the state, schoolteachers enjoyed a more secure salary scheme and better welfare coverage, but they also faced more restrictions to participate in anti-government activities. Fortunately, the closure of English primary schools in the 1970s reversed the crisis for the Chinese education movement. It even pitched Chinese primary schools as the most sought after academic institutions in the country.

Fierce competition to enrol into Chinese schools opened up sponsorship and donations as another source of sustainable income, for making sponsorships and donations to one of these popular schools guaranteed entry into them. Schools in rural and less populated areas, however, suffered from low enrolment and faced the threat of closure, which led many to seek assistance from politicians to be relocated to urban areas.

Although formal and institutional rules are important, but when these structural elements are weakened by the state, cultural and historical sentiments become core incentives for movement actors. The third finding of this chapter is that the strong cultural sentiments that Malaysian Chinese attached to their ethnic identity became the force that drove the continuous involvement of the Chinese community in the Chinese education movement. These actors included ethnic Chinese school principles, ethnic Chinese politicians, and ethnic Chinese businessmen. Nevertheless, the movement faced the internal challenge of uniting members whose cultural sentiments differed albeit being members of the same ethnic and lingual heritage. The division in cultural sentiments may be described as the fraction between the conservatives (represented by the central committee of the Chinese education movement) and moderates (largely those from converted Chinese schools). Most members of the former insisted that the movement should remain exclusive and maintain its narrowly-defined objectives and principles at the risk of losing collective support.

The fourth finding from this chapter is the transformation of the relationship between *Dongzong* and *Jiaozong*, from one of co-existence into a symbiosis. *Jiaozong's* capacity in leading the Chinese education movement plunged significantly as a result of diminishing participation from Chinese schoolteachers at the grassroots. Strong institutional bonds between these sister organizations based on shared identity and strong inter-leadership collaboration sustained the movement and had helped them survive state oppression. However, *Jiaozong's* weak capacity in mobilizing and sustaining its movement organizations and supporters was also becoming a burden for the movement. Not only had it been hijacked by political players who held it hostage against *Dongzong's* open criticisms of the Ministry of Education and the government, it had also become (and will likely continue to be) a potential threat to the continuity of the Chinese education movement. If the movement's current leaders continue to deny that their institutions are crumbling internally or dismiss them as a 'normal' process in collaboration, this could become the single major factor leading to the termination and failure of the movement.

Notes

1. The author used the term "school committee" to refer to individuals who actively take part in the administration of the revenues or property or in the management of an educational institution. They are defined as school managers (for primary schools) and school governors (for secondary schools and institutions for higher education) under the 1961 Education Act. See FM (1961).

2. Fully assisted schools are schools built on government premises, and are entitled to full financial assistance from the state for capital grants. Capital grant is defined in 1961 Education Act as "a payment from public funds to an educational institution for the provision of land or buildings, the alteration to or extension of existing premises, and the provision of furniture or equipment for new altered or extended premises". Ibid., part 1.2.

3. Chai Yah Han (蔡亚汉) (former chairman, Penang Chinese School Alumni Association 槟州华校校友会联合会), interview by the author, Penang, 17 January 2009; Lim K.C. (pseudonym, retired Chinese primary school teacher), interview by the author, Penang, 24 February 2008; and Lu X.F. (pseudonym, retired Chinese primary school principal), interview by the author, Penang, 10 February 2008.

4. Quek Suan Hiang (former chairman, *Dongzong*), interview by the author, Johore, 23 March 2010.

5. Liu (1986, pp. 19–26); and Yeoh Ban Eng (former vice chairman, *Jiaozong*), interview by the author, Penang, 7 January 2009.

6. Huang K.L. (pseudonym, retired school teacher), interview by the author, Penang, 17 January 2009.

7. Sim Mow Yu, interview by the author, Malacca, 26 March 2008.

8. MLHGSBJZ (1990, pp. 1, 64–78); and *Sinchew Daily*, 22 October 1962.

9. UCSTAM (1987*b*, p. 576); and Loot Ting Yee, interview by the author, Kuala Lumpur, 24 March 2008.

10. Er Joo Tiong (余裕忠) (senior executive officer, Department of Resource and Research, *Jiaozong*), interview by the author, Selangor, 22 July 2010.

11. UCSCAM (1995, p. 43); and Loot Ting Yee, interview by the author, Kuala Lumpur, 24 March 2008.

12. *Sinchew Daily*, 30 May 1994.

13. *China Press*, 11 April 1994; and *Sinchew Daily*, 12 April 1994.

14. *Nanyangshangpao*, 25 April 1994.

15. *Sinchew Daily*, 25 April 1994.

16. Yeoh L.C. (pseudonym, retired Chinese secondary school principal), interview by the author, Penang, 20 January 2009.

17. Yeoh Ban Eng, interview by the author, Penang, 7 January 2009.

18. Yeoh L.C., interview by the author, Penang, 20 January 2009; and Sim C.T. (pseudonym, retired Chinese secondary school principal), interview by the author, Penang, 15 January 2009.

19. Yeoh Ban Eng, interview by the author, Penang, 7 January 2009.

20. Sim Mow Yu, interview by the author, Malacca, 26 March 2008; and Yeoh L.C., interview by the author, Penang, 20 January 2009.

21. *Sinchew Daily*, 3 November 1998.

22. *Sinchew Daily*, 9 September 2004.

23. *Kwongwahyitpoh*, 22 September 2004.

24. *Oriental Daily*, 15 October 2004.

25. *Oriental Daily*, 17 November 2004; and Chai Yah Han, interview by the author, Penang, 17 January 2009.

26. The previous principals who were forced to leave were Li Yi Qiang (李毅强) in July 2004; Lin Yu Lian (林玉莲) in March 2005, and Ye Xia Guang in January 2006. See Zhang, G.H. (2006).

27. This television programme (就事论事) invited three guest speakers: *Dongzong* chief executive officer Bock Tai Hee (莫泰熙), Democratic Action Party Sungai Pinang state assembly member Teng Chang Khim (邓章钦), and Selangor Petaling Jaya District Chinese Primary Schools Parents Association (八打灵县华小家长会) Vice Chairman Teh Hon Seng (郑云城). See Lim, H.S. (2006*b*).
28. *Nanyangshangpao*, 19 February 2006.
29. Shum Thin Khee (沈天奇) (head, Department of Organization and Publicity, *Dongzong*), interview by the author, Selangor, 27 February 2009.
30. Leong Tzi Liang (林子量) (retired movement activist), interview by the author, Penang, 17 January 2009.
31. Choong Ee Hoong (钟一泓) (assistant executive officer, Department of Organization Affairs, *Dongzong*), interview by the author, Selangor, 27 July 2010.

4

LEADERS, ALLIANCES, AND POLITICS

INTRODUCTION

While Chapter 3 focused on the challenges and complexity of the intra-movement collaboration, this chapter studies the overall momentum of the Chinese education movement, in particular, the roles of national leaders and inter-movement alliance, within a larger political context. Due to limited access to political institutions, social movements of non-liberal democratic states tend to rely on strong leadership and inter-agency capital to share information, build coalitions, strengthen networks, and mobilize collective support from the larger community to resist the state.

The capacity of a leader is primarily concerned with the bureaucratic ability to implement and consolidate the movement's organizational principles, and with the effectiveness of tactical decision-making (Roche and Sachs 1969, pp. 208–9). Despite differences in styles and preferences in movement campaigns, all movement leaders must rise above given constraints to sustain the movement. The formation of inter-movement coalitions enable movement leaders to maximize pre-existing social structures to facilitate the movement's development, and may lead to enrichment of shared resources, enhancement of public visibility and better coordination of plans (Zald and Ash 1969, p. 475).

This chapter argues that inter-movement coalitions within non-liberal democracies are likely be engaged and sustained through movement leaders' personal ties and capacity, rather than through formal structural arrangements. Movement repertoires and interactional experiences are not static, but adapt and evolve throughout the movement's trajectories to reduce risks and increase chances of attaining the movement's ultimate objectives.

This chapter begins by analysing strategies adopted by a leader of the Chinese education movement, Lim Fong Seng (林晃升), which were to capitalize on grievances arising from the implementation of the 1971 New Economic Policy to mobilize support from the Chinese community. Such strategies included the independent Chinese secondary schools revival movement (1973), the Merdeka University's petition (1978), and the lawsuit of Merdeka University (1980–86).[1]

The second section of this chapter studies the movement's transformation as it moved out of its comfort zone to form strategic alliances with other Chinese organizations and political parties in response to increasing assimilative policies imposed by the state. As a result, the Chinese education movement began to play an important role in mobilizing the Alliance of Three campaign (1982), the Alliance of Fifteen Leading Chinese Guilds and Associations (1983), the national Chinese primary schools sit-in protest (1987), and the promotion of a dual coalition system with opposition parties (1990).

The third section of this chapter illustrates the shift in the repertoires of the Chinese education movement after the failure of the 1990 dual coalition system campaign. Progressive co-optation by the state successfully weakened alliances within the Chinese community, prompting the leaders of the Chinese education movement to change their original strategy of mobilizing resistances to mobilizing resources, and to channel more efforts towards securing underground collaboration with various government ministers. The chapter ends with an analysis of the movement's repertoires and dilemmas after the political tsunami of 2008, and evaluates if these political opportunities might lead to ultimate success, or mark the beginning of the movement's devastation.

POLITICAL PRESSURE, PROCESS, AND OPPORTUNITIES

When Abdul Razak Hussein became the second prime minister of Malaysia (1970–76), he embarked on a series of social engineering programmes through the New Economic Policy (1971) (GM 1971c). For starters, he geared the government towards the creation of a new political culture with the formation of a BN coalition in 1973 (NSTP 1976, p. 58).

The *bumiputera* equity quota was introduced and forcefully implemented across the public and private sectors, inevitably marginalizing minority groups (Ho, K.L. 1988). Even more controversial of a country proclaiming itself as a democracy was the amendment to the Federal Constitution of Malaysia and introduction of Article 153, which made it an offence to question provisions on the Malay language, Malay special rights, position of the Malay rulers, and the citizenship rights of the immigrant races (GM 1971*d*, pp. 1–7).

Facing increasing assimilative measures from the state, the minority communities grew increasingly insecure about their ability to defend and preserve their ethnic and cultural identities. These extraordinary times, however, saw the rise of ordinary people to become extraordinary leaders of the movement. A mining businessman from Selangor, Lim Fong Seng, was selected as *Dongzong* chairman in 1973 and soon became the movement's most substantive leader. Addressing his supporters at the meeting of the United Chinese School Committees' Association of Selangor and Kuala Lumpur in March 1973, Lim framed the Chinese education movement as follows:

> The problems we face at Chinese schools are political problems. The future of Chinese schools and Chinese education depends on the country's political developments and the way to save Chinese education is not to sit around, wait, and do nothing. We must fully mobilize, prepare ourselves adequately, and be effective advocates for our cause (UCSCAM 1988, p. 30; and Zhan 2003, p. 301).

As will be detailed in the next chapter, Lim transformed the successful Perak independent Chinese secondary schools revival movement from a state movement into a national movement. He initiated the Malaysian Independent Chinese Secondary Schools Working Committee in December 1973 to reform the curriculum and academic system of independent Chinese secondary schools in Malaysia. In 1974, Lim, who was also the chairman of Merdeka University Company, proposed the formation of Merdeka College (独立学院) to fulfil one of the movement's missions of establishing an independent Chinese tertiary education institution in Malaysia. However, the proposal was rejected by the ruling regime on the ground that the primary language of instruction, Chinese, was contrary to the 1971 National Educational Policy and the 1971 Universities and University Colleges Act.[2]

The failure to launch Merdeka College forced Lim and his followers to draw back and concentrate on affairs related to independent Chinese secondary schools.[3] In 1975, the Malaysian Independent Chinese Secondary Schools Working Committee proposed to issue the Unified Examination Certificate (华文独中高初中统一考试) as a national examination to assess the academic credentials of the students of independent Chinese secondary schools. However, two months before the examination, the then Education Minister Mahathir Mohamad demanded cancellation of the examination on the ground that the conduct of the Unified Examination Certificate by *Dongjiaozong* "might disrupt the status quo of mainstream national education and causing unnecessary ethnic tensions" (Zhen 2006, pp. 100–5).

Dongjiaozong took a firm stand and insisted that the implementation of this examination was not contravening the law. In his defence, Lim, with support from his colleagues from the Chinese education movement, pointed out that the Unified Examination Certificate was intended as an internal examination for students of independent Chinese secondary schools and thus should be deemed as legal as the London Chamber of Commerce and Industry Qualifying Examination, which offered recognition in accountancy.[4] Lim's audacity in engaging in open rebuttal of the state was motivated by frustration of being marginalized by the state after the 1969 ethnic riots, and the urgent need to protect the Chinese identity from being assimilated by pro-*bumiputera* national policies. Therefore, despite warnings and pressure from Mahathir, the examination was conducted at forty-two locations nationwide (including Sabah and Sarawak in East Malaysia) in December 1975.

Motivated by his triumph in the Unified Examination Certificate dispute, Lim decided to put up a fight and demanded approval from the state to establish Merdeka University. He first enhanced the movement's legal capacity by inviting enthusiastic young lawyers, such as Kerk Choo Ting (郭洙镇), Soo Thien Ming (苏天明), Low Sik Thong (刘锡通), and Ngeow Yin Ngee (饶仁毅), amongst others, as the movement's legal advisors. They carefully studied various limitations imposed by the National Education Policy and the Universities and University Colleges Act, and drafted the Petition for Incorporation Order for the Establishment of Merdeka University (呈最高元首请求恩准创办独立大学请愿书).

Dongjiaozong mobilized support from 4,238 Chinese guilds and associations to sign the petition, which was submitted to the King in

January 1978, who rejected the petition without a second thought. Dissatisfied with the outcome, *Dongjiaozong* filed a suit against the government and challenged the rights of the Chinese community to establish Merdeka University on constitutional grounds. The One-Person, One-Dollar for Merdeka University Legal Fee (一人一元独大法律基金) fundraising campaign was launched in 1978 and successfully collected a total donation of 292,713 ringgit by 1980.[5] This financial resource enabled *Dongjiaozong* to hire a Queen's Counsel, Michael Beloff, and ten Malaysian Chinese lawyers to file their case at the Kuala Lumpur High Court in September 1980.[6] The hearing began a year later but the court eventually ruled against the establishment of Merdeka University in November 1981 on the following grounds:

1. The proposed university was contrary to the National Education Policy, since the medium of instruction would be in Chinese;
2. It would be set up by a private organization;
3. It would only be admitting students from independent Chinese secondary schools;
4. It violated the 1971 Universities and University Colleges Act, whereby any university, public or private, is a "public authority" and as such, has to use Malay language (*Bahasa Melayu*) for official purposes, which is consistent with the Constitution, Article 152 (1) (MUB 1978*b*, pp. 349, 355, 362; and OCJKL 1981).

By July 1982, the Federal Court ruled against *Dongjiaozong*'s appeal (FCKL 1981). Four judges supported the High Court's decision, citing that Merdeka University was a public institution and therefore had no right to use Chinese language as its official language. The fifth, and the only ethnic Chinese judge, opined that the usage of Chinese language was not against the Constitution. A subsequent attempt to appeal the case through the Privy Council in London was unsuccessful due to the involvement of the case with the Constitution, which was beyond the statutory powers of the Privy Council, thus marking the end of the whole court battle.

Many years later, Lim Fong Seng made the following statement in his recapitulation of the Merdeka University lawsuit:

> The founding of Merdeka University caused disputes because it was a struggle between ethnic rights activists versus political opportunists and racist politicians; [Merdeka University] was banned, proving the

suppression of vernacular language and education in this country. The lawsuit demonstrated Merdeka University Company's determination to uphold civil rights and the rule of law. The verdict served to expose the flaws of the Constitution's ability to protect the status of Malaysian people's vernacular languages. It is a setback to the civil rights movement in Malaysia (DNICSSDWC 1993, p. 3).

Dongjiaozong might have lost the verdict, but the Merdeka University lawsuit won applause from both the Chinese community and recognition by the government for its determination as well as courage in defending its goal. In addition, Tunku Abdul Rahman College (拉曼学院), which was under MCA's patronage, was established as the feeder college for the needy Chinese community in direct response to the Merdeka University episode. Tunku Abdul Rahman College became the most affordable and accessible tertiary education institution for Chinese secondary schools graduates in the 1970s. The first Chinese community-funded college, Southern College (南方学院), was established in Johore twenty years later, after liberalization of the National Education Policy in 1990.

Another important consequence from the Merdeka University lawsuit was the participation of young lawyers in the central decision-making process of the Chinese education movement. Highly appreciated by Lim Fong Seng, these lawyers were given direct access to the movement's central committee as appointed committee members. The injection of much-needed vibrancy and valour of these professional middle-class activists into the movement significantly influenced the movement's repertoires in the 1980s.

ALLIANCE OF THE CHINESE CIVIL SOCIETIES

The Merdeka University lawsuit highlighted the reality that democratic institutions in Malaysia are at times easily manipulated by the ruling regime, and *Dongjiaozong* would have little chance of success without strong political support; it was this consideration that prompted Lim Fong Seng to participate in electoral politics in 1982. Lim's ambitious plan was, however, strongly opposed by the pro-MCA faction of the Chinese education movement. *Jiaozong* Chairman Sim Mow Yu referred to Lim's plan as naïve, and questioned the logic of an education movement organization getting involved in contentious party politics.[7]

On the other hand, Lim's plan also had strong supporters, many who were politically ambitious and wanted to use *Dongjiaozong* as a stepping stone to a political career.[8] According to movement veteran Loot Ting Yee, Lim and his supporters once considered forming a *Dongjiaozong* political party. However, the plan was foiled due to a lack of resources.[9] Lim launched the Alliance of Three campaign prior to the 1982 General Election and invited collaboration from ethnic Chinese politicians (both from the ruling regime and opposition parties) to defend the rights of the Chinese community (Koh 1986). To his dismay, ethnic Chinese politicians from MCA, the strongest ethnic Chinese party in the ruling government, and Democratic Action Party (DAP), the strongest opposition party at the time, showed little interest in the collaboration.

It was through mediation by MCA-turned-Gerakan politicians, Chen Wing Sum (曾永森) and Lim Keng Yaik (林敬益), that the deal was eventually sealed between *Dongjiaozong* and Gerakan, the multi-ethnic but increasingly Chinese-dominated political party from BN. To officiate this collaboration, Lim Fong Seng led about twenty Chinese educationalists to join Gerakan in March 1982 and made a pledge of "Join BN, Rectify BN" (打进国阵, 纠正国阵) (Chian 1994, p. 82). Amongst them, Kerk Choo Ting and Koh Tsu Koon contested as Gerakan candidates during the 1982 General Election, while Ong Tin Kim (王添庆) and Kang Chin Seng (江真诚) contested in the 1986 General Election.[10]

Kerk contested in Kepong constituency against DAP candidate Tan Seng Giaw (陈胜尧), while Koh competed against DAP candidate Chian Heng Kai (陈庆佳).[11] DAP was particularly unhappy with the line up, as both DAP candidates were also active Chinese educationalists at the local level. Pitting Chinese educationalists against each other was a lose-lose game for both DAP and *Dongjiaozong*. As a result, DAP saw a reduction of its parliamentary seats from fifteen in 1978 to nine in 1982. Gerakan turned out to be the largest winner of this campaign, winning five out of seven parliamentary seats contested — the best performance in the party's history (GM 1983, pp. 132–33; Lim, K.S. 1985; and Mauzy 1983*b*, p. 501).

Dongjiaozong also emerged as a loser from this campaign, as its dream of rectifying BN was badly shattered when all four educationalists who ran for office (Kerk, Koh, Ong, and Kang) were reformed by BN. Not only did they fail to deliver the promise of defending the interests of the Chinese education movement in the BN government, they were muted from criticizing the state's marginalization policies by their desire to accumulate political capital for themselves within the reality of intra-party power struggle.

In addition, amongst these four candidates, only Kerk was an active member in the *Dongzong* committee. The other three men had brief encounters with *Dongjiaozong*: Kang was a newly appointed member of the Malaysian Independent Chinese Secondary Schools Working Committee; Ong was one of the lawyers in the legal team in the Merdeka University lawsuit; and Koh was totally new to *Dongjiaozong*. Their loose engagement with *Dongjiaozong* meant that their commitment to Chinese education was rather weak, and gradually they began to put the interests of Gerakan and politics before those of the Chinese education movement.[12] Lacking a shared political goal amongst the four also made it impossible for them to overcome the domination of UMNO within BN, despite holding important positions within Gerakan.[13] It was not until 1990 that Lim Fong Seng admitted publicly that the campaign had been "immature" and failed his expectations (Zhan 2003).

Mahathir Mohamad became the fourth prime minister of Malaysia in 1981. In order to boost his popularity within UMNO, Mahathir's administration imposed a series of assimilative policies in the 1980s to strengthen the Malays' domination in the country (Chandra 1989*b*, pp. 31–35). For example, the narrowly defined National Cultural Policy (*Dasar Kebudayaan Negara*) was implemented in 1981 (GM 1981*a*). Activities that were perceived as contradictory to Malay culture and Islam were prohibited. Notably, the police refused to release permits for Chinese lion dance performances other than during Chinese New Year. The usage of Chinese text on commercial signboards was also restricted (SCAH 2004, p. 78). To make *Bahasa Melayu* (Malay language) the dominant medium of education in the country, the English-medium Higher School Certificate was replaced by the Malay-medium Malaysian Higher School Certificate (*Sijil Tinggi Persekolahan Malaysia*) in 1982 (GM 1981*b*, p. 390). In 1983, the Malaysian National Primary Syllabus (*Kurikulum Bersepadu Sekolah Rendah*) was implemented, amongst others (GM 1979; 1981*b*, p. 403; and MEM 1985*b*).

All these acts of discrimination fuelled insecurity within the Chinese community, especially amongst the post-independence generation who regarded Malaysia as their homeland and believed that all Malaysian citizens should enjoy equal rights.[14] In response, Selangor Chinese Assembly Hall activist Chong King Liong (张景良), supported by Chairman Khoo Seong Chi (邱祥炽), began to lobby for the support of Chinese guilds and associations to draft the Memorandum on National Cultural Policy (国家文化备忘录) as a countermeasure against the National Cultural Policy. The memorandum demanded more inclusive and multicultural representation in national cultural policies (Zhang, J.L. 1983). This timely effort received affirmative and encouraging responses from Chinese guilds and associations nationwide. Representatives from all state-level Chinese assembly halls, Chinese chambers of commerce, Chinese school committee associations, and Chinese schoolteachers' associations agreed to overcome their regional, linguistic, kinship, and occupational differences to defend the common interests of the Chinese community.

In March 1983, the first Chinese Cultural Congress (全国华人文化节) was organized in Penang as a platform to establish the Alliance of Fifteen Leading Chinese Guilds and Associations, one of the largest coalitions of the Chinese community in Malaysia (see Map 4.1).[15] During the congress, the alliance endorsed the Memorandum on National Cultural Policy. The memorandum was submitted to Anwar Ibrahim, the then Minister of Youth and Sports, but was rejected on the ground that the National Cultural Policy had already been finalized (SCAH 2004, p. 63).

Facing a regime that rejected bottom-up input to its policymaking highlighted the importance of strong associational bonds amongst the minority communities in boosting their political influence. Therefore, the National Chinese Guilds and Associations Cultural Working Committee (全国华团文化工作委员会) was established in August 1984 to strengthen bonds amongst Chinese guilds and associations. The working committee promoted sharing of intellectual and financial resources, enabled routine interactions and built intimate working relationships amongst leading activists within the alliance. The strengthening of associational links increased the Alliance of Fifteen's capacity to emerge as the most outspoken political pressure group in the 1980s.

In 1985, the Alliance of Fifteen established the Chinese Resource and Research Centre (华社资料研究中心) as a strategic think-tank, whose first and most important contribution was to draft the Joint Declaration of National Chinese Guilds and Associations (全国华团联合宣言) (SCAH 1985). The declaration demanded political reforms, greater democratization, and equal opportunities for all Malaysians, regardless of ethnicity.

MAP 4.1

The Alliance of Fifteen Leading Chinese Guilds and Associations

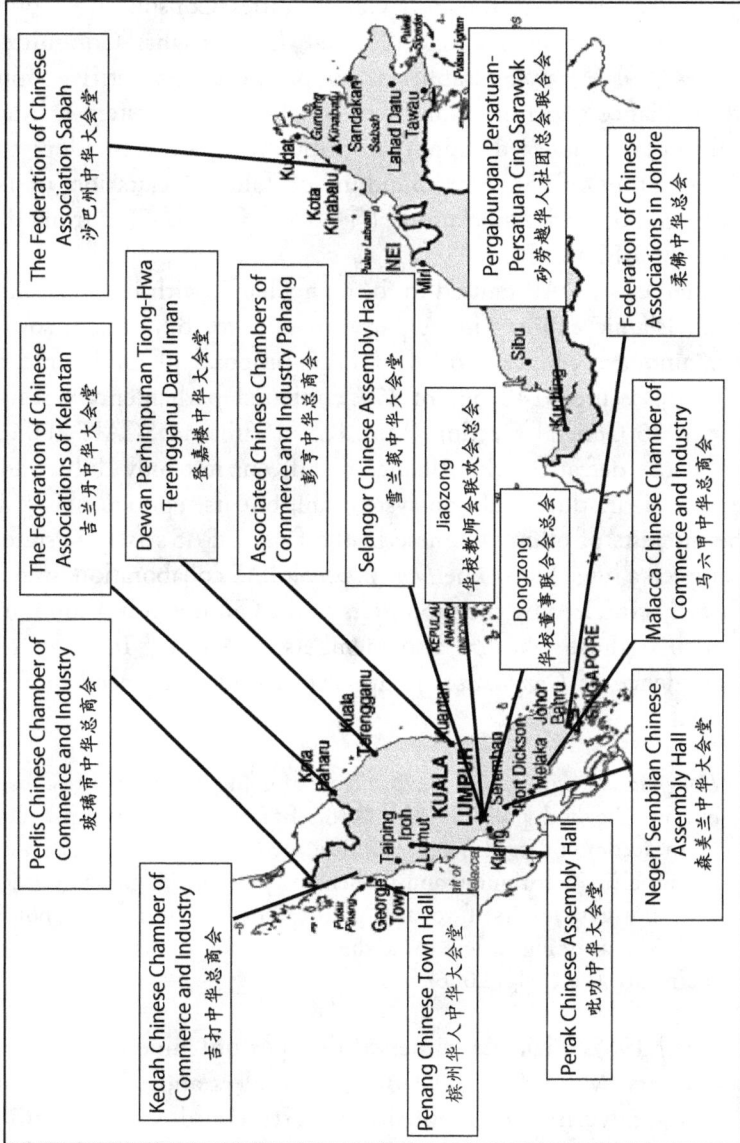

The Federation of Chinese Association Sabah
沙巴州中华大会堂

Pergabungan Persatuan-Persatuan Cina Sarawak
砂劳越华人社团总会联会会

Federation of Chinese Associations in Johore
柔佛中华总会

Perlis Chinese Chamber of Commerce and Industry
玻璃市中华总商会

The Federation of Chinese Associations of Kelantan
吉兰丹中华大会堂

Dewan Perhimpunan Tiong-Hwa Terengganu Darul Iman
登嘉楼中华大会堂

Associated Chinese Chambers of Commerce and Industry Pahang
彭亨中华总商会

Selangor Chinese Assembly Hall
雪兰莪中华大会堂

Jiaozong
华校教师会联会总会

Dongzong
华校董事联合会总会

Malacca Chinese Chamber of Commerce and Industry
马六甲中华总商会

Kedah Chinese Chamber of Commerce and Industry
吉打中华总商会

Penang Chinese Town Hall
槟州华人大会堂

Perak Chinese Assembly Hall
吡叻中华大会堂

Negeri Sembilan Chinese Assembly Hall
森美兰中华大会堂

Source: The author.

In September that year, the Alliance of Fifteen expanded their lobbying efforts by bridging the Malay-dominated PAS. With Lim Fong Seng representing *Dongjiaozong* in a dialogue of understanding between *Dongjiaozong* and PAS, the PAS Communities Consultative Council was formed. In 1986, the National Chinese Civic Rights Committee (全国华团民权委员会) was established to promote competitive opposition political alliance and formation of the dual coalition system in Malaysia.[16] The alliance also lobbied support from political parties to adopt the 1986 Implementation of the Memorandum of Joint Declaration of National Chinese Guilds and Associations (贯彻华团联合宣言) during the 1986 election (SCAH 1986).

Nonetheless, DAP refused to form an alliance with PAS, which insisted upon an Islamic country in its party's manifesto. BN, which sowed seeds of fear amongst Chinese voters of PAS' proposal of an Islamic country, successfully secured 148 out of 177 contested parliamentary seats in the August 1986 General Election (Lim, K.S. 1986; and SCAH 2004, p. 84). It was a sore defeat for the Alliance of Fifteen: not only did its ambitious campaign of the dual coalition system fail, but its reputation as a defender of the interests of ethnic Chinese in the face of PAS's Islamic state agenda also suffered a huge blow. The *Dongjiaozong*-PAS collaboration, in particular, was heavily criticized by the supporters of the Chinese education movement, in particular those who are also members of MCA.[17] In order to regain the confidence of *Dongjiaozong*'s upporters, Lim announced in September 1986 that,

> *Dongjiaozong* will uphold the principle of going beyond political party but not beyond politics (超越政党, 不超越政治). This will allow us to accommodate different political views, and, at the same time, remain alert in critiquing and influencing policymaking. *Dongjiaozong* shall not restrict itself to any political party but it shall not be apolitical, as doing so will cause the organization to detach itself from the reality (Lee, P.K. 2006).

In October 1987, Malaysia witnessed the apex of Chinese political strength and solidarity. More than 3,000 Chinese leaders and representatives from the ruling government, opposition parties and Chinese guilds and associations nationwide participated in the Protest Assembly of National Chinese Guilds and Associations and Political Parties (全国华团政党抗议大会议) at *Tianhou* Temple (天后宫), Kuala Lumpur. They protested against the Ministry of Education's appointment of more than a hundred non-Chinese-speaking teachers to take over senior positions in Chinese primary schools.

The protest assembly had an all-star turnout, with some of the most ardent critics from the Chinese community, such as Chong King Liong (Selangor Chinese Assembly Hall), Lim Fong Seng (*Dongzong*), Sim Mow Yu (*Jiaozong*), Lim Kit Siang (林吉祥, DAP), and others, taking turns to woo the audience with their impassioned speeches.[18] Together with supporters, they uniformly demanded the government to resolve the controversy by removing the "unqualified" schoolteachers within three days, or face a nationwide strike of Chinese primary schools (UCSCAM 1988, p. 9; and *Xinwanbao*, 4 October 1987).

Recognizing the assembly's power, Mahathir Mohamad relented. He appointed Deputy Prime Minister Ghafa Baba to head a mediation committee to put an end to the stalemate. Cabinet members cum Mediation Committee members, Lee Kim Sai and Lim Keng Yaik, acted as the government's bridge, and successfully persuaded the Chinese leaders to compromise and delay the strike. However, due to the lack of prompt and effective communication channels, they failed to terminate the movement at the grassroots level, where anti-government emotions ran high (UCSCAM 1998, p. 10). Eventually, school strikes were carried out in Penang (fourth-six schools), Malacca (seven schools), Kuala Lumpur-Selangor (seven schools), and Perlis (one school).[19] Subsequent strikes spread like wildfire, with at least a quarter of Chinese primary schools in Malaysia joining the strike.[20]

In response, Najib Razak, acting chief of UMNO Youth, organized an anti-Chinese protest with some 7,000 demonstrators at Merdeka Stadium (Case 1996, p. 197). Mounting ethnic tensions created an opportunity for Mahathir to carry out his infamous *Operasi Lalang* to contain escalating political tension.[21] The police detained 107 activists, which included Lim Fong Seng, Sim Mow Yu, Thuang Pik King (庄迪君, vice chairman, *Jiaozong*), Kua Kia Soong (director, Chinese Resource and Research Centre), Lim Kit Siang, amongst others, under the Internal Security Act (UCSCAM 1989, pp. 26–30). The Ministry of Internal Affairs also temporarily revoked the publishing licences of three newspapers, namely, the English-medium newspaper, *The Star*, Malay-medium *Watan*, and Chinese-medium *Sinchew Daily*, on the grounds that they publicized sensitive issues and ignored the possible impact of these issues on the peace and harmony amongst ethnic groups and on state security.[22]

Leader of the Alliance of Fifteen, Chong King Liong, who narrowly escaped detention, mobilized support from Chinese guilds and associations nationwide to demand the release of these detainees (FLCGAM 1988). However, crippled by fear of a second wave of *Operasi Lalang*, most people hesitated. The fear instilled by *Operasi Lalang* is best exemplified by the refusal of *Dongzong* General Secretary Low Sik Thong — who was by default second in line to lead the organization — to take over. Instead, Lim Geok Chan (林玉静), a movement activist from Selangor state, who at the time of appointment did not hold any position within *Dongzong*, stepped forward to lead *Dongzong* as acting chairman during this critical time.[23]

The controversy ended in April 1988 with the implementation of the Four-One Resolution. The resolution proposed that four senior positions in Chinese primary schools, namely, school principal, first and second deputy principals, and head of the afternoon session, must be equipped with qualifications of Chinese proficiency. The chief of curriculum activities could be exempted from this regulation. After the proposal was implemented, Chinese education movement leaders, Lim Fong Seng and Sim Mow Yu, were released in June the same year, followed by Thuang Pik King and Kua Kia Soong. The last detainee released from the *Operasi Lalang* was DAP father-and-son team, Lim Kit Siang and Lim Guan Eng, who were imprisoned until April 1989 (UCSCAM 1989, pp. 26–30).

The 1987 mass arrest changed both the Chinese education movement and the BN regime. For the former, new positions, such as deputy chairman and vice chairman, were introduced to strengthen the management efficiency of the movement (UCSCAM 1989, pp. 51–52; 2004a, pp. 45–47). In order to quell anti-government sentiments and to appease its opponents, the BN regime invited 150 representatives from political parties, minority groups, and social organizations to take part in the National Economic Advisory Council (*Majlis Perundingan Ekonomi Negara*) in January 1989 (NEAC 1991, pp. 327–50). Despite knowing that the invitation was more political than economic, *Dongzong*, *Jiaozong*, and Selangor Chinese Assembly Hall represented the Alliance of Fifteen to join the council (UCSCAM 1990, p. 18).

The three organizations proposed the replacement of the ethnic quota in national universities by a merit system, and demanded transparency in state decision-making processes. However, these suggestions were deliberately excluded from the council's report (UCSCAM 1990, p. 3.) The 150 representatives withdrew from the council eight months later, in protest against the discriminatory verbal insults by the council's officers, and the lack of transparency in the council's decision-making processes (UCSCAM 1990, pp. 3, 18–28, 32–33).

Despite this, the BN regime continued to engage the Chinese education movement community through the Education Act Advisory Council (*Majlis Perundangan Akta Pendidikan*) in August 1990. *Dongzong*, *Jiaozong*, Selangor Chinese Assembly Hall, Nanyang University Alumni Association of Malaya (马来亚南大校友会), and Federation of Alumni Associations of Taiwan Universities of Malaysia (马来西亚留台校友会联会总会) accepted the invitation with mixed feelings.[24] This invitation marked the first official recognition of the status of these two associations. It was a symbolic breakthrough for the Chinese education movement as the BN regime had been refusing to acknowledge the qualifications of graduates from Nanyang University and Taiwanese universities since the 1950s.[25] Although sceptical of the intentions of the council, these Chinese education representatives nevertheless submitted the Proposals on the Draft of the 1990 Education Act (对1990年教育法令草案的修改建议) to the government in March 1991 (UCSCAM 1992c, pp. 21–28; and UCSCAM et al. 1991). Not surprisingly, none of the proposals was included in the 1990 Education Act.

Frustrated, disappointed and feeling helpless from repeatedly hitting the wall, Chinese education movement leader Lim Fong Seng decided to take one of the riskiest decisions in the movement's history: in 1990, he participated in the General Election, and once again, yielded to the formation of the dual coalition system.[26] Although his decision was embraced by *Dongzong* General Secretary Low Sik Thong, *Dongzong* Vice Chairman Chin Choong Sang, and others, the majority of *Dongjiaozong* leaders opposed the decision.[27]

Jiaozong Chairman Sim Mow Yu, State of Johore Chinese School Managers and Teachers' Association (柔佛州华校董教联合会) Chairman Quek Suan Hiang, and their supporters, voiced their strong preference for the Chinese education movement to remain politically neutral.[28]

The division forced *Dongjiaozong* to release an official statement in August 1990 to reaffirm its principle of "beyond political party but not beyond politics":

> *Dongjiaozong*, as a social organization (社团), cannot and will not assign representatives to participate in the upcoming elections. However, operating on the principal of promoting democratization through the formation of a dual coalition system in Malaysia, *Dongjiaozong* encourages the participation of Chinese individuals in party politics (UCSCAM 1991, p. 18).

To avoid implicating the Chinese education movement, Lim Fong Seng and twenty-six Chinese educationalists resigned from their positions in *Dongjiaozong* prior to joining DAP.[29] DAP fully utilized the Chinese educationalists to garner support from Chinese voters. Lim Fong Seng was appointed as DAP advisor and former *Dongzong* Chief Executive Secretary Lee Ban Chen (李万千) was appointed as DAP vice president.[30] These former Chinese educationalists joined the People's Coalition (*Gagasan Rakyat*), an opposition front comprising DAP, PAS, *Parti Melayu Semangat 46*, *Parti Bersatu Sabah*, and the All Malaysian Indian Progressive Front, to challenge BN's political domination.[31]

Unfortunately, although DAP successfully acquired twenty parliamentary seats and forty-five state assembly seats in the 1990 General Election, the rejection of *Parti Melayu Semangat 46* by the Malay community prevented the People's Coalition from toppling the BN ruling regime. Lim Fong Seng's legacy in DAP soon ended with his withdrawal from the party in early 1991 prompted by his disagreement on DAP's approaches on the Chinese education (Lai, X.J. 2001). In June 1991, Foo Wan Thot (胡万铎), a former MCA Perak state activist, was selected as the new *Dongzong* chairman. Foo emphasized a negotiation-oriented approach as a more effective way to solve the problems of Chinese education. In order to affirm the stability of *Dongzong's* new leadership, Lim made the following remarks to his supporters in October 1991:

> Some have characterized my era as an era of confrontation while Foo's as era of negotiation. *Dongjiaozong* is a pressure group not because of its leaders' objectives or decisions, but rather, the subjective factors influencing decisions at the time.[32]

Foo's diplomatic strategy began with friendly visits and closed door conversations with Gerakan and MCA leaders. The meeting with MCA President Ling Liong Sik (林良实) was particularly promising as it improved *Dongjiaozong*-MCA relationship and restored their collaboration in the development of Chinese education. Two significant commitments were reached by MCA at the meeting: location of funds for the development of independent Chinese secondary schools and recognition of the Unified Examination Certificate as an entrance qualification to Tunku Abdul Rahman College.[33]

Foo's efforts, however, were overshadowed by the 1992 controversy of Lick Hung Chinese Primary School (力行华文小学).[34] This school had shifted to Subang Jaya in 1991 due to a shortage of students at its old premises at Bangsar. The controversy arose after Selangor Education Department ordered the replacement of the school committee with a financial management committee (*lembaga pengurus kewangan*) — a less powerful school authority that had commonly existed in national schools only. Lick Hung's school committee, headed by Chairperson Chew Saw Eng (周素英), protested against the replacement and alleged it as a ploy to transform the school into a national school.[35]

The controversy became more complicated when Chew and her deputy Wang Wen Han (王文汉) each hosted a new school committee. Both claimed that they were the legitimate leaders of the school committee and refused to give in. The dispute snowballed when Chew, who was also *Dongzong*'s treasurer, roped in the support of her colleagues in *Dongzong*, while Wang was backed up by members of MCA's Selangor Branch.[36] Debates between supporters from both parties were intense. By November 1992, Selangor and Kuala Lumpur state-level MCA leaders proposed that MCA members, who constituted about 70 per cent of the Chinese school committees, should enter, rectify, and form a new *Dongjiaozong*.[37]

Fortunately, MCA President Ling Liong Sik's timely intervention successfully prevented further escalation.[38] As a gesture of appreciation to Ling, Foo Wan Thot attended the launch of MCA Langkawi Project in February 1993, much to the displeasure of his fellow *Dongjiaozong* colleagues. Many of Foo's colleagues felt that the Langkawi Project, which involved fundraising for new Chinese villages (新村) and independent Chinese secondary schools nationwide, was yet another political attempt to replace *Dongjiaozong* in the long run.[39] Foo, however, insisted on his pro-MCA strategy, which subsequently cost him his popularity within the Chinese education movement, particularly amongst followers of former leader Lim Fong Seng. Foo became one of the shortest serving *Dongzong* chairman in the movement's history, and was replaced by Quek Suan Hiang in 1993.

CHINESE DIVERGENCE

The Lick Hung incident and the call to establish an alternative *Dongjiaozong* exposed the divisions within the Chinese education movement's community. The divisions worsened in the 1990s with an increasing number of politically ambitious, pro-BN individuals taking over the leadership of various Chinese guilds and associations. These pro-BN individuals compromised to external suppression from the state and internal threats from within. Most importantly, the differences in ambitions and agendas amongst those at the helm of Chinese guilds and associations dichotomized the politics of collaboration and politics of pressure of Chinese guilds and associations in Malaysia, and directly impacted the collective support received by the Chinese education movement.

The intra-Chinese rift was widened in the formation of the Unified Federation of Malaysian Chinese Assembly Hall (马来西亚中华大会堂联合会, renamed as Federation of Chinese Associations Malaysia 马来西亚中华大会堂总会 in 1997) (FCAM 1997). Attempts to establish the federation were first proposed by the Alliance of Fifteen in 1982. However, the BN regime delayed its establishment until October 1991, soon after MCA had gained control of almost all state-level Chinese assembly halls (SCAH 2004, p. 59).

Conflicts between the collaborative versus the confrontational factions within the former Alliance of Fifteen community reached boiling point during the first committee election for the federation in December 1991. Those of the confrontational faction did not want the pro-collaborative leader, who was also Selangor Chinese Assembly Hall Chairman Lim Geok Chan, to win the presidency uncontested; so they persuaded Sim Mow Yu, then *Jiaozong* chairman and president of the Malacca Chinese Assembly Hall, to compete.

Ultimately, Lim Geok Chan won by an overwhelming majority (130 votes to forty) and his victory saw the pro-collaborative rift gradually dominating the central leadership of the Unified Federation of Malaysian

Chinese Assembly Hall. Sim's involvement in the politics of power struggle between the two factions caused relationship between *Dongjiaozong* and the federation to deteriorate.[40] The soured relationship reached its nadir when *Dongjiaozong* withdrew from the drafting of the National Chinese Guilds and Associations Cultural Programme (全国华团文化工作总纲领) in 1996.

Dongjiaozong was dissatisfied with Lim Geok Chan and his supporters who tried to amend the 1983 Memorandum on National Cultural Policy and the Joint Declaration of National Chinese Guilds and Associations (UCSCAM 1998, pp. 33, 67). *Dongjiaozong* saw these changes as sacrificing the Chinese's interests and the independence of Chinese organizations. In return, Lim accused *Dongjiaozong* of unwelcomed, unsolicited interference in the drafting of the memorandum.[41]

This marked the beginning of the departure of these two organizations from each other. Although *Dongjiaozong* adopted a strategy characterized by a mixture of resistance and negotiation in their interaction with the state, but it was firm in its defence of the original principles of the demands made by the Alliance of Fifteen. On the other hand, vested economic interests and intimate relationship with MCA saw most of the leaders of the federation supporting the authorities unconditionally. As a result, both organizations began to distance themselves from each other and to form new coalitions with their preferred alliances (UCSCAM 1998, pp. 67–70).

RESOURCE MOBILIZATION

The Chinese education movement entered a new phase when Quek Suan Hiang was selected as the new *Dongzong* chairman in 1993. Amongst the first tasks Quek managed was the ambitious development project of 8.5 acres of land in Kajang. This piece of land was owned by the trustees of Kajang Fah Kiew Chinese School (加影华侨学校产业受托会), and rented to Merdeka University Company in 1974 as the university's campus. UMNO-led Selangor state government reclaimed the land in 1978 but it was "returned" to the trustees in 1981 after successful intervention by Chinese politicians (Huajiaoshenghui 1993, pp. 38, 55–57; and UCSCAM 1992c, p. 331).

In 1989, driven by the fear of losing the land again and by the imperative to boost the spirit of Chinese educationalists after *Operasi*

Lalang, Lim Fong Seng proposed to develop the Kajang premises into a new headquarters for the Chinese education movement. To facilitate this project, the land was transferred to Merdeka University Company in 1989 and leased to *Dongzong* for thirty years at one ringgit per annum.[42] Quek and his team transformed the Chinese education movement into a resource-mobilizing engine in the 1990s. A series of fundraising campaigns, such as charity performances, food sales and singing contests, were conducted (Huajiaoshenghui 1993, p. 79). The Chinese Education Torch Relay (华教火炬行) spread across all independent Chinese secondary schools in West Malaysia and raised nearly 2 million ringgit in 1992 (Huajiaoshenghui 1993, p. 74; and UCSCAM 1992*c*, p. 54; 1993, p. 28; 2002*b*, pp. 21–25). The completion of the four-storied administrative building was celebrated with an elaborate opening ceremony in December 1993.

With insufficient funds to purchase facilities and equipment for the new building, *Dongzong* used the opening ceremony as a strategic platform to launch a second wave of fundraising campaigns.[43] It started with the tree-planting ceremony (百万松柏献华教) at which more than 2,000 pine trees were planted by donors, and the event generated almost 2.5 million ringgit in donations (UCSCAM 1995, p. 36). The pine tree symbolizes persistency, while tree-planting signifies efforts to provide a better future for the next generation — an apt metaphoric reference to the movement's determination in preserving Chinese schools in Malaysia.[44]

A room adoption programme was launched in 1994 to generate large sums of donations from the generous rich for the development of the headquarters. The programme enabled those who donated more than 20,000 ringgit to name a room in the new administrative building, while those who donated more than 500,000 ringgit could name a floor.[45] Hope Foundation (1 million ringgit), Gerakan (527,561 ringgit), and MCA (500,000 ringgit) topped the list of donors (UCSCAM 1997, p. 19). In particular, the donation from Hope Foundation was delivered by its chairman, Khoo Kay Peng (邱继炳), in a high-profile ceremony witnessed by Deputy Prime Minister Anwar Ibrahim — the most senior UMNO politician to have ever attended *Dongjiaozong's* activities (UCSCAM 1995, pp. 7, 42).

Other than being remembered as the chairman who was skilled at mobilizing donations, Quek Suan Hiang was also known for his well-rounded interactions with the BN regime.[46] Quek's good relationship with ethnic Chinese ministers in the cabinet gave *Dongzong* an advantage in the accommodative political milieu in the 1990s to introduce amicable bilateral negotiations with the regime. Amongst the most significant outcomes from these negotiations were the granting of school registration status to twenty-one independent Chinese secondary schools and the conduct of special schoolteachers' training programmes to overcome the shortage of Chinese primary schoolteachers.

Quek's charisma as a leader shone through during the controversy of Vision Schools Project (*Rancangan Sekolah Wawasan*). Proposed under the seventh Malaysia Plan in 1994, the government recycled the blueprint of the Integrated Schools Project (*Rancangan Sekolah Integrasi*) to promote ethnic integration amongst schoolchildren through sharing of school facilities.[47] However, previous bad experiences with the state's education policies and suspicions of the Vision Schools Project as yet another pretext to systematically eliminate Chinese schools in Malaysia saw strong opposition from the Chinese education movement supporters.[48] Quek's soft, yet determined approach successfully persuaded school committees from all five short-listed Chinese primary schools not to participate in the Vision Schools Project.[49] Collective boycott from the Chinese schools became one of the crucial factors that had led to the cancellation of the project in the 2000s.[50]

In September 1998, a political scuffle between Deputy Prime Minister Anwar Ibrahim and Prime Minister Mahathir resulted in the former's expulsion from his political appointments. A few days later, Anwar was arrested on trumped-up charges of corruption and sodomy. The cloud of conspiracy and despotism surrounding Anwar's overnight political demise led to the birth of an anti-Mahathir *reformasi* movement.[51] The movement was supported largely by the Malay middle class engineered from state-sponsored schemes created during Mahathir's twenty-two years' reign. Ironically, these ethnic Malays turned away from their patrons and supported the People's Justice Party, which contested against BN during the 1999 General Election (Khoo 2003, pp. 195–99).

With the Malay voters sturdily divided, BN was forced to depend on non-Malays votes to sustain its political domination. This political opportunity was exploited by the Selangor Chinese Assembly Hall Civic Rights Committee, which initiated the Malaysian Chinese Organisations' Election Appeals Committee (*Suqiu* Committee) (MCOEAC 2002, p. 15).

Quek Suan Hiang was named as the committee's chairman. Quek revealed the little known reason behind his appointment as chairman of the committee at the interview for this study:

> As the demands made by the *Suqiu* Committee were related to the collective interests of the Chinese community in this nation, the committee had to be led by leaders from national-level Chinese guilds and associations. Such an arrangement would strengthen the inclusiveness and collectiveness of this committee. Therefore, although Chairman Ngan Ching Wen (颜清文) of the Selangor Chinese Assembly Hall wanted to be the chairman, he was not entitled to do so as he was a leader for one of the state-level Chinese guilds and associations. On the other hand, the leader from the largest Chinese guilds and associations in Malaysia, Federation of Chinese Associations Malaysia [formerly known as Unified Federation of Malaysian Chinese Assembly Hall], had rejected this position, as Federation President Chong Chin Shoong (张征雄) did not want to offend the government. In the end, I, as the chairman of *Dongzong*, was nominated and selected to lead the committee.[52]

The *Suqiu* Committee suggested a reform programme comprising seventeen proposals, including the removal of the *bumiputera* and non-*bumiputera* dichotomy, abolishment of the ethnic quota system, and reform of the affirmative action from ethnic-based into needs-based, amongst others (MCOEAC 2002, p. 15). The Federation of Chinese Associations Malaysia and the Association of Chinese Chambers of Commerce and Industry of Malaysia (马来西亚中华总商会) refused to endorse these proposals on the ground that they were too aggressive and would infuriate the Malays.[53] As a result, only some 2,098 Chinese guilds and associations endorsed these demands, about half of the total that endorsed the 1983 Memorandum on National Cultural Policy.

Mahathir capitalized on the division in the committee by criticizing the committee for "not having the support of all Chinese in Malaysia"[54] and remarking that Malaysian Chinese were being deployed as "a means to pressurize the government" by a small group of people.[55] Despite this, pressures to win the 1999 General Election saw leaders of BN Chinese political parties, namely MCA, Gerakan, and Sarawak United People's Party, make a joint announcement in September 1999 that "the cabinet, in principal, accepted the *Suqiu* Committee demands".[56] BN's timely response managed to salvage its support from the Chinese community and allow it to maintain its two-thirds majority at the polls, despite a considerable decline (from 65 per cent in 1995 to 56 per cent in 1999) in its overall popular votes (Funston 2000, p. 49).

The fact that UMNO had failed to win Malay-majority support in the 1999 General Election threatened its status quo in BN (Maznah 2003, pp. 67, 77). A leading Malaysian studies scholar, Khoo Boo Teik, correctly pointed out that in his attempts to recapture Malay support, Mahathir resultantly played the card of "the contrivance of a Chinese threat to Malay rights" by attacking the *Suqiu* Committee (Khoo 2003, p. 126). A series of events in August 2000 supported Khoo's observation. The first was the anti-*Suqiu* Committee demonstration, participated by about 200 UMNO Youth members. These UMNO members protested outside Selangor Chinese Assembly Hall to demand the withdrawal of the petition and an apology to the Malay community to be made.[57] The protest was followed by Mahathir's open condemnation of the *Suqiu* Committee in the National Day speech on 31 August 2000. He criticized the committee as being "not much different than communists who tried to destroy the special status of Malays in the country and shared a similar approach to *Al-Maunah*" (Tan, K. 2000). After a series of closed-door negotiations with UMNO, the committee chairman, Quek Suan Hiang, was forced to rescind seven of the committee's appeals.

This was a huge setback for Quek and the *Dongjiaozong*. Quek bore the blame of "bowing down to UMNO pressure" although he was not the progenitor of the demands.[58] *Dongjiaozong* was also blamed for crossing movement boundaries and its former alliance, the Federation of Chinese Associations Malaysia, withdrew its support. In response, *Dongjiaozong* established the Alliance of Seven Chinese Education-Related Guilds and Associations (华教界七华团) in 2002 to strengthen their collectiveness (see Figure 4.1). This Alliance of Seven was led by *Dongzong* and consisted of *Jiaozong*, Federation of Alumni Associations of Taiwan Universities of Malaysia, Nanyang University Alumni Association of Malaya, United Chinese School Alumni Association (华校校友会联合会总会), Malaysian Seven Major Clans Associations (七大乡团协调委员会), and Federation of Chinese Associations Malaysia.[59] The Federation of Chinese Associations Malaysia held a symbolic membership and has remained passive from most of the decision-making within the alliance (Ho, K.L. 1992*b*, p. 5). The roles of this new alliance will be discussed in the next chapter.

FIGURE 4.1
The Alliance of Seven Chinese Education-Related Guilds and Associations

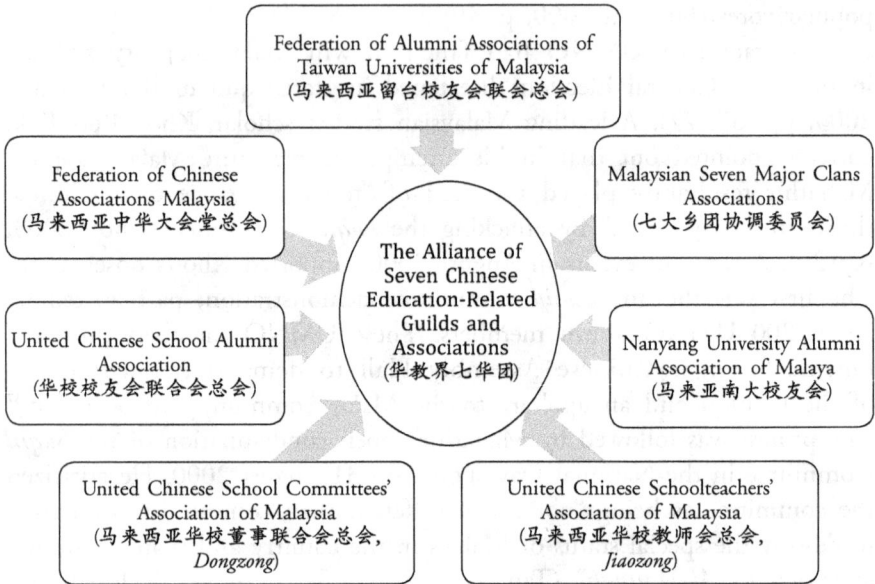

Federation of Alumni Associations of
Taiwan Universities of Malaysia
(马来西亚留台校友会联会总会)

Federation of Chinese
Associations Malaysia
(马来西亚中华大会堂总会)

Malaysian Seven Major Clans
Associations
(七大乡团协调委员会)

The Alliance of
Seven Chinese
Education-Related
Guilds and
Associations
(华教界七华团)

United Chinese School Alumni
Association
(华校校友会联合会总会)

Nanyang University Alumni
Association of Malaya
(马来亚南大校友会)

United Chinese School Committees'
Association of Malaysia
(马来西亚华校董事联合会总会,
Dongzong)

United Chinese Schoolteachers'
Association of Malaysia
(马来西亚华校教师会总会,
Jiaozong)

Source: The author.

POST-MAHATHIR MALAYSIA

Mahathir retired in October 2003. Abdullah Badawi, who had been known for his amicable Islamic credentials, succeeded the premiership. Abdullah's administration was well received by the rural Malay electorate through the "civilizational and comprehensive Islam" (*Islam hadhari*) programme (Abdullah 2006, pp. 1–29; and Fauwaz 2001). His publicized war on corruption involving arresting and charging several high-ranking officials convinced the urban class of his determination to shape a new and more transparent administration. The timely upturn of the economy after the Severe Acute Respiratory Syndrome crisis in early 2003 and the constituency delineation of electoral boundaries exercise in April 2003 also significantly maximized BN's political strength (Liow 2005, pp. 909–12). These factors ensured a landslide victory of more than 90 per cent of the contested parliamentary seats for Abdullah's administration during the 2004 General Election.

Over the same period, new leadership in the MCA and the Chinese education movement also came into power. Ong Ka Ting (黄家定) and Hon Choon Kim (韩春锦) became the new MCA president and deputy president, respectively, in 2003 after the MCA had been troubled by internal party factions.[60] Intensified power struggles within MCA effectively took away the two new MCA leaders' capacity and interest to facilitate demands from *Dongjiaozong*. The relationship between MCA and *Dongjiaozong* did not improve even after Yap Sin Tian succeeded Quek Suan Hiang as *Dongzong* chairman in 2005.

In addition, the rapid rise of Abdullah Badawi's son-in-law, Khairy Jamaluddin, in UMNO Youth was posing a considerable challenge to Hishammuddin Hussein's political position as the chief of UMNO Youth. Hence, in his attempts to assert his domination and superiority, Hishammuddin refused to meet any *Dongjiaozong* representatives in public or respond to the memorandums of the Chinese education movement submitted during the early days of his term as minister of education (2004–09).[61] Lack of support from MCA and cessation of all communication channels from the minister of education forced *Dongjiaozong* to seek new supporters through inter-ethnic collaboration. In 2007, for the first time in the history of the Chinese education movement, *Dongjiaozong* engaged the Tamil Foundation of Malaysia to jointly submit a Memorandum for the Return of Vernacular Education (还我母语教育备忘录) in protest against the implementation of the Teaching and Learning Science and Mathematics in English Programme (*Pengajaran dan Pembelajaran Sains dan Matematik dalam Bahasa Inggeris*).[62]

Two years later, *Dongjiaozong* conducted dialogues with the Malay advocacy group, Movement to Eliminate Teaching and Learning Science and Mathematics in English Programme (*Gerakan Mansuhkan Pengakaran dan Pembelajaran Sains dan Metematik dalam Bahasa Inggeris*) and explored joint strategies to pressure the government to withdraw the programme.[63] The stalemate ended with the withdrawal of the programme after BN suffered a significant political setback in the 2008 General Election.[64]

The political storm that struck Malaysia in 2008 had been brewing steadily since 2007. Although Abdullah's administration had made a glorious entrance into politics, Malaysians were getting increasingly impatient and disappointed with the administration's inability to fulfil its promises. The Malaysians' frustration culminated in the Coalition for Clean and Fair Election (*Gabungan Pilihanraya Bersih dan Adil*) rally in November 2007. More than 40,000 supporters attended the rally to demand reform in the country's electoral and political system (Xie 2007). A few days later, the Hindu Rights Action Force mobilized a second wave of mass protest over the failure of Malaysian Indian Congress to represent the interests of the Indian community in Malaysia (Case 2009, p. 329; and *Straits Times*, 26 November 2007).

Eventually it was the rise of Anwar Ibrahim, after his release from prison in September 2004, as a *de facto* leader that led to the formation of a strong inter-ethnic opposition political coalition under People's Alliance (*Pakatan Rakyat*, PR). The result was a switchover of an overwhelming number of votes to PR at the 2008 General Election. For the second time in Malaysia's history, BN lost its two-thirds dominance in the parliament. PR also gained control of five state-level governments in the Peninsula.[65] BN's weakened political domination was further threatened by Anwar Ibrahim's landslide victory in the Permatang Pauh parliamentary by-election in August 2008, after Anwar had fulfilled the legal bar to hold political office. The victory marked a comeback for Anwar. The formation of a significant, albeit unstable, dual coalition system for the first time in Malaysia's history was welcomed with a mixture of excitement and anxiety.[66]

The BN-PR competition intensified after Najib Razak succeeded Abdullah as prime minister in April 2009. Najib sought to revive his party and BN coalition by launching the "One Malaysia" campaign that promised economic reforms through the New Economic Model.[67] PR and BN also adopted more accommodative principles towards the demands of various pressure groups, including those from the Chinese education movement.[68] PR state governments offered, for instance, waiver of land taxes for schools, land allocation, and financial aid to vernacular schools in their respective states. Notably, DAP-led Penang government allocated 1 million ringgit in 2009 and 2 million ringgit a year later to five independent Chinese secondary schools in Penang.[69] People's Justice Party-led Selangor government donated a total of 6 million ringgit to the Chinese schools and independent Chinese secondary schools, and the PAS-led Kelantan government donated 2,229 acres of land to Kelantan Chung Wah Independent High School (吉兰丹中华独立中学).[70]

As mentioned earlier, BN agreed to revert to teaching Mathematics and Science in vernacular language in all primary schools with effect from 2012.[71] Najib's administration also responded positively to demands by the Chinese education movement. For instance, Unified Examination

Certificate holders are now allowed to apply for the state education loan starting from May 2010 (PTPTN 2010). Chinese classes have also been introduced in the national schools, marking the formal entrance of Chinese education into Malaysia's mainstream education system. Yap Sin Tian also used the opportunity to foster closer collaboration with MCA ministers, to demand for recognition of Unified Examination Certificate as an entry qualification into the national universities, and to upgrade *Dongjiaozong*-funded New Era College into a full university. Nevertheless, intense conflicts within *Dongjiaozong* had significantly reduced its capacity to exploit this political opportunity to the fullest. This caused the movement to miss a golden opportunity in achieving its ultimate aims of securing the status of Chinese education, Chinese schools, and Chinese language in Malaysia.

CONCLUSION

The opportunity for movement mobilization varies with the transitioning realities of political circumstances, especially the political circumstances constrained by a non-liberal democratic political context. Due to limited political access, the success of movement strategies is often determined by critical factors in leadership, brokerage, and external networks.

The leadership of the Chinese education movement has been selected through a bottom-up democratic process, and therefore the movement and its leadership have managed to secure legitimacy in mobilizing its supporters and launching various campaigns in resisting state suppression. Strong leadership is not inherited naturally but is structurally created through the leaders' ability to gather think-tanks, utilize their social capital in engaging support from leaders of other organizations, engage with MCA leaders for critical information, and take advantage of their positions as *Dongjiaozong* leaders to mobilize appropriate strategies.

Most importantly, leaders must outsmart external political constraints to sustain the movement's goals by adapting the movement's repertoires according to the changes in the movement supporters' mentalities, as well as according to the state's responses. The impacts of these factors have been shown in this chapter, in particular the shift of movement repertoires adopted by movement leaders, which varied from resistance-oriented to negotiation-oriented approaches. Chinese educationalists led by Lim Fong Seng resisted the state through a series of collective action and mass participation in politics (directly and indirectly) as a means to achieve their movement objectives in the 1970s and 1980s. However, these efforts failed to garner sufficient support from movement supporters who were divided by their various political affiliations, with many of them viewing such attempts to be too costly, as the state had the power and tendencies to manipulate its law enforcement system to crack down movement supporters.

Learning from past consequences, Foo Wan Thot softened the movement's approach in 1991 and fostered closer collaboration with MCA. However, Foo's pro-MCA strategy was poorly received by the movement supporters. Subsequent leaders such as Quek Suan Hiang and Yap Sin Tian revised their strategies to take on a politically neutral, collaborative, and negotiation-oriented approach. Instead of having a pro-MCA position, Quek was able to work amicably with the authorities through brokerage and facilitation by MCA ministers. Such indirect collaboration was better received by the movement supporters, and the Chinese education movement was also able to deliver its demands for changes effectively. The impact of these lobbying efforts went beyond policymaking to the policy-executing level, and the result of these efforts is promising rewards for the movement.

The movement has also relied on the support of its alliances through networking with other Chinese guilds and associations in the country. This relationship is best exemplified by the Alliance of Fifteen Leading Chinese Guilds and Associations formed in the 1980s in the face of increasing threats of assimilation from the state. The Chinese education movement leaders, Lim Fong Seng and Sim Mow Yu, collaborated with an activist of leading Chinese guilds and association, Chong King Liong, to form a formidable alliance, and the trio led a series of Chinese civic movements in the 1980s. The cause of the Chinese education movement in this era was framed as a fight for the values inherent in a democracy and a fight for human rights, beyond vernacular education rights.

Facing mounting challenges from the Chinese community, the state responded by deploying a series of carrot-and-stick measures. Through cohesive suppression (*Operasi Lalang*) and co-optation (formation of Unified Federation of Malaysian Chinese Assembly Hall), the state successfully weakened the influence of *Dongjiaozong* by breaking up the latter's relationship with the influential leaders of some of the Chinese guilds and associations' leaders. As the once-influential Alliance of Fifteen entered into a decline, the movement was forced to establish new alliances with the other Chinese guilds and associations and non-Chinese organizations. Although support from the non-Chinese communities held the promise of kick-starting the movement into a powerful momentum, but the exclusive nature of the Chinese education movement has prevented the collaboration from blossoming.

After 2008, the competition between BN and PR has provided valuable political opportunities for the Chinese education movement. BN leader, Najib Razak, who became Malaysia's prime minister in 2009, has adopted a more accommodative approach towards the demands from the Chinese education movement. At the same time, the state governments controlled by PR have also been implementing various pro-vernacular education policies and allocating financial resources to the Chinese schools in their states.

It remains a pity that despite increasing political opportunities for movement mobilization in Malaysia after 2008, mounting internal factionalism within the Chinese education movement has distracted movement leaders from exploiting these political opportunities to their fullest potential as they have been preoccupied with managing and resolving internal movement problems. Perspectives of, and the impacts of internal factionalism on the Chinese education movement will be discussed in Chapter 5.

Notes

1. For further details on Merdera University Petition, see MUB (1978*a*).
2. Announced by Education Minister Musa Hitam during UMNO Annual National Assemble on 17 September 1978. See DNICSSDWC (1993, p. 24); and GM (1971*b*; 1971*f*; 2006*a*).
3. The issue was also discussed during the National Independent Chinese Secondary Schools Committees and School Principals Joint Meeting (全国独中董事及校长联席会议) on 10 August 1974.
4. Such consensus was made during an emergency meeting held at Selangor Chinese Assembly Hall on 30 November 1975. The meeting was attended by 142 representatives from state-level Chinese school committees' associations, Chinese schoolteachers' associations, and Chinese school alumni associations.
5. The figure represents the total fund collected by 10 September 1980. See MUB (1978*b*); and Zhen (2006, p. 86).
6. These lawyers were Ker Kim Tin, Soo Thien Ming, Tan Chek Yoke, J.C. Bernatt, Soo Lim Pang, Lee Shan Too, Ong Tin Kim, Low Sik Thong, Ngeow Yin Ngee, and Siew Yew Ming.
7. Lee, P.K. (2006, p. 56); and *Sinchew Daily*, 21 August 1990.

8. Sim Mow Yu, interview by the author, Malacca, 26 March 2008.

9. Hew (1997); Thock (1994*a*, pp. 21–27; 1994*b*); and Loot Ting Yee, interview by the author, Kuala Lumpur, 24 March 2008.

10. During the 1986 General Election, Ong won the Anson parliamentary seat while Kerk won the Taiping parliamentary. Sim Mow Yu, interview by the author, Malacca, 26 March 2008.

11. Chian Heng Kai was an Internal Security Act detainee (1976–81) for criticizing government's discrimination policy on Chinese education. He won the 1978 Batu Gajah parliamentary seat election despite being detained under the Internal Security Act.

12. *Dongjiaozong* criticized Kerk Choo Ting as "no longer took an active interest in Chinese education matters since being appointed a deputy minister". See UCSCAM (1987*a*, pp. 15–17).

13. Kerk served as Gerakan deputy president for sixteen years before he retired in 2005. Kang was the party deputy vice president prior to retirement in 1999. Ong was appointed as Perak state secretary but passed away in 1997. Koh became the Penang chief minister (1990–2008) and party president since 2008. See Chin, J. (2006, p. 79); Khor and Khoo (2008, pp. 86–87); and Koh (1986, pp. 6–7).

14. Leong Tzi Liang, interview by the author, Penang, 3 February 2010.

15. Chinese assembly hall is the highest Chinese guilds and association authority in a state. Four states (Malacca, Kedah, Perlis, and Pahang) that do not have a Chinese assembly hall are represented by the Chinese chamber of commerce. In total, these two organizations have about 5,000 Chinese guilds and associations under their umbrella. See SCAH (2004, p. 62); and Yen (1981, pp. 62–63; 2000, p. 3). For the origins and development of the Chinese Cultural Congress from 1984 to 2000, see FCAM (2001).

16. *Nanyangshangpao*, 1 September 1986.

17. Sim Mow Yu, interview by the author, Malacca, 26 March 2008.

18. Other speakers in this gathering included Mah Cheok Tat (马卓达, Penang representative), Xu Min Yan (余明炎, Malacca representative), Hou Heng Hua (侯亨桦, Social Democratic Party), Huang Zhen Bu (黄振部, *Parti Sosialis Rakyat Malaysia*), Ong Tin Kim (Gerakan), Lee Kim Sai (李金狮, MCA), and Loot Ting Yee (*Jiaozong*).

19. *China Press*, *Nanyangshangpao*, and *Sinchew Daily*, 16 October 1987.

20. UCSCAM (2001*a*, p. 243); and Sim Mow Yu, interview by the author, Malacca, 26 March 2008.

21. For the list of the detainees, see Tan, S.G. (1989, pp. 129–33). For the official accounts of this operation, see GM (1988).

22. These newspapers received a new operation permit in March 1988. See DAP (1988, pp. 116–17); and Freedman (2000, p. 83).

23. Sim Mow Yu, interview by the author, Malacca, 26 March 2008.

24. Due to political constraint, Nanyang University alumnus in Malaysia has yet to successfully establish a national association. The alumnus organizations (Selangor, Penang, Kuala Lumpur, Johore, Perak, Malacca, and Sarawak) operate at the state level; while the Kuala Lumpur branch has been the default representative of Nanyang University alumnus in various *Dongjiaozong* related activities due to its strategic logistic location. For more, see Lee, Y.L. (2004, p. 421); NUAAM et al. (1982, pp. 83, 87–102); and UCSCAM (1991, p. 54; 1993, p. 32).

25. Many of these marginalized communities are strong supporters and core components of the Chinese education movement. By 2010, forty out of sixty principals, and one forth of 3,650 teachers who is serving at independent Chinese secondary schools were Nanyang University or Taiwanese universities graduates. See Yau (2008, pp. 6–7); Low Hing King (movement activist), interview by the author, Kuala Lumpur, 23 February 2009; and Yau Teck Kong (姚迪刚) (president, Federation of Alumni Associations of Taiwan Universities of Malaysia), interview by the author, Selangor, 18 February 2009.

26. CMCS (1990); *Nanyangshangpao*, 9 August 1990; *Sinchew Daily*, 9 August 1990; and Thock (1994a; 1994b).

27. *Nanyangshangpao*, 26 July, 1 August, and 4 August 1990.

28. They included Council of Perak Chinese School Committees (吡叻华校董事会联合会) Chairman cum *Dongzong* Deputy Chairman Foo Wan Thot, *Jiaozong* Vice Chairman Loot Ting Yee, and *Jiaozong* Vice Chairman Thuang Pik King. See *China Press*, 15 August 1990; *Nanyangshangpao*, 3 August, 6 August, 7 August, 8 August, and 18 August 1990; *Sinchew Daily*, 18 August 1990; and *Tongbao*, 7 August 1990.

29. These educationalists included Kua Kia Soong, Lee Ban Chen, Ngeow Yin Ngee, Yang Pei Keng (杨培根), Ng Wei Siong (吴维湘), and Chong Joon Kin (张永庆). For more, see UCSCAM (1991, pp. 39–40); *Nanyangshangpao*, 5 August 1990; and *Sinchew Daily*, 7 August 1990.

30. *Nanyangshangpao*, 20 August 1990.

31. This coalition ends in 1996 after the withdrawal of *Parti Bersatu Sabah* and the dissolution of *Parti Melayu Semangat 46*. See Case (1992, pp. 183–205); UCSCAM (1991, p. 37); Lim, K.S. (1990); and *Sinchew Daily*, 8 August and 17 August 1990.

32. UCSCAM (1992c, pp. 35–36); and *Sinchew Daily*, 20 October 1991.

33. *Sinchew Daily*, 16 October and 17 October 1991.

34. Chew Saw Eng (chairperson, Malaysia United Chinese School Alumni Association), interview by the author, Kuala Lumpur, 17 February 2009.

35. *China Press*, 4 May, 8 June and 16 June 1992; *Nanyangshangpao*, 27 July 1992; and *Sinchew Daily*, 5 May and 6 May 1992.

36. *Nanyangshangpao*, 8 August 1992; and *Sinchew Daily*, 17 May 1992.

37. *China Press*, 21 May and 11 August 1992; and *Sinchew Daily*, 27 July and 28 July 1992.
38. *China Press* and *Nanyangshangpao*, 26 May 1992.
39. Chinese New Villages are settlements created during British rule to segregate Chinese communities from the Malayan Communist Party in the 1950s. For more, see Daniel (1995, p. 115); and Loh (2000).
40. *Nanyangshangpao*, 13 February 1992.
41. *Nanyangshangpao*, 25 May 1992.
42. DHLC (2008*b*); Zhen (2006, p. 257); and Lee Hing (吕兴) (deputy chairman, Merdeka University Berhad), interview by the author, Selangor, 28 July 2010.
43. Quek Suan Hiang, interview by the author, Johore, 23 March 2010.
44. In the same evening, a fundraising dinner (风雨同路为华教万人宴) collected another 43.6 million ringgit. See UCSCAM (1994, p. 33; 1995, pp. 30, 36).
45. Quek Suan Hiang, interview by the author, Johore, 23 March 2010.
46. Sim Mow Yu, interview by the author, Malacca, 26 March 2008.
47. Strong opposition from the Chinese community successfully persuaded the Ministry of Education to replace the Integrated Schools Project with a less controversial Student Integration Programme (*Rancangan Integrasi Murid Untuk Perpaduan*) in 1986. The latter was well-received by the vernacular communities, as it enabled the vernacular schools to retain their original identity, while the students benefited from more effective integration efforts through collectively-organized extra-curriculum activities. For more, see MEM (1985*a*; 1985*b*; 1995); *Nanyangshangpao*, 22 August 1985; *Sinchew Daily*, 9 August 1985; UCSCAM (2000*a*, pp. 2–8; 2001*a*, pp. 189–219); and *Utusan Malaysia*, 7 August 1985.
48. *Sinchew Daily*, 21 November 2000; and UCSCAM (2000*a*, p. 2).
49. These schools included Soon Jian Chinese Primary School in Alor Setar, Kedah (循然华文小学); Khing Ming Chinese Primary School in Kuala Kubu Bharu, Selangor (竟明华文小学); Ladang Hillside Chinese Primary School in Negeri Sembilan (丘晒园华文小学); Eng Ling Chinese Primary School (永宁华文小学) and Wai Sin Chinese Primary School in Perak (维新华文小学); and Segamat Central Site Chinese Primary School in Johore (中央华文小学). See Ng, T.E. (2003, pp. 184–204).
50. The Ministry of Education launched five pilot Vision Schools in 2000, namely the Subang Jaya Vision School Complex house the Datuk Jaafar Onn National Primary School, Tun Tan Cheng Lock Chinese Primary School (陈祯禄华文小学), and Tun Sambantan Tamil Primary School. The other four Vision Schools Complexes were located at the Pekan Baru (Parit Buntar, Perak), Taman Aman (Alor Setar, Kedah), Tasik Permai (Penang), and Pundut (Seri Manjung, Perak). However, only the Subang Jaya Vision Schools was successful. The Johore version was terminated due to the presence of

too many national schools, while the Vision School in Pundut was troubled by the controversy between the administration of the national schools and Tamil schools. See *Nanyangshangpao*, 2 and 10 December 2000; *Star*, 25 May 2002; UCSCAM (1996, pp. 70–78); and Quek Suan Hiang, interview by the author, Johore, 23 March 2010.

51. On *reformasi* pictorial and chronology, see Petra (2001). On analysis of *reformasi* movement and its post-impact on Malaysia politics, see Freedman (2000, p. 52); Ganesan (2004, p. 72); and Loh and Saravanamuttu (2003).

52. Quek Suan Hiang, interview by the author, Johore, 23 March 2010.

53. Loh (2009); *Nanyangshangpao*, 9 September 1999; Ng, T.E. (2003, p. 198); and *Sinchew Daily*, 27 and 29 August 1999.

54. *Sinchew Daily*, 14 September 1999.

55. *Berita Harian*, 21 September 1999.

56. *Nanyangshangpao* and *Sinchew Daily*, 24 September 1999.

57. The event was widely covered (in different perspectives) in both Chinese and Malay newspapers. For the pro-*Suqiu* Committee coverage, see *Nanyangshangpao* and *Sinchew Daily*, 19–23 August 2000. On pro-UMNO coverage, see *Utusan Malaysia*, 18–23 August 2000.

58. Quek Suan Hiang, interview by the author, Johore, 23 March 2010.

59. The Malaysian Seven Major Clans Associations comprised of custodian-based clan associations, guilds, occupation- and region-based Chinese guilds and associations: Malaysian Federated San Kiang Association (马来西亚三江总会), Federation of Hainan Association Malaysia (马来西亚海南公会联合会), Guangxi Association Malaysia (马来西亚广西公会总会), Federation of Hakka Association Malaysia (马来西亚客家公会联合会), Federation of Teochew Association Malaysia (马来西亚潮州公会联合会), Federation of Hokkien Association Malaysia (马来西亚福建社团联合会), and Federation of Kwangtung Association Malaysia (马来西亚广东会馆联合会).

60. Back in 1999, contentions between MCA President Ling Liong Sik's team A (supported by Ong Ka Ting) and Deputy President Lim Ah Lek's (林亚礼) team B (supported by Chan Kong Choy, 陈广才) over the nomination of their respective *protégés* for the presidential post had to be temporarily frozen by Mahathir's "peace formula". Both Ling and Lim had not sought re-election and had agreed to retire in May 2003, paving the way for Ong and Chan's appointment to full ministerial positions. Although Ong won the party president election eventually, the resultant bad blood between the two factions destabilized the party enough to dilute its decision-making influence within BN. See Phoon (2006).

61. *Sun*, 24 March 2009. The memorandums submitted included the *Dongjiaozong's* overall opinion on the Malaysia Education Blueprint 2001–2010 (董教总对2001至2010年教育发展大蓝图总体意见书) (2002); Suggestions on the Ninth Malaysia Plan (第九大马计划的建议书) (2005); Suggestions on

the Ninth Malaysia Plan (第九大马计划的建议书) (2005); *Dongjiaozong's* opinion on the Malaysia Education Blueprint 2006–2010 (董教总对2006 至2010年教育发展大蓝图总体意见书) (2007).

62. Implemented in all primary schools since January 2003, the programme aimed to raise English proficiency amongst the schoolchildren by enforcing the teaching of mathematics and science in English. Student with little exposure to English language had suffered from this programme. For more, see Dongjiaozong (2004); *Nanyangshangpao*, 10 August and 31 October 2002; PPPPK (2007); *Sinchew Daily*, 8 August and 10 October 2002; and Wong, J. (2002).

63. *Merdeka Review*, 13 March 2009; and Shum Thin Khee, interview by the author, Selangor, 27 February 2009.

64. *News Straits Times* and *Sinchew Daily*, 9 July 2009.

65. Better known as the Perak Constitutional Crisis, BN regained control of Perak state after three PR state assembly members quit their parties and BN, together with the support of these three members, won a slim majority of over twenty-eight seats. See *Harakah*, 23 September 2010.

66. For analysis on the impact of the post-2008 General Election, see Tan and Lee (2008).

67. Guided by three principles, namely, high income, sustainability, and inclusiveness, the model hoped to improve the country's economic growth in capital and productivity for all Malaysians. See NEAC (2010, pp. 3–30).

68. Chen (2008); and *Merdeka Review*, 14 March 2008.

69. *Sinchew Daily*, 25 April 2010.

70. *Guangming Daily*, 30 August 2009; and *Kwongwahyitpoh*, 21 August 2010.

71. *News Straits Times* and *Sinchew Daily*, 9 July 2009.

5

MOBILIZATION MACHINERY

INTRODUCTION

After exploring the interactions, alliances, and rivals of the Chinese education movement in the earlier chapters, the focus now turns to the movement's internal institutions and mobilization machinery. This chapter explores three key components of the movement's institutions, namely, the Malaysian Independent Chinese Secondary Schools Working Committee, the *Dongjiaozong* Chinese Primary Schools Working Committee, and the *Dongjiaozong* Higher Learning Centre. Together, these three components play the role of a *de facto* education ministry for the Chinese community in Malaysia, and became the movement's machinery for mobilizing resources. As the size of the movement continues to grow and financial expenses increase, some of the components become more successful and sustainable, while others are not. Over time, the diverse development of these components thus transformed the relationship between *Dongzong* and *Jiaozong* from one of symbiosis into one of commensalism.

Through exploring the power relationships amongst these components, this chapter also analyses the decision-making hierarchy of the Chinese education movement from the 1970s to 2010s. Divided into the managerial (led by the elected committees) and operative (led by the salaried executives) levels, the movement functioned within a bureaucratic system that is predominantly agent-based and formulated around loosely-defined rules. Although professionalism eventually grew out of this hybrid system, the working dynamics and outcomes of the collaboration varied according to the interpersonal relationships.

The chapter ends with a discussion on the impact of the increasing economic value of the Chinese language on the Chinese education movement, transforming the movement from a national into a transnational movement. Even though the movement tried to expand its collaborative networks internationally through the Southeast Asian Chinese Language Teaching Convention (东南亚华文教学研讨会) and the New Era College, the impacts remained limited. This chapter will also evaluate the factors that had divided the movement into two (or more) confrontative factions.

THE INDEPENDENT CHINESE SECONDARY SCHOOLS REVIVAL MOVEMENT

After implementation of the 1961 Education Act, only sixteen Chinese secondary schools in the Peninsula Malaysia opted not to receive financial aid from the government and operated outside the national education system as independent Chinese secondary schools in order to preserve their authority over the school's management.

To appease angry Chinese communities and protect the social interests of the school committees that had acceded to the conversion project in the 1960s, the Ministry of Education allowed the converted schools to set up new or affiliated independent Chinese secondary schools within a shared school campus.[1] A total of thirty-three affiliated independent Chinese secondary schools (国民型华文中学董事部兼办独立中学) were established under these circumstances in the Peninsula. In Sabah and Sarawak, a total of seventeen new independent Chinese secondary schools were established between 1962 and 1969.[2]

Nevertheless, the development of independent Chinese secondary schools was stalled after the Malayan Secondary School Entrance Examination was abolished in 1963, for the abolishment of this examination resulted in the automatic enrolment of all primary school graduates into secondary schools (Leong and Tan 1997, p. 308). Subsequently in 1964, the implementation of nine years of free education for all citizens also drew new enrolment away from independent Chinese secondary schools that collected fees. On top of that, converted schools (which received financial aid from the government) offering better salaries also drew schoolteachers away from independent Chinese secondary schools.

Unable to surpass these constraints, five out of fourteen independent Chinese secondary schools in Perak were shut down by 1969. The remaining nine independent Chinese secondary schools in Perak, which hosted merely about 1,500 students altogether, were barely surviving in the late 1960s and early 1970s.[3] The threat to survival of independent Chinese secondary schools nationwide meant that the continuity of the Chinese education movement was also under threat. Therefore, as soon as the Emergency Decree was lifted in June 1972, the Grand Three Associations of Chinese Education hosted a nationwide meeting and established the Independent Chinese Secondary Schools Development Committee (独中发展小组) to strategize ways to salvage the plunging status of Chinese schools in Malaysia (UCSCAM 1987d, p. 614).

In Perak, Zeng Dun Hua (曾敦化) and Shen Ting (沈亭) from Poi Lam High School (培南独中) laid the groundwork for inter-independent Chinese secondary schools collaboration by gathering all related school principals in November 1972, and extended the invitation to chairmen of school committees a month later. By April 1973, the legendary Perak independent Chinese secondary schools revival movement was kick-started with full support from the Perak state-level Chinese school committees' association, the Council of Perak Chinese School Committees.[4]

The Perak Independent Chinese Secondary Schools Development Working Committee (吡叻州发展华文独中工作委员会) launched a successful fundraising campaign highlighting the concept of $yì$ (义), a voluntary and righteous behaviour to protect the weak. Donations were generated through charity campaigns involving sales of food, fishing, trishaw riding, and "One Person, One Dollar" donations, amongst others (Zhen 1996, pp. 46–48). The campaign garnered support from the Chinese community in Perak and nationwide, particularly from those who had suffered under the Emergency Decree and who were dissatisfied with the New Economic Policy system. The 1 million ringgit target was reached and the money was used for the expansion of school buildings and facilities, the hiring of more schoolteachers, and the setting up of scholarships and loans for independent Chinese secondary school students.[5]

The campaign also encouraged and persuaded parents to send their children to independent Chinese secondary schools. Student enrolment increased from about 2,500 in 1970 to roughly 5,100 in 1976 in the nine independent Chinese secondary schools in Perak (Shen 1975). Encouraged by increasing enrolment and improved public image, all nine schools collaboratively drafted a unified school curriculum and uniform textbooks, with each school responsible for developing a designated subject textbook.[6]

In March 1973, the Seminar on Independent Chinese Secondary Schools (华文独中研讨会) was organized in Selangor to draft the *Guiding Principles of Malaysian Independent Chinese Secondary Schools* (华文独立中学建议书). The draft was later used as the blueprint for reforming independent Chinese secondary schools at the national level. Although Perak was the leading state in the efforts channelled into reforming independent Chinese secondary schools, the dominance of Selangor state-level movement leaders in the *Dongzong* central committee saw the latter overtaking the leadership of the reformation. In December 1973, the national revival movement was inaugurated at the National Conference for Independent Chinese Secondary Schools Development (全国发展华文独中运动大会).

The Malaysian Independent Chinese Secondary Schools Working Committee was established as a *de facto* education ministry for the Chinese community. As it was not registered under the 1966 Society Act, this working committee was subordinated under *Dongzong* to secure operation legality, and safeguard financial resources and properties of the working committee.[7] As illustrated in Figure 5.1, organizationally, the working committee comprises of a general committee, a standing committee, and seven working units. Thirteen representatives each from *Dongzong* and *Jiaozong* formed the general committee; thirteen committee members from the Chinese education movement affiliated organizations would be appointed at the first meeting.

At this first meeting too, committee positions of the fifteen-member standing committee would be decided. Senior positions in the standing committee, such as chairman (主席), general secretary (总务), and treasurer (财政), were classified as reserved positions (当然常务委员) and were held by *Dongzong*'s office bearers by default. The positions for the deputy chairman, deputy general secretary, and deputy treasurer were reserved by default for office bearers from *Jiaozong*. Other positions within the standing committee were decided through elections. The working committee could also assign a maximum of seventeen appointed standing committee members (委任委员务) when necessary.

FIGURE 5.1

Organizational Chart of *Dongzong* and Malaysian Independent Chinese Secondary Schools Working Committee

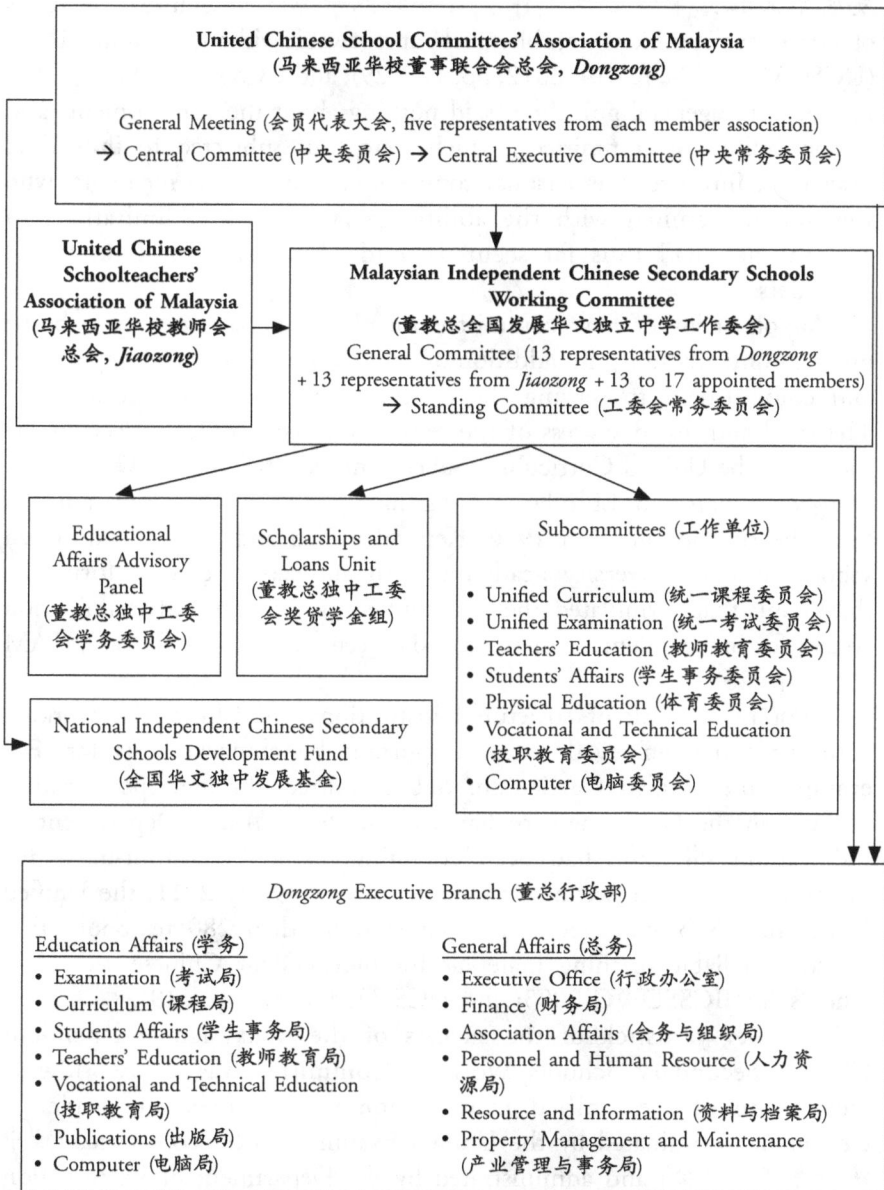

United Chinese School Committees' Association of Malaysia
(马来西亚华校董事联合会总会, *Dongzong*)

General Meeting (会员代表大会, five representatives from each member association)
→ Central Committee (中央委员会) → Central Executive Committee (中央常务委员会)

United Chinese Schoolteachers' Association of Malaysia
(马来西亚华校教师会总会, *Jiaozong*)

Malaysian Independent Chinese Secondary Schools Working Committee
(董教总全国发展华文独立中学工作委员会)
General Committee (13 representatives from *Dongzong* + 13 representatives from *Jiaozong* + 13 to 17 appointed members)
→ Standing Committee (工委会常务委员会)

Educational Affairs Advisory Panel
(董教总独中工委会学务委员会)

Scholarships and Loans Unit
(董教总独中工委会奖贷学金组)

National Independent Chinese Secondary Schools Development Fund
(全国华文独中发展基金)

Subcommittees (工作单位)

• Unified Curriculum (统一课程委员会)
• Unified Examination (统一考试委员会)
• Teachers' Education (教师教育委员会)
• Students' Affairs (学生事务委员会)
• Physical Education (体育委员会)
• Vocational and Technical Education (技职教育委员会)
• Computer (电脑委员会)

Dongzong Executive Branch (董总行政部)

Education Affairs (学务)
• Examination (考试局)
• Curriculum (课程局)
• Students Affairs (学生事务局)
• Teachers' Education (教师教育局)
• Vocational and Technical Education (技职教育局)
• Publications (出版局)
• Computer (电脑局)

General Affairs (总务)
• Executive Office (行政办公室)
• Finance (财务局)
• Association Affairs (会务与组织局)
• Personnel and Human Resource (人力资源局)
• Resource and Information (资料与档案局)
• Property Management and Maintenance (产业管理与事务局)

Source: Compiled by the author with reference to UCSCAM (2011, pp. 127–45).

The functions of these committees were briefly deliberated on the three-page *Organizational Rules and Regulations of the Malaysian Independent Chinese Secondary Schools Working Committee* (董教总全国发展华文独立中学运动工作委员会组织规章).[8] For example, the terms of service for all positions were biannual but renewable without maximum limits (UCSCAM 1987*d*, p. 614; 2012, pp. 127–29); and UCSTAM 1983*c*, p. 25). However, the general guidelines said nothing about the commitments and responsibilities of committees, which were thus subjected to individual discretion. Intimate interpersonal connections between the members, who were highly familiar with the abilities, characters, and limitations of one another, had thus far secured bonds, built trust and prevented free riders.

Appointment of new committee members, in particular, was based on recommendations, in addition to the candidate's social reputation and commitment to serving the development of Chinese education.[9] The tried and tested success of the selection process could be seen in the success of the Unified Curriculum Subcommittee (独中统一课程编委会). *Dongzong* chairman Lim Fong Seng handpicked Kerk Choo Ting to head the subcommittee in 1976. Kerk identified and invited committed schoolteachers, university academics and subject experts to form the think-tank that formulated the first unified curriculum and examination system for independent Chinese secondary schools in Malaysia (UCSTAM 1983*c*, p. 26).

Despite the lack of structured institutional guidelines, the working committee had achieved a few important benchmarks thus far. For example, the Unified Curriculum Subcommittee, through specialization of work in the Department of Curriculum (课程局) and Department of Publications (出版局), had been designing textbooks custom-made for independent Chinese secondary schools since 1979. By 2011, the Unified Curriculum Subcommittee had designed more than 280 textbooks that served as reliable teaching materials for independent Chinese secondary schools (DNICSSDWC 2005; and UCSCAM 1987*d*, p. 619).

Another yardstick of the success of the Malaysian Independent Chinese Secondary Schools Working Committee was the worldwide recognition of the Unified Examination Certificate as an academic credential. Coordinated by the Unified Examination Subcommittee (独中统一考试委员会) and administered by the Department of Examination (考试局), this examination was prepared and evaluated collaboratively

FIGURE 5.2

Distribution of Unified Examination Certificate Candidates

(1973–2011)

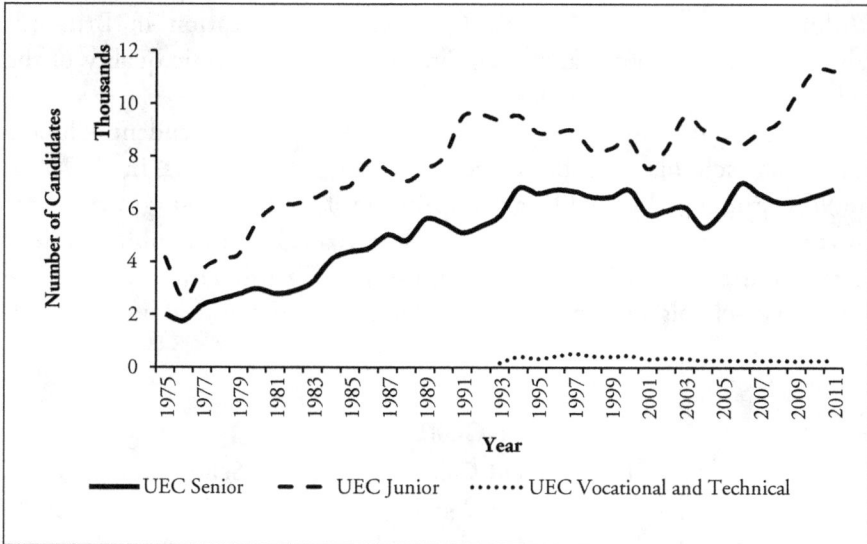

Source: Compiled by the author with data extracted from UCSCAM (2011, p. 290; 2012, p. 61).

by an extensive network of schoolteachers of independent Chinese secondary schools. Divided into three levels, namely, the senior, junior, vocational and technical levels, the examination was a unified academic assessment and credential of the students of independent Chinese secondary schools.

As illustrated in Figure 5.2, the popularity of this examination can be seen by the increase in the number of candidates taking the examination. By 2011, an accumulative total of 481,598 candidates had taken the three categories of examinations since it was first introduced in 1975. Senior-level candidates had risen dramatically, from 1,993 students in 1975 to 6,748 students by 2011. Candidates for the junior-level examinations also increased from 4,150 to 11,259 students over the same period. The vocational and technical candidates climbed comparatively slower, from 167 students in 1993 to 277 students in 2011.

By 2011, milestones continued to be made as Unified Examination Certificate holders were qualified for exemption from entrance examinations at all universities in Singapore; it was recognized as a qualification for high school education in the United States, and as the equivalent of the Ordinary Level of the General Certificate of Education in Britain.[10] These milestones boost parents' confidence on the academic quality of the independent Chinese secondary schools.

As such, the number of students enrolled in independent Chinese secondary schools had increased from 28,318 students in 1973 to 66,968 students by 2011, an impressive 136 per cent growth over thirty-nine years, as illustrated in Figure 5.3. Sustainable student enrollments also stablized the number of independent Chinese secondary schools at sixty since the launch of the revival movement.[11]

FIGURE 5.3

Distribution of Independent Chinese Secondary School Students in Malaysia

(1973–2011)

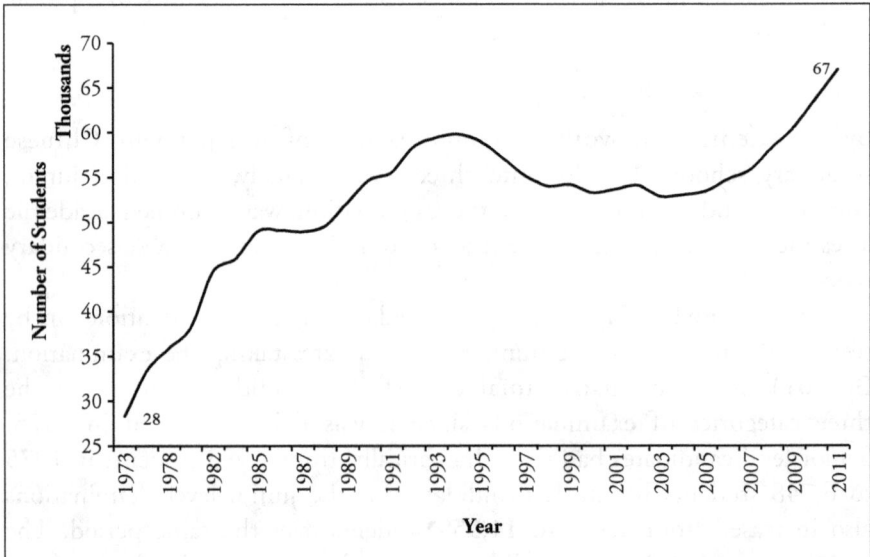

Source: UCSCAM (2012, p. 316).

By 2005, the *Guiding Principles of Educational Reform of Malaysian Independent Chinese Secondary Schools* (独中教育改革纲领) was introduced as a new blueprint for these schools, with the aim of making the curricula more comprehensive, scientific, and less exam-oriented (DNICSSDWC 1997).

The achievements and operation of the national independent Chinese secondary schools revival movement does not come free. Although the committee members worked on a voluntary basis, the hiring of executives, purchase of materials, and administration of decisions cost money. To ensure there were sufficient funds to support the revival movement, the National Independent Chinese Secondary Schools Development Fund (全国华文独中发展基金) was launched in March 1974. The working committee rode on the extensive network of the Chinese education movement and launched one of the most successful fundraising campaigns in the history of the Chinese education movement. Almost 3 million ringgit was collected within the first nine months after the launch of the fundraising campaign (UCSCAM 1987*d*, p. 616). The extensive mobilization power demonstrated by the supporters surprised state authorities, which subsequently prohibited all media (Chinese newspapers in particular) from covering news related to the fundraising campaign.[12]

To solicit donations and encourage participation from movement supporters on a more regular and on-going basis, the Independent Chinese Secondary Schools Development Sponsorship Programme (全国华文独中发展基金常年赞助人) was introduced in 1984 (UCSCAM 1987*b*, p. 617). Unfamiliar and foreign to such a fundraising mechanism, responses from movement supporters were unremarkable, with about 350 sponsors yearly. A "direct sales" networking strategy was adopted by the programme in 1996 and successfully boosted the number of sponsors and donations for the programme. In a year's time, the pool of sponsors broke the thousandth mark, with the total donations received skyrocketing from 36,055 ringgit in 1996 to 167,994 ringgit in 1997 (see Table 5.1). To enhance transparency and to instil public confidence, all donations received through the programme were detailed at the Malaysian Independent Chinese Secondary Schools Working Committee and *Dongzong* annual working reports. The financial expenses reports were also audited and checked by sponsors at the annual sponsors meeting.[13]

TABLE 5.1

Malaysian Independent Chinese Secondary Schools Working Committee Sponsorship Programme
(1985–2011)

Year	Number of Sponsors	Donations Received (ringgit)
1985	634	50,030
1986	394	31,120
1987	375	31,562
1988	343	28,529
1989	379	31,430
1990	324	28,110
1991	289	27,650
1992	262	25,030
1993	328	31,830
1994	297	83,610
1995	298	64,529
1996	382	36,055
1997	1,796	167,994
1998	1,402	160,383
1999	1,159	141,059
2000	1,083	116,746
2001	731	113,641
2002	n.a.	209,710
2003	n.a.	108,000
2004	n.a.	123,000
2005	n.a.	490,956
2006	n.a.	177,060
2007	n.a.	281,218
2008	n.a.	238,000
2009	n.a.	136,090
2010	n.a.	209,674
2011	n.a.	168,616

Note: Dongzong no longer made public the number of sponsors after year 2002. Therefore the data is listed as not available (n.a.).

Source: Compiled by the author with data from UCSCAM (1988–91; 1992*c*; 1993–99; 2000*b*; 2001*b*; 2002*a*; 2003*b*; 2004*d*; 2005; 2006*a*; 2007; 2008*a*; 2009–12).

GREY ZONE POWER STRUGGLES

Dongzong hired very few salaried executives in its early days. Li Da Ting (李达庭), one of the first salaried staff of the movement, served as the sole general officer (座办) from 1953 to 1973. Like many general officers of the smaller Chinese guilds and associations in Malaysia, Li had to manage all the operational and administrative duties alone (UCSCAM 1987*b*). The success of the Unified Education Certificate examinations and production of independent Chinese secondary schools' textbooks saw an increasing need for additional staff to assist in administrative work. Profits from the sales of textbooks and from the collection of examination fees provided sustainable financial resources for the movement to hire qualified candidates with more attractive compensation packages.[14]

All executive matters of the Malaysian Independent Chinese Secondary Schools Working Committee were managed and administrated by the *Dongzong* executive branch. The executive branch expanded quickly after the mid-1970s. As illustrated in Figure 5.4, staff member in the executive

FIGURE 5.4

Growth of *Dongzong*'s Executive Branch

(1953–2011)

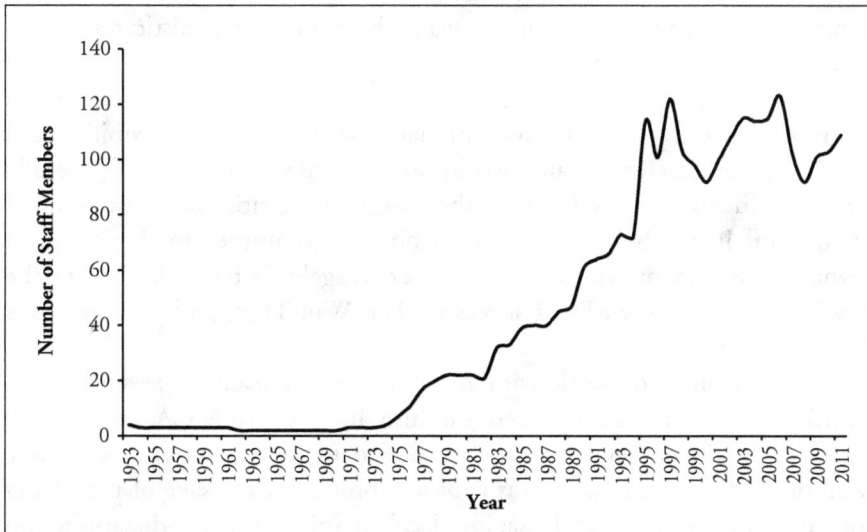

Source: UCSCAM (2012, p. 316).

branch grew from 21 in 1982 to 109 in 2011, and became the largest executive branch amongst social movements in Malaysia. Divided broadly into the General Affairs and the Education Affairs sections, more than one hundred staff served in thirteen departments. General Affairs attended to *Dongzong*'s managerial and mobilization needs, while Education Affairs executed matters related to independent Chinese secondary schools.[15]

The executive branch operates in a Western-style bureaucratic system formulated around loosely defined rules, although having a constitution and regulated systems (such as staff benefits, salary ranking and staff training programmes) have edged the traditional management operating style towards modernity. Recruiting professional executives has helped overcome the potential free rider problems that could arise from the movement's large and extensive grassroots support base.

Despite this, the decision-making process remained top-down and leader-centric (UCSCAM 1997, p. 21). Such an arrangement enables the movement to be more responsive and to achieve more result-oriented outcomes in the ever-changing political hothouse of Malaysia. Interpersonal capital and trust between the leaders and their subordinates dominated decision-making processes, as exemplified by the collaboration between movement leader Lim Fong Seng and movement executives with whom he worked side-by-side, such as Lee Ban Chen, Kua Kia Soong, and Chong Joon Kin. Together, they veered away from the failing traditional approach of seeking compromises through brokerage, towards bold and antagonistic resistances against state suppression.[16]

Unfortunately, relational capital is a double-edged sword: over-reliance on relational capital stunts institutional development, for flexibility is a loophole that can erode an institution internally. The lack of carefully written guidelines on the limits to the power an executive can have resulted in the shift in the balance of power from the committee to the executive branch. The antagonistic reality of power struggles is best observed in the power struggle between Lim's successor, Foo Wan Thot, and the executives from Lim's era.

Foo's inability to work with his predecessor's team of executives, in addition to the pressure placed on him by the pro-MCA controversy discussed in the earlier chapters, forced Foo to step down after only one term in office.[17] The dispute was kept low profile for the sake of preserving the movement's unity and "saving face" despite growing dissatisfaction from amongst the movement supporters. The dispute, which exposed a fundamental institutional weakness in the Chinese education movement, was left unresolved and eventually led to a more complicated controversy a few years later.

The infamous incident involved Chief Executive Officer Bock Tai Hee and *Dongzong* Chairman Yap Sin Tian. Bock had joined *Dongzong* as a junior executive officer in 1981 but rose through the ranks quickly to become the head of the executive branch just four years later. Bock's power and influence accelerated during the administration of Chairman Quek Suan Hiang, who led the movement from 1993 to 2005. As Quek was residing in Johore, he was unable to personally oversee the activities of the movement headquarters in Selangor on a daily basis. Therefore, Bock was entrusted and empowered to manage the executive branch during Quek's absence. Moreover, as most of the other Selangor- and Kuala Lumpur-based *Dongzong* office bearers were also busy with their own full-time occupation, they visited the movement headquarters only to sign documents. Eventually, the role of the committee eroded from that of a decision-maker to a mere "rubber stamp" (DNICSSDWC 1995, p. 12).

This vacuum allowed Bock to make decisions on behalf of *Dongzong* and the Malaysian Independent Chinese Secondary Schools Working Committee. From staff appointments, salary scales, contents of press statements, preparation and allocation of annual budget, Bock exercised his power as chief of the executive branch to the fullest. Assisted by the heads of all departments in the executive branch, Bock established one of the most robust and professional executive branches of a social movement organization in Malaysia.

Problems started to arise in 2005 when Quek's successor, Yap Sin Tian, who sought to reinstall to the committee's authority and retake control of power from the executives to the movement committee. Fearful of the changes that Yap would introduce after Bock's retirement (which had been delayed since 1999) and eager to vie for the position of chief executive officer, some executive members exploited Bock's retirement as an issue to attack Yap.[18] To resolve the dispute, Yap compromised to establish a committee (comprising of three senior officers from the executive branch) to take over the duties of the chief executive officer for six months before a new candidate was appointed.[19] Bock also agreed to officially retire from his position in January 2007.[20]

After the transitional period, Yap quickly consolidated his position by installing the soft-spoken Kuang Hee Pang (邝其芳) as chief executive officer, accompanied by a series of major changes in the chain of command of the executive branch. The heads of departments in the executive branch must report directly to the chairman of the Malaysian Independent Chinese Secondary Schools Working Committee, a position dominated by the chairman of *Dongzong*, making Yap the key — not a phantom — decision-maker. These changes effectively reduced the executive branch to a subordinate body within the system. It also undermined the confidence and limited the performance of the staff members.[21] Staff morale was low as they felt they were treated as "salaried staff" and no longer appreciated as "contributors" to the movement.[22] In response to the changes, five heads of department and more than thirty staff members resigned from the executive office in 2007.[23]

One thing, however, remained unchanged for the executive branch: decision-making was still top-down and person-centred. Yap continues to dominate the chairmanship of *Dongzong* at the time of writing, and the Malaysian Independent Chinese Secondary Schools Working Committee will need to put in extra efforts in hiring the right people and not be constrained by Yap to hire only the people he knows or prefers. It is only with healthy competition and more transparency in all decision-making processes (such as in hiring and promoting staff members) that the factions within *Dongzong* would find a common ground. In the meantime, the reformist faction that was forced to leave the executive branch, comprising Bock and his supporters, have been trying to establish the Independent Chinese Secondary School Principals Association (独中校长理事会) and the Independent Chinese Secondary Schools' Education Alliance (独中教育联盟) as alternative organizations to *Dongzong*.[24]

DONGJIAOZONG CHINESE PRIMARY SCHOOLS WORKING COMMITTEE

The development of independent Chinese secondary schools can only be successful with the continued existence and development of Chinese primary schools. The importance of Chinese primary schools to independent Chinese secondary schools was recognized as early as in 1974 during the Perak independent Chinese secondary schools revival movement (Shen 1975, p. 73). Council of Perak Chinese School Committees took the lead in organizing state-level working committees for the development of Chinese primary schools.

The mission to protect Chinese primary schools as the foundation of Chinese education became a national endeavour after *Dongzong* established the *Dongjiaozong* Chinese Primary Schools Working Committee in 1977.

Lim Fong Seng from *Dongzong* was selected as the leader of the Chairmen Group (主席团). Chairmen from all state-level Chinese school committees associations, Chinese schoolteachers associations, and Chinese school alumni were automatically enrolled as members of the Chairmen Group (UCSCAM 1987*d*, p. 638; and UCSTAM 2008*a*). It was hoped that by consolidating power, it could attract more individuals — especially youths — outside of *Dongjiaozong* to defend the use of Chinese as the medium for teaching and administration in Chinese primary schools (UCSCAM 1987*d*, p. 639).

However, the Chinese Primary Schools Working Committee was not as successful as many had expected. Unequal distribution of Chinese primary schools in each state and county made it difficult to establish uniform mobilization. The Chinese population in Kelantan and Terengganu was too small, while Malacca and Perlis housed a limited number of Chinese primary schools. Schoolteachers and school committees in Sabah and Sarawak had already been collaborating for years at the state level and therefore did not see the need to establish yet another working committee. However, Chinese educationalists in Penang found a better working platform under the Penang Chinese Education Working Committee (槟城州华文教育工作委员会), which received financial assistance from the state government.

Thirty years later, in July 1993, the *Dongjiaozong* Chinese Primary Schools Working Committee was "reintroduced" by *Dongjiaozong* as a subordinate unit of *Jiaozong*. It was believed that this move would enable funding to be channelled from the more successful Malaysian Independent Chinese Secondary Schools Working Committee to *Dongjiaozong* Chinese Primary Schools Working Committee, and thus help to support *Jiaozong's* activities.[25] The new Chinese Primary Schools Working Committee was headed by a central-level committee with various state-level working committees. The state-level working committees were administrated independently by the respective state's Chinese school committees associations, and only collaborated with the central-level working committee in large-scale fundraising campaigns. Thus far, only Johore, Perak, Selangor, and Pahang have had a functional state-level working committee (PJCPSDWC 2004).

The central-level working committee comprised of a general committee, a standing committee, and six working units. Seven representatives each from *Dongzong* and *Jiaozong* formed the general committee. The positions of chairman, general secretary, and treasurer in the standing committee

FIGURE 5.5

Organizational Chart of *Jiaozong* and the *Dongjiaozong* Chinese Primary Schools Working Committee

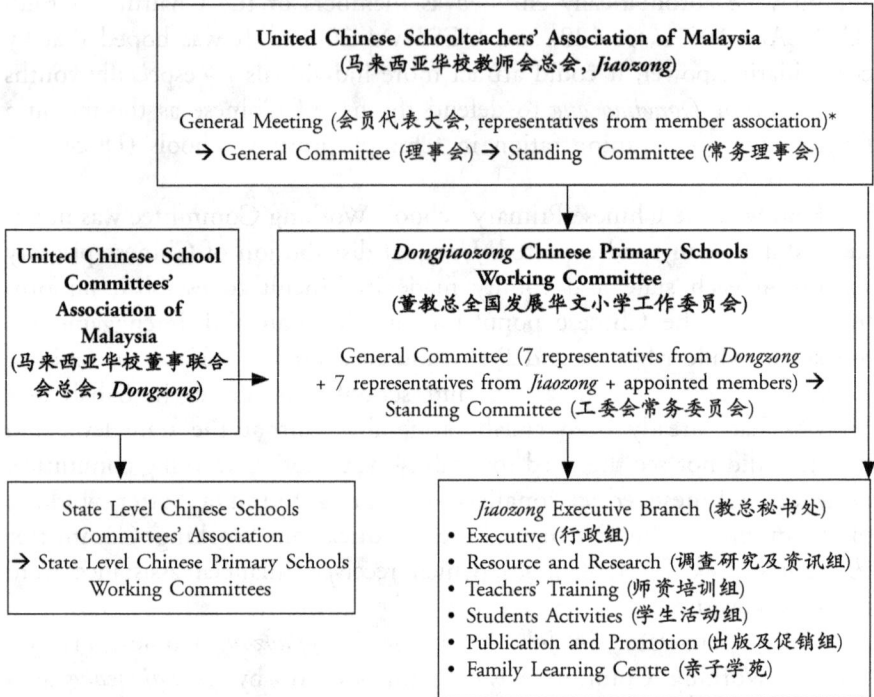

```
┌──────────────────────────────────────────────────────────────┐
│        United Chinese Schoolteachers' Association of Malaysia  │
│              (马来西亚华校教师会总会, Jiaozong)                    │
│                                                                │
│   General Meeting (会员代表大会, representatives from member association)* │
│   → General Committee (理事会) → Standing Committee (常务理事会)   │
└──────────────────────────────────────────────────────────────┘
```

```
┌─────────────────────┐      ┌───────────────────────────────────────┐
│ United Chinese School│      │ Dongjiaozong Chinese Primary Schools    │
│     Committees'      │      │         Working Committee               │
│    Association of    │      │    (董教总全国发展华文小学工作委员会)        │
│      Malaysia        │      │                                         │
│  (马来西亚华校董事联合 │ →    │ General Committee (7 representatives from Dongzong │
│   会总会, Dongzong)   │      │ + 7 representatives from Jiaozong + appointed members) → │
└─────────────────────┘      │    Standing Committee (工委会常务委员会)   │
                             └───────────────────────────────────────┘
```

```
┌─────────────────────────┐   ┌───────────────────────────────────────┐
│ State Level Chinese Schools│  │ Jiaozong Executive Branch (教总秘书处)   │
│  Committees' Association   │  │ • Executive (行政组)                    │
│ → State Level Chinese Primary Schools │ • Resource and Research (调查研究及资讯组) │
│    Working Committees     │  │ • Teachers' Training (师资培训组)        │
└─────────────────────────┘   │ • Students Activities (学生活动组)       │
                              │ • Publication and Promotion (出版及促销组) │
                              │ • Family Learning Centre (亲子学苑)       │
                              └───────────────────────────────────────┘
```

Notes: *Quota of association representatives depend on total members of the association:
100 members (two representatives), 101 to 200 members (three representatives),
201 to 300 members (four representatives), 301 to 400 members (five representatives),
401 to 500 members (six representatives), 501 to 600 members (seven representatives).
Source: Compiled by the author with resources provided by *Jiaozong*.

were held by *Jiaozong*'s office bearers; the positions for the deputy chairman, deputy general secretary, and deputy treasurer were reserved for office bearers from *Dongzong*. Other positions within the standing committee were decided through elections. The working committee could also appoint additional committee members when necessary.

All administrative matters of the working committee were managed by *Jiaozong* executive branch, which numbered about fifteen full-time staff. From 1985 till 2006, the executive branch also served all administrative matters of the Lim Lian Geok Cultural Development Centre.[26] This tiny executive branch played key roles in organizing the annual Chinese Education Festival (华教节) held in December to commemorate the demise of former *Jiaozong* Chairman Lim Lian Geok.[27] The festival hosted activities such as a memorial ceremony, seminars, fundraising dinners, and the Lim Lian Geok Award (林连玉精神奖) presentation ceremony, as symbolic reminders of the continuous struggle of the Chinese education movement. The fundraising dinner, in particular, generated a key source of income to sustain *Jiaozong* and its executive branch.

However, after the Lim Lian Geok Cultural Development Centre was declared as an independent organization in 2006, *Jiaozong* had been having an annual deficit of some 20,000 ringgit, in addition to having its executive staff reduce to about one fourth of its former strength.[28] Unlike its sister organization, the Malaysian Independent Chinese Secondary Schools Working Committee, which had a steady income, the expenses of the *Dongjiaozong* Chinese Primary Schools Working Committee was generated through public donations during events and under the Sponsorship Programme for Chinese Primary Schools Development (全国华文小学发展基金常年赞助人), which averaged about 10,000 ringgit annually (see Table 5.2).[29]

Having very little financial income, the *Jiaozong* administration had to conduct movement activities by way of carefully-planned budgets to prevent the organization from running into a deficit. However, the organization's commitment to movement-related programmes, and the pressure to sustain continuous visibility made it difficult to do so. For example, seminars on important topics such as teaching methods for new schoolteachers and sustainable psychological health for teachers were conducted with minimal registration fees. Attended by an annual average of 1,500 schoolteachers, these activities aimed to "return to the fundamentals of education and reintroduce *Jiaozong* to the schoolteachers community as an organization that supports the Chinese community".[30]

Nonetheless, the pressing need to sustain the movement's everyday expenses financially *vis-à-vis* the need to maintain supporters' confidence is, in practice, difficult to balance. Too much emphasis on soliciting financial resources from supporters may be perceived as exploitative and raise questions about the sincerity of the movement's ultimate goal; yet, having insufficient resources had placed the movement and the executive officers in a position where they had to make the impossible possible.

TABLE 5.2
Sponsorship Programme for Chinese Primary Schools Development
(1989–2011)

Year	Number of Sponsors	Donations Received (ringgit)
1989	176	53,374
1990	156	41,688
1991	120	27,091
1992	139	19,094
1993	109	15,322
1994	109	30,308
1995	61	7,350
1996	65	7,215
1997	47	6,265
1998	52	22,980
1999	88	36,900
2000	9	10,751
2001	81	14,488
2002	56	14,307
2003	42	4,000
2004	59	6,500
2005	102	14,150
2006	128	21,691
2007	144	24,505
2008	114	15,950
2009	108	13,130
2010	93	12,690
2011	99	13,970

Source: Compiled by the author with data extracted from UCSTAM (1990–2006; 2007*c*; 2008*b*; 2009–12).

As a result of financial constraints and insufficient human resources, the executive branch and *Jiaozong* at large no longer sought to challenge state authorities contentiously, as "it is beyond our current ability" as Yap Hon Kiat remarked.[31] Not only does Yap's lamentation reflect his frustrated ambition to do more for the office, but it reflects the fact that, very often, the potential of the executive office to achieve the goals of the Chinese education movement is limited by internal operative constraints, limited resources, and the conservativeness of its leaders.

DONGJIAOZONG HIGHER LEARNING CENTRE AND NEW ERA COLLEGE

One of the ambitions of the Chinese education movement is to establish a complete Chinese education system in Malaysia. However, the BN regime has, time and again, rejected the movement's proposal to establish Merdeka University and Merdeka College, as the proposed medium of instruction, that is, Chinese, violated the 1971 Universities and University Colleges Act. The act was liberalized in the 1990s after Prime Minister Mahathir Mohamad proposed the Vision 2020 campaign. To meet the call of Vision 2020 for Malaysia to be a developed, industrial state by year 2020, the regime began to allow the formation of non-Malay-speaking private universities. It was under this backdrop that the first Chinese community-funded college, Southern College, was established in the state of Johore. This breakthrough and the growing importance of the Chinese language with China's rapid economic ascendancy gave hope to *Dongjiaozong* leaders of the possibility of establishing a movement-sponsored tertiary education institution in Malaysia.

The *Dongjiaozong* Higher Learning Centre was established in 1994 as the maiden company for New Era College (UCSCAM 1994, p. 53). Consisting of representatives from Merdeka University Company, *Dongzong*, and *Jiaozong*, this was the largest cross-organization collaboration in the history of Chinese education movement. The Merdeka University Company leased the plot of land at Kajang as New Era's premises for minimal fees; *Dongzong* provided an interest-free loan of 100,000 ringgit to Higher Learning Centre and allocated four annual study loans of 5,000 ringgit for New Era College' students in 1995 (UCSCAM 1996, p. 24; 1998, p. 28). *Jiaozong*, despite not being able to contribute financially, supported the project as a collaborator.

After four years of continuous lobbying and brokerage efforts by MCA cabinet members, the Ministry of Education approved the operation of the New Era College in 1997 (DHLC 2008*b*, p. 40; and UCSCAM 1995, p. 305). According to Quek Suan Hiang, former *Dongzong* Chairman who was also the head of the centre and college board,

> The most challenging task after we received the operating licence was to ensure sustainable development for the college within the competitive private tertiary education market in Malaysia. *Dongjiaozong* was an empty box and had limited resources. Therefore, we had a difficult beginning. Having only 148 students at its first intake, the college

had a deficit of about 300,000 ringgit in the first year. Most lessons were conducted in temporary containers in 1998, as fundraising for the construction of the college building was still underway.[32]

The overwhelming need for financial resources saw Quek spend all his three terms as *Dongzong* chairman fundraising for the movement. Amongst the largest fundraising campaign he conducted was the campaign held in collaboration with the United Chinese School Alumni Association, which generated some 1.5 million ringgit.[33] Substantial donations were generated from large organizations and wealthy individuals through the lobbying efforts of movement leaders. Notable examples were 600,000 ringgit donations by the Lee Foundation (李氏基金) and 30,000 ringgit by Chiew Swee Peow Chinese Education Trust Fund (周瑞标教育基金) (UCSCAM 2002*b*, p. 75). These funds were critical for the construction of New Era's teaching building and student dormitory, which were completed in 2002 (DHLC 2008*b*, p. 33).

The Chinese community, however, was beginning to show signs of fatigue at having to pay a "second income tax" — a term used to refer to donations made to Chinese education activities — due to the continuous line-up of fundraising campaigns. In order to generate financial donations from the community in a sustainable way, the *Dongjiaozong* Higher Learning Centre and New Era College Development Fund (董教总教育中心基金, 新纪元学院建设及发展基金) and the New Era College Sponsorship Programme (新纪元学院发展基金赞助人) were launched in 1998 (see Table 5.3).[34] The sponsorship programme amassed an average donation of about 170,000 ringgit annually, which covered a significant part of the expenses for the college's operation and infrastructure. Another significant source of income was derived from the centre's role as the sole overseas representative for the Higher Education in China Exhibition (中国高等教育展) in Malaysia and the official student enrolment representative for Xiamen University in China in 1996.[35]

As an academic institution, the best source of income — and the most sustainable — is derived from having sufficient intake of students each year. However, due to the lack of accreditation from the National Accreditation Board (*Lembaga Akreditasi Negara*) and Malaysian Qualifications Agency (*Agensi Kelayakan Malaysia*), the New Era College was not able to issue bachelor degrees to its students during its early days. Graduates had to continue their studies with affiliated universities to obtain a full bachelor degree. In order to compete with other private universities and colleges in Malaysia, New Era offered lower school fees, provided numerous scholarships

TABLE 5.3
New Era College Sponsorship Programme
(1998–2011)

Year	Number of Sponsors	Donations Received (ringgit)
1998	1,400	109,172
1999	2,400	209,751
2000	679	49,999
2001	523	89,341
2002	1,178	222,351
2003	1,384	229,375
2004	1,306	208,390
2005	1,331	216,774
2006	1,245	193,014
2007	1,140	195,686
2008	1,088	175,757
2009	769	120,416
2010	822	142,673
2011	733	129,869

Source: Compiled by the author with data extracted from DHLC (1999–2008*a*; 2009–12).

and loans, and more importantly, targeted Chinese-speaking students from independent Chinese secondary schools for recruitment.

Movement leaders, such as Quek Suan Hiang, utilized their extensive personal networks in China to establish collaborations with universities in China, such as Beijing Normal University (北京师范大学), South China Normal University (华南师范大学), for academic credit transfer (DHLC 1999, p. 20; and UCSCAM 1995, p. 8). By 2011, about ninety universities worldwide, including forty universities in China and thirty-one universities in Taiwan, had signed memorandums of understanding for credit transfer with New Era College.[36] The college also provided on-the-job training for schoolteachers of independent Chinese secondary schools, especially those who did not have prior education-related training, under the Professional Teaching Programme (教育专业系). These strategies paid off, with the number of new enrolment rising above 1,000 students in 2002, and from then onwards, the college began to generate income, as illustrated in Figure 5.6.[37]

FIGURE 5.6
Distribution of New Era College Students
(1998–2011)

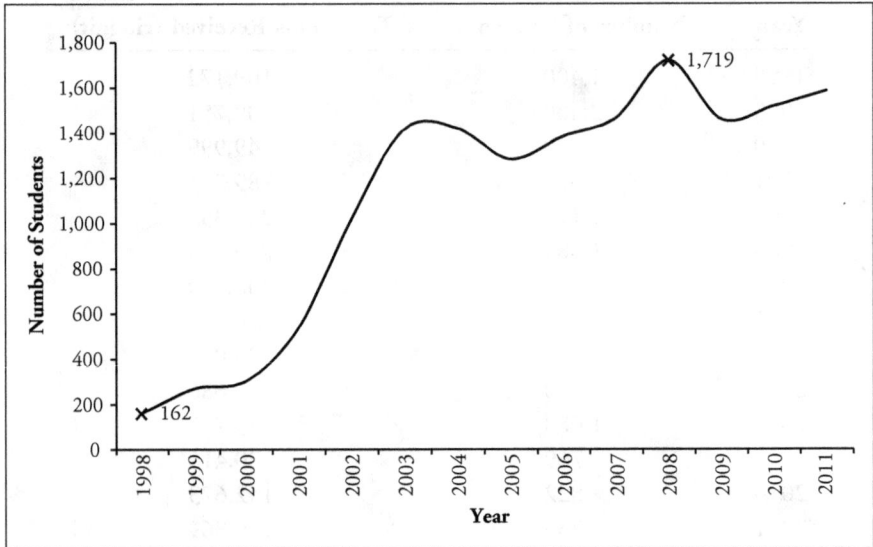

Source: Compiled by the author with data extracted from DHLC (1999–2008*a*; 2009–12).

Renewed interest in Chinese language in the 1990s saw the gradual liberalization of policies on the teaching of Chinese language by the governments in the Southeast Asia region (UCSCAM 1998, p. 73; Leo 2007, pp. 335–36; and Lin, H.D. 2000). Riding on the opportunity, *Dongjiaozong*, as the leading and the most established Chinese education institution in the region, played a crucial role in sharing its experiences and assisting neighbouring affiliations in their establishment efforts.[38] In 1995, the *Dongjiaozong* Higher Learning Centre organized the first Southeast Asian Chinese Language Teaching Convention to promote exchanges on the teaching of Chinese, provide platforms on exchanges of information, and strengthen collaboration between participating organizations (see Map 5.1).

This biennial regional conference, hosted in rotation by the convention's members, had been attracting participation of representatives from Chinese educationalists and advocates from Southeast Asia, as well as government officials from China, since its inception.[39] *Dongzong*'s executive branch acted as the convention's secretariat and was responsible for publishing

MAP 5.1

Southeast Asian Chinese Language Teaching Convention

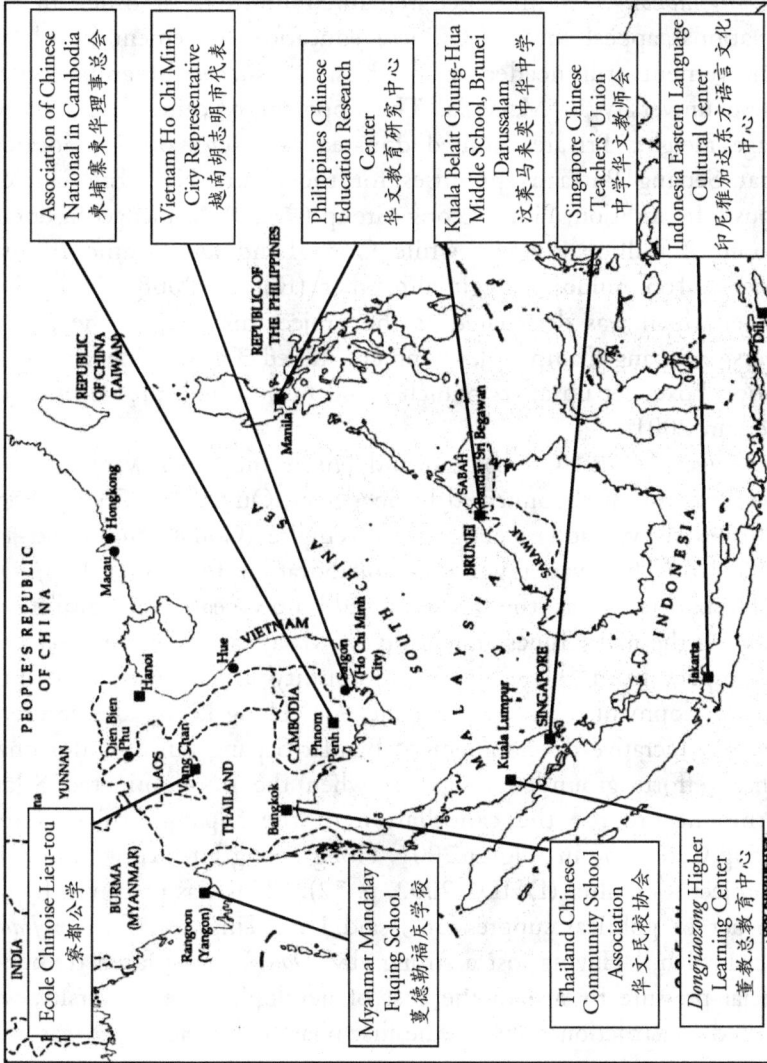

Ecole Chinoise Lieu-tou 寮都公学

Association of Chinese National in Cambodia 柬埔寨柬华理事总会

Vietnam Ho Chi Minh City Representative 越南胡志明市代表

Philippines Chinese Education Research Center 华文教育研究中心

Kuala Belait Chung-Hua Middle School, Brunei Darussalam 汶莱马来奕中华中学

Singapore Chinese Teachers' Union 中学华文教师会

Indonesia Eastern Language Cultural Center 印尼雅加达东方语言文化中心

Myanmar Mandalay Fuqing School 曼德勒福庆学校

Thailand Chinese Community School Association 华文民校协会

Dongjiaozong Higher Learning Center 董教总教育中心

Source: The author.

the annual newsletter — *Southeast Asia Chinese Education Bulletin* (东南亚华文教育通讯), and the convention's seminar papers (东南亚华文教学研讨会特辑).

Although the convention successfully launched a regional platform for *Dongjiaozong*, its influence remained limited. In order to create international appeal for the Chinese education movement in Malaysia, the movement still needed to establish a (successful and reputable) Chinese university in Malaysia. The opportunity came in 2000, when Vintage Heights Private Limited donated 100 acres of land located in Bandar Sepang Putra as premises for the future New Era University campus.[40] In addition, Hong Leong Group (丰隆集团) pledged a donation of about 2 million ringgit, while GuocoLand and Hume Industries donated 1.163 million ringgit altogether (Fauwaz 2008). Hong Leong Finance, which was designated as the project manager of the New Era University-Sepang Campus development, raised 3.38 million ringgit from donation boxes set up at its branches and from a high profile fundraising concert in 2001.

Vintage Heights, GuocoLand and Hume Industries were subsidiaries of the politically well-connected businessman, Quek Leng Chan (郭令灿), and his extensive Hong Leong Group empire (Gomez and Jomo 1997, pp. 66–72). This was a win-win collaboration for both *Dongjiaozong* and Hong Leong, as the former could now realize its ambition of developing the first Chinese university in Malaysia, while the latter earned great respect from the Chinese community as generous contributors to the development of vernacular education. Hong Leong also secured the potentially lucrative development of Bandar Sepang Putra. Unfortunately, all these efforts grounded to a halt when the BN-dominated Selangor government ordered the cancellation of the Sepang Project Ground Breaking Ceremony in August 2001. Hong Leong Finance withdrew from this project soon after (DHLC 2002, p. 32). "This was perceived by many as an act of political suppression", said Loot Ting Yee, former *Jiaozong* vice chairman.[41] Having lost a strong ally, *Dongjiaozong* faced tremendous financial pressure to sustain the cost of developing the university, whose estimated construction costs for the first phase of development was at least 16 million ringgit.

Dongjiaozong was later caught in a legal deadlock with Hong Leong over the contract of transfer of the donated land. It contained a clause stipulating that "all land not developed by August 2007 must be returned to the developers".[42] A new memorandum of understanding was signed between the two on 19 February, two weeks prior to the 2008 General Election, in a high-profile ceremony at MCA headquarters. Witnessed by Selangor Chief Minister Mohd Khir Toyo, attended by Quek Leng Chan and MCA politicians, Yap Sin Tian, and the key members of *Dongjiaozong* conceded to being used for political gains for the sake of salvaging the Sepang campus.[43]

At the same time, the centre also collaborated closely with Hou Kok Chung (何国忠), the deputy minister of higher education, in upgrading New Era to a university.[44] Compared with other colleges that have successfully been granted university status, New Era faced more than its share of obstacles. Not only did it fall short of having sufficient academic calibre, variety in its academic programme, and a complimentary upgrading plan, past controversies involving Merdeka University between the movement and the BN regime also made the approval by the BN government of such status difficult.[45]

The presence of Principal Kua Kia Soong in New Era College, who was known for being outspoken about his anti-BN views, did not help resolve the controversies surrounding the upgrade of New Era (DHLC 2002, p. 15). Kua's opinions on the college's management and development also conflicted with those of the college's board.[46] For example, Kua refused to execute the Xiamen University Nanyang Research Institute Project (厦门大学南洋研究院研究计划案), a collaborative research project initiated by the New Era Board of Governors.[47] According to Kua, "[the project] was too expensive [about 300,000 ringgit] and there was no real academic advantage for the college" (Kua 2009, pp. 7–8). In response, Quek Suan Hiang criticized Kua for not understanding the sentiments behind the collaboration with Xiamen University, which was set up by the prominent Chinese Malayan philanthropist, Tan Kah Kee (陈嘉庚).[48]

Tensions between Kua and the board of directors escalated in 2008, when the new head of board and chair of the college senate, Yap Sin Tian, refused to renew Kua's contract. Although Kua reached the legal retirement age in 2005, but his retirement was delayed in search of a suitable and qualified successor from amongst senior staff. Yap's decision threatened the status quo of the college and the interests of the senior staff,[49] resulting in heated internal fights. More than twenty staff signed a petition and mobilized students to conduct sit-ins in protest over Yap's decision.

To quell one of the worst internal conflicts to have occurred in the history of the Chinese education movement, movement veterans, such as Foo Wan Thot, Quek Suan Hiang, Sim Mow Yu, and Loot Ting Yee, called for self-restraint amongst the stakeholders. Four highly respected figures among movement supporters, Khew Khing Ling (丘琼润), Yoong Suan (杨泉), Tan Yew Sing (陈友信), and Toh Kin Woon (杜乾焕), were appointed as mediators, but they failed to get both parties to reach a consensus.[50]

To break the deadlock, representatives of Chinese school committees' associations from Malacca, Negeri Sembilan, and Johore jointly called for a *Dongzong* Extraordinary Delegates Meeting — the first in the history of the movement.[51] In this Extraordinary Delegates Meeting, *Dongzong* members voted (ten to three) in favour of hiring a new principal. Due to differences in opinion between the chairmen of state-level Chinese school committee associations and some state delegates, the votes, which were cast in confidence by the chairman, were not necessarily representative of the entire association; rather, they were more reflective of the personal inclinations of individual delegates.[52] In addition, some argued that the results of the extraordinary meeting represented only the views of *Dongzong*, and neglected inputs from other stakeholders of the *Dongjiaozong* Higher Learning Centre.

Failing to renew his contract, Kua left New Era in December 2008. In protest, five heads of department resigned, citing that they were acting on the principle of "death is better than life with humiliation" (士可杀不可辱).[53] Pua Eng Chong (潘永忠) became New Era's third principal in January 2009 and continued his predecessors' work until New Era College was eventually upgraded to a full-fledged university.[54]

With the departure of Bock, Kua and their supporters from the movement, Yap began to rebuild the Chinese education movement with his trusted team members in the hopes of establishing a more inclusive, representative, and internally democratic movement. Nevertheless, Yap's autonomy continued to be challenged by his fellow colleagues at the local and state levels: Yap lost the Kuala Lumpur Confucian School Committee re-election in 2008, but was able to defend his leadership at the United Chinese School Committees' Association of Selangor and Kuala Lumpur, as well as at the *Dongzong* election in 2009.

CONCLUSION

The formation of the Malaysian Independent Chinese Secondary Schools Working Committee in the 1970s successfully gathered experts and academics from the Chinese community to revive and reform the curriculum and educational system for independent Chinese secondary schools. The *Dongjiaozong* independent Chinese secondary schools revival movement created and transformed the image of independent Chinese secondary schools into that of a popular private secondary school, especially in the central and southern regions of West Malaysia. It also generated important sustainable financial resources for *Dongzong* through the sales of textbooks and collection of fees for the Unified Examination Certificate examinations. These financial resources enabled *Dongzong*, as the caretaker of working committee, to expand the size and strength of the Chinese education movement. As the work of the working committee grew, so did the need for more full-time staff. The movement hired and cultivated full-time, salaried and highly-educated (university degree holders) professional executives to sustain various operational and mobilization needs of the movement.

Nevertheless, the lack of a clear delineation of roles, boundaries, and authority allowed the executive officers of the Malaysian Independent Chinese Secondary Schools Working Committee to manipulate their commitments to their own ends, resulting in a precarious power imbalance between the executive officers and the committee members during the post-Lim Fong Seng era. Lacking clarity of rules and a systematic division of work, the leaders of the Chinese education movement were over burdened by multiple roles within the movement. This eventually put a noticeable strain on their effectiveness and commitment in the delivery of their responsibilities. Such reliance on individual capacity rather than on a carefully planned and executed structured system is a common phenomenon in social movements situated within non-liberal democratic states. Although such a lax and flexible system allowed social movement leaders to deal with the unpredictability of non-liberal democratic states more promptly and effectively, the system also allowed opportunists to abuse their close relationships with the leaders to fulfil their personal agendums.

Another point worth noting is the failure of the movement to sustain the *Dongjiaozong* Chinese Primary Schools Working Committee in the 1980s despite having adopted a working structure similar to the Malaysian Independent Chinese Secondary Schools Working Committee. *Jiaozong* had been significantly weakened by shrinking membership and low participation rate at the local as well as national level. In an effort to revive the weakening *Jiaozong*, the *Dongjiaozong* Chinese Primary Schools Working Committee was re-introduced in 1994 to assist with the organization's administrative and secretariat work.

Although efforts in terms of financial and human resources were injected into the *Dongjiaozong* Chinese Primary Schools Working Committee, these efforts did not solve *Jiaozong*'s fundamental problems of declining membership and lack of sustainable financial resources. *Jiaozong*'s activities became less appealing in particular after Lim Lian Geok Cultural Development Centre no longer came under *Jiaozong* management since 2004. When Yap Sin Tian became *Dongzong* chairman in June 2005, he led a transformation to strengthen the role of the movement central committee. Thus, the pressure to sustain and strengthen its relationship with the authorities in return for political assistance to upgrade New Era College into a full university also necessitated a clean-up within the social movement organization.

Overbearing executive officers, such as Bock Tai Hee, Kua Kia Soong and others, left the movement. Many talented staff members also left due to their inability to adapt to the new leadership because the latter regarded the executive staff as "salaried members" and no longer a comrade of the movement. The internal changes in the Chinese education movement disappointed many; however, in the opinion of the current leadership, it was the only way to secure trust from state authorities, and to obtain approval for the upgrade of New Era College.

Though the Chinese education movement was openly divided into two (or more) factions at the time of writing, there are many lessons to be learnt from the personal controversies that plagued the movement and its social movement organizations in 2006 and 2008. The controversies indicated that the capability of the Chinese education movement to make demands for vernacular rights was thwarted by individuals who turned the movement organizations into battlegrounds for personal gains. The controversy also revealed that the current movement institution lacked an appropriate mechanism to manage internal conflicts. The New Era crisis highlighted the need to establish a commission of enquiries empowered to arbitrate internal disputes and pass judgement.

Many movement veterans expressed their dismay over the future of the movement. However, competition for power and control over leadership of the movement would only intensify within the movement's national institutions (*Dongzong*, Merdeka University Company, and *Jiaozong*), amongst its state-level networks, as well as in the schools. What these bickering parties failed to realize was that continued internal fighting and regrouping into factions would only benefit their common enemy, that is, the state authorities, to the detriment of the movement in the long run. Movement veteran, Lee Hing, commented,

> We have donated our time, money and effort to the Chinese education
> movement. In so doing, we should exercise self-restraint and not engage
> in personal politics. However, what has been happening [to the Chinese
> education movement] in the past years is disappointing. If things get
> too complicated, and everyone has to choose a camp, then I would
> rather spend more time with my grandchildren at home than to face
> all this nonsense."[55]

Perhaps it is time for the leaders of the Chinese education movement to
review the system to strengthen its mechanisms for checks and balances.
The movement has been riding on state suppression and depending on
external suppression to foster solidarity amongst its supporters. Despite
the movement's successful persistence over the years, the lack of efforts in
developing a more structured movement institution to enhance its internal
strength has seen the movement troubled by factionalism. In order to
be successful in mobilizing the necessary support to achieve its ultimate
objectives, a movement should be inclusive, both internally and externally.
The issues of academic institutions aside, *Dongjiaozong* must tackle the
more fundamental goal of installing the Chinese language with official
status in the Federal Constitution of Malaysia, as doing so is the only way
to secure and develop Chinese schools and Chinese universities as part of
the educational landscape in Malaysia.

Notes

1. By 1998, twenty-one converted schools had set up affiliated independent
   Chinese secondary schools, sharing school facilities such as libraries, school
   halls, fields and canteens with their converted counterparts. The number
   of independent Chinese secondary schools eventually rose from sixteen in
   the 1961 into sixty nationwide by 2008. A majority of dropouts from the
   Chinese converted schools were those who failed the English-medium Lower
   Certificate for Education after completing Form Three, and therefore did not
   qualify for enrolment into Form Four. For more, see Shen (1975, p. 8); Tay
   (1998c, pp. 266, 271–73); and Sim Mow Yu, interview by the author, Malacca,
   26 March 2008.
2. For the list of these schools, see Appendix 3.
3. These schools are Sekolah Menengah Yik Ching Yik Ching (育青中学),
   Shen Jai High School (深斋中学), Sekolah Menengah San Min (Suwa)
   (安顺三民独中), Tsung Wah Private Secondary School (崇华中学),
   Sekolah Tinggi Nan Hwa Ayer Tawar (南华独中), Hua Lian High School
   (太平华联中学), Sekolah Menengah Pei Yuan (Private) KPR (培元独中),
   Poi Lam High School, and Yuk Choy High School (Private) (育才独立中学).

4. *Sinchew Daily*, 10 April 1975.

5. Straits dollar was replaced by Malaysian dollar in 1967 as the currency for Malaysia. It was later replaced by ringgit in 1975. See Loh, Phang, and Saravanamuttu (1981, pp. 61–62).

6. Chinese language by Pei Yuan, English language by Yuk Choy, Malay language by Nan Hwa, mathematics by Hua Lian, history by San Min, geography by Yik Ching, commerce by Shen Jai, and science by Poi Lam. See Zhen (1996, p. 82) and Lim, G.A. (2004).

7. Choong Wei Chuan (钟伟前) (head, Department of Resource and Information Affairs, *Dongzong*), interview by the author, Selangor, 17 March 2008.

8. UCSCAM (2012, pp. 127–29). For earlier version of the constitution, see DNICSSDWC (1990; 1995).

9. Sim Mow Yu, interview by the author, Malacca, 26 March 2008.

10. See UCSCAM (2004c) for the detailed description of the curriculum planning for science (pp. 39–47), commerce (pp. 48–57), and technical education (pp. 58–68). For the list of *Dongzong* in-house publications, see UCSCAM (1997, pp. 93–97). For further discussion on the Unified Examination Certificate, see DNICSSDWC (1997); and UCSCAM (1989, p. 34).

11. Comparatively, independent Chinese secondary schools in the central and southern region of West Malaysia are doing much better than those located at the northern region of West Malaysia, Sabah, and Sarawak. At the time of writing, there are twenty-four medium-scale (with 300 to 1,000 students) and fourteen small-scale (less than 300 students) independent Chinese secondary schools nationwide that still need further assistance from the working committee to achieve sustainable growth. Continuous lobbying efforts by the movement activities and timely political opportunities in 1999 have led to the establishment of Foon Yew High School (宽柔中学). It was the first independent Chinese secondary school to be approved by the Ministry of Education after a long freeze since 1969. See UCSCAM (1991, p. 30; 1992b, p. 32; 1999, pp. 60–61).

12. Sim Mow Yu, interview by the author, Malacca, 26 March 2008.

13. These sponsors also received a certificate of appreciation, newsletter on Chinese education (华教导报), annual working reports, and were rewarded as members with the Chinese Education Card (华教卡), which allowed them to enjoy discounts on *Dongjiaozong*'s publications.

14. Together, the Department of Examination and the Department of Curriculum generated about 40 per cent of total incomes annually. These financial resources sustained the expenses of other non-profit making departments, especially the departments that maintained the movement operational needs. *Dongzong* uses eight units in its salary scheme according to academic qualifications and years of service. Therefore, a senior officer such as the chief executive officer who has served more than fifteen years can earn up to 9,000 ringgit per month. On top of that, all heads of department enjoy a special allowance of 500 ringgit per month. See UCSCAM (2008b, p. 10).

15. There were six departments at the General Affairs section (executive officer, finance, association affairs, personnel and human resources, resource and information, property management and maintenance) and seven departments at the Education Affairs section (examination, curriculum, students affairs, teachers' education, vocational and technical education, publications, computer). Details of the ages and education qualifications of the executive staff can be found in Appendix 4. For more, see UCSCAM (1987*b*, p. 208; 1987*c*, pp. 381, 616; 1996, pp. 8–14; 1997, pp. 13, 26).

16. Sim Mow Yu, interview by the author, Malacca, 26 March 2008.

17. Loot Ting Yee, interview by the author, Kuala Lumpur, 24 March 2008.

18. Liu D.C. (pseudonym, executive officer, *Dongzong*), interview by the author, Selangor, 27 July 2010.

19. Members of this three-person committee included Li Yue Tong (李岳通) (Head, Department of General Affairs), Choong Pai Chee (庄白绮) (Head, Department of Meeting and Organization), and Zhang Xi Chong (张喜崇) (Head, Department of Curriculum). See UCSCAM (2008*a*, p. 35).

20. *Merdeka Review*, 20 October 2006.

21. Eng L.O. (pseudonym, executive officer, *Dongzong*), interview by the author, Selangor, 29 July 2010.

22. Choong Woei Chuan, interview by the author, Selangor, 17 March 2008.

23. The heads who resigned were Zhang Xi Chong from the Department of Curriculum, Liang Sheng Yi (梁胜义) from the Department of Student Affairs, Chen Li Qun (陈利群) from the Department of Personnel, Li Hui Jin (李惠祚) from the Department of Teachers' Training, and Lin Mei Yan (林美燕) from the Department of Technical Education. See *Oriental Daily*, 10 December 2007.

24. *Malaysiakini*, 2 October 2009.

25. UCSTAM (1994, p. 15); and Loot Ting Yee, interview by the author, Kuala Lumpur, 24 March 2008.

26. Prior to 1994, all *Jiaozong*'s administrative work is conducted by the Education Research Centre (教育研究中心). Former executives who served this centre included Yow Lee Fung (姚丽芳), Tang Ah Chai (陈亚才), and Liew Kan Ba (刘崇汉). See KLCSTAAMEC (2000, pp. 661–63); and UCSTAM (1983*b*, p. 636).

27. The Department of Executive organized and executed *Jiaozong* meeting decisions, facilitated work on propaganda, fundraising, finance and human resource; Department of Resource and Research collected and compiled data; Department of Teachers' Training conducted training programmes; Department of Students Activities conducted annual Chinese-speaking competitions, holiday camps and seminars; Department of Publication and Promotion was responsible for in-house publications; Department of Early Childhood Education conducted parenting and pre-school education programmes. See UCSTAM (2007*c*, pp. 12, 14, 177, 198).

28. Yap Hon Kiat (叶翰杰) (chief administrative secretary, *Jiaozong*), interview by the author, Selangor, 22 July 2010; and Er Joo Tiong, interview by the author, Selangor, 22 July 2010.

29. Donations were generated during Sim Mow Yu's eightieth birthday celebration in 1992, and *Jiaozong*'s fifty-fifth anniversary celebration in 2006. Each of these occasions generated anywhere from 60,000 to 80,000 ringgit, sums large enough to sustain the organization's annual expenses for about three to five years. Yap Hon Kiat and Er Joo Tiong, interview by the author, Selangor, 22 July 2010.

30. Yap Hon Kiat, interview by the author, Selangor, 22 July 2010.

31. Ibid.

32. Quek Suan Hiang, interview by the author, Johore, 23 March 2010.

33. State-level fundraising dinner generated 158,000 ringgit; United Chinese School Alumni Association at Perak, Selangor, Malacca and Johore donated 20,000 ringgit each; Thousand Men Fundraising Dinner in December 1996 (1214千万心宴) generated a total of 1.34 million ringgit. For details of these events, see UCSCAM (1996, p. 29; 2002*b*, pp. 75–77, 85–103); and *Nanyangshangpao*, 18 December 1996.

34. Those who donated more than 1,000 ringgit were named honorary sponsors (荣誉赞助人), 500 ringgit as permanent sponsor (永久赞助人), and 50 ringgit as normal sponsors. See UCSCAM (1998, pp. 145–49).

35. Back in 1998, the college only consisted of four departments (accounting, finance and business, Chinese language and literature, information technology). By 2012, the college consisted four schools (business, humanities and social sciences, media and creative arts, science) and eight departments (business, Chinese business in society, Chinese language and literature, education, guidance and counselling psychology, arts and design, drama and visual, media studies, information sciences, and computing studies).

36. According to the college's Public and International Relation Office in 2011, New Era's Memorandums of Understanding partners includes universities in China (forty), Taiwan (thirty-one), United Kingdom (ten), Malaysia (eight), Australia and New Zealand (two each), and Hong Kong (one).

37. Wong Wai Keat (黄伟豪) (executive officer, Department of Student Enrolment, New Era College), interview by the author, Selangor, 27 July 2010.

38. For example, the centre donated a set of textbooks to Chinese schools in Cambodia, and waived copyright fees to allow these schools to reprint the books for use in the country. New Era also introduced a programme titled Teaching of Chinese Language to Non-Chinese Teachers (对外汉语教学) to train non-Chinese school teachers (mainly those from Indonesia and Thailand) in teaching Chinese in their vernacular language. Hong Woan Ying (孔婉莹) (head, Public and International Relation Office, New Era College), interview by the author, Selangor, 26 July 2010. See DHLC (2009, pp. 105–15).

39. The convention normally begins with reports and country overview of Chinese language teaching, and paper presentations and discussions on Chinese ontology, materials, teaching methods, teachers' training, and evaluation.

40. Vintage Heights was a joint venture amongst GuocoLand (Malaysia) Limited, Selangor Development Corporation (*Perbadanan Kemajuan Negeri Selangor*) — a state development agency controlled by UMNO Selangor state government prior to 2008, Hap Seng Consolidated Limited, Crescent Capital Private Limited, and Cheltenham Investments Private Limited.

41. Loot Ting Yee, interview by the author, Kuala Lumpur, 24 March 2008.

42. *Star*, 20 February 2008.

43. *Sinchew Daily*, 20 February 2008.

44. Ministry of Higher Education separated from Ministry of Education on March 2004 to become a full ministry responsible for all higher education-related matters with the aim of transforming Malaysia into a centre of excellence for higher education.

45. Ministry of Higher Education required that a university must have at least 20 per cent doctorate holders and 60 per cent master degree holders as staff. However, New Era had only three Ph.D. holders amongst the 125 staff members. By December 2009, only fifteen out of thirty-four programmes received the stamp of approval from the Malaysian Qualifications Agency (with ten of them under provisional accreditation), and three received full accreditation from the Ministry of Higher Education. See DHLC (2010, pp. 66, 242–47).

46. Chai Yah Han, interview by the author, Penang, 17 January 2009.

47. New Era College Board of Governors consisted of seven representatives from *Dongjiaozong* Higher Learning Centre, the college principal and deputy principal, and two representatives each from the college academics, alumnus, and students. For details regarding the project, see UCSCAM (1996, p. 287). For details regarding the board's structure, see DHLC (2001, p. 7).

48. Quek Suan Hiang, interview by the author, Johore, 23 March 2010.

49. Lim Ming King (林明镜) (executive committee member, *Dongzong*), interview by the author, Malacca, 6 February 2009.

50. Chai Yah Han, interview by the author, Penang, 17 January 2009.

51. These representatives are Yang Yin Chong (杨应俊) and Pang Siew Fian (冯秋萍) from Malacca Chinese Education and Progressive Association (马六甲华校董事会联合会), Tew Say Kop (张志开) from Negeri Sembilan Chinese School Committees Council, and Tan Tai Kim (陈大锦) from the State of Johore Chinese School Managers and Teachers' Association.

52. Lim Ming King, interview by the author, Malacca, 6 February 2009.

53. They are Zhan Yuan Rui, Chong Joon Kin, Zhang Ji Zuo, and Liang Sheng Yi.

54. Pua Eng Chong (principal, New Era College), interview by the author, Selangor, 27 February 2009.

55. Lee Hing, interview by the author, Selangor, 28 July 2010.

6

SOCIAL MOBILIZATION IN NON-LIBERAL DEMOCRACIES

INTRODUCTION

This study has identified two institutions, namely, structural and relational institutions, that have been crucial to the mobilization capacity and persistency of the Chinese education movement in Malaysia. As democratic institutions within non-liberal democracies are often constrained and easily manipulated by the ruling regime, social movements in these states rely instead on relational institutions to channel their needs and demands for change. The flexibility of relational institutions based on informal interpersonal networks compliment the rigidity of their structured counterparts, thus enabling social movements in non-liberal democracies to persist in pushing its agenda despite facing ongoing constraints imposed by the state.

Dynamic state-movement interactions result in movement mobilization mechanisms and repertoires that are adapted to the local political environment, indigenous norms and cultural influences. Although these mechanisms and repertoires may differ from those practised in liberal democratic societies, they have proven to be enduring in sustaining movements in suppressive states. Using the Chinese education movement in Malaysia as a case study, this study has demonstrated that despite rapid industralization and urbanization, primordial-based social movements — of which the Chinese education movement is a type — remain a significant social force in Malaysia.

This concluding chapter is divided into three sections. It first summarizes each of the previous chapters and details their significance to the main argument of the study. The second section explores three significant trends on social mobilization identified from studying the Chinese education movement: (1) the strategies and sustainence of resource mobilization efforts of the Chinese education movement activists; (2) the role of brokers and interpersonal networks in sustaining movement-regime interactions within a non-liberal democratic setting; and (3) the challenges faced by the movement in sustaining unification.

In the final section, the role of institutions, in particular the non-formal relational institutions, is evaluated in terms of the institutions' impact on the endurance of social mobilization within a suppressive regime. This section emphasizes the importance of adapting movement repertoires and mobilization mechanisms, especially those that have evolved through interactions with the regime over the years, as the key drivers of the movement. As one of the oldest nationwide social movements in Asia, the Chinese education movement is an instructive example from which important lessons may be drawn and shared with activists of similar movements within non-liberal democratic settings.

CHAPTER SUMMARIES AND THEIR SIGNIFICANCE

Chapter 1 laid the foundation of the book and traced the rise of social movement studies in non-liberal democratic contexts. The roles of extra-institutional variables in the execution of structural institutions were delivered in three perspectives: the intra-movement relationship explored the roles of social movement organizations and movement leaders in mobilizing movement activities; the movement-state relationship was characterized by dynamic interactions of these conflicting parties through constant adaptation of movement and suppression repertoires; the inter-movement perspective asserted the importance of interpersonal bonds in engaging networks and building alliances with other social movements in the country.

Chapter 2 demonstrated the path-dependent qualities of the Chinese education movement during Malaya's transition from a British colony to independence. Intimate collaboration between the movement and the MCA under the framework of the Grand Three Associations of Chinese Education succesfully procured political compromises from the Malay political elites to incorporate Chinese schools into the national education system (rather than face extermination), and accommodate more political rights for Chinese immigrants as citizens of Malaya in the 1950s. In return, the Alliance coalition government received support from Chinese voters (and other vernacular communities) and succeeded in gaining independence from the British in 1957. Nevertheless, constitutional deadlocks over the installation of the Chinese' vernacular language as an official language resulted in the most severe setback for the Grand Three. Pro-vernacular MCA leaders were forced to leave the party; movement leaders were punished; and the movement's capacity was significantly weakened by a series of discriminative regulations imposed by the gradually oppressive UMNO-dominated regime. All these forced the Chinese education movement to form an alliance with Chinese guilds and associations outside the MCA to continue its self-help mission to defend the distinctiveness of Chinese culture in Malaysia.

Chapter 3 analysed the dynamic interactions between the ruling regime and the Chinese education movement following the 1969 ethnic riots. Although an elected government was restored after two years of emergency rule under the National Operation Council, pro-Malay policies, such as the New Economic Policy in 1970, were also imposed. Chinese schools were marginalized by the national education system, and received little financial support to sustain their development or to maintain their facilities. Movement leaders from *Jiaozong* were punished by the authorities, instilling fear amongst the movement communities and supporters. Meanwhile, Chinese schoolteachers were incorporated as civil servants, resulting in a massive drain of both human and financial resources for *Jiaozong*. The Chinese education movement was revived when leaders from *Dongzong*, the sister organization of *Jiaozong*, took over leadership. *Dongzong* launched the national-level independent Chinese secondary schools revival movement to mobilize the Chinese community to support the movement. More importantly, the timely forced closure of all English primary schools by the state in the late 1970s turned the wheels of fortune in favour of the movement — not only did it increase the popularity of Chinese primary schools, it also reinstated the role and importance of the Chinese school committees, which had traditionally been acting as the management arm of Chinese primary schools.

Chapter 4 revealed the role of leaders, brokers, and alliances in mobilizing the movement within Malaysia's testing political landscape. This chapter in particular traced the movement repertoires adopted by four leaders, namely, Lim Fong Seng, Foo Wan Thot, Quek Suan Hiang, and Yap Sin Tian, which varied from competitive resistance to cooperative collaboration. The variation in strategies often relied on each leader's capacity to engage support from Chinese politicians in the ruling regime and the opposition parties, the capability of the movement to mobilize participation and financial resources from supporters, and the strength of the leader's alliance with Chinese guilds and associations.

Chapter 5 was dedicated to evaluating and affirming the movement's capability for learning and adaptation, which resulted in the creation of the Malaysian Independent Chinese Secondary Schools Working Committee, the *Dongjiaozong* Chinese Primary Schools Working Committee, and the *Dongjiaozong* Higher Learning Centre as the movement's mobilization machinery. The machinery was organized in terms of national, state and thematic working committees, with extensive support from full-time executive branches to maintain the everyday needs of the movement. Through systemic intra-movement networks as well as alliances with Chinese guilds and associations, the machinery has been critical to the mobilization of participants for the Chinese education movement.

Chapter 5 also detailed the success of the Independent Chinese Secondary Schools Working Committee in generating financial resources for the movement. However, its success also resulted in the domination of *Dongzong* leaders in the movement. Overburdened by multiple roles within the movement, the leaders manifested noticeable strain in their effectiveness and commitment in delivering their responsibilities, which, in turn, resulted in the increasing domination of the executive staff in maintaining the movement's daily activities. Delayed efforts to restore the balance of power resulted in open conflict between the factions and consequent division of the movement community.

SOCIAL MOBILIZATION IN NON-LIBERAL DEMOCRACIES

Thus far, the study has pondered over the survival of social movements in repressive states and questioned the role of institutions in sustaining social movement activities, prolonging their existence, and increasing their opportunities for success. This section identifies three criteria, namely, constant resource mobilization, relationship with the non-liberal democratic regime, and unification of diversity, as key variables to such understanding.

Constant Resource Mobilization

Resource mobilization has been one of the most visible yardsticks for measuring the popularity of a movement and the influence of its leaders. Constant needs for financial resources to sustain the development of

Chinese schools at the local level and to maintain movement activities at the national level resulted in the evolution of various mobilization mechanisms that have been adapted to the political norms in twentieth-century Malaysia.

Although all Chinese primary schools and converted Chinese secondary schools have been incorporated into the national system and are thus entitled to state's education budget, promotion of Malay-medium national schools by the BN ruling regime as the school for all Malaysians has resulted in unequal distribution of state resources. As discussed in Chapter 3, the Malay-medium schools have become the sole beneficiary of the national budget since independence, while other vernacular schools have been facing severe financial scarcity in sustaining, let alone developing, themselves.

Such structural constraints have forced Chinese schools to depend on public donations to survive. Education is an expensive enterprise. Although teachers' salaries are supported by the government, other expenses are not. These expenses require substantial sums of money annually and therefore involve constant, wearying fundraising. The contribution from the Chinese communities in Malaysia, ranging from wealthy business entrepreneurs to the urban-middle-class and working-class citizens, varied according to their economic capacity.

Chinese schools, as the most autonomous yet fundamental units of the Chinese education movement, depend on two primary mechanisms to mobilize the local Chinese community to contribute financially: school committees and fundraising campaigns. Chinese schools rely on members of school committees to contribute a "second income tax" as the schools' core financial income. The willingness of school committee members to donate stems from culturally-, socially-, economically- and politically-driven motivations. Culturally, individuals with financial resources or political connection are expected to take the lead in safeguarding the community's common goods. Communal pressure, which could be self- or other-imposed, has ensured the continuous commitment of community elites in supporting the needs of Chinese schools. Such expectations are strongly felt, especially within dense Chinese communities, where the ties remain intimate and are based predominantly on interpersonal interactions. The benefits of paying a "second income tax" are multiple. School committee members generally receive respect and praise from the community for their altruism. Social recognition strengthens social capital and expands business opportunities. As many Chinese entrepreneurs are constrained by *bumiputera* economic policies in Malaysia, they have to rely on interpersonal relationships and day-to-day social connections to sustain and expand their small- and medium-sized enterprises.

While financially-advantaged businessmen are still the dominant forces in Chinese school committees, interaction between the business and middle classes has increased since the 1980s. As a result of Malaysia's rapid industrialization and urbanization, more Chinese have moved from rural areas to cities for work and business opportunities. At the same time, the state's promotion of national schools stalled the development of vernacular schools. Therefore, the Chinese community faced fierce competition to enrol their children into Chinese schools in urban neighbourhoods, most of which were already overcrowded. To ensure successful enrolment into their preferred schools, many urban middle-class parents sought to establish patronage relationships with school committees to have the upper hand over the school committees' quota for recommending new enrolments.

The other mechanism most Chinese schools have been depending upon for income is the fundraising campaign. The income resulting from these activities go towards maintaining school equipment (such as tables, chairs, and library facilities), developing school facilities (such as computer room, school hall, and sports complex), expanding school premises and so on. Middle-class parents have been willing to support these donation campaigns primarily to ensure that their children have access to better facilities and thus, a head start in a competitive and result-oriented education system. However, the participation of these parents in the donation campaigns is at best passive and limited. Most of them donate to the school that hosts their children, and are less committed to support other Chinese schools. They are willing to donate financially but rarely organize or participate as members of fundraising committees, and many of them tend to stop donating to the school upon their child's graduation.

Although the financially- and socially-inferior working-class communities are on the periphery of the Chinese schools' structure, they have been the most loyal and fervent supporters of the local mobilization campaigns. Albeit contributing a much less significant amount compared with their business-class counterparts, their participation rate has been disproportionately higher, as was demonstrated in the success of the "one-person, one-dollar" donation campaign popularized in the 1950s. The campaign remains as one of the most popular fundraising repertoire today. Although novices in social movements, working-class supporters are driven by the simple desire to ensure their children and future generations of the Chinese community in Malaysia have access to Chinese education.

While the financial needs of Chinese schools at the local level have been met through periodic fundraising campaigns and donations from the school committees, those of the movement headquarters at the national level are met through national mechanisms. Over the course of the past six decades, *Dongzong* has grown from a conceptual national collaboration between Chinese school committees to one of the largest, most well-established, and most resourceful social movement organization in Malaysia. The success of the independent Chinese secondary schools revival movement in the 1970s and 1980s has generated a sustainable source of income to support the executive expenses of *Dongzong*.

In contrast, the weaker partner of the Chinese education movement, *Jiaozong*, continues to face annual financial deficits in its operations. The reintroduction of the Chinese Primary Schools Working Committee in 1994 failed to generate a sustainable source of income for *Jiaozong*. Plagued by conservative leaders and passive members who constrained *Jiaozong*'s potential for expansion, the fading Chinese schoolteachers organization failed to produce new appealing issues to compete with other Chinese organizations for resources and support. In 2001, *Jiaozong* also lost its key source of income from the annual fundraising dinner of the Lim Lian Geok Cultural Development Centre's Chinese Education Festival after the latter declared its "independence" from *Jiaozong*.

Facing mounting deficits year after year, executive officers at *Jiaozong* had to rely on sporadic and piecemeal fundraising programmes for public donations. For example, it conducts small-scale seminars, which have been the only visible activities that kept *Jiaozong* connected to its remaining audience, namely, Chinese schoolteachers. The content of the seminars usually centre on motivation, training, and topics closely related to the contemporary needs of Chinese schoolteachers. A minimal registration fee is collected to cover the cost of the activities. Although the seminars harness great potential as a means to generate income to replenish *Jiaozong*'s bleeding coffers, the non-profit nature of *Jiaozong* has prevented it from exploiting these activities as a source of income. As for the movement's executives, they would rather *Jiaozong* remain in the red than risk being perceived to be profit-driven by its few remaining supporters.

In the history of the Chinese education movement, various fundraising campaigns at the national level have been conducted when significant sums of money were needed. A series of campaigns was conducted in the early 1990s to support the construction of the movement organization's new headquarters in Kajang. Movement leaders were responsible for planning the campaigns and tapping on their social capital to garner support from the community at large. The execution and administration of these fundraising campaigns fell on full-time executive officers at *Dongzong* and *Jiaozong*, which totalled about 120 staff members. The organized networks and processes enabled the central branches of both organizations to mobilize extensive support from grassroots members for the fundraising campaigns.

The collective cultural identity represented by the Chinese education movement has been a key factor to the successful mobilization of resources nationwide over the years. *Dongjiaozong* has always framed itself as a defender of Chinese culture to attract ardent support from the Chinese-speaking community. It employs repertoires that are closely identified with the elements and trappings of Chinese culture in all of its campaigns. As this study has demonstrated, fundraising dinners, bazaars, traditional plays and similar events that highlight the concept of charitable, voluntary and righteous actions to protect the weak, have attracted extensive community participation. Large amounts of donations have also been collected through the "one-person, one-dollar" campaign and during ceremonial events such as anniversaries, weddings and religious celebrations. These campaigns generate amongst the participants much passion and a sense of renewed awareness of the importance of preserving Chinese education.

Nevertheless, it became apparent in the mid-1990s that fundraising was taking a toll on the two organizations as some campaigns fell short of their targeted amount. As time wore on and the movement aged, ossification set in and the movement repertoires became less impulsive and more rigid. Movement leaders, in particular those who had come into power in the 1990s, preferred to work within moderate- and low-risk settings rather than in settings that were extreme or aggressive. The preference stemmed from the leaders' experience that these moderate settings had survived the narrow and fluid liberal civil space in Malaysia. Taking a moderate stance has not irritated the regime, and thus far, it has been the most effective approach for delivering the movement's demands within the political setting of contemporary Malaysia.

The movement also tried to publicize the positive results of its campaigns in the Chinese vernacular press from time to time — visual, physical, or symbolic — to boost the morale and confidence of its supporters. Publicizing the results of its campaigns also highlighted the movement organization's transparency and check-and-balance mechanisms to instil public confidence. In spite of these efforts, the aging movement, overwhelmed by the impact of ossification, bureaucratization and centralization, is slowly losing its dynamism and momentum. Since the 2008 General Election, the movement has been presented with increasing political opportunities as the BN ruling regime began to show signs of relent in its approval of the establishment of the New Era University, and re-installation of independent Chinese secondary school in Pahang. At the time of writing, MCA senior politicians continue to broker between the BN regime and leaders of the Chinese education movement led by Yap Sin Tian on these matters. However, the vast amount of resources needed to support these massive projects divided movement leaders, as some questioned the ability and capacity for the movement to run a university or establish an independent Chinese secondary school.

In addition, there are calls from movement supporters, especially the reformist cluster, to re-examine the movement's goals, directions and strategies in the face of globalization and changing needs of the Chinese community. If the New Era University project were to go ahead, the movement must confront the pressing need to change its approach to be more inclusive, and to engage support from non-ethnic Chinese populations in Malaysia, as well as ethnic Chinese from Southeast Asia and the rest of the world.

Relationship with the Non-Liberal Democratic Regime

Opportunities for movement mobilization vary with the changing realities of political circumstances. Social movements constrained under a non-liberal democratic political context and an oppressive state face more difficulties in encapsulating their demands. The Chinese education movement has been able to co-exist with the heavy-handed state by exploiting the limited space in the non-liberal democratic system of Malaysia, manoeuvring to have its interests represented through brokerage by MCA politicians, and drawing opportunities by constantly adapting its movement strategies.

The movement has been condemned by the BN ruling regime, in particular, the Malay-ethnic political party, UMNO — a dominant partner in BN — as a threat to national unity. Demands from the movement have threatened the interests of ethnic Malays, forcing the UMNO-led regime to face considerable political pressure to maintain its image as the guardian of the Malay community's "inherent" rights in the country. Over the years, the regime has imposed constraints on the movement through various strategies: threats, manipulation (by way of resource distribution, retraction of schoolteachers' teaching permits and citizenship), and co-optation of movement leaders, amongst others.

Although the regime can, and has been, manipulating the electoral procedures to its own advantage to narrow the room for contenders to curb politicking, it cannot limit civil liberties outright by arresting and incarcerating opponents and civilians. Thus, the electoral system remains a significant mechanism in legitimatizing the regime's domestic power. As the majority of the constituencies in Malaysia are mixed, contesting parties need the support of voters from all ethnic groups to secure victory in the elections. Therefore, although tensions between the movement and the state have sometimes been high, the BN ruling regime risks offending the larger Chinese community in Malaysia — thus losing their electoral support — if it employs overly coercive measures to suppress or terminate the movement.

Moreover, long-term confrontation between the regime and the Chinese-dominated MCP from 1949 to 1989 had been a costly battle for the regime, economically and politically. To discourage the Chinese community from supporting the communists, the regime allowed it to express its grievances through non-violence means, such as by participating in its education movement. Thus, the state tolerated the movement during the years of battling the communists, which in turn explained the movement's continued existence.

While social movements in matured democratic states can demonstrate and adopt explicit anti-state stances to express grievances in achieving demands, these forms of resistance tend to provoke strong reactions from the state. The BN regime, for example, has been containing, co-opting and suppressing movements by proactive, albeit often covert, repressive measures or through counter-movement strategies. In turn, the Chinese education movement activists have learnt to adapt their repertoires in order to lower risks. This is the second factor that led to the movement's prolonged existence.

Chapter 4 also showed how the movement developed parallel institutions in reaction to opportunities available within the tightly contended political environment. The onslaught of discriminative and assimilative state-imposed policies gave the movement leaders little choice but to move out of their comfort zone in the 1980s to form strategic alliances with larger, more comprehensive, Chinese civic societies. *Dongjiaozong* collaborated with Gerakan in the Alliance of Three campaign in 1982 and established the Alliance of Fifteen Leading Chinese Guilds and Associations in 1983. The collaborations led to the height of the Malaysian Chinese civic movement at the mass assembly at *Tianhou* Temple in 1987.

In the face of the rising of a powerful social force from the Chinese civic community and mounting challenges from a severe internal faction within UMNO, Prime Minister Mahathir Mohamad decreed the infamous *Operasi Lalang* in 1987 to contain escalating political tension. Four activists from the education movement were amongst the 107 detained for purportedly fanning anti-government sentiments and threatening national security. *Operasi Lalang* not only enabled Mahathir to freeze political challenges and divert focus away from internal party faction to inter-ethnic relations, it was also an important wake-up call for the movement. After 1987, the Chinese education movement embarked on strengthening the movement's internal structural institution. Overwhelming pressure from the regime also prompted the movement's chairman, Lim Fong Seng, to form a political alliance with the leading opposition party, DAP, to challenge BN in the 1990 General Election. Nevertheless, political alliance (with ruling regime or opposition parties) failed to garner sufficient support from the movement community, which was affiliated to different political parties.

There were times when *Dongjiaozong* successfully pressured the state into compromising on these demands, best exemplified by the issue over the tender rights of school canteens and cooperative shops in the late 1990s, and the Vision School project in the early 2000s. More often than not, the movement was able to obtain only limited concessions from the state, as was the case with the controversy in the early 2000s regarding the use of English as the medium of instruction for mathematics and science in schools. The credit for the successful endurance of the Chinese education movement also has to go to MCA, and to some extent, Gerakan, for their brokerage efforts. Conflicting interests between UMNO and *Dongjiaozong* had limited the degree of trust between these two stakeholders. Therefore, the role of brokers, especially those from BN, was important. MCA politicians shuttled between UMNO and *Dongjiaozong* to mediate interactions, bridge the needs of both sides, and enable compromises through negotiations. In doing so, MCA has established a working relationship with the Chinese education movement leaders and even exploited the relationship as a political model for MCA to gain support from the Chinese community. Through this approach, the movement found the most efficient channel for having its interests represented and for influencing and pressuring for change in the state's process of agenda-setting. The UMNO-led BN regime has also contained the movement and its leaders by occasionally responding to the movement's demands.

During the peak of consociational politics between the Alliance coalition government in the 1950s, the impact of brokerage is exemplified by the successful efforts of MCA's first president, Tan Cheng Lock, who persuaded UMNO's president, Abdul Rahman, to attend a secret negotiation with the movement's leaders at Tan's residence in Malacca in 1955. The negotiation led to a social contract between the movement and the Alliance coalition government. As head of the Grand Three, Tan also solidified his status amongst the Chinese education movement community.

MCA's second president, Lim Chong Eu, was an equally progressive broker for the movement. The pressure to garner support from Chinese voters in competition against the growing socialist front forced Lim and his team to be more committed to accommodating the demands of the Chinese education movement, such as advocating for a more open and inclusive education policy and according official status to the Chinese language in the Federal Constitution. Lim achieved substantial success in excluding the regime's controversial ultimate objective of making Malay as the main medium of instruction in all schools as stated in Article 12 of the 1957 Education Ordinance. His success is a key factor that ensured the continued existence of Chinese schools in post-independence Malaysia. Expectedly, such a pro-movement and pro-Chinese community stand became a great threat to UMNO and non-Chinese–speaking MCA elites. The reality that Malaysian politics is elite-based forced Lim to resign. He was replaced by a more submissive, pro-UMNO leader, Tan Siew Sin, in 1962.

The fall of the Alliance coalition in 1969 marked the end of the consociational model of mutual respect in Malaysia politics. Since then, although there had been no lack of passionate sympathizers of the movement who came into power in MCA, the weakening of MCA within the BN coalition limited the impact of brokerage significantly. These intermediate agencies could only act as buffers, providing timely tip-offs and strategic suggestions that helped the movement obviate state suppression. For example, the MCA National Education Bureau would process memorandums based on the proposals drafted by Chinese education movement activists. MCA ministers would then bring these documents to the BN cabinet's meetings for negotiation. Although the contents of these memorandums were essentially the same, the BN regime, however, had been more willing to accede to the demands of its component parties than those made directly by movement activists.

By the beginning of the 1990s, MCA had grown increasingly reliant on Chinese education-related issues to gain political support from Chinese voters. To gain support from Chinese voters in the general elections, MCA reported regularly on the number of rural Chinese schools that had been successfully relocated to urban areas and the special funds received by the Chinese schools from the state. Although such "self-advertisement" was successful in the 1990s, its effects gradually faded.

The interactions between the state and the movement had been neither rigid nor linear; instead, they had evolved through continual interactions. In the 2008 General Election, the Chinese community harshly criticized MCA's over-reliance on its intermediate political strategies as insufficient to secure the minority's rights. As a result, BN lost its traditional two-thirds dominance of the parliament in 2008, and MCA suffered one of its worst and most humiliating battles since independence, or at least since 1969. Although the BN regime has never been supportive of the Chinese education movement, to date it has yet to terminate the movement by force.

The movement's prolonged existence is proof that a movement can co-exist successfully with a suppressive regime. Facing a state that has the power and tendencies to manipulate its law enforcement system to crack down on anti-state social movements, the Chinese education movement activists have learnt that it is strategic to adopt a negotiation-oriented rather than a resistance-oriented approach. However, even though a negotiation-oriented approach effectively reduces the risks and costs of sustaining the movement and therefore prolongs the movement's existence, it decreases the movement's capacity to reach its ultimate aims.

Unification of Diversity

As one of the largest social movements in Malaysia, the Chinese education movement is supported by a vast number of heterogeneous agencies. The vast numbers of supporters, each playing different roles, have varied levels of commitment to, and expectations from the movement, which impeded the movement's efforts in unification. The internal divisions that plagued the Chinese education movement are, namely, (1) the division between *Dongzong* and *Jiaozong*, (2) problems of movement exclusiveness, and (3) tensions between the conservatives and the reformists.

The movement is commonly perceived by its supporters and the public as a collaboration between the national umbrella association of *Dongzong* and *Jiaozong*. However, power relationships between these two sister organizations have not been equal. Outspoken *Jiaozong* leaders successfully led the movement's resistance in the 1950s and 1960s. However, strong suppression from the state — such as the revocation of *Jiaozong* chairman, Lim Lian Geok's citizenship; deportation of *Jiaozong* advisor, Yan Yuan

Zhang; and the dismissal of *Jiaozong* vice chairman, Sim Mow Yu, from all political positions in MCA, amongst others — drastically reduced *Jiaozong's* leadership capacities.

Jiaozong's activities plunged dramatically when the state drafted all Chinese schoolteachers into the civil servant system and limited their involvement in anti-state activities. The establishment of the officially-recognized National Union of the Teaching Profession in 1974 replaced *Jiaozong's* role as the sole representative organization for schoolteachers. Failing to overcome these changes, *Jiaozong's* role in the movement weakened from that of a leader to that of a collaborator in the 1980s. The collaborative relationship between *Jiaozong* and *Dongzong* was forged during the 1980s when they were housed under the same roof in the *Jiaozong* building in downtown Kuala Lumpur. Movement-related activities were conducted within a shared workspace, enabling like-minded individuals to develop emotional bonds and trust that helped to strengthen and unify the movement. Strong interpersonal relationships amongst leaders, through which information, human resources and financial resources were shared, solidified the movement.

Unfortunately, the disparities in resource capacities between *Jiaozong* and *Dongzong* magnified with the growing accomplishment of the latter in the 1990s. Rising as the leader of the movement, *Dongzong* continued to make milestones with the completion of a larger and better equipped movement headquarters at Kajang. In contrast, with dwindling membership and resources, *Jiaozong's* significance amongst Chinese schoolteachers continued to fade, leading to the domination of the Chinese school principals in *Jiaozong*. Today, *Jiaozong* has become a mere shadow of its past. It has softened its approach in its dealings with the state to protect the interests of Chinese schoolteachers. By adopting a less risky and more moderate approach, the *Dongzong*-led Chinese education movement is often perceived as conservative by many, but such an approach remains the best way to resolve the dilemma between the sister organizations.

Another obstacle to movement unification has been the division between conservatives and reformists. The former comprised core leaders of the movement, while the latter comprised predominantly senior members of the movement's executive branch. In the 1970s, thematic working committees were established to facilitate the needs of the independent Chinese secondary schools revival movement. Since then, increasing numbers of full-time and professional personnel joined the executive branch to meet the managerial and operational needs of the movement. The participation of these dynamic non-business and non-teaching individuals was significant in sustaining the movement.

With the successful establishment of this executive community, decision-making in the movement was divided into two levels: the leadership branch consisting of elected movement committee members dealt with external matters, and the salaried executive branch that managed day-to-day operations of the movement. These two levels of decision-making successfully generated amicable social capital between the Chinese guilds and associations and the Chinese education movement's activists in joint pursuit of their shared goal of furthering the interests of Chinese Malaysians.

Conflicts between the conservatives and the reformists began to surface after *Dongzong* chairman, Lim Fong Seng's retirement from the movement. Failure of the dual coalition system campaign with DAP in 1990 resulted in a clear division between the pro-MCA and pro-DAP supporters. Members of both factions — the former dominating the leadership branch and committees, and the latter dominating the executive branch — began to manipulate the unwritten norms of the movement to exert their influence on the movement's organization. Although the movement developed characteristics of a matured structured institution over time, such as written constitutions, rules and regulations, these institutional characteristics only served to fulfill procedural needs and were symbols of formality, rather than channels for meaningful participation. Unwritten norms dominated the actual implementation of the movement.

Quek Suan Hiang was able to accommodate the interests of both sides by focusing most of the movement's attention on accumulating financial resources to support the construction of the movement's headquarters in Kajang. Nevertheless, the tug of war between the factions continued in the 2000s. To consolidate power and control of the institutions and operations of the movement, both factions installed their preferred candidates as new committee members of the movement. By 2008, competition for power between the reformists and the conservatives had escalated into a full-blown conflict that eventually led to the departure of the reformist faction. The conflict divided the movement largely into three factions. The first comprises conservatives who now control *Dongjiaozong*. The second comprises reformists who were forced to leave *Dongjiaozong* and were later reassembled under the Lim Lian Geok Cultural Development Centre and demanded for structural reform of the Chinese education movement. The third faction — mostly veterans of the movement — comprises those who were frustrated by the power struggle between the former two factions. Although the reformists have yet to succeed in overthrowing the core leaders of *Dongjiaozong* at the time of writing, infighting nevertheless has had a destructive influence on the movement.

Ironically, factionalism stems in part from the movement's exclusiveness. To strengthen internal unity, sustain collective identity, and justify its legitimacy as defenders of the Chinese community, the movement's leaders constructed the movement's activities based on the injustice and discrimination suffered by the Chinese community. The exclusiveness of the injustice frame has been effective in mobilizing support from the Chinese community. The greater the suppression by the state, the higher the mobilization capacity and support the movement received from the Chinese community nationwide. Continuous attempts from the state to convert Chinese schools into a Malay-dominated national system in the 1980s unwittingly led to unification of the political power of the Chinese-speaking community, apparent in the demonstration staged at *Tianhou* Temple in 1987.

To enhance and maintain the movement's exclusiveness, the Chinese education movement has been staffed exclusively by ethnic Chinese-educated Chinese. Preference is given to graduates from institutions that are not yet recognized by the state, such as independent Chinese secondary schools, Nanyang University or Taiwanese universities. Many outsiders see this as a form of Chinese chauvinism, stemming from inferior complex and a lack of appreciation of the multicultural reality of the Malaysian society. In fact, the policy of exclusion has isolated many individuals with great potential from accessing the movement's leadership.

The domination of an exclusive community within the movement has also prevented the movement from establishing interethnic alliances. The language barrier has been the hardest hurdle to overcome as most members of the Chinese education movement lack the linguistic capacity to reach out to supporters of other linguistic groups. Moreover, as one of the oldest social movements in Malaysia, the disparity in strength may have made it more difficult for the Chinese education movement to collaborate with other smaller, newer social movements.

Although the support of non-ethnic Chinese individuals in the controversy over the use of English as the medium of instruction for science and mathematics had presented great potential for interethnic collaboration, leaders of the Chinese education movement failed to capitalize on this opportunity. By 2008, while other movement groups in Malaysia had taken advantage of the political opportunity to broach a number of issues ranging from human rights, equal opportunities for minority groups and state reformation, *Dongjiaozong's* response — or rather, the lack of response — was disappointing.

Factionalism may potentially create more space for democracy, competition, dynamism and choice. However, failure to manage internal rivalry may do more harm. Burdened by exclusiveness, conservatism and internal faction, *Dongjiaozong* failed to extend itself beyond a contained pressure group to play a more significant role in domestic contentious politics, despite its longevity.

CONCLUSION

This study has demonstrated that the capacities for social mobilization and endurance of a social movement depend on structural and relational institutions. The former delineate the roles and responsibilities of each agency within the movement, install legitimate status upon social movement leaders to lead the movement, and enable these leaders to mobilize support from movement members and the larger community.

As social movements comprise large numbers of agencies and individuals, having formal structural institutions is on its own insufficient for inducing strong inter-agency commitment to the movement. Here is where relational institutions, with their more organic, dynamic and adaptive nature, can supplement and fill the gaps of structural institutions.

Due to the lack of access to democratic institutions, social movement leaders develop working relationships with members of the ruling regime to achieve their demands through brokerage efforts. Brokers enable an informal but important channel for conflicting parties to seek common grounds. Through bridging and enabling constructive interactions between conflicting parties, brokers strengthen their political significance within the regime's entity and receive support from the movement community for putting forth the movement's demands to the state's core decision-making bodies. However, the impact of brokerage is supplementary rather than primary, for brokerage alone seldom procures the ultimate goals of a social movement.

Movement repertoires may vary from aggressive to collaborative, manifest to latent. Unlike social movement activists in democratic states who enjoy freedom from fear to express their demands openly, the choice of movement repertoires in non-liberal democratic states are determined by the lessons social movement activists learnt from their previous interactions with the state. As interactions between social movement and the state are considerably influenced by the local political structure and social environment, social movement activists adjust their activities and repertoires according to the local milieu. Therefore, movement leaders who are constrained by a non-liberal democratic setting have to choose the most efficient, most rewarding and least risky approach to mobilize support from the community.

The rigidity and ineffectiveness of democratic institutions within suppressive states has also given rise to strategies that rely on interpersonal relationships to meet the movement's demands rather than through formal channels. Movement leaders expand their influence through social capital, and form networks and alliances with like-minded individuals and organizations. Although this form of collaboration may be fragile and can collapse upon changes in leadership, it remains the most accessible and fastest approach for social movements to form a strong anti-state alliance under oppressive conditions.

Although political opportunities and resources available to a social movement may be scarce, the internal movement solidarity is the most significant factor to successful social mobilization. Tensions between factions are unavoidable; therefore, it is vitally important for a movement to be equipped with the ability to manage these challenges through a well-structured institution or through a well-respected and authorized leader. A united movement will be able to resist strong repression from its traditional enemy, the state, but a divided movement will be too fragile and easily torn apart by disunity from within.

APPENDICES

APPENDIX 1
List of *Jiaozong's* Members

Year Registered	Name
1937	Batang Padang Chinese Schoolteachers' Association 马登巴冷华校教师公会
1939	Muar Chinese Schoolteachers' Association 麻坡华校教师公会
1940	Malacca Chinese Schoolteachers' Association 马六甲华校教师公会
1940	Penang Chinese Schoolteachers' Association 槟城华校教师会
1940	Sarikei Chinese Schoolteachers' Association 泗里街华人教师公会
1940	Sibu Chinese Schoolteachers' Association 诗巫华人教师公会
1945	Meradong Chinese Schoolteachers' Association 马拉端华小教师公会
1946	Batu Gajah Chinese Schoolteachers' Association 华怡乡区华校教师公会
1946	Ipoh Chinese Schoolteachers' Association 怡保市华校教师公会
1946	Manjung Chinese Schoolteachers' Association 曼绒华校教师公会
1946	Negeri Sembilan Chinese Schoolteachers' Association 森美兰华校教师公会
1946	Northern Perak Chinese Schoolteachers' Association 北吡叨华校教师公会
1947	Hilir Perak Chinese Schoolteachers' Association 下吡叨区华校教师公会
1947	Perak United State-Level Chinese Schoolteachers' Association 吡叨州华校教师会联合会
1948	Segamat Chinese Schoolteachers' Association 昔加末华校教师公会

APPENDIX 1 (Cont'd)

Year Registered	Name
1949	Kampar and Gopeng Chinese Schoolteachers' Association 金宝务边区华校教师公会
1949	Kuala Lumpur Chinese Schoolteachers Association 吉隆坡华校教师公会
1949	Northern Kedah Chinese Schoolteachers' Association 吉北华校教师公会
1950	Central Kedah Chinese Schoolteachers' Association 吉中华校教师公会
1950	Raub Chinese Schoolteachers' Association 劳勿华校教师公会
1951	Perlis Chinese Schoolteachers' Association 玻璃市华校教师公会
1952	Kluang Chinese Schoolteachers' Association 居銮区华校教师公会
1952	Southern Johore Chinese Schoolteachers' Association 柔南华校教师公会
1953	Eastern Pahang Chinese Schoolteachers' Association 东彭华校教师公会
1953	Selangor Chinese Schoolteachers' Association 雪兰莪华校教师公会
1953	Southern Kedah Chinese Schoolteachers' Association 吉南华校教师公会
1955	Temerloh and Bera Chinese Schoolteachers' Association 淡马鲁暨百乐县华校教师公会
1955	Terengganu Chinese Schoolteachers' Association 登嘉楼华校教师公会
1957	Kuala Lipis Chinese Schoolteachers' Association 立卑华校教师公会
1961	Pontian Chinese Schoolteachers' Association 笨珍华校教师公会

APPENDIX 1 *(Cont'd)*

Year Registered	Name
1962	Central Johore Chinese Schoolteachers' Association 柔中区华校教师公会
1968	Kelantan Chinese Schoolteachers' Association 吉兰丹华校教师公会
1969	Johore United State-Level Chinese Schoolteachers' Association 柔佛州华校教师公会联合会
1974	Bentong Chinese Schoolteachers Association 文冬华校教师公会
1979	Pahang United State-Level Chinese Schoolteachers' Association 彭亨州华校教师公会联合会
1980	Cameron Highlands Chinese Schoolteachers' Association 金马仑华校教师公会
1984	Jerantut Chinese Schoolteachers' Association 而连突华校教师公会
1995	Kuala Kangsar Chinese Schoolteachers' Association 江沙县华校教师公会
1997	Kuching and Samarahan Chinese Primary Schoolteachers' Association 晋汉省华小教师公会
1999	Sri Aman Kuching and Samarahan Chinese Primary Schoolteachers' Association 斯里阿曼木中省华小教师公会
2002	Sarawak United State-Level Chinese Primary Schoolteachers' Association 砂拉越华小教师会联合会
2005	Sabah Chinese Schoolteachers' Association 沙巴州华校教师总会
2007	Bintulu Kuching and Samarahan Chinese Primary Schoolteachers' Association 民都鲁华小教师公会

Source: The author.

APPENDIX 2
List of *Dongzong's* Members

Year Registered	Name
1949	State of Johore Chinese School Managers and Teachers' Association 柔佛州华校董教联合会
1952	Council of Perak Chinese School Committees 吡叻华校董事会联合会
1953	Negeri Sembilan Chinese School Committees Council 森美兰华校董事会联合会
1953	Penang and Province Wellesley United Chinese School Management Association 槟威华校董事会联合会
1954	United Chinese School Committees' Association of Selangor and Wilayah Persekutuan Kuala Lumpur 雪兰莪暨吉隆坡联邦直辖区华校董事会联合会
1954	Kelantan Chinese School Committees and Teacher's Association 吉兰丹华校董事教师联合会
1955	Malacca Chinese Education and Progressive Association 马六甲华校董事会联合会
1956	United Chinese School Committees' Association of Kedah 吉打华校董事会联合会
1979	United Association of Private Chinese Secondary School Committees Sabah 沙巴华文独立中学董事会联合会总会
1988	Sarawak United Association of Private Chinese Secondary School Management Committee 砂拉越华文独立中学董事会联合会总会
1989	United Chinese School Committee of Managers Pahang 彭亨华校董事会联合会
1990	Sarawak United Association of Chinese Primary Aided School Committee 砂拉越津贴华文小学董事联合
1996	United Chinese School Committees' Association of Perlis 玻璃市华校董事会联合会
2001	United Chinese School Committees' Association of Terengganu 登嘉楼华校董事会联合会

Source: The author.

APPENDIX 3
List of Independent Chinese Secondary Schools in Malaysia

	Refused Conversion Offer	Converted and Established Affiliated School	New School in the 1960s
Johore			
1. Chinese High School, Batu Pahat 峇株吧辖华仁中学	*		
2. Chung Hwa High School 中化中学	*		
3. Foon Yew High School 宽柔中学	*		
4. Kluang Chong Hwa High School 居銮中华中学	*		
5. Pei Hwa High School 利丰港培华独立中学		*	
6. Sekolah Menengah Chong Hwa S.B.R. 新文龙中华中学	*		
7. Sekolah Menengah Pei Chun 培群独中		*	
8. Yong Peng High School 永平中学	*		
Kedah			
9. Keat Hwa High School 亚罗士打吉华独立中学		*	
10. Sekolah Menengah Sin Min 亚罗士打新民独立中学		*	
11. Sekolah Menengah Sin Min Sungai Petani 新民独立中学		*	
Kelantan			
12. Kelantan Chung Hwa Independent High School 吉兰丹中华独立中学		*	

APPENDIX 3   *(Cont'd)*

	Refused Conversion Offer	Converted and Established Affiliated School	New School in the 1960s
Kuala Lumpur			
13. Chong Hwa High School 吉隆坡中华独立中学		*	
14. Confucian Private Secondary School 尊孔独立中学		*	
15. Kuen Cheng High School 坤成中学	*		
16. Tsun Jin High School 吉隆坡循人中学	*		
Malacca			
17. Pay Fong High School 培风中学	*		
Negeri Sembilan			
18. Chung Hua High School Seremban 芙蓉中华中学	*		
19. Sekolah Menengah Chung Hua Port Dickson 波德申中华中学	*		
Penang			
20. Chung Ling Private High School 钟灵独立中学		*	
21. Han Chiang High School 韩江中学	*		
22. Jit Sin Independent High School 大山脚日新独立中学		*	
23. Penang Chinese Girls' Private High School 槟华女子独立中学		*	
24. Phor Tay Private High School 菩提独立中学		*	

APPENDIX 3   *(Cont'd)*

	Refused Conversion Offer	Converted and Established Affiliated School	New School in the 1960s
Perak			
25. Hua Lian High School 太平华联中学		*	
26. Sekolah Menengah Pei Yuan (Private) KPR 培元独中		*	
27. Poi Lam High School 培南中学		*	
28. Sekolah Menengah San Min (Suwa) 安顺三民独中		*	
29. Sekolah Menengah Yik Ching 育青中学	*		
30. Sekolah Tinggi Nan Hwa Ayer Tawar 南华独中		*	
31. Shen Jai High School 深斋中学	*		
32. Tsung Wah Private Secondary School 崇华中学		*	
33. Yuk Choy High School (Private) 育才独立中学		*	
Sabah			
34. Beaufort Middle School 保佛中学			*
35. Kian Kok Middle School 建国中学			*
36. Lahad Datu Middle School 拿笃中学			*
37. Papar Middle School 吧巴中学			*
38. Pei Tsin High School 古达培正中学			*

APPENDIX 3   *(Cont'd)*

	Refused Conversion Offer	Converted and Established Affiliated School	New School in the 1960s
39. Sabah Chinese High School 斗湖巴华中学			*
40. Sabah Tshung Tsin Secondary School 沙巴崇正中学			*
41. Tenom Tshung Tsin Secondary School 丹南崇正中学			*
42. Yu Yuan Secondary School 育源中学			*
Sarawak			
43. Batu Kawa Min Lit Secondary School 石角民立中学			*
44. Catholic High School 诗巫公教中学			*
45. Chung Hua Middle School No. 1 古晋中华第一中学	*		
46. Chung Hua Middle School No. 3 古晋中华第三中学	*		
47. Chung Hua Middle School No. 4 古晋中华第四中学	*		
48. Citizen Middle School 诗巫公民中学			*
49. Guong Ming Middle School 诗巫光民中学	*		
50. Kai Dee Middle School 民都鲁开智中学	*		
51. Kiang Hin Middle School 诗巫建兴中学	*		
52. Ming Lik Secondary School, Sarikei 泗里奎民立中学			*
53. Pei Min Middle School 培民中学			*

APPENDIX 3   *(Cont'd)*

	Refused Conversion Offer	Converted and Established Affiliated School	New School in the 1960s
54. Riam Road Secondary School 廉律中学			*
55. Serian Public Secondary School 西连民众中学			*
56. Wong Nai Siong Secondary School 诗巫黄乃裳中学			*
Selangor 57. Hin Hua High School 巴生兴华中学	*		
58. Kwang Hua Private High School 光华独中		*	
59. Pin Hwa High School 滨华中学	*		
60. Sekolah Menengah Chung Hua Klang 巴生中华独立中学		*	
Subtotal	22	21	17
Total	60		

Source: The author.

APPENDIX 4

Distribution of *Dongzong* Executive Branch Staff by Academic Qualification, Age, and Years of Service (1995–2011)

Year	1995	1996	1997	1998	1999	2000	2001	2002	2003	2004	2005	2006	2007	2008	2009	2010	2011	Average
Total Staff Members	114	101	122	103	98	92	100	108	115	114	115	123	102	92	101	103	109	107.5
Academic Qualification																		
Ph.D.	1	1	2	0	0	0	0	0	0	0	0	0	0	0	0	0	0	0.2
Master	1	2	7	4	5	5	5	v7	8	9	9	9	7	9	9	9	10	6.8
Bachelor	35	38	42	41	36	32	34	39	44	45	47	54	51	35	38	41	43	40.9
Certificate	15	10	12	11	13	9	10	12	14	15	16	23	18	19	18	13	19	14.5
Form VI	56	46	55	43	39	42	45	43	40	35	33	35	23	24	32	40	37	39.3
Form III	6	4	4	4	5	4	6	7	9	10	10	2	5	5	4	—	—	9.5
Age																		
< 30	—	—	—	—	—	—	—	—	—	—	68	64	46	29	35	33	34	44.1
31—40	—	—	—	—	—	—	—	—	—	—	21	36	32	37	34	35	37	33.1
41—50	—	—	—	—	—	—	—	—	—	—	15	15	16	16	18	19	20	17.0
51—55	—	—	—	—	—	—	—	—	—	—	6	3	4	5	6	10	10	6.3
> 56	—	—	—	—	—	—	—	—	—	—	5	5	4	5	8	6	8	5.9
Years of Service																		
< 1	—	—	—	—	—	—	—	18	24	15	19	24	15	13	11	9	12	16.0
1—5	—	—	—	—	—	—	—	33	36	44	43	48	35	25	33	36	41	37.4
6—10	—	—	—	—	—	—	—	30	30	26	28	20	18	15	18	16	17	21.8
11—15	—	—	—	—	—	—	—	16	15	14	12	19	19	16	16	16	12	15.5
16—20	—	—	—	—	—	—	—	3	3	6	4	5	8	11	10	12	16	7.8
21—25	—	—	—	—	—	—	—	2	1	2	2	2	1	7	2	4	5	2.8
> 25	—	—	—	—	—	—	—	6	6	7	7	5	6	5	3	3	6	5.4
Contract	—	—	—	—	—	—	—	—	—	—	—	—	—	—	—	7	—	—

Source: Compiled by the author with data extracted from UCSCAM (1988—91; 1992c; 1993—99; 2000b; 2001b; 2002a; 2003b; 2004a; 2005; 2006a; 2007; 2008a; 2009—12).

BIBLIOGRAPHY

Abdul Fauzi Abdul Hamid. "Political Dimensions of Religious Conflict in Malaysia: State Response to an Islamic Movement". *Indonesia and the Malay World* 28, no. 80 (2000): 32–65.

Abdul Rahman. *Looking Back: Monday Musings and Memories*. Kuala Lumpur: Pustaka Antara, 1977.

———. *Lest We Forget: Further Candid Reminiscences*. Petaling Jaya: Eastern Universities, 1983.

———. *Malaysia: The Road to Independence*. Petaling Jaya: Pelanduk, 1984.

———. *Challenging Times*. Petaling Jaya: Pelanduk, 1986a.

———. *Political Awakening*. Petaling Jaya: Pelanduk, 1986b.

Abdullah Ahmad Badawi. *Islam Hadhari: A Model Approach for Development and Progress*. Selangor: MPH, 2006.

Abraham, Collin. *Divide and Rule: The Roots of Race Relation in Malaysia*. Kuala Lumpur: INSAN, 1997.

Adams, Jacqueline. "Art in Social Movements: Shantytown Women's Protest in Pinochet's Chile". *Sociological Forum* 17, no. 1 (March 2002): 21–26.

Alberoni, Francesco. *Movement and Institution*. Translated by Patricia C. Arden Delmoro. New York: Columbia University Press, 1984.

Anderson, Benedict. *Imagined Communities: Reflections on the Origin and Spread of Nationalism*. 2nd ed. London, New York: Verso, 1991.

Anderson, Lisa. *The State and Social Transformation in Tunisia and Libya, 1830–1980*. Princeton: Princeton University Press, 1986.

Andrain, Charles and David Apter. *Political Protest and Social Change: Analyzing Politics*. London: Macmillan, 1995.

Andrews, Kenneth. "Creating Social Change: Lessons from the Civil Rights Movement". In *Social Movements: Identity, Culture and the State*, edited by David Meyer, Nancy Whittier, and Belinda Robnett. New York: Oxford University Press, 2002.

Armony, Ariel and Hector Schamis. "Babel in Democratization Studies". *Journal of Democracy* 16, no. 4 (October 2005): 113–28.

Bandy, Joe and Jackie Smith, eds. *Coalitions Across Borders: Transnational Protest and the Neoliberal Order*. Oxford: Rowman and Littlefield, 2005.

Bashevkin, Sylvia. "Interest Groups and Social Movements". In *Comparing Democracies*, edited by Lawrence LeDuc, Richard Niemi, and Pippa Norris. California: Sage, 1996.

Benford, Robert. "You Could Be the Hundredth Monkey: Collective Action Frames and Vocabularies of Motive Within the Nuclear Disarmament Movement". *Sociological Quarterly* 34 (1993): 195–216.

Berita Harian. "Barisan Tidak Akan Layan Ugutan: PM" [Prime Minister: Barisan will not respond to threats]. 21 September 1999.

Blumer, Herbert. "Collective Behavior". In *An Outline of the Principles of Sociology*, edited by Robert Ezra Park. New York: Barnes and Noble, 1939.

Boudreau, Vincent. "State Repression and Democracy Protest in Three Southeast Asian Countries". In *Social Movements: Identity, Culture and the State*, edited by David Meyer, Nancy Whittier, and Belinda Robnett. New York: Oxford University Press, 2002.

————. *Resisting Dictatorship: Repression and Protest in Southeast Asia*. Cambridge: Cambridge University Press, 2004.

Bourdieu, Pierre. "The Forms of Capital". In *Handbook of Theory and Research for the Sociology of Education*, edited by John G. Richardson. Westport: Greenwood, 1986.

CACE (Central Advisory Committee for Education, Federation of Malaya). *Minutes of Meetings, file no. 31/51*. Kuala Lumpur: Central Advisory Committee for Education, 1951.

Callaghy, Thomas. "The State and the Development of Capitalism in Africa: Theoretical, Historical and Comparative Reflections". In *The Precarious Balance: State and Society in Africa*, edited by Donald Rothchild and Naomi Chazan. Boulder: Westview, 1988.

Campbell, John. *Institutional Change and Globalization*. Princeton: Princeton University Press, 2004.

Camroux, David. "State Responses to Islamic Resurgence in Malaysia: Accommodation, Co-Option and Confrontation". *Asian Survey* 36, no. 9 (September 1996): 852–68.

Carey, John. "Parchment, Equilibria and Institutions". *Comparative Political Science* 33, nos. 6–7 (2000): 735–61.

Carothers, Thomas. "The End of the Transition Paradigm". *Journal of Democracy* 13, no. 1 (January 2002): 5–21.

Case, William. *Semi-Democracy in Malaysia: Pressures and Prospects for Change*. Canberra: Australian National University Press, 1992.

————. *Elites and Regimes in Malaysia: Revisiting a Consociational Democracy*. Australia: Monash Asia Institute, 1996.

————. "New Uncertainties for an Old Pseudo-Democracy: The Case of Malaysia". *Comparative Politics* 37, no. 1 (October 2004): 83–104.

————. "How's My Driving? Abdullah's First Year As Malaysian PM". *Pacific Review* 18, no. 2 (2005): 137–57.

———. "Electoral Authoritarianism in Malaysia: Trajectory Shift". *Pacific Review* 22, no. 3 (2009): 311–33.

———. "Transition from Single-Party Dominance? New Data from Malaysia". *Journal of East Asian Studies* 10 (2010): 91–126.

CC (Constitutional Commission). *Report of the Federation of Malaya Constitutional Commission 1957*. London: Her Majesty's Stationary Office, 1957.

Chai, Hon Chan. *Education and Nation Building in Plural Societies: The West Malaysian Experience*. Canberra: Australian National University Press, 1977.

Chan, Heng Chee. "The Malayan Chinese Association". Master's thesis, University of Singapore, 1965.

Chandra Muzaffar. *Islamic Resurgence in Malaysia*. Petaling Jaya: Penerbit Fajar Bakti, 1987.

———. *Challenges and Choices in Malaysian Politics and Society*. Penang: Aliran, 1989*a*.

———. *The NEP: Development and Alternative Consciousness*. Penang: Aliran, 1989*b*.

Cheah, Boon Kheng. *Red Star Over Malaya*. Singapore: Singapore University Press, 1983.

———. *Malaysia: The Making of a Nation*. Singapore: Institute for Southeast Asian Studies, 2002.

Chen, Shaua Fui 曾薛霏. "Xinzhengju You Xinguandao Fanying Huajiao Wenti, Yexintian Zanyang Minlian Zhouzhengfu Xinzuofeng" 新政局有新管道反映华教问题, 叶新田赞扬民联州政府新作风 [New political situation provides new opportunity to reflect Chinese education related problems, Yap Sin Tian compliments Pakatan Rakyat state governments new approaches]. *Merdeka Review*, 8 April 2008 <http://www.merdekareview.com/news.php?n=6463> (accessed 9 September 2013).

Cheong, Yuen Keong. "Gerakan Pendidikan Cina Di Malaysia: Satu Kajian Tentang Perjuangan Dong Jiao Zong (1970–2002)" [Chinese education movement in Malaysia: Case study on Dong Jiao Zong (1970–2002)]. Ph.D. dissertation, Faculty of Arts and Social Sciences, University of Malaya, Malaysia, 2007.

Chew, Kong Huat. "Chinese Education in Malaysia". In *Sociology Working Paper*, edited by Steward Gardner. Penang: Penerbit Universiti Sains Malaysia, 1975.

Chian, Heng Kai 陈庆佳. *Yanshou Gangwei: Wode Zhenglunxuan* 严守岗位: 我的政论选 [Dedications and commitments to my roles and positions: Collection of my political essays]. Kuala Lumpur: Oriengroup 东方企业, 1994.

Chin, B.N. Christine. "The State of the 'State' in Globalization: Social Order and Economic Restructuring in Malaysia". *Third World Quarterly* 21, no. 6 (December 2000): 1035–57.

Chin, James. "New Chinese Leadership in Malaysia: The Contest for the MCA and Gerakan Presidency". *Contemporary Southeast Asia* 28, no. 1 (2006): 70–87.

Chin, Peng. *My Side of History*. Singapore: Media Masters, 2003.

China Press 中国报. "Binnisishi De Jiaoyu Baogaoshu" 宾尼斯氏的教育报告书 [Barnes' Education Report]. 12 June 1951.

————. "Mahuagonghui Suo Changjian Zhi Daxue Xianxiu Yuanxiao Jihua Wancheng Gongbu" 马华公会所倡建之大学先修院校计划完成公布 [Annoucement on the completion of the pre-university college established by Malaysian Chinese Association]. 15 July 1968.

————. "Bingzhou Bake Huaxiao Jizengzhi Liushijian, Bake Hanglie Gengzhuangda" 槟州罢课华小激增至六十间, 罢课行列更壮大 [The number of Chinese primary schools participating in the school strike at Penang reaches sixty]. 16 October 1987.

————. "Dongjiaozong Yaocuisheng Liangdangzhi, Zhichi Huatuan Renshi Jiaru Minxing Canxuan" 董教总要催生两党制, 支持华团人士加入民行参选 [*Dongjiaozong* wants to mobilize the formation of dual coalition system and supports individuals from Chinese guilds and associations to participate in the elections under Democratic Action Party]. 15 August 1990.

————. "Zanzhuren Yao Zhuijiu Huaxiao Dahui Xiaozhang Zixing Gaiqi" 赞助人要追究华小大会校长自行改期 [School sponsors want to investigate why the school principal rescheduled the date of school general meeting without prior notice]. 4 May 1992.

————. "Xiaocuoren Yitu Nandecheng Dongzong Jianjue Zhichi Lixing Huaxiao Dongshihui" 小撮人意图难得逞 董总坚决支持力行华小董事会 [United Chinese School Committees' Association of Malaysia vows to support the school committee of Lick Hung Chinese Primary School]. 21 May 1992.

————. "Lutingyu: Yingsheli Gongzhenghui Rang Youguanzhe Bianjie" 陆庭谕: 应设立公证会让有关者辩解 [Loot Ting Yu: Should establish public hearing session to provide explanation opportunities for the affected parties]. 26 May 1992.

————. "Pingjing De Chitangli Youeyu, Xinjiaoyu Faling Xiuding Dongzong Yu Wu Diaoyi Qingxin" 平静的池塘里有鳄鱼, 新教育法令修订董总吁勿掉以轻心 [There are crocodiles under the still water ponds, United Chinese School Committees' Association of Malaysia warns not to underestimate the new Education Act]. 8 June 1992.

————. "Shishi Xinjiaoyu Faling Dongshibu Bian Caiwuzu" 实施新教育法令董事部变财务组 [The new Education Act changes school committee into a financial management committee]. 16 June 1992.

————. "Mahua Minzheng An Guozhao" 马华民政暗过招 [Malaysian Chinese Association and Malaysian People's Movement Party are competing in secret]. 11 August 1992.

————. "Huhuoshan Youyi Wending Sendonglianhui Zhuxi" 胡火山有意问鼎森董联会主席 [Hu Huo Shan is interested in being the chairman of Negeri Sembilan Chinese School Committees' Association]. 11 April 1994.

Chwe, Suk Young Michael. "Structure and Strategy in Collective Action". *American Journal of Sociology* 105 (1999): 128–56.

Clutterbuck, Richard. *Long Long War: Counterinsurgency in Malaya and Vietnam.* New York: Praeger, 1966.

CMCS (Centre for Malaysian Chinese Studies 华社研究中心), ed. *Lun Huatuan Renshi Canzheng* 论华团人士参政 [Debates on the participation of individuals from Chinese guilds and associations in politics]. Kuala Lumpur: Selangor Chinese Assembly Hall, 1990.

Coleman, James. "Social Capital in the Creation of Human Capital". *American Journal of Sociology* 94 (1990): S95–120.

Coy, Patrick, ed. *Research in Social Movements, Conflicts and Change*. Greenwich: JAI, 1978.

Crouch, Harold. "Authoritarian Trends, the UMNO Split and the Limits to State Power". In *Fragmented Vision: Culture and Politics in Contemporary Malaysia*, edited by Joel Kahn and Loh Kok Wah Francis. Sydney: Allen and Unwin, 1992.

———. "Malaysia: Neither Authoritarian nor Democratic". In *Southeast Asia in the 1990s: Authoritarian, Democracy and Capitalism*, edited by Kevin Hewison, Richard Robison, and Garry Rodan. Sydney: Allen and Unwin, 1993.

———. *Government and Society in Malaysia*. Sydney: Allen and Unwin, 1996.

Daniel, G.P. *Dr Ling Liong Sik and the Politics of Ethnic Chinese Unity*. Selangor: Times, 1995.

DAP (Democratic Action Party). *The Real Reason: Operation Lalang ISA Arrests October 27, 1987*. Petaling Jaya: Democratic Action Party, 1988.

———. *25 Years of Struggle: Milestones in DAP History*. Petaling Jaya: Democratic Action Party, 1991.

Davis, Gerald, Doug McAdam, W. Richard Scott, and Mayer Zald, eds. *Social Movements and Organization Theory*. New York: Cambridge University Press, 2005.

de Tarde, Gabriel. *On Communication and Social Influence: Selected Papers*. Chicago: University of Chicago Press, 1969.

della Porta, Donatella and Manuela Caiani. *Social Movements and Europeanization*. New York: Oxford University Press, 2009.

della Porta, Donatella and Mario Diani. *Social Movements: An Introduction*. London: Blackwell, 1999.

DHLC (*Dongjiaozong* Higher Learning Centre 董教总教育中心). *Dongjiaozong Jiaoyu Zhongxin Feiyingli Youxian Gongsi Dongjiaozong Xinjiyuan Xueyuan 1998 Nian Gongzuo Baogaoshu* 董教总教育中心非营利有限公司 董教总新纪元学院 1998年工作报告书 [*Dongjiaozong* Higher Learning Center and *Dongjiaozong* New Era College 1998 working report]. Selangor: *Dongjiaozong* Higher Learning Center, 1999.

———. *Dongjiaozong Jiaoyu Zhongxin Feiyingli Youxian Gongsi Dongjiaozong Xinjiyuan Xueyuan 1999 Nian Gongzuo Baogaoshu* 董教总教育中心非营利有限公司 董教总新纪元学院 1999年工作报告书 [*Dongjiaozong* Higher Learning Center and *Dongjiaozong* New Era College 1999 working report]. Selangor: *Dongjiaozong* Higher Learning Center, 2000.

———. *Dongjiaozong Jiaoyu Zhongxin Feiyingli Youxian Gongsi Dongjiaozong Xinjiyuan Xueyuan 2000 Nian Gongzuo Baogaoshu* 董教总教育中心非营利

有限公司 董教总新纪元学院 2000年工作报告书 [*Dongjiaozong* Higher Learning Center and *Dongjiaozong* New Era College 2000 working report]. Selangor: *Dongjiaozong* Higher Learning Center, 2001.

———. *Dongjiaozong Jiaoyu Zhongxin Feiyingli Youxian Gongsi Dongjiaozong Xinjiyuan Xueyuan 2001 Nian Gongzuo Baogaoshu* 董教总教育中心非营利有限公司 董教总新纪元学院 2001年工作报告书 [*Dongjiaozong* Higher Learning Center and *Dongjiaozong* New Era College 2001 working report]. Selangor: *Dongjiaozong* Higher Learning Center, 2002.

———. *Dongjiaozong Jiaoyu Zhongxin Feiyingli Youxian Gongsi Dongjiaozong Xinjiyuan Xueyuan 2002 Nian Gongzuo Baogaoshu* 董教总教育中心非营利有限公司 董教总新纪元学院 2002年工作报告书 [*Dongjiaozong* Higher Learning Center and *Dongjiaozong* New Era College 2002 working report]. Selangor: *Dongjiaozong* Higher Learning Center, 2003.

———. *Dongjiaozong Jiaoyu Zhongxin Feiyingli Youxian Gongsi Dongjiaozong Xinjiyuan Xueyuan 2003 Nian Gongzuo Baogaoshu* 董教总教育中心非营利有限公司 董教总新纪元学院 2003年工作报告书 [*Dongjiaozong* Higher Learning Center and *Dongjiaozong* New Era College 2003 working report]. Selangor: *Dongjiaozong* Higher Learning Center, 2004.

———. *Dongjiaozong Jiaoyu Zhongxin Feiyingli Youxian Gongsi Dongjiaozong Xinjiyuan Xueyuan 2004 Nian Gongzuo Baogaoshu* 董教总教育中心非营利有限公司 董教总新纪元学院 2004年工作报告书 [*Dongjiaozong* Higher Learning Center and *Dongjiaozong* New Era College 2004 working report]. Selangor: *Dongjiaozong* Higher Learning Center, 2005.

———. *Dongjiaozong Jiaoyu Zhongxin Feiyingli Youxian Gongsi Dongjiaozong Xinjiyuan Xueyuan 2005 Nian Gongzuo Baogaoshu* 董教总教育中心非营利有限公司 董教总新纪元学院 2005年工作报告书 [*Dongjiaozong* Higher Learning Center and *Dongjiaozong* New Era College 2005 working report]. Selangor: *Dongjiaozong* Higher Learning Center, 2006.

———. *Dongjiaozong Jiaoyu Zhongxin Feiyingli Youxian Gongsi Dongjiaozong Xinjiyuan Xueyuan 2006 Nian Gongzuo Baogaoshu* 董教总教育中心非营利有限公司 董教总新纪元学院 2006年工作报告书 [*Dongjiaozong* Higher Learning Center and *Dongjiaozong* New Era College 2006 working report]. Selangor: *Dongjiaozong* Higher Learning Center, 2007.

———. *Dongjiaozong Jiaoyu Zhongxin Feiyingli Youxian Gongsi Dongjiaozong Xinjiyuan Xueyuan 2007 Nian Gongzuo Baogaoshu* 董教总教育中心非营利有限公司 董教总新纪元学院 2007年工作报告书 [*Dongjiaozong* Higher Learning Center and *Dongjiaozong* New Era College 2007 working report]. Selangor: *Dongjiaozong* Higher Learning Center, 2008*a*.

———. *Xinjiyuan Xueyuan Jianxiao Shinian Jinian Zhuanji* 新纪元学院建校十年纪念专辑 1998–2008 [Commemoration magazine of New Era College's tenth anniversary]. Selangor: *Dongjiaozong* Higher Learning Center, 2008*b*.

———. *Dongjiaozong Jiaoyu Zhongxin Feiyingli Youxian Gongsi Dongjiaozong Xinjiyuan Xueyuan 2008 Nian Gongzuo Baogaoshu* 董教总教育中心非营利

有限公司 董教总新纪元学院 2008年工作报告书 [*Dongjiaozong* Higher Learning Center and *Dongjiaozong* New Era College 2008 working report]. Selangor: *Dongjiaozong* Higher Learning Center, 2009.

———. *Dongjiaozong Jiaoyu Zhongxin Feiyingli Youxian Gongsi Dongjiaozong Xinjiyuan Xueyuan 2009 Nian Gongzuo Baogaoshu* 董教总教育中心非营利有限公司 董教总新纪元学院2009年工作报告书 [*Dongjiaozong* Higher Learning Center and *Dongjiaozong* New Era College 2009 working report]. Selangor: *Dongjiaozong* Higher Learning Center, 2010.

———. *Dongjiaozong Jiaoyu Zhongxin Feiyingli Youxian Gongsi Dongjiaozong Xinjiyuan Xueyuan 2010 Nian Gongzuo Baogaoshu* 董教总教育中心非营利有限公司 董教总新纪元学院 2010年工作报告书 [*Dongjiaozong* Higher Learning Center and *Dongjiaozong* New Era College 2010 working report]. Selangor: *Dongjiaozong* Higher Learning Center, 2011.

———. *Dongjiaozong Jiaoyu Zhongxin Feiyingli Youxian Gongsi Dongjiaozong Xinjiyuan Xueyuan 2011 Nian Gongzuo Baogaoshu* 董教总教育中心非营利有限公司 董教总新纪元学院 2011年工作报告书 [*Dongjiaozong* Higher Learning Center and *Dongjiaozong* New Era College 2011 working report]. Selangor: *Dongjiaozong* Higher Learning Center, 2012.

Diamond, Larry Jay. *Developing Democracy: Toward Consolidation*. Baltimore: Johns Hopkins University Press, 1999.

———. "Thinking About Hybrid Regimes". *Journal of Democracy* 13, no. 2 (April 2002): 21–35.

Diani, Mario. "Social Movements and Social Capital: A Network Perspective on Movement Outcomes". *Mobilization: An International Journal* 2, no. 2 (1997): 129–47.

DiMaggio, Paul J. and Walter Powell. "The Iron Cage Revisited: Institutional Isomorphism and Collective Rationality in Organizational Fields". *American Sociological Review* 48 (1983): 147–60.

DNICSSDWC (*Dongjiaozong* National Independent Chinese Secondary School Development Working Committee 董教总全国华文独中发展工作委员会). *Duda Shiliaoji* 独大史料集 [Documentary collection of Merdeka University]. Kuala Lumpur: Merdeka University Berhad, 1993.

———. *Dongjiaozong Quanguo Huawen Duzhong Gongzuo Weiyuanhui Zuzhi Xize* 董教总全国华文独中工作委员会组织细则 [Organizational Rules and Regulations of the Malaysian Independent Chinese Secondary Schools Working Committee]. Office document. Kuala Lumpur: United Chinese School Committees' Association of Malaysia, 1990.

———. *Dongjiaozong Quanguo Huawen Duzhong Gongzuo Weiyuanhui Zuzhi Xize* 董教总全国华文独中工作委员会组织细则 [Organizational Rules and Regulations of the Malaysian Independent Chinese Secondary Schools Working Committee]. Office document. Selangor: United Chinese School Committees' Association of Malaysia, 1995.

———. *Duzhong Jiaogai Chutan: 1996 Nian Tantao Huawen Duzhong Xuezhi, Kecheng Yukaoshi Gexin Fangxiang Gongzuoying Ziliao Huibian* 独中教改初探: 1996年探讨华文独中学制、课程与考试革新方向工作营资料汇编 [Preliminary evaluation of independent Chinese secondary school education reforms: Collection of materials on the Workshop on Education System, Curriculum, and Examination Evaluation and Reforms for Independent Chinese Secondary Schools 1996]. Selangor: United Chinese School Committees' Association of Malaysia, 1997.

———. *Malaixiya Huawen Duli Zhongxue Jiaoyu Gaige Gangling* 马来西亚华文独立中学教育改革纲领 [Guiding principles of educational reform in Malaysian independent Chinese secondary schools]. Selangor: United Chinese School Committees' Association of Malaysia, 2005.

Dongjiaozong 董教总. *Huajiao Gongzuozhe Shouce* 华教工作者手册 [Handbook for Chinese education workers]. Kuala Lumpur: United Chinese School Committees' Association of Malaysia, 1989.

———. *Malaixiya Huawen Xiaoxue Dongshihui Gongzuo Shouce Yangben* 马来西亚华文小学董事会工作手册样本 [Sample of working guidelines for Malaysia Chinese primary schools' school committees]. Selangor: United Chinese School Committees' Association of Malaysia, June 1998 <http://www.djz.edu.my/resource/images/doc/JueXing/zhangcheng02.pdf> (accessed 4 September 2013).

———. "Dongjiaozong Muyu Jiaoyu Xuanyan" 董教总母语教育宣言 [*Dongjiaozong's* declaration on mother tongue education]. Memorandum. 1999.

———. "Xiaoxue Shuli Yinghua Shijian Gaoquanguo Huaxiao Jiazhangshu Dongjiaozong Fandui Huaxiao Yi Yingyu Jiaoshou Shulike De Wendalu" 小学数理英化事件 告全国华小家长书 董教总反对华小以英语教授数理科的问答录 [List of questions and answers on *Dongjiaozong's* opposition on the teaching of Science and Mathematic subjects with English language at Chinese primary schools]. In *Dongzong 50 Nian Tekan: 1954–2004* 董总50年特刊: 1954–2004 [Commemoration magazine of United Chinese School Committees' Association of Malaysia's fiftieth anniversary: 1954–2004], edited by United Chinese School Committees' Association of Malaysia. Selangor: United Chinese School Committees' Association of Malaysia, 2004.

———. *Huaxiao Guanli Jizhi Zhinan* 华小管理机制指南 [Management handbook for Chinese primary schools]. Selangor: United Chinese School Committees' Association of Malaysia, 2006.

———. "Dongjiaozong Yu Mahuagonghui Dui Yixia Shuxiang Huajiao Keti Jinxing Jiaoliu" 董教总与马华公会对以下数项华教课题进行交流 [Discussions between *Dongjiaozong* and Malaysian Chinese Association on the following Chinese education related topics]. Office document. 13 April 2010 <http://www.djz.edu.my/resource/images/pic/wenxian/20100413_DJZ%20&%20MCA.pdf> (accessed 4 September 2013).

DSGM (Department of Statistics, Government of Malaysia). *Buku Tahunan Perangkaan Malaysia 2011* [Yearbook of Statistics Malaysia 2011]. Putrajaya: Department of Statistics, Malaysia, 2011.

Durkheim, Emile Durkheim. *The Rules of Sociological Method*. Chicago: University of Chicago Press, 1938.

Edelman, Marc. "Social Movements: Changing Paradigms and Forms of Politics". *Annual Review of Anthropology* 30 (2001): 285–317.

Escobar, Arturo and Sonia Alvarez, eds. *The Making of Social Movements in Latin America: Identity, Strategy and Democracy*. Boulder: Westview, 1992.

Evans, Peter. "Predatory, Developmental and Other Apparatuses: A Comparative Political Economy Perspective on the Third World State". *Sociological Forum* 4, no. 4 (1989): 561–87.

Farish Noor. *The Hindu Rights Action Force (HINDRAF) of Malaysia: Communitarian Across Borders?* Singapore: S. Rajaratnam School of International Studies, 2008.

Fauwaz Abdul Aziz. "PM: ACA to Be Fully Independent". *Malaysiakini*, 28 April 2001 <http://www.malaysiakini.com/news/81664> (accessed 9 September 2013).

———. "Old Project 'Revived' As MCA Election Goody". *Malaysiakini*, 19 February 2008 <http://www.malaysiakini.com/news/78265> (accessed 2 September 2013).

FCAM (Federation of Chinese Associations Malaysia 马来西亚中华大会堂总会). "Quanguo Huatuan Wenhua Gongzuo Zonggangling" 全国华团文化工作总纲领 [Guiding principals of National Chinese Guilds and Associations Cultural Program]. 22 June 1997.

———. *Malaixiya Huaren Wenhuajie Ziliaoji* 马来西亚华人文化节资料集 [Collection of materials on Malaysian Chinese Cultural Festival]. Kuala Lumpur: Federation of Chinese Associations Malaysia, 2001.

FCKL (Federal Court Kuala Lumpur). *Civil Appeal no. 236 of 1981. Merdeka University Berhad v. Government of Malaysia* <http://ilms.agc.gov.my:88/online/uploaded/fc/[1982]%201%20LNS%201%20MERDEKA%20UNIVERSITY%20BERHAD%20v.%20GOVERNMENT%20OF%20MALAYSIA%20.pdf> (accessed on 11 September 2013).

Fishman, Joshua. "National Languages and Languages of Wider Communication in Developing Nations". *Anthropological Linguistics* 11, no. 4 (April 1969): 111–35.

FLC (Federal Legislative Council). *Educational Policy: Statement of the Federal Government on the Report of the Special Committee on the Implementation of Educational Policy Together with the Report of That Committee*. Kuala Lumpur: Government Press, 1954.

FLCGAM (Fifteen Leading Chinese Guilds and Associations of Malaysia 全国十五华团领导机构). "Yaoqiu Shifang Huayi Lingxiu Beiwanglu" 要求释放华裔领袖备忘录 [Memorandum to demand the release of ethnic Chinese leaders]. Memorandum submitted to Prime Minister Mahathir Mohamad. 11 March 1988.

FM (Federation of Malaya). *Chinese Schools and the Education of Chinese Malayans: The Report of a Mission Invited by the Federation Government to Study the Problem of the Education of Chinese in Malaya*. Kuala Lumpur: Government Press, 1951*a*.

———. *Report of the Committee on Malay Education, Federation of Malaya*. Kuala Lumpur: Government Press, 1951*b*.

———. *Report on the Barnes Report on Malay Education and the Fenn-Wu Report on Chinese Education*. Kuala Lumpur: Government Press, 1951*c*.

———. *Education Ordinance 1952*. Kuala Lumpur: Government Press, 1952*a*.

———. *Report of the Registrar-General on Population, Births, and Deaths*. Kuala Lumpur: Government Press, 1952*b*.

———. *Report of the Special Committee Appointed on the 20th Day of September, 1951*. Kuala Lumpur: Government Press, 1952*c*.

———. *Report of the Special Commission Appointed by the High Commissioner in Council to Consider Ways and Means of Implementing the Policy Outlined in the Education Ordinance 1952, in the Context of Diminishing Financial Resources of the Federation 1954 (Council Paper no. 67 of 1954)*. Kuala Lumpur: Government Press, 1954.

———. *Report by the Chief Minister of the Federation of Malaya on the Baling Talks*. Kuala Lumpur: Government Press, 1956*a*.

———. *Report of the Education Committee, 1956*. Kuala Lumpur: Government Press, 1956*b*.

———. *Education Ordinance 1957*. Kuala Lumpur: Government Press, 1957*a*.

———. *Population Census of the Federation of Malaya (Report no. 14)*. Kuala Lumpur: Government Press, 1957*b*.

———. *Report of the Education Review Committee 1960*. Kuala Lumpur: Government Press, 1960.

———. *Education Act 1961*. Kuala Lumpur: Government Press, 1961.

FMCGA (Federation of Malaya Chinese Guilds Association 马来亚华人行业社团总会). "Quanma Huaren Zhuce Shetuan Daibiao Dahui Zhengqu Gongminquan Xuanyan" 全马华人注册社团代表大会争取公民权宣言 [The Memorandum to Acquire for Citizenship by the National Convention of Chinese Registered Guilds and Associations in Malaya]. 26 April 1956.

Forsyth, Timothy. "Environmental Social Movements in Thailand: How Important is Class?". *Asian Journal of Social Sciences* 29, no. 1 (2001): 35–51.

Foster, George. "The Dyadic Contract: A Model for the Social Structure of a Mexican Peasant Village". *American Anthropologist* 63 (1961): 1173–92.

Foweraker, Joe. *Theorizing Social Movements*. London: Pluto, 1995.

Freedman, Amy. *Political Participation and Ethnic Minorities: Chinese Overseas in Malaysia, Indonesia and the United States*. New York, London: Routledge, 2000.

Fujio, Hara. "The Japanese Occupation of Malaya and the Chinese Community". In *Malaya and Singapore during the Japanese Occupation*, edited by Paul Kratoska. Singapore: Singapore University Press, 1995.

Fukuyama, Francis. "Democracy's Future: The Primacy of Culture". *Journal of Democracy* 6, no. 1, (January 1995): 7–14.

Funston, John. "Malaysia's Tenth Elections: Status Quo, Reformasi or Islamization?". *Contemporary Southeast Asia* 22, no. 1 (April 2000): 23–59.

Furnivall, John Sydenham. *Colonial Policy and Practice: A Comparative Study of Burma and Netherlands India*. London: Cambridge University Press, 1948.

Gamson, William. *The Strategy of Social Protest*. Homewood: Dorsey, 1975.

Ganesan, Narayanan. "Malaysia in 2003: Leadership Transition with a Tall Shadow". *Asian Survey* 44, no. 1 (January–February 2004): 70–77.

GM (Government of Malaysia). *National Language Act 1963*. Kuala Lumpur: Government Press, 1963.

———. *National Educational Policy 1971*. Kuala Lumpur: Jabatan Cetak Kerajaan, 1971*a*.

———. *National Language Act* (Revised) *1971*. Kuala Lumpur: Jabatan Cetak Kerajaan, 1971*b*.

———. *New Economic Policy 1971*. Kuala Lumpur: Jabatan Cetak Kerajaan, 1971*c*.

———. *Parliamentary Debates on the Constitution Amendment Bill 1971*. Kuala Lumpur: Jabatan Cetak Kerajaan, 1971*d*.

———. *Second Malaysia Plan 1971–1975*. Kuala Lumpur: Jabatan Cetak Kerajaan, 1971*e*.

———. *University and University Colleges Act*. Kuala Lumpur: Jabatan Cetak Kerajaan, 1971*f*.

———. *Third Malaysia Plan 1976–1980*. Kuala Lumpur: Jabatan Cetak Kerajaan, 1976.

———. *Cabinet Committee Report on the Implementation of Education Policies*. Kuala Lumpur: Jabatan Cetak Kerajaan, 1979.

———. *Dasar Kebudayaan Negara* 1981 [National Cultural Policy 1981]. Kuala Lumpur: Jabatan Percetakan Negara, 1981*a*.

———. *Fourth Malaysia Plan 1981–1985*. Kuala Lumpur: Jabatan Percetakan Negara, 1981*b*.

———. *Report of the Malaysian General Elections, 1982*. Kuala Lumpur: Jabatan Percetakan Negara, 1983.

———. *Fifth Malaysia Plan 1986–1990*. Kuala Lumpur: Jabatan Percetakan Negara, 1986.

———. *Ke Arah Memelihara Keselamatan Negara* [Towards the protection of National Security]. Kertas Perintah 14, tahun 1988. Kuala Lumpur: Jabatan Percetakan Negara, 1988.

———. *Akta Pendidikan 1990* [Education Act 1990]. Kuala Lumpur: Jabatan Percetakan Negara, 1990.

————. *Sixth Malaysia Plan 1991–1995*. Kuala Lumpur: Jabatan Percetakan Negara, 1991.

————. *Rancangan Malaysia Ketujuh 1996–2005* [Seventh Malaysia Plan 1996–2005]. Kuala Lumpur: Jabatan Percetakan Negara, 1995.

————. *Rancangan Malaysia Kelapan 2001–2005* [Eighth Malaysia Plan 2001–2005]. Putrajaya: Jabatan Percetakan Negara, 2001.

————. *National Language Acts 1963/67*. Kuala Lumpur: Jabatan Percetakan Negara, 2006*a*.

————. *Rancangan Malaysia Kesembilan 2006–2010* [Ninth Malaysia Plan 2006–2010]. Putrajaya: Jabatan Percetakan Negara, 2006*b*.

Goldstone, Jack, ed. *States, Parties and Social Movements*. New York: Cambridge University Press, 2003.

Gomez, Edmund Terence. *Political Business: Corporate Involvement of Malaysian Political Parties*. Queensland: James Cook University of North Queensland Press, 1994.

Gomez, Edmund Terence and K.S. Jomo. *Malaysia's Political Economy: Politics, Patronage and Profits*. Cambridge: Cambridge University Press, 1997.

Goodwin, Jeff, James Jasper, and Jaswinder Khattra. "Caught in a Winding, Snarling Vine: The Structural Bias of Political Process Theory". *Sociological Forum* 14, no. 1 (March 1999): 27–54.

GTACE (Grand Three Associations of Chinese Education 三大机构华文教育中央委员会). "Benbang Huaren Dui Jiaoyu Zongyaoqiu" 本邦华人对教育总要求 [Memorandum of Demands on Chinese Education by Chinese Citizens in the Federation]. *Jiaoshi Zazhi* 教师杂志 [Teacher's Journal] 1, no. 5 (1960): 24–26.

Guangming Daily 光明日报. "Pizhengfu Zeng 9 Duzhong Qianqing Tudi, Yidi Yangxiao Lirun Chong Xingzheng Jingfei" 霹政府赠9独中千顷土地, 以地养校利润充行政经费 [Perak state government donates one thousand hectares of land to nine independent Chinese secondary schools in the state, profits generated from these lands will be used to support school administrative expenses]. 30 August 2009.

Gusfield, Joseph. "The Reflexivity of Social Movements: Collective Behavior and Mass Society Theory Revisited". In *New Social Movements: From Ideology to Identity*, edited by Enrique Larana, Hank Johnston, and Joseph Gusfield. Philadelphia: Temple University Press, 1994.

Hara, Fujio. *Malayan Chinese and China: Conversion in Identity Consciousness 1945–1957*. Tokyo: Institute of Developing Economies, 1997.

Harakah. "Revisiting the Perak Crisis". 23 September 2010.

He, Baogang. *The Democratization of China*. London: Routledge, 1996.

Heinz, John, Edward Laumann, Robert Nelson, and Robert Salisbury. *The Hollow Core: Private Interest in National Policy Making*. Cambridge: Harvard University Press, 1993.

Helmke, Gretchen and Steven Levitsky. *Informal Institutions and Democracy: Lessons from Latin America*. Baltimore: John Hopkins University Press, 2006.

Heng, Pek Koon. "The Social and Ideological Origins of the Malayan Chinese Association". *Journal of Southeast Asian Studies* 14, no. 2 (September 1983): 290–311.

———. *Chinese Politics in Malaysia: The History of the Malaysian Chinese Association*. Singapore: Oxford University Press, 1988.

Hew, Kuan Yau 丘光耀. *Disantiao Daolu: Malaixiya Huaren Zhengzhi Xuanze Pipan* 第三条道路: 马来西亚华人政治选择批判 [The third option: Criticism on the Malaysian Chinese political selection]. Selangor: Diqiucun Wangluo 地球村网络, 1997.

Hilton, Matthew. *Choice and Justice: Forty Years of the Malaysian Consumer Movement*. Penang: Penerbit Universiti Sains Malaysia, 2009.

Hirofumi, Hayashi. "Massacre of Chinese in Singapore and Its Coverage in Postwar Japan". In *New Perspectives on the Japanese Occupation in Malaya and Singapore 1941–1945*, edited by Akashi Yoji and Yoshimura Mako. Singapore: National University of Singapore Press, 2008.

Ho, Khai Leong. "Accountability in the Malaysian Bureaucracy: Politics and Administration". Working Papers 18. Department of Political Science, National University of Singapore, 1988.

———. "Aggrandizement of Prime Minister's Power: The Transformation of the Office of the Prime Minister in Malaysia". *Internationales Asienforum* 23, nos. 1–2 (1992*a*): 227–43.

———. "The Malaysian Chinese Guilds and Associations As Organized Interests in Malaysian Politics". Working Papers. Department of Political Science, National University of Singapore, 1992*b*.

Ho, Kin Chai. *Malaysian Chinese Association: Leadership Under Siege*. Kuala Lumpur: Ho Kin Chai, 1984.

Hodgson, Geoffrey. *The Evolution of Institutions: Agency, Structure and Darwinism, American Institutionalism*. London, New York: Routledge, 2004.

Horowitz, Donald. *Ethnic Groups in Conflict*. Berkeley: University of California Press, 1985.

Huajiaoshenghui Gongweihui Shiliaozhanzu 华教盛会工委会史料展组. *Huaguang Yongyao* 华光永耀 [Glory of Chinese education will shine forever]. Kuala Lumpur: United Chinese School Committees' Association of Malaysia, 1993.

Huang, Guan Qin 黄冠钦. "Malaixiya Jiaoyu Zhengce Yu Huawen Jiaoyu Wenti Zhiyanjiu" 马来西亚教育政策与华文教育问题之研究 [Education policies in Malaysia and its contentions with the Chinese education]. Master's thesis, Chinese Culture University, Taipei, 1984.

Huang, Xue Jing 黄雪晶, ed. *Zhangyashan De Huajiao Gushi* 张雅山的华教故事 [Teo Gah San' contributions to Chinese education]. Selangor: United Chinese School Committees' Association of Malaysia, 2002.

Huang, Zhao Fa 黄招发, ed. *Huajiao Bainian Kankelu: Shalauyue Huawen Zhongxue Fendoushi* 华教百年坎坷路: 砂劳越华文中学奋斗史 [Hundred years of difficult journey of Chinese education: History of Chinese secondary school development in Sarawak]. Sarawak: Law Yew Muk 刘友光, 2004.

Hunt, Scott and Robert Benford. "Identity Talk in the Peace and Justice Movement". *Journal of Contemporary Ethnography* 22 (1994): 488–517.

Huntington, Samuel. *Political Order in Changing Societies.* New Heaven: Yale University Press, 1968.

Hussin Mutalib. *Islam in Malaysia: From Revivalism to Islamic State?* Singapore: Singapore University Press, 1993.

Ingham, Barbara and Colin Simmons, eds. *Development Studies and Colonial Policy.* London, Totowa: Frank Cass, 1987.

Jain, Ravindra K. *Indian Transmigrants: Malaysian and Comparative Essays.* Gurgaon, Haryana, India: Three Essays Collective, 2009.

Jenkins, J. Craig and Charles Perrow. "Insurgency of the Powerless: Farm Worker Movements 1946–1972". *American Sociological Review* 42 (1977): 249–68.

Jennet, Christine and Randal Stewart. "Introduction". In *Politics of the Future: The Role of Social Movements,* edited by Christine Jennett and Randal Stewart. Australia: Macmillan, 1989.

Jesudason, James. "Malaysia: The Syncretic State". In *Political Oppositions in Industrialising Asia,* edited by Garry Rodan. London: Routledge, 1996.

Johan Saravanamuttu. "Malaysian Civil Society–Awakenings?" In *Risking Malaysia: Culture, Politics and Identity,* edited by Maznah Mohamad and Wong Soak Koon. Bangi: Penerbit Universiti Kebangsaan Malaysia, 2001.

Jomo K.S. and Patricia Todd. *Trade Unions and the State in Peninsular Malaysia.* Kuala Lumpur: Oxford University Press, 1994.

Jones, David Martin. *Political Development in Pacific Asia.* Cambridge: Polity, 1997.

Jopple, Christian. *East German Dissidents and the Revolution of 1989: Social Movement in a Leninist Regime.* London: Macmillan, 1995.

K.J. Ratnam. *Communalism and the Political Process in Malaya.* Kuala Lumpur: University of Malaya Press, 1965.

Kerkvliet, Benedict. *The Power of Everyday Politics: How Vietnamese Peasants Transformed National Policy.* Singapore: Institute for Southeast Asian Studies, 2005.

Kessler, Clive S. "Malaysia: Islamic Revivalism and Political Disaffection in a Divided Society". *Southeast Asia Chronicle* 75 (October 1980): 3–11.

Key, Valdimer Orlando. *Politics, Parties and Pressure Groups.* 5th ed. New York: Crowell, 1964.

Keylor, William. *A World of Nations: The International Order Since 1945.* New York: Oxford University Press, 2003.

Khoo, Boo Teik. "Democracy and Authoritarianism in Malaysia Since 1957: Class, Ethnicity and Changing Capitalism". In *Democratization in Southeast and East Asia*, edited by Anek Laothamatas. Singapore: Institute for Southeast Asian Studies, 1997.

―――. *Beyond Mahathir: Malaysian Politics and its Discontents*. London: Zed Books, 2003.

Khor, Jin Kong and Khoo Kay Peng. *Non-Sectarian Politicians in Malaysia: The Case of Parti Gerakan Rakyat Malaysia*. Kuala Lumpur: Trafalgar, 2008.

Kinkwok Daily News 建国日报. "Huawu Jiaoyu Baogaoshu Pingyi" 华巫教育报告书平议 [Reviews on the Chinese and Malay education reports]. 12 July 1951.

Kitschelt, Herbert. "Landscapes of Political Interest Intermediation. Social Movements, Interest Groups and Parties in the Early Twenty-First Century". In *Social Movements and Democracy*, edited by Pedro Ibarra. Houndsmill, Basingstoke: Palgrave-MacMillan, 2003.

Klandermans, Bert. "A Theoretical Framework for Comparisons of Social Movement Participation". *Sociological Forum* 8, no. 3 (September 1993): 383–402.

Klandermans, Bert and Sjoerd Goslinga. "Media Discourse, Movement Publicity and the Generation of Collective Action Frames: Theoretical and Empirical Exercises in Meaning Construction". In *Comparative Perspectives on Social Movements*, edited by Doug McAdam, John McCarthy, and Mayer Zald. Cambridge: Cambridge University Press, 1996.

Klandermans, Bert, Hanspeter Kriesi, and Sidney Tarrow. *From Structure to Action: Comparing Social Movement Research Across Cultures*. Greenwich: JAI, 1988.

KLCSTAAMEC (Kuala Lumpur Chinese Schoolteachers' Association Anniversary Magazine Editing Committee 吉隆坡教师公会纪念特刊编委会). *Jilongpo Jiaoshi Gonghui 1949–1999 Wenxian Ji Shiliao Huibian Jingxi Huiqing Jinian Tekan* 吉隆坡教师公会1949–1999文献及史料汇编—金禧会庆纪念特刊 [Commemoration magazine of Kuala Lumpur Chinese Schoolteachers Association's fiftieth anniversary with collection of articles and materials from 1949 to 1999]. Kuala Lumpur: Kuala Lumpur Chinese Schoolteachers Association, 2000.

Knight, Jack. *Institutions and Social Conflict*. New York: Cambridge University Press, 1992.

Koh, Tsu Koon 许子根. *Xuzigen Boshi Canzheng Sinian Yanlun Xuanji Zhiyi* 许子根博士参政四年言论选集之一 [Selection of speeches from Dr. Koh Tsu Koon's first four years in politics 1]. Penang: Syarikat Perniagaan Toh and Tan, 1986.

Kok, Wah Ying 郭华盈. "Dongxiao Fengbo Jieshu, Jianli Guanli Shoufei Jizhi Dujue Lanquan" 董校风波结束, 建立管理收费机制杜绝滥权 [The end of the controversy between school committee and school principal, establishment of financial management institution to prevent corruption in the future]. *Merdeka Review* 独立新闻在线, 18 March 2006 <http://www.merdekareview.com/news.php?n=1376> (accessed 4 September 2013).

Koopmans, Ruud. "Movements and Media: Selection Processes and Evolutionary Dynamics in the Public Sphere". *Theory and Society* 33, no. 3/4 (June–August 2004): 367–91.

Kriesi, Hanspeter, Ruud Koopmans, and Jan Duyvendak. *The Politics of New Social Movements in Western Europe: A Comparative Analysis.* Minneapolis: University of Minnesota Press, 1995.

Ku, Hung Ting 古鸿廷. *Jiaoyu Yu Rentong: Malaixiya Huawen Zhongxue Jiaoyu Zhi Yanjiu, 1945–2000* 教育与认同: 马来西亚华文中学教育之研究, 1945–2000 [Education and identity: Research on Chinese secondary schools' education in Malaysia, 1945–2000]. Xiamen: Xiamen University Press 厦门大学出版社, 2003.

Kua, Kia Soong. *The New Era College Controversy and the Betrayal of Dong Jiao Zong.* Kuala Lumpur: Oriengroup, 2009.

Kwongwahyitpoh 光华日报. "Xuexiao Shitang Zhaobiao Zhuquan Jiaoxianjiaoju, Duqianhuan Jiangwei Huaxiao Zhenghui Quanyi" 学校食堂招标主权交县教局, 杜乾焕将为华校争回权益 [Surrender of rental rights of school canteen to the district education department, Toh Kin Woon will retrieve these rights for the Chinese schools]. 22 September 2004.

———. "Mahanshun: Pi 9 Duzhong Yidi Yangxiao, Zhouzhengfu Bokuan Jiang Shouhui" 马汉顺: 霹9独中以地养校, 州政府拨款将收回 [Ma Han Shun: Nine independent Chinese secondary schools in Perak will sustain the school expenses through profits from land, the state government will revert financial aid]. 21 August 2010.

Lai, Suat Yan. "Participation of the Women's Movement in Malaysia: The 1999 General Election". In *Civil Society in Southeast Asia*, edited by Lee Hock Guan. Denmark and Singapore: Nordic Institute of Asian Studies and Institute for Southeast Asian Studies, 2004.

Lai, Xiao Jian 廖小健. "Malaixiya Liangxianzhi Chubu Xingcheng" 马来西亚两线制初步形成 [The formation of dual coalition system in Malaysia]. *Dangdai Yatai* 当代亚太 [Contemporary Asia Pacific] 4, no. 4 (2001): 19–23.

Laothamatas, Anek. "Development and Democratization: A Theoretical Introduction with Reference to the Southeast Asian and East Asian Cases". In *Democratization in Southeast and East Asia*, edited by Anek Laothamatas. Singapore: Institute for Southeast Asian Studies, 1997.

LCHR (Lawyers Committee for Human Rights). *Malaysia: Assault on the Judiciary.* New York: Lawyers Committee for Human Rights, 1990.

Lee, C.H. Julian. *Islamization and Activism in Malaysia.* Singapore: Institute for Southeast Asian Studies, 2010.

Lee, Kam Hing. "The Political Position of the Chinese in Post-Independence Malaysia". In *The Chinese Diaspora: Selected Essays* 2, edited by Wang Ling Chi and Wang Gung Wu. Singapore: Times Academic, 1998.

Lee, L.M. Raymond. "Patterns of Religious Tension in Malaysia". *Asian Survey* 28, no. 4 (April 1988): 400–18.

———. "The State, Religious Nationalism and Ethnic Rationalization in Malaysia". *Ethnic and Racial Studies* 13, no. 4 (October 1990): 482–502.

Lee, Leong Sze 利亮时. "Malaixiya Huawen Jiaoyu De Shanbian 1945–1970" 马来西亚华文教育的嬗变 1945–1970 [Transformation of Chinese education in Malaysia 1945–1970]. Master's thesis, National University of Singapore, 1999.

Lee, Phun Koon 李亚遨. "Linlianyu: Xiaoxiao De Kaoju" 林连玉: 小小的考据 [Lim Lian Geok: Some criticism]. In *Zhuhun Linlianyu Xubian* 族魂林连玉续编 [Soul of Malaysian Chinese Lim Lian Geok continuation edition], edited by Lee Phun Koon. Selangor: Lim Lian Geok Cultural Development Center 林连玉基金会, 2005.

———. *Wanjie Piaoxiang Xubian* 晚节飘香续编 [Biography of Sim Mow Yu 2]. Selangor: United Chinese Schoolteachers' Association of Malaysia, 2006.

Lee, Yip Lim 李业霖. *Nanyang Daxue Shilunji* 南洋大学史论集 [Collection of articles on Nanyang University]. Selangor: Nanyang University Alumni Association of Malaya 马来亚南大校友会, 2004.

Leo, Suryadinata. "Ethnic Chinese Political Participation and the Revival of Chinese Culture: Post-Suharto Developments". In *Chinese Diaspora Since Admiral Zhenghe*, edited by Leo Suryadinata. Singapore: Chinese Heritage Centre, 2007.

Leong, Choon Heng and Tan Siew Hoey. "Malaysia: Social Development, Poverty Reduction and Economic Transformation". In *Development with a Human Face: Experiences in Social Achievements and Economic Growth*, edited by Santosh Mehrotra and Richard Jolly. Oxford: Oxford University Press, 1997.

Levitsky, Steven and Lucan Way. "The Rise of Competitive Authoritarianism". *Journal of Democracy* 13, no. 2 (April 2002): 51–65.

Lew, Bon Hoi 廖文辉. *Huaxiao Jiaozong Ji Qirenwu (1951–2005)* 华校教总及其人物 (1951–2005) [The United Chinese Schoolteachers' Association of Malaysia and its activists (1951–2005)]. Selangor: United Chinese Schoolteachers' Association of Malaysia, 2006.

Lew, Bon Hoi and Loot Ting Yee 陆庭谕, eds. *Shenmuyu Shiji Xinian* 沈慕羽事迹系年 [Life story of Sim Mow Yu]. Kuala Lumpur: United Chinese Schoolteachers' Association of Malaysia, 1997.

Lijphart, Arend. "Typologies of Democratic Systems". *Comparative Political Studies* 1 (1968): 3–43.

———. "Comparative Politics and the Comparative Method". *American Political Science Review* 65, no. 3 (September 1971): 682–93.

———. "Non-Majoritarian Democracy: A Comparison of Federal and Consociational Theories". *Publius* 15, no. 2 (Spring 1985): 3–15.

———. *Thinking About Democracy*. London and New York: Routledge, 2008.

Lim, Guo An 林国安. "Malaixiya Huawen Duli Zhongxue Kecheng Mubiao Yanjiu" 马来西亚华文独立中学课程目标研究 [Study on the curriculum objectives of independent Chinese secondary schools in Malaysia]. *Malaixiya*

Huawen Jiaoyu 马来西亚华文教育 [Chinese education in Malaysia] 2 (December 2004): 6–19.

Lim, Hong Siang 林宏祥. "Jingwu Dongshizhang Jubao Xiaozhang Juankuan Cunru Buzhiming Hukou" 精武董事长举报校长捐款存入不知名户口 [Chairman of Chen Moh's school committee reveals that the school principal deposited donations into an unknown bank account]. *Merdeka Review*, 24 November 2005 <http://www.merdekareview.com/news.php?n=122> (accessed 4 September 2013).

———. "Jingwu Huaxiao Dongshihui Yu Xiaozhang De Jiaoli" 精武华小董事会与校长的角力 [Disputes between Chen Moh's school committee and school principal]. *Merdeka Review*, 3 March 2006*a* <http://www.merdekareview.com/news_v2.php? n=1287> (accessed 4 September 2013).

———. "Xiaozhang Tanwu Zhengduan: Jianyan Zhongwen Baozhang Zhenmianmu" 校长贪污争端: 检验中文报章真面目 [Disputes on corrupted school principal: The truth about Chinese press]. *Merdeka Review*, 9 March 2006*b* <http://www.merdekareview.com/news_v2.php?n=1327> (accessed 4 September 2013).

———. "Sizhang Zongzhi Erwan Zhipiao Xialuo Buming, Jingwu Qiongzhui Bushe Bizou Jiaoyu Juzhang?" 四张总值二万支票下落不明, 精武穷追不舍逼走教育局长? [Unable to explain the whereabouts of four cheques with total sum of RM20,000, pressure from Chen Moh forces the departure of the Head of the Education Department]. *Merdeka Review*, 19 June 2006*c* <http://www.merdekareview.com/ news.php?n=1954> (accessed 4 September 2013).

Lim, Kit Siang. "Call on Malaysian Chinese to be Aware of New Election Gimmicks Like Merger or Joint Councils to Bring About a Repeat of the 1982 General Elections Results". Speech. 10 March 1985 <http://bibliotheca.limkitsiang.com/1985/03/10/call-on-malaysian-chinese-to-be-aware-of-new-election-gimmicks-like-'merger'-or-'joint-councils'-to-bring-about-a-repeat-of-the-1982-general-elections-results/> (accessed 9 September 2013).

———. "Call on Tung Chiau Chung Officials Responsible for the 1982 Strategy of 'Attack into the Barisan Nasional to Recrify Barisan Nasional' to Admit the Grave Error of Their Decision, and to Direct these like Ker Choo Ting, Koh Tsu Koon and Others Who joined Gerakan on This Mission to Withdraw from Barisan or to Lose All Forms of Tung Chiau Chung support". Speech. 28 May 1986 <http://bibliotheca.limkitsiang.com/1986/05/28/call-on-tungchiau-chung-officials-responsible-for-the-1982-strategy-of-'attack-into-the-barisan-nasional-to-recrify-barisan-nasional'-to-admit-the-grave-error-of-their-decision-and-t/> (accessed 9 September 2013).

———. "Two-Coalition System to Crush the Monopoly of Political Power and Save Democracy in Malaysia". Speech. 18 August 1990 <http://bibliotheca.limkitsiang.com/1990/08/18/two-coalition-system-to-crush-the-monopoly-of-political-power-and-save-democracy-in-malaysia/> (accessed 9 September 2013).

Lim, Lian Geok 林连玉. "Wo Weishenme Shiwang" 我为什么失望 [Why I was disappointed]. *Jiaoshi Zazhi* 教师杂志 [Teacher's Journal] 1, no. 5 (1960): 3.

———. *Huiyi Pianpianlu* 回忆片片录 [My memoir]. Kuala Lumpur: United Chinese Schoolteachers' Association of Malaysia, 1965.

———. *Fengyu Shibanian Shangji* 风雨十八年上集 [Eighteen years of challenges 1]. Kuala Lumpur: United Chinese Schoolteachers' Association of Malaysia, 1988.

———. "Linlianyu Gongminquan An" 林连玉公民权案 [Civil rights of Lim Lian Geok]. Kuala Lumpur: Lim Lian Geok Cultural Development Center, 1989.

———. *Fengyu Shibanian Xiaji* 风雨十八年下集 [Eighteen years of challenges 2]. Kuala Lumpur: United Chinese Schoolteachers' Association of Malaysia, 1990.

———. *Linliang Gongan* 林梁公案 [Controversies between Lim Lian Geok and Liang Yu Gao]. Kuala Lumpur: Lim Lian Geok Cultural Development Center, 1998.

Lin, Hua Dong 林华东. "Zouxiang Shiji De Dongnanya Huawen Jiaoyu Yu Jiaoxue" 走向21世纪的东南亚华文教育与教学 [Chinese education and teachings in Southeast Asia towards the Twenty-First Century]. *Journal of Quanzhou Normal College* 泉州师范学院学报 18, no. 5 (2000): 35.

Lin, Wu Cong 林武聪 Wang Zong Lin 王宗麟, and Xu De Fa 许德发, eds. *Xiankai Huaxiao De Ditan: Xiaozhang Shetan Zhengyiji* 掀开华小的地毯: 校长涉贪争议集 [Controversy over alleged corruption among Chinese Primary Schools' principals]. Kuala Lumpur: Suirenshi 燧人氏事业, 2006.

Linz, Juan José. "Totalitarian and Authoritarian Regimes". In *Handbook of Political Science* 3, edited by Fred Greenstein and Nelson Polsby. Reading: Addison-Wesley, 1975.

Liow, Joseph. "The Politics Behind Malaysia's Eleventh General Election". *Asian Survey* 45, no. 6 (November-December 2005): 907–30.

Lipsky, Michael. "Protest As a Political Resource". *American Political Science Review* 62 (1968): 1144–58.

Liu, Bo Kui 刘伯奎. *Xingtan Ershinian: Zhongzhong Ershinian* 杏坛二十年: 中中二十年 [Twenty years at Zhonghua High School]. Singapore: South Seas Society 南洋学会, 1986.

Loh, Kok Wah Francis. *The Politics of Chinese Unity in Malaysia: Reform and Conflict in the Malaysian Chinese Association 1971–1973*. Singapore: Institute for Southeast Asian Studies, 1982.

———. "Chinese New Villages". In *The Chinese in Malaysia*, edited by Lee K.H. and C.B. Tan. Kuala Lumpur: Oxford University Press, 2000.

———. *Old vs. New Politics in Malaysia: State and Society in Transition*. Petaling Jaya: Strategic Information and Research Development Centre and Aliran, 2009.

Loh, Kok Wah Francis and Johan Saravanamuttu, eds. *New Politics in Malaysia*. Singapore: Institute for Southeast Asian Studies, 2003.

Loh, Kok Wah Francis and Khoo Boo Teik, eds. *Democracy in Malaysia: Discourses and Practices*. Surrey: Curzon, 2002.

Loh, Kok Wah Francis, Phang Chung Nyap, and Johan Saravanamuttu. *The Chinese Community and Malaysia-China Ties: Elite Perspectives*. Tokyo: Institute of Developing Economies, 1981.

Lomperis, Timothy. *From People's War to People's Rule: Insurgency, Intervention and the Lessons of Vietnam*. Chapel Hill: University of North Carolina Press, 1996.

Lounsbury, Michael and Bill Kaghan. "Organizations, Occupations and the Structuration of Work". *Research in the Sociology of Work* 10 (2001): 25–51.

Lyon, Margo. "The Dakwah Movement in Malaysia". *Review of Indonesian and Malayan Affairs* 13, no. 2 (1979): 34–45.

Mackie, Jamie A.C. *Konfrontasi: The Indonesia-Malaysia Dispute 1963–1966*. Kuala Lumpur: Oxford University Press, 1974.

Mainwaring, Scott. "Introduction: Democratic Accountability in Latin America". In *Democratic Accountability in Latin America*, edited by Scott Mainwaring and Christoper Welna. Oxford: Oxford University Press, 2003.

Makmor Tumen. *Wanita di Malaysia: Perjuangan Menuntut Hak* [Women in Malaysia: Struggles for rights]. Kuala Lumpur: Penerbit Universiti Malaya, 2006.

Malay Mail. "Tan Siew Sin: It Would Be Easier for Hell to Freeze Over Than for Merdeka University to Be Established under the Prevailing Circumstances in Malaysia". 17 April 1969.

Malaysiakini, "Motaixi Changzu 'Duzhong Jiaoyu Lianmeng', Dongzongping: Tu Cuanduo Huajiao Lingdaoquan" 莫泰熙倡组"独中教育联盟", 董总抨: 图篡夺华教领导权 [Bock Tai Hee proposes the establishment of the Independent Chinese Secondary Schools Education Alliance, United Chinese School Committee's Association of Malaysia criticises it as an attempt to overtake the leadership of the Chinese education movement]. 2 October 2009 <http://www.malaysiakini.com/news/114087> (accessed on 3 November 2013).

March, James and Johan Olsen. "The New Institutionalism: Organizational Factors in Political Life". *American Political Science Review* 78 (1984): 734–49.

Marsden, Peter. "Brokerage Behavior in Restricted Exchange Networks". In *Social Structure and Network Analysis*, edited by Peter Marsden and Nan Lin. Beverly Hills: Sage, 1982.

Marsh, Ian. "Introduction". In *Democratization, Governance and Regionalism in East and Southeast Asia: A Comparative Study*, edited by Ian Marsh. New York: Routledge, 2006.

Mason, Frederic. *The Schools of Malaya*. Singapore: Donald Moore, 1954.

Mauzy, Diane. *Barisan Nasional: Coalition Government in Malaysia*. Kuala Lumpur: Marican and Sons, 1983a.

———. "The 1982 General Elections in Malaysia: A Mandate for Change?". *Asian Survey* 23, no. 4 (April 1983b): 497–517.

Mauzy, Diane and Robert Stephen Milne. "The Mahathir Administration in Malaysia: Discipline through Islam". *Pacific Affairs* 56, no. 4 (Winter 1983): 617–48.

Maznah Mohamad. "The Contest for Malay Votes in 1999: UMNO's Most Historic Challenge?". In *New Politics in Malaysia*, edited by Loh Kok Wah Francis and Johan Saravanamuttu. Singapore: Institute for Southeast Asian Studies, 2003.

————. *Paradoxes of State Islamization in Malaysia: Routinization of Religious Charisma and the Secularization of the Syariah*. Singapore: Asia Research Institute, 2009.

MCACEB (Malaysian Chinese Association Central Education Bureau). "Mahua Gonghui Quanguo Huaxiao Xiaodi Diaocha Baogao" 马华公会全国华小校地调查报告 [Report on Chinese primary schools' land ownership status, a national survey conducted by Malaysian Chinese Association]. *Sinchew Daily*, 16 October 2008.

McAdam, Doug. *Political Process and the Development of Black Insurgency, 1930–1970*. Chicago: University of Chicago Press, 1982.

————. "The Framing Function of Movement Tactics: Strategic Dramaturgy in the American Civil Rights Movement". In *Comparative Perspectives on Social Movements: Political Opportunities, Mobilizing Structures and Cultural Framings*, edited by Doug McAdam, John McCarthy, and Mayer Zald. Cambridge: Cambridge University Press, 1996.

McAdam, Doug, John McCarthy, and Mayer Zald, eds. *Comparative Perspectives on Social Movements: Political Opportunities, Mobilizing Structures and Cultural Framings*. Cambridge: Cambridge University Press, 1996.

McAdam, Doug, Sidney Tarrow, and Charles Tilly. "Toward An Integrated Perspective on Social Movements and Revolution". In *Comparative Politics: Rationality, Culture and Structure*, edited by Mark Irving Lichbach and Alan Zuckerman. New York: Cambridge University Press, 1997.

————. *Dynamics of Contention*. New York: Cambridge University Press, 2001.

McCarthy, John, Jackie Smith, and Mayer Zald. *The Trend of Social Movements in America: Professionalization and Resource Mobilization*. Morristown: General Learning, 1973.

McCarthy, John and Mayer Zald. "Resource Mobilization and Social Movements: A Partial Theory". *American Journal of Sociology* 82 (1977): 1212–41.

MCOEAC (Malaysian Chinese Organisations' Election Appeals Committee 马来西亚华人社团大选诉求委员会). *Malaixiya Huaren Shetuan Daxuan Suqiu Ziliao Huibian* 1999–2001 *Dier Fence* 马来西亚华人社团大选诉求资料汇编 1999–2001 第二分册 [Collection of documents on the Malaysian Chinese Organisations' Election Appeals Committee 1999–2001 vol. 2]. Selangor: United Chinese School Committees' Association of Malaysia, 2002.

Means, Gordon. "Public Policy toward Religion in Malaysia". *Pacific Affairs* 51 (Fall 1978): 384–405.

————. *Malaysian Politics: The Second Generation*. Singapore: Oxford University Press, 1991.

Melucci, Alberto. "The New Social Movements: A Theoretical Approach". *Social Science Information* 19, no. 2 (1980): 199–266.

————. "The Symbolic Challenge of Contemporary Movements". *Social Research* 52 (1985): 789–816.

————. *Nomads of the Present: Social Movements and Individual Needs in Contemporary Society*. London: Hutchinson Radius, 1989.

————. *Challenging Codes, Collective Action in the Information Age*. Cambridge: Cambridge University Press, 1996.

MEM (Ministry of Education Malaysia). *Educational Statistics of Malaysia 1974/1975*. Kuala Lumpur: Dewan Bahasa dan Pustaka, 1978.

————. *Draf Buku Panduan Rancangan Integrasi Murid-Murid* [Draft guidebook for Student Integration Program]. Kuala Lumpur: Kementerian Pelajaran Malaysia, 1985*a*.

————. *Sukatan Pelajaran Sekolah Rendah 1983* [Integrated Curriculum for Primary Schools 1983]. Kuala Lumpur: Dewan Bahasa dan Pustaka, 1985*b*.

————. *Educational Statistics of Malaysia 1980–1985*. Kuala Lumpur: Dewan Bahasa dan Pustaka, 1986*a*.

————. *Perangkaan Pendidikan Malaysia 1986* [Educational Statistics of Malaysia 1986]. Kuala Lumpur: Dewan Bahasa dan Pustaka, 1986*b*.

————. *Perangkaan Pendidikan Malaysia 1987* [Educational Statistics of Malaysia 1987]. Kuala Lumpur: Dewan Bahasa dan Pustaka, 1990.

————. *Perangkaan Pendidikan Malaysia 1991* [Educational Statistics of Malaysia 1991]. Putrajaya: Ministry of Education Malaysia, 1991.

————. *Sekolah Wawasan: Konsep dan Pelaksanaan* [Vision School: Concepts and implementations]. Kuala Lumpur: Jabatan Pelajaran Malaysia, 1995.

————. *Perangkaan Pendidikan Malaysia 2007* [Malaysia Educational Statistics 2007]. Putrajaya: Ministry of Education Malaysia, 2007.

————. *Perangkaan Pendidikan Malaysia 2008* [Malaysia Educational Statistics 2008]. Putrajaya: Ministry of Education Malaysia, 2008.

————. *Perangkaan Pendidikan Malaysia 2009* [Malaysia Educational Statistics 2009]. Putrajaya: Ministry of Education Malaysia, 2009.

————. *Perangkaan Pendidikan Malaysia 2010* [Malaysia Educational Statistics 2010]. Putrajaya: Ministry of Education Malaysia, 2010.

————. *Perangkaan Pendidikan Malaysia 2011* [Malaysia Educational Statistics 2011]. Putrajaya: Ministry of Education Malaysia, 2011.

Merdeka Review. "Motaixi Qingchu Biaoming Buliuren, Yangyungui: Buxuyue Nai Changwei Jueding" 莫泰熙清楚表明不留任, 杨云贵: 不续约乃常委决定 [Bock Tai Hee indicates that he will not stay, Yang Yun Gui says that the decision of not renewing Bock's contract was made by the Standing Committee]. 20 October 2006 <http://www.merdekareview.com/news.php?n=2799> (accessed 2 September 2013).

———. "Liangxianzhi Fazhan Shi Quanmin Shengli, Dongjiaozong Ti Qida Jiaoyu Yaoqiu" 两线制发展是全民胜利, 董教总提七大教育要求 [The development of dual coalition system is a victory for all people, *Dongjiaozong* proposes seven educational demands]. 14 March 2008 <http://www. merdekareview.com/news_v2.php?n=6250> (accessed 2 September 2013).

———. "Bada Huatuan Yu Hashanamo Jiaoliu, Yizhi Tongyi Huifu Muyu Jiaoshuli" 八大华团与哈山阿末交流, 一致同意恢复母语教数理 [Eight Chinese guilds and associations exchange ideas with Hassan Ahmad and mutually agree to restore the teachings of Mathemathic and Science subjects using mother tongue]. 13 March 2009 <http://www.merdekareview.com/news/ n/9067.html> (accessed 2 September 2013).

Meyer, David and Sidney Tarrow. "A Movement Society: Contentious Politics for a New Century". In *The Social Movement Society: Contentious Politics for a New Century*, edited by David Meyer and Sidney Tarrow. Oxford: Rowman and Littlefield, 1998.

Migdal, Joel. *Strong Societies and Weak States*. Princeton: Princeton University Press, 1988.

Milne, Robert Stephen. "Malaysia". *Asian Survey* 4, no. 2 (February 1964): 695–701.

———. "Malaysia and Singapore, 1975". *Asian Survey* 16, no. 2, part II (February 1976): 186–92.

Milne, Robert Stephen and Diane Mauzy. *Malaysian Politics under Mahathir*. London: Routledge, 1999.

MLHGSBJZ (Malaiya Lianhebang Huawen Gaoji Shifan Biye Jiaoshi Zhigonghui 马来亚联合邦华文高级师范毕业教师职工会). *Gaoshi Sishinian (1949–1989) Malaiya Lianhebang Huawen Gaoji Shifan Biye Jiaoshi Zhigonghui Jinian Tekan* 高师四十年 (1949–1989) 马来亚联合邦华文高级师范毕业教师职工会纪念特刊 [Commemoration magazine of Senior Normal Graduate Schoolteachers Association's fortieth anniversary (1949–1989)]. Kuala Lumpur: Malaiya Lianhebang Huawen Gaoji Shifan Biye Jiaoshi Zhigonghui, 1990.

Mohamad Abu Bakar. "Islamic Revivalism and the Political Process in Malaysia". *Asian Survey* 21, no. 10 (October 1981): 1040–59.

Mohamed Salleh Abas. *May Day for Justice: The Lord President's Version*. Kuala Lumpur: Magnus Books, 1989a.

———. *The Role of the Independent Judiciary*. Kuala Lumpur: Promarketing, 1989b.

Morrill, Calvin. *The Executive Way: Conflict Management in Corporations*. Chicago: University Chicago Press, 1995.

MPSSMCM (Majlis Pengetua Sekolah-Sekolah Menengah Conforming Malaysia 全国华中校长理事会), ed. *Malaixiya Guominxing Huawen Zhongxue Zhinan* 马来西亚国民型华文中学指南 [Directory of Confirming Chinese Secondary Schools in Malaysia]. Kuala Lumpur: Majlis Pengetua Sekolah-Sekolah Menengah Conforming Malaysia, 2006.

MU (Malayan Union). *Annual Report on Education in the Malayan Union for the Period 1st April 1946 to 31st December 1946.* Council Paper no. 53 of 1946. Kuala Lumpur: Government Press, 1947.

MUB (Merdeka University Berhad 独大有限公司). "Cheng Zuigaoyuanshou Qingqiu Enzhun Chuangban Duli Daxue Qingyuanshu" 呈最高元首请求恩准创办独立大学请愿书 [Petition Submitted to Yang Dipertuan Agong of Malaysia for Incorporation Order for the Establishment of Merdeka University]. 30 January 1978*a*.

———. *Duda Wengaoji* 独大文告集 [Collection of articles on Merdeka University]. Kuala Lumpur: Merdeka University Berhad, 1978*b*.

Nanyangshangpao 南洋商报, "Ping Baien Weiyuanhui Baogaoshu" 评拜恩委员会报告书 [Review of the Barnes Report]. 13 June 1951.

———. "Huawen Jiaoyu Baogaoshu Zhengyi De Zhuzhang" 华文教育报告书正义的主张 [The rightful position of the Chinese Education Report]. 9 July 1951.

———. "Lun Muyu Jiaoyu De Zhongyaoxing" 论母语教育的重要性 [Discussion on the importance of mother tongue education]. 19 July 1951.

———. "Zailun Huawen Ying Liewei Guanfang Yuwen" 再论华文应列为官方语文 [Another discussion on instating Chinese language as official language]. 20 October 1954.

———. "Fangyan Jiaoyu Yu Guomin Jiaoyu" 方言教育与国民教育 [Vernacular and national education]. 23 October 1954.

———. "Zhengyi Yongqi, Zuihou Jueze" 正义勇气, 最后抉择 [The final option]. 10 November 1954.

———. "Wei Weihu Huawen Jiaoyu Er Fendou" 为维护华文教育而奋斗 [Striving to protect the Chinese education]. 15 November 1954.

———. "Shoujian Zonghe Xiaoxue Kaishi Shangke" 首间综合小学开始上课 [First integrated school starts operation]. 22 August 1985.

———. "Sanjiehe Yu Liangge Zhenxian Gainian Shutu Tonggui, Junwei Kangju Zhongzu Zhuyi, Dongzong Zhuxi Linhuangsheng" 三结合与两个阵线概念殊途同归, 均为抗拒种族主义, 董总主席林晃升 [United Chinese School Committees' Association of Malaysia Chairman Lim Fong Seng: The alliance of three and the dual coalition shares the goal of opposing racism]. 1 September 1986.

———. "57 Jian Huaxiao Quanmian Bake, Binjiapoxuezhi Yu Sanwan Xuesheng Wei Shangke" 57间华小全面罢课, 槟甲坡雪直逾三万学生未上课 [Fifty-seven Chinese primary schools participate in the protest, more than 30,000 students in Penang, Malacca, Perlis, Selangor, and Kuala Lumpur skip school]. 16 October 1987.

———. "Xingdongdang, Siliu, Huatuan Quxiang Dajiehe, Liuhuajiao Renshi Cheng Huojian Shangzhen" 行动党, 四六, 华团趋向大结合, 六华教人士乘火箭上阵 [Unity of Democratic Action Party, Semangat 46, and the

Chinese guilds and associations, six Chinese educationalists will contest in the general elections under Democratic Action Party]. 26 July 1990.

————. "Xinshengdai De Zhengzhi Linian He Shijian" 新生代的政治理念和实践 [Political ideas of the new generation and its implementation]. 1 August 1990.

————. "Lianhe Xuanyan Xia Zhengzhi Daohuoxian, Huatuan Canxuan Yijian Fenqi" 联合宣言下争执导火线, 华团参选意见分歧 [Disputes over joint manifesto, conflict of opinions on the participation of Chinese guilds and associations in general elections]. 3 August 1990a.

————. "Pidonglianhui Yu Zhouduzhong Gongweihui, Mingtian Zhaokai Tebie Lianxi Huiyi Shang Huajiao Renshi Canzheng Xuanshi" 霹董联会与州独中工委会, 明天召开特别联席会议商华教人士参政参选事 [Perak Chinese School Committees' Association and Perak State Independent Chinese Secondary Schools Working Committee will hold a special joint meeting tomorrow to discuss the issue of Chinese educationalists' participation in politics]. 3 August 1990b.

————. "Quanguo Dongzong Fuzhuxi: Gongping Duidai Huajiao Canxuan Renshi" 全国董总副主席: 公平对待华教参选人士 [Deputy chairman of United Chinese School Committees' Association of Malaysia: Treat the Chinese educationalists who participated in general elections with justice]. 3 August 1990c.

————. "Zantong Benbao Shelun Kanfa, Dui Huajiao Renshi Canxuan Wenti Bufang Yi Kaifang Xionghuai Kandai—Chensongsheng Lushi" 赞同本报社论看法, 对华教人士参选问题不妨以开放胸怀看待—陈松生律师 [Chen Song Seng agrees with the opinions posted in *Nanyangshangpao* on being open to the participation of Chinese educationalists in politics]. 4 August 1990.

————. "Huajiao Jigou Buzhanran Zhengzhi Secai: Dongjiaozong Chengyuan Canxuan Xucizhi" 华教机构不沾染政治色彩: 董教总成员参选须辞职 [Chinese education institutions will not associate with politics: *Dongjiaozong* members must resign]. 5 August 1990.

————. "Linhuangsheng Biaoming Yuan Canxuan, Dongzong Zhuxi Fenxi Xingshi Zhi Zhizhengdang Taiqiang, Huajiao Renshi Jiaru Fanzhen Keqi Junheng Zuoyong" 林晃升表明愿参选, 董总主席分析形势指执政党太强, 华教人士加入反阵可起均衡作用 [Lim Fong Seng announces his willingness to compete in the general elections, the current ruling regime is too powerful, Chinese educationalists may help to balance the situation by joining the opposition]. 6 August 1990.

————. "Laijie Daxuan Shiyu Liutaisheng Jiangzai Fanduidang Qixia Chuzhan" 来届大选十余留台生将在反对党旗下出战 [About ten Taiwanese university graduates will participate in the upcoming general elections as candidates of the opposition parties]. 7 August 1990.

————. "Senzhonghua Gongshang Lianzong Shuli Huizhang Lizun Renwei, Ruowei Canxuan Er Chanzheng, Shexian Mou Zhengzhi Sili" 森中华工商联总署

理会长李俊认为, 若为参选而参政, 涉嫌谋政治私利 [Negeri Sembilan Chinese Chamber of Commerce Deputy President Li Zun thinks that those who participated in the general elections in order to enter politics are highly suspicious of seeking personal advantages]. 8 August 1990.

———. "Qian Dongzong Zhixingmishu Liwanqian, Juchuan Jue Jingxuan Bajili Guoxi" 前董总执行秘书李万千, 据传决竞选峇吉里国席 [Former United Chinese School Committees' Association of Malaysia Chief Executive Officer Lee Ban Chen may be contesting at Bakri parliamentary constituency]. 9 August 1990.

———. "Jiaoyu Xieshang Lishihui Mingdan Puguang Zhengdang Shou Yao Dong Jiao Zong Shang Bang" 教育协商理事会名单曝光: 12政党受邀董教总上榜 [Twelve political parties are invited to participate in *Dongjiaozong*'s Education Negotiation Committee]. 18 August 1990.

———. "Linhuangsheng Ren Xingdongdang Guwen, Liwanqian Dang Quanguo Fuzhuxi" 林晃升任行动党顾问, 李万千当全国副主席 [Lim Fong Seng appointed as Democratic Action Party advisor and Lee Ban Chen as the vice president]. 20 August 1990.

———. "Huazi Yijiao Wenti Xuehuatang You Juanru Jiufen, Linyujing Cheng Douzheng Jiaodian" 华资移交问题雪华堂又卷入纠纷, 林玉静成斗争焦点 [Another dispute on the transfer of Huazi Resource and Research Centre to Selangor Chinese Assembly Hall, Lim Geok Chan becomes dispute's focal point]. 13 February 1992.

———. "Sanhuatuan Danwei Zhendui Wuyueshiri Yian Fanan, Tanglian Weixin Shoutiaozhan" 三华团单位针对五月十日议案发难, 堂联威信受挑战 [Three Chinese guilds and associations challenge the prestige of Unified Federation of Malaysian Chinese Assembly Hall by criticising the meeting on 10 May]. 25 May 1992.

———. "Shoubangshi Lihang Huaxiao Fengbo Shimo" 首邦市力行华小风波始末 [The whole story on the controversy of Lick Hung Chinese Primary School]. 26 May 1992.

———. "Huwanduo: Ruguo Huaxiao Dongshihui Diwei Bubao Dongjiaozong Kaolu Fanan" 胡万铎: 如果华小董事会地位不保董教总考虑发难 [Foo Wan Thot: *Dongjiaozong* will revolt if the status of the Chinese primary schools' committees are threatened]. 27 July 1992.

———. "Qianji Quanguo Huaxiao Dongshihui Zhuquan Wenti Dongzong Jue Jieshou Chuli Lihang Fengbo" 迁及全国华小董事会主权问题董总决接手处理力行风波 [United Chinese School Committees' Association of Malaysia decides to intervenes in the Lick Hung controversy as the issue will affect the authority of all Chinese primary schools committees in Malaysia]. 8 August 1992.

———. "Sendonglianhui Chuxuan, Huhuoshan Jumoxi, Chensongshengpai Dahuo Quansheng" 森董联会初选, 胡火山居末席, 陈松生派大获全胜 [Elections of Negeri Sembilan Chinese School Committees' Association, Hoo Huo Shan ranked at the bottom most, Chin Choong Sang's fraction won all contested seats]. 25 April 1994.

———. "Qianzhi Lazhu Dianran Huajiaoxin" 千支蜡烛点燃华教心 [Thousands of candles light up the heart of Chinese education movement supporters]. 18 December 1996.

———. "Zhi Jizhe Cuowu Quanshi Tanhua, Zhangzhengxiong Fouren Pingji Suqiu" 指记者错误诠释谈话, 张征雄否认评击诉求 [Chong Chin Shoong blames the reporters for misinterpreted his conversation and denies that he criticized the Malaysian Chinese Organisations' Election Appeals Committee]. 9 September 1999.

———. "Guoquanqiang Ganxie Neige Guanzhu, Yanjiu Ruhe Luoshi Suqiu" 郭全强感谢内阁关注, 研究如何落实诉求 [Quek Suan Hiang appreciates the attention from the cabinet and will research on the implementation of the appeals]. 24 September 1999.

———. "Xiechunrong: Chuncui Wuhui, Suqiu Gongwei Wuxu Daoqian" 谢春荣: 纯粹误会, 诉求工委无须道歉 [Ser Choon Ing: It is merely a misunderstanding, Malaysian Chinese Organisations' Election Appeals Committee does not need to apologize]. 19 August 2000.

———. "Disanzhe Yu Wuqing Jieqia, Anpai Yu Gongweihui Xieshang" 第三者与巫青接洽, 安排与工委会协商 [Third party will contact United Malays National Organisation Youth to broker negotiation platform with the Malaysian Chinese Organisations' Election Appeals Committee]. 20 August 2000.

———. "Suqiu Gongwei Yao Jingfang Guanzhu Dongyan Fen Xuehuatang Kouhao" 诉求工委要警方关注恫言焚雪华堂口号 [Malaysian Chinese Organisations' Election Appeals Committee demands the police to pay attention on the threats to burn down the Selangor Chinese Assembly Hall]. 21 August 2000.

———. "Huatuan Huashe Song Hualan Mianli Suqiu Gongweihui" 华团华社送花篮勉励诉求工委会 [Chinese guilds and associations sent flower baskets as support to Malaysian Chinese Organisations' Election Appeals Committee]. 22 August 2000.

———. "Suqiu Gongweihui Zhihan Xisang, Yaoqiu Yu Wuqing Duihua" 诉求工委会致函希桑, 要求与巫青对话 [The Malaysian Chinese Organisations' Election Appeals Committee sends letter to Hishamuddin and demands dialogue opportunities with United Malays National Organisation Youth]. 23 August 2000.

———. "Zhengfu Zunzhong Yiyuan, Zanting Guchui Bumianqiang 5 Huaxiao Hongyuan Xuexiao" 政府尊重意愿, 暂停鼓吹不勉强5华小宏愿学校 [The government will not force five shortlisted Chinese primary schools to participate in the Vision Schools Program]. 2 December 2000.

———. "Jiaorong Jihua Jingfeida, Quanmian Luoshi Burongyi" 交融计划经费大, 全面落实不容易 [Full scale implementation of the Integration Program may not be possible due to expensive cost]. 10 December 2000.

————. "Guozhuzhen: Xu Jiaqiang Yingwen Jiaodao, Minzheng Zhichi Huawen Jiao Shuli" 郭洙镇: 须加强英文教导, 民政支持华文教数理 [Kerk Choo Ting: Malaysian People's Movement Party supports the teaching of Mathematic and Science subjects in Chinese, but must enhance the teaching of English subject]. 10 August 2002.

————. "Linjingyi: Sidang Tongyi 2-3-3 Fangan, 8 Jieke Jiao, 3 Xinkemu" 林敬益: 四党同意2-3-3方案, 8节课教, 3新科目 [Lim Keng Yaik: Four political parties agreed at the 2-3-3 resolution, eight periods to teach three new subjects]. 31 October 2002.

————. "Yangqingliang: Jiu Xuexiao Shitang Zhaobiao, Dongzong Buying Weinan Xiaozhang" 杨清亮: 就学校食堂招标, 董总不应为难校长 [Yang Qing Liang: United Chinese School Committees' Association of Malaysia should not oppress school principals and making things difficult for school principals on the issue of the rental rights of school canteens]. 19 February 2006.

NEAC (National Economic Advisory Council). *Laporan Majlis Perundingan Ekonomi Negara* [Report of the National Economic Advisory Council]. Kuala Lumpur: Jabatan Percetakan Negara, 1991.

————. *New Economic Model for Malaysia 2010*. Putrajaya: National Economic Advisory Council, 2010.

News Straits Times. "New Deal for Education: Policy Reversed but English Hours Extended for Schools". 9 July 2009.

Ng, Choon Sim Cecilia. "The Women's Movement: Towards Multi-Cultural Dialogue and Peace Building". In *Building Bridges, Crossing Boundaries: Everyday Forms of Inter-Ethnic Peace Building in Malaysia*, edited by Loh Kok Wah Francis. Jakarta: Ford Foundation, 2010*a*.

————. *The Hazy New Dawn: Democracy, Women and Politics in Malaysia*. Singapore: Asia Research Institute, 2010*b*.

Ng, Choon Sim Cecilia, Maznah Mohamad, and Tan Beng Hui. *Feminism and the Women's Movement in Malaysia: An Unsung (R)evolution*. Milton Park, Abingdon, Oxon; New York: Routledge, 2006.

Ng, Tien Eng. "The Contest for the Chinese Votes: Politics of Negotiation or Politics of Pressure?". In *New Politics in Malaysia*, edited by Loh Kok Wah Francis and Johan Saravanamuttu. Singapore: Institute for Southeast Asian Studies, 2003.

NOC (National Operations Council). *The May 13 Tragedy: A Report*. Kuala Lumpur: National Operations Council, 1969.

Norani Othman, ed. *Muslim Women and the Challenge of Islamic Extremism: Sisters in Islam*. Petaling Jaya: Vinlin, 2005.

North, Douglass. *Institutions, Institutional Change and Economic Performance*. Cambridge: Cambridge University Press, 1990.

NSTP (News Straits Times Press), ed. *Seluruh Hidupnya untuk Malaysia* [All his life for Malaysia]. Kuala Lumpur: New Straits Times Press, 1976.

NUAAM et al. (Nanyang University Alumni Association of Malaya 马来亚 南大校友会, Nanyang University Alumni Association of Perak 吡叻南大 校友会, Nanyang University Alumni Association of Penang 槟城南大校友会, Nanyang University Alumni Association of Johore Bahru 新山南大校友会, and Nanyang University Alumni Association of Sarawak 砂劳越南大校友会), eds. *Jinian Nanyang Daxue Chuangxiao 25 Zhounian Tekan* 纪念南洋大学 创校25周年特刊 [Commemoration magazine of Nanyang University's twenty-fifth anniversary]. Kuala Lumpur: Nanyang University Alumni Association of Malaya, Nanyang University Alumni Association of Perak, Nanyang University Alumni Association of Penang, Nanyang University Alumni Association of Johore Bahru, and Nanyang University Alumni Association of Sarawak, 1982.

O'Balance, Edgar. *Malaya: The Communist Insurgent War, 1948–1960*. Hamden: Archon, 1966.

Oberschall, Anthony. *Social Movements: Ideologies, Interests and Identities*. New Brunswick: Transaction, 1993.

OCJKL (OCJ Kuala Lumpur). *2 MLJ 356. Merdeka University Berhad v. Government of Malaysia*. 1981. <http://ilms.agc.gov.my:88/online/uploaded/fc/271112030905 MERDEKA_UNIVERSITY%20BERHAD%20v%20GOVERNMENT% 20OF%20MA.pdf> (acessed 11 September 2013).

Offe, Claus. "New Social Movements: Challenging the Boundaries of Institutional Politics". *Social Research* 52, no. 4 (1985): 817–68.

Oliver, Pamela and Gerald Marwell. "Mobilizing Technologies for Collective Action". In *Frontiers in Social Movement Theory*, edited by Aldon Morris and Carol McClurg Mueller. New Haven, London: Yale University Press, 1992.

Olson, Mancur. *The Logic of Collective Action: Public Goods and the Theory of Groups*. Cambridge: Harvard University Press, 1965.

———. *The Rise and Decline of Nations*. New Haven, London: Yale University Press, 1982.

Ongkili, James. *Nation Building in Malaysia, 1946–1974*. Singapore: Oxford University Press, 1985.

Oriental Daily 东方日报. "Jiaozhang, Quanli Jiaohui Dongshihui, Shitang Zhaobiao Huifu Yuanzhuang" 教长, 权力交回董事会, 食堂招标恢复原状 [Minister of Education restores the rental rights of school's canteen to the school committee]. 15 October 2004.

———. "Jingwu Huaxiao Fanmaibu" 精武华小贩卖部 [Cooperative shop of Chen Moh Chinese Primary School]. 17 November 2004.

———. "Dongzong Dadizhen Xingzhengbu 7 Ju Zhuren Cicheng" 董总大地震 行政部7局主任辞呈 [Seven head of departments of United Chinese School Committees' Association of Malaysia administrative office resigned]. 10 December 2007.

Ottaway, Marina. *Democracy Challenged: The Rise of Semi-Authoritarianism*. Washington: Brookings Institution and Carnegie Endowment for International Peace, 2003.

Panizza, Francisco. "Human Rights in the Processes of Transition and Consolidation of Democracy in Latin America". *Political Studies* 43 (August 1995): 168–88.

Park, Robert Ezra. *Society: Collective Behavior, News and Opinion, Sociology and Modern Society*. Glencoe: Free Press, 1955.

Parsons, Talcott. *The Structure of Social Action*. New York: McGraw-Hill, 1937.

Peattie, Mark. "Nanshin: 'The Southward Advance' 1931–1941, as a Prelude to the Japanese Occupation of Southeast Asia". In *The Japanese Wartime Empire, 1931–1945*, edited by Ramon Hawley Myers, Mark Peattie, Zhou Wan Yao, and Peter Duus. Princeton: Princeton University Press, 1996.

Petra Kamarudin. *The Reformasi Trail*. Kuala Lumpur: Raja Petra Kamarudin, 2001.

Phatharathananunth, Somchai. *Civil Society and Democratization: Social Movements in Northeast Thailand*. Denmark: Nordic Institute of Asian, 2006.

Phoon, Wing Keong 潘永强. "Mahuagonghui Paixi Zhengzhi Chutan (2000–2003)" 马华公会派系政治初探 (2000–2003) [A preliminary study of fractional politics in Malaysian Chinese Association (2000–2003)]. *New Era College Academic Journal* 3 (July 2006): 63–88.

PJCPSDWC (Petaling Jaya Chinese Primary Schools Development Working Committee 八打灵发展华小工委会). *Badaling Fazhan Huaxiao Gongweihui 2001–2004 Nian Huodong Xilie Ji Lianhuan Wanhui Tekan* 八打灵发展华小工委会 2001–2004 年活动系列暨联欢晚会特刊 [Special magazine of Petaling Jaya Chinese Primary Schools Development Working Committee with records of activities conducted from 2001 to 2004]. Selangor: Petaling Jaya Chinese Primary Schools Development Working Committee, 2004.

Powell, Walter and Paul DiMaggio, eds. *The New Institutionalism in Organizational Analysis*. Chicago: University of Chicago Press, 1991.

PPPPK (Pertubuhan-Pertubuhan Pendidikan Pelbagai Kaum). "Huanwo Muyu Jiaoyu" 还我母语教育 [Restoration of mother tongue education]. Memorandum submitted to Prime Minister Abdullah Ahmad Badawi. 27 November 2007.

PTPTN (Perbadanan Tabung Pendidikan Tinggi Nasional). "Pengecualian syarat lulus Sijil Pelajaran Malaysia untuk memohon pembiayaan pendidikan bagi pelajar-pelajar kelulusan Unified Examination Certificate di Institusi Pendidikan Tinggi Swasta" [Educational loan application exemption conditions for Unified Examination Certificate holders who study at Private Higher Education Institutions]. Surat pekeliling Perbadanan Tabung Pendidikan Tinggi Nasional bilangan 2 tahun 2010 [Perbadanan Tabung Pendidikan Tinggi Nasional circular letter no. 2 year 2010]. 3 May 2010.

Purcell, Victor. *The Chinese in Malaya*. London: Oxford University Press, 1948.

———. *Malaya: Communist or Free?* London: Victor Gollancz, 1954.

———. *The Chinese in Malaya*. Kuala Lumpur: Oxford University Press, 1967.

Purdue, Derrick. "Conclusion: Civil Society, Governance, Social Movements and Social Capital". In *Civil Societies and Social Movements: Potentials and Problems*, edited by Derrick Purdue. London and New York: Routledge, 2007.

Putnam, Robert. *Bowling Alone: The Collapse and Revival of American Community*. New York: Simon and Schuster, 2000.

PWCRCAGM (Protem Working Committee of Representatives of Chinese Associations and Guilds of Malaysia 马来西亚华人注册社团代表大会筹备工作委员会). "Wei Zhengqu Huawen Diwei Xiang Shouxiang Dongguadulaman Chengsong Beiwanglu" 为争取华文地位向首相东姑阿都拉曼呈送备忘录 [Memorandum to the Prime Minister Tunku Abdul Rahman for a rightful place of the Chinese language]. Kuala Lumpur, 4 November 1965.

Pye, Lucian. *Lessons from the Malayan Struggle against Communism*. Cambridge: Massachusetts Institute for Technology, 1957.

Ramakrishna, Kumar. "Transmogrifying Malaya: The Impact of Sir Gerald Templer 1952–1954". *Journal of Southeast Asian Studies* 32, issues 1 (February 2001): 79–92.

———. *Emergency Propaganda: The Winning of Malayan Hearts and Minds 1948–1958*. Surrey: Curzon, 2002.

Ramasamy, Nagiah and Chris Rowley. "Trade Unions in Malaysia: Complexity of a State-Employer System". In *Trade Unions in Asia: An Economic and Sociological Analysis*, edited by John Benson and Ying Zhu. London: Routledge, 2008.

Roche, John and Stephen Sachs. "The Bureaucrat and the Enthusiast: An Exploration of the Leadership of Social Movements". In *Studies in Social Movements: A Social Psychological Perspective*, edited by Barry McLaughlin. New York: Free Press, 1969.

Roff, Margaret. "The Malayan Chinese Association, 1948–1965". *Journal of Southeast Asian History* 6 (1965): 40–53.

Roger, Kershaw. "Within the Family. The Limits of Doctrinal Differentiation in the Malaysian Ruling Party Election of 1987". *Review of Indonesian and Malaysian Affairs* 23 (1989): 125–93.

Roy, Kartik and Jörn Sidera. "Institutions, Globalisation and Empowerment: An Overview of Issues". In *Institutions, Globalization and Empowerment*, edited by Kartik Roy and Jörn Sideras. Cheltenham: Edward Elgar, 2006.

Rudner, Martin. "The Malaysian General Election of 1969: A Political Analysis". *Modern Asian Studies* 4, no. 1 (1970): 1–21.

S.M. Mohamed Idris. *Malaysian Consumers and Development*. Penang: Consumers' Association of Penang, 1986.

Sandhu, Kernial Singh. "Emergency Resettlement in Malaya". *Journal of Tropical Geography* 18 (1964): 157–83.

SCAH (Selangor Chinese Assembly Hall 雪兰莪中华大会堂). "Quanguo Huatuan Lianhe Xuanyan" 全国华团联合宣言 [Joint declaration of Chinese guilds and associations in Malaysia]. Unpublished document. 12 October 1985.

———. "Guanche Huatuan Lianhe Xuanyan Diyijieduan Jiudamubiao" 贯彻华团 联合宣言: 第一阶段九大目标 [Implementation of the joint declaration of Chinese guilds and associations in Malaysia]. Memorandum. 18 May 1986.

———. *Xuelane Zhonghua Dahuitang Bashi Zhounian Tangqing Jinian Tekan 1923–2003* 雪兰莪中华大会堂八十周年堂庆纪念特刊 1923–2003 [Commemoration magazine of Selangor Chinese Assembly Hall's eightieth anniversary 1923–2003]. Kuala Lumpur: Selangor Chinese Assembly Hall, 2004.

Schedler, Andreas. "The Menu of Manipulation". *Journal of Democracy* 13, no. 2 (April 2002): 36–50.

Scheingold, Stuart. *The Politics of Rights: Lawyers, Public Policy and Political Change.* 2nd ed. Ann Arbor: University of Michigan Press, 2004.

Scott, James. *The Moral Economy of the Peasant: Rebellion and Subsistence in Southeast Asia.* New Haven: Yale University Press, 1976.

———. "Resistance without Protest and without Organization: Peasant Opposition to the Islamic Zakat and the Christian Tithe". *Comparative Studies in Society and History* 29, no. 3 (July 1987): 417–52.

Shamsul A.B. "Religion and Ethnic Politics in Malaysia". In *Asian Visions of Authority: Religion and the Modern States of East and Southeast Asia*, edited by Charles Keyes, Laurel Kendall, and Helen Hardcores. Honolulu: University of Hawaii Press, 1994.

Sheila Nair. "Constructing Civil Society in Malaysia: Nationalism, Hegemony and Resistance". In *Malaysian Studies I: Rethinking Malaysia*, edited by Jomo K.S. Kuala Lumpur: Malaysian Social Science Association, 1999.

Shen, Ting 沈亭. *Bilizhou Huawen Duzhong Fuxingshi* 吡叻州华文独中复兴史 [History of the Perak independent Chinese secondary schools revival movement]. Perak: Perak Independent Chinese Secondary Schools Working Committee 吡叻州独中工委会, 1975.

Shevtsova, Liliia Fedorovna and Mark Eckert. "Russia's Hybrid Regime". *Journal of Democracy* 12, no. 4 (October 2001): 65–70.

Sia, Keng Yek. *S.R.J.K. (Cina) Dalam Sistem Pendidikan Kebangsaan: Dilema dan Kontroversi* [Chinese primary schools in the national education system: Dilemmas and controversies]. Kuala Lumpur: Penerbit University Malaya, 2005.

Silcock, Thomas and Ungku Abdul Aziz. "Nationalism in Malaya". In *Asian Nationalism and the West: A Symposium Based on Documents and Reports of the Eleventh Conference Institute of Pacific Relations*, edited by William Holland. New York: Octagon, 1953.

Sinchew Daily 星洲日报. "Fenni Jiaoyu Diaochatuan De Keti" 芬尼教育调查团 的课题 [Topics related to the Fenn-Wu education survey committee]. 8 July 1951.

———. "Huaxiao Yuwen Yu Jiaocai Wenti: Sanlun Fenni Wudeyao Huawen Jiaoyu Baogaoshu" 华校语文与教材问题: 三论芬尼吴德耀华文教育报告书

[Problems on Chinese schools' medium of teaching and teaching materials: The third discussion on Fenn-Wu Education Report on Chinese Education]. 10 July 1951.

———. "Huajiao Jiaoyu Jichu De Tantao" 华教教育基础的探讨 [Exploration on the foundation of Chinese education]. 31 October 1954.

———. "Wanjiu Lianhebang De Huaxiao Jiaoyu" 挽救联合邦的华校教育 [Saving the Chinese education in the Federation of Malaya]. 9 November 1954.

———. "Huajiao Dahui Bimu, Tongguo Cheng Beiwanglu Qing Lianmeng Mingnian Daxuan Zhenggang Jiang Huawen Liewei Guanfangyuyan" 华教大会闭幕, 通过呈备忘录请联盟明年大选政纲将华文列为官方语言 [Closing of the Chinese Education Convention, will submit a memorandum to the Alliance government to demand instating of Chinese language as an official language in the Alliance's election manifesto next year]. 23 September 1958.

———. "Dafu Binwei Gaoshi Jiaoshi Zhigonghui Fenhui Yijianshu" 答复槟威高师教师职工会分会意见书 [Response to Penang Senior Normal Graduate Schoolteachers Association's opinion letter]. 22 October 1962.

———. "Huajiao Gongzuo Weiyuanhui Yitongguo Huawen Daxue Mingcheng Dingwei Duli Daxue" 华教工作委员会议通过华文大学名称定为独立大学 [Chinese Education Committee will name the new Chinese university as Merdeka University]. 25 February 1968.

———. "Pizhou Dongshi Lianhehui Yuezhong Jiang Huishang, Choumu Baiwanyuan Jijin Zhu Zhounei Duzhong Fazhan" 霹州董事联合会月中将会商, 筹募百万元基金助州内独中发展 [Perak Chinese School Committees' Association will raise financial aid to support development of independent Chinese secondary schools in the state]. 10 April 1975.

———. "Dongjiaozong Huyu Gejie Miqie Guanzhu Jiaoyubu Tuixing Zonghe Xuexiao Jihua" 董教总呼吁各界密切关注教育部推行综合学校计划 [*Dongjiaozong* calls the public to be vigilant on the Integration School Program introduced by the Ministry of Education]. 9 August 1985.

———. "Tiaopan Butiao Chuxian Xiaoliwai: Jiaoyu Wenti Bei Yanbianwei Zhongzu Jiufen, Bingzhou Maqing Baojing Yaozhuo Shandong Fenzi" 挑畔布条出现校篱外: 教育问题被演变为种族纠纷, 槟州马青报警要捉煽动份子 [Banners with provoking messages are hung outside schools: Penang Branch of Malaysian Chinese Association Youth files police report to arrest provoking parties]. 16 October 1987.

———. "Xinshan Liutai Tongxuehui, Zhichi Liutaisheng Canxuan" 新山留台同学会, 支持留台生参选 [Johore Bahru Taiwanese Universities Graduates Association supports formal Taiwanese Universities graduates to contest in the general elections]. 7 August 1990.

———. "Linhuangsheng Deng 27 Ren Jiaru Xingdongdang" 林晃升等27人加入行动党 [Lim Fong Seng and twenty-seven individuals joined Democratic Action Party]. 8 August 1990.

———. "Kejiaxun: Duoming Huatuan Renshi Youyi Canzheng, Zhizai Xiezhu Zhuangda Fanduidang, Foujue Guozhen Sanfener Xiwei" 柯嘉逊: 多名华团人士有意参政, 旨在协助壮大反对党, 否决国阵三分二席位 [Kua Kia Soong: Many individuals from the Chinese guilds and associations have indicated their interest to participate in politics in order to strengthen the opposition parties and to reject Barisan Nasional's two thirds majority in the parliament]. 9 August 1990.

———. "Linhuangsheng Chengren Dangnian Neianling Xia Beikou, Shi Jueding Canzheng Cuihuaji, Gengzhuyao Yuanyin: Tuidong Liangxianzhi Shixian" 林晃升承认当年内安令下被扣, 是决定参政催化剂, 更主要原因: 推动两线制实现 [Lim Fong Seng admits that being arrested under the Internal Security Act has motivated him to participate in politics, more importantly he wants to mobilize the formation of a dual coalition system]. 17 August 1990.

———. "Linhuangsheng Biaoming You Xingdongdang Jueding Shifou Chulai Jingxuan, Weiba Dongjiaozong Zhaopai Guazai Shenshang" 林晃升表明由行动党决定是否出来竞选, 未把董教总招牌挂在身上 [Lim Fong Seng clarifies that he did not exploit *Dongjiaozong* for personal political gain and will follow the decision of Democratic Action Party about his possibility to contest in the general elections]. 18 August 1990.

———. "Shenmuyu: Huatuan Renshi Canzheng, Xiangzheng Yizhong Minzu Qiyi" 沈慕羽: 华团人士参政, 象征一种民族起义 [Sim Mow Yu: Participation of individuals from Chinese guilds and associations in politics can be perceived as an ethnic-based uprising]. 21 August 1990.

———. "Xiang Zhengfu Zhengqu Zizhu Ji Tigong Jiaoxue Xunlian: Dongzong Yaoqiu Mahua Zhu Duzhong" 向政府争取资助及提供教学训练: 董总要求马华助独中 [United Chinese School Committees' Association of Malaysia requests Malaysian Chinese Association to assist independent Chinese secondary school in securing financial aid and teachers trainings assistance from the government]. 16 October 1991.

———. "Jianli Wengu De Xieshang Jichu" 建立稳固的协商基础 [Formation of a strong and dependable foundation for negotiation]. 17 October 1991.

———. "Zhengqu Quanyi, Lajin Zhengdang Guanxi, Dongzong Gai Paodao Xieshang Luxian" 争取权益, 拉近政党关系, 董总改跑道协商路线 [United Chinese School Committees' Association of Malaysia adopts negotiation approach, closer ties with political parties to secure benefits]. 20 October 1991.

———. "Lixing Huaxiao Ling 14 Ming Zanzhuren Buchengren Xindongshihui" 力行华小另14名赞助人不承认新董事会 [Fourteen school sponsors from Lick Hung Chinese Primary School refused to acknowledge the new school committee]. 5 May 1992.

———. "Lutingyu Yi Lixing Huaxiao Shijian Weili Yu Quanguo Huaxiao Dongshibu Guanzhu Mingcheng Shifou Youbian" 陆庭谕以力行华小事件为例吁全国

华小董事部关注名称是否有变 [Loot Ting Yee uses the Lick Hung Chinese Primary School as an example to remind all Chinese school committees to check if the status and name of their organization has changed]. 6 May 1992.

———. "Lixing Huaxiao Dongshibu Renwei Wuxu Zaikai Zanzhu Dahui Yimian Zhengzhi Jinyibu Hunluan" 力行华小董事部认为无需再开赞助大会以免争执进一步混乱 [To avoid further disputes and confusion, the school committee of Lick Hung Chinese Primary School will not host another school sponsors meeting]. 17 May 1992.

———. "Buman Huaxiao Dongshibu Bian Caiwu Xiaozu Dongzong Yu Mahua Minzheng Quebao Huaxiao Bubianzhi" 不满华小董事部变财务小组董总吁马华民政确保华小不变质 [United Chinese School Committees' Association of Malaysia is dissatisfied with the replacement of school committee by financial management committee and requests Malaysian Chinese Association and Malaysian People's Movement Party to protect the original identity of Chinese schools]. 27 July 1992.

———. "Jijian Huaxiao Dongshihui Yibiancheng Caiwu Xiaozu? Fengzhenan Jinxing Diaocha" 几间华小董事会以变成财务小组？冯镇安进行调查 [Fong Chan Onn will investigate how many Chinese primary school's school committee have been replaced by financial management committee]. 28 July 1992.

———. "Lixing Shijian Shi Daohuoxian Zhiyi, Jingxuan Sendonglian Zhuxi Huhuoshan Xishuo Yuanwei" 力行事件是导火线之一，竞选森董联主席，胡火山细说原委 [Hoo Huo Shan explains that Lick Hung controversy was one of the motivations for him to compete in the Negeri Sembilan Chinese School Committees' Association's chairmanship election]. 12 April 1994.

———. "Sendonglianhui Gaixuan Jin Yiren Luobai, Chensongshengpai Jihuo Quansheng Huhuoshan Yi Zuidifen Depiao Jishen Chuxuan Lishi" 森董联会改选仅一人落败，陈松生派几获全胜胡火山以最低分得票跻身初选理事 [Only one person lost in the election of Negeri Sembilan Chinese School Committees' Association, Chin Choong Sang's fraction won almost all contested positions, Hoo Huo Shan entered the committee with the least votes]. 25 April 1994.

———. "Jiaozong Mubiao Buhui Gaibian, Wangchaoqun Ni Gongzuo Fangzhen" 教总目标不会改变，王超群拟工作方针 [Objectives of United Chinese Schoolteachers' Association of Malaysia will not change, Ong Kow Ee will identify new working direction]. 30 May 1994.

———. "Fengzhenan: Shu Dongshibu Zhuquan, Huaxiao Shitang Yizhao Chuantong Zhaobiao" 冯镇安：属董事部主权，华小食堂依照传统招标 [Fong Chan Onn: Rental rights of school canteen belongs to the school committee]. 3 November 1998.

———. "Wufa Zantong Tichu Shiji Ji Biaoda Fangshi, Shanglianhui Buqian Suqiu" 无法赞同提出时机及表达方式，商联会不签诉求 [United Chinese Chambers of Commerce Association will not sign the Malaysian Chinese Organisations'

Election Appeals as the association disagrees with the approach and timing of the appeals were presented]. 27 August 1999.

———. "Buhui Naru Huazong Jianyi, Suqiu Neirong Buxiugai" 不会纳入华总建议, 诉求内容不修改 [Will not include suggestions proposed by Federation of Chinese Associations Malaysia, contents of the Malaysian Chinese Organisations' Election Appeals will not be amended]. 29 August 1999.

———. "Xuelonghangzong Buqian Suqiu, Yu Shuxia Tuanti Bufa Yizhi" 雪隆行总不签诉求, 吁属下团体步伐一致 [Selangor and Kuala Lumpur Occupational Associations refused to endorse the Malaysian Chinese Organisations' Election Appeals]. 14 September 1999.

———. "Yu Neige Xiaozu Jiaoliu Qude Chengguo, Suqiu Gongweihui Gan Xinwei" 与内阁小组交流取得成果, 诉求工委会感欣慰 [The Malaysian Chinese Organisations' Election Appeals Committee is satisfied with the fruitful outcomes from the seminar with Cabinet subcommittee]. 24 September 1999.

———. "Gongweihui Shangxin Neirong Beiqujie, Bushouhui Suqiu Bu Daoqian" 工委会伤心内容被曲解, 不收回诉求不道歉 [The committee is saddened with the misinterpretation of the appeals but insists that they will not apologize or revoke the appeals]. 19 August 2000*a*.

———. "Kangyi Suqiu Qingxujiang, Wuqing Xuehuatangwai Shiwei" 抗议诉求情绪将, 巫青雪华堂外示威 [United Malays National Organisation Youth protested outside the Selangor Chinese Assembly Hall and accused the Malaysian Chinese Organisations' Election Appeals for triggering sensitive issues]. 19 August 2000*b*.

———. "Wuqing Xian Huatuan Yizhounei Feichu Suqiu Daoqian" 巫青限华团一周内废除诉求道歉 [United Malays National Organisation Youth requests the Chinese guilds and associations to withdraw the appeals and apologize within one week]. 19 August 2000*c*.

———. "Caitianqiang: Liyong Tequan Wenti, Wutong Zhuanyi Renmin Shixian" 蔡添强: 利用特权问题, 巫统转移人民视线 [Chua Tian Chang: United Malays National Organisation is using the special rights issues to divert people's attention]. 20 August 2000*a*.

———. "Mahua Tiaojieren Juese Bucunzai, Chenguangcai: Huatuan Wuxu Daoqian" 马华调解人角色不存在, 陈广才: 华团无须道歉 [Chan Kong Choy: No broker from Malaysian Chinese Association, there is no need for the Chinese guilds and associations to apologize]. 20 August 2000*b*.

———. "Wuqing Baoan Zhisuqiu Shandong, Wengshijie: Gongweihui Ruo Ganshou Weixie Kebaojing" 巫青报案指诉求煽动, 翁诗杰: 工委会若感受威胁可报警 [United Malays National Organisation Youth filed police report and accused the Malaysian Chinese Organisations' Election Appeals Committee for offending the Sedition Act, Ong Tee Keat comments that if the committee felt threatened they can also report to the police]. 20 August 2000*c*.

————. "Zhendui Wuqingtuan Xingdong, Xuehuatuan Shengan Yihan" 针对
巫青团行动, 雪华团深感遗憾 [Selangor Chinese Assembly Hall is deeply
repentant by the actions of United Malays National Organisation Youth].
20 August 2000*d*.

————. "Gongweihui Jushouhui Suqiu, Layishi: Han Zhengzhi Yitu" 工委会
拒收回诉求, 拉益士: 含政治意图 [Rais: Political intension is the main
reason for the committee to refuse revoking the appeals]. 21 August
2000*a*.

————. "Wuqing Kouhao Ju Weixiexing, Suqiu Gongweihui Xiang Jingfang
Beian" 巫青口号具威胁性, 诉求工委会向警方备案 [The committee files
police report as slogans posted by United Malays National Organisation Youth
are threatening]. 21 August 2000*b*.

————. "Zhi Wuqing Yinqi Jinzhang Jushi, Huazong Yaoqiu Fukui Chashou"
指巫青引起紧张局势, 华总要求副揆插手 [Federation of Chinese Associations
Malaysia requests intervention from the deputy prime minister]. 21 August
2000*c*.

————. "Renmin Songhualan, Shengyuan 2 Tuanti" 人民送花篮, 声援2团体
[Support from the people for the two organizations]. 22 August 2000.

————. "Jianyi She Tuanjie Zilihui, Jiejue Gezu Maodun Zhengduan" 建议设
团结咨理会, 解决各族矛盾争端 [Form a unity advisory committee to solve
conflicts between ethnic groups]. 23 August 2000.

————. "Zhendui Hongyuan Xuexiao Jihua, Jiaozhang Yuanyu Dongzong
Huitan" 针对宏愿学校计划, 教长愿与董教总会谈 [Minister of Education
is willing to discuss the Vision Schools project with *Dongjiaozong*].
21 November 2000.

————. "Linliangshi: Jiyu Zhengdang Shijian Diaocha, Neige Weishang Yingyu
Jiao Shuli" 林良实: 给予政党时间调查, 内阁未商英语教数理 [Lim Liong
Sik: The Cabinet is providing time for the political parties to conduct
research on the issue of teaching of Science and Mathematics in English].
8 August 2002.

————. "Huaji Zhengdang Jianyi Tuixing 2-3-3 Fangchengshi, Huaxiao Shang
8 Jie Yingyu Jiaodao Kemu" 华基政党建议推行2-3-3方程式, 华小上8节
英语教导科目 [Chinese based political parties suggest to implement a 2-3-3
formula, Chinese primary schools will have eight periods of classes using
English to teach the subjects]. 10 October 2002.

————. "Binhuaxiao Shitang Zhaobiaoquan Beiduo, Jiao Xianjiaoyuju Chuli,
Donglianhui Fandui" 槟华小食堂招标权被夺, 交县教育局处理, 董联会
反对 [Penang Chinese School Committees' Association objects the involvement
of district education department to manage the school canteen rental rights
controversy]. 9 September 2004.

————. "Mahuagonghui Fenglong Jiang Choukuan 300 Wan, Xinjiyuan Xinxiao
Niannei Donggong" 马华公会丰隆将筹款300万, 新纪元新校年内动工
[Malaysian Chinese Association and Hong Leong will collect a donation of

RM3 million, New Era College's new campus will be constructed within this year]. 20 February 2008.

————. "2012 Nian Yingyu Jiaoshuli Feichu" 2012 年英语教数理废除 [Abolishment of the teaching of Science and Mathematics subjects in English by 2012]. 9 July 2009.

————. "Zanyang Zhiduhua Bokuan Duzhong, Xiaoyou Lianzong Kending Bingzhengfu" 赞扬制度化拨款独中, 校友联总肯定槟政府 [United Chinese School Alumni Association complements Penang state government for institutionalized financial aid for the independent Chinese secondary schools]. 25 April 2010.

Skocpol, Theda. *States and Social Revolutions: A Comparative Analysis of France, Russia and China*. Cambridge, New York: Cambridge University Press, 1979.

————. "Bringing the State Back in: Strategies of Analysis in Current Research". In *Bringing the State Back In*, edited by Peter Evans, Dietrich Rueschemeyer, and Theda Skocpol. New York: Cambridge University Press, 1985.

Smelser, Neil. *Theory of Collective Behavior*. New York: Free Press, 1963.

Smith, Anthony. "State-Making and Nation-Building". In *States in History*, edited by John Hall. New York: Blackwell, 1986.

Smith, Jackie. *Social Movements for Global Democracy*. Maryland: Johns Hopkins University Press, 2008.

Snow, David, E. Burke Rochford Jr., Steven Worden, and Robert Benford. "Frame Alignment Processes, Micro Mobilization and Movement Participation". *American Sociological Review* 51, no. 4 (August 1986): 464–81.

Snow, David and Robert Benford. "Ideology, Frame Resonance and Participant Mobilization". *International Social Movement Research* 1 (1988): 197–217.

————. "Master Frames and Cycles of Protest". In *Frontiers in Social Movement Theory*, edited by Aldon Morris and Carol McClurg Mueller. New Haven: Yale University Press, 1992.

Snyder, David and Charles Tilly. "Hardship and Collective Violence in France, 1830–1960". *American Sociological Review* 37 (1972): 520–32.

Springhall, John. *Decolonization Since 1945: The Collapse of European Overseas Empires*. New York: St. Martin's, 2000.

Staggenborg, Suzanne. "The 'Meso' in Social Movement Research". In *Social Movements: Identity, Culture and the State*, edited by David S. Meyer, Nancy Whittier, and Belinda Robnett. New York: Oxford University Press, 2002.

Star. "Encouraging Response to First Vision School Project". 25 May 2002.

————. "Sepang Picked As Site of New Era College". 20 February 2008 <http://www. thestar.com.my/Story.aspx?file=%2F2008%2F2%2F20%2Felection2008%2F20382065&sec=Election2008> (accessed 2 September 2013).

Steinberg, Marc. "The Talk and Back Talk of Collective Action: A Dialogic Analysis of Repertoires of Discourse among Nineteenth-Century English Cotton Spinners". *American Journal of Sociology* 105, no. 3 (1999): 736–80.

Stenson, Michael. *Industrial Conflict in Malaya: Prelude to the Communist Revolt of 1948*. London, New York: Oxford University Press, 1970.

Stockwell, A.J. "Imperialism and Nationalism in South East Asia". In *The Oxford History of the British Empire*. Vol. 4 of the Twentieth Century, edited by Judith Brown and William Roger Louis. Oxford: Oxford University Press, 1999.

Straits Times. "Kuala Lumpur Rally Poses Challenge to Leading Indian Party". 26 November 2007.

Sun. "Hishamuddin: Dong Jiao Zong Needs to Change". 24 March 2009.

Tan, Ai Mei 陈爱梅. *Dama Huaxiao Zouxiang Hefang: Cong Dongxiao Fengbo Kan Huaxiao Jianglai De Fazhan* 大马华小走向何方: 从董校风波看华小将来的发展 [The future of Chinese primary schools in Malaysia]. Selangor: Strategic Information and Research Development Centre 策略资讯与社会研究中心, 2006.

Tan, Beng Hui and Ng Choon Sim Cecilia. "Embracing the Challenge of Representation: The Women's Movement and Electoral Politics in Malaysia". In *New Politics in Malaysia*, edited by Loh Kok Wah Francis and Johan Saravanamuttu. Singapore: Institute for Southeast Asian Studies, 2001.

Tan, Jun E and Zawawi Ibrahim. *Blogging and Democratization in Malaysia: A New Civil Society in the Making*. Petaling Jaya: Strategic Information and Research Development Centre, 2008.

Tan, Kevin. "PM Likens Suqiu's Actions to Communists and Al-Ma'unah". *Malaysiakini*, 30 August 2000 <http://www.malaysiakini.com/news/465> (accessed 13 October 2013).

Tan, Kim Hong. *The Chinese in Penang: A Pictorial History*. Penang: Areca, 2007.

Tan, Lee Ooi. *Dinamik Ruang Siber dalam Gerakan Reformasi di Malaysia* [The roles of dynamic cyber space in Malaysia's reformasi movement]. Selangor: Penerbit Universiti Kebangsaan Malaysia, 2010.

Tan, Liok Ee. "Politics of Chinese Education in Malaya, 1945–1961". Ph.D. dissertation, Faculty of Arts and Social Sciences, Universiti Malaya, 1985.

———. "Tan Cheng Lock and the Chinese Education Issue in Malaya". *Journal of Southeast Asian Studies* 19, no. 1 (1988): 48–61.

———. *The Politics of Chinese Education in Malaya, 1945–1961*. Kuala Lumpur: Oxford University Press, 1997.

Tan, Nathaniel and John Lee, eds. *Political Tsunami: An End to Hegemony in Malaysia?* Kuala Lumpur: Kinibooks, 2008.

Tan, Seng Giaw. *The First 60 Days: The 27th October ISA Arrests*. Petaling Jaya: Democratic Action Party, 1989.

Tan, Yao Sua. *Politik Dongjiaozong dalam Pendidikan Vernakular Cina di Semenanjung Malaysia, 1960–1982* [Politics of *Dongjiaozong* in vernacular Chinese education in Peninsula Malaysia 1960–1982]. Pulau Pinang: Penerbit Universiti Sains Malaysia, 2005.

Tang, Tze Ying 陈子鹦. "Malaixiya Huawen Zhongxue Gaizhi: Wangyongnian yu Zhongling Zhongxue Weili" 马来西亚华文中学改制: 汪永年与钟灵中学为例 [Conversion of Chinese secondary schools in Malaysia: An example of Wang Yong Nian and Chung Ling High School]. Master's thesis, Graduate School of Southeast Asian Studies, National Chi Nan University, Taiwan, 2004.

Tarrow, Sidney. *Power in Movement: Social Movements, Collective Action and Politics*. Cambridge, New York: Cambridge University Press, 1994.

Tay, Lian Soo 郑良树. "Dulihou Huawen Jiaoyu" 独立后华文教育 [Chinese education after independence]. In *Malaixiya Huarenshi Xinbian Dierce* 马来西亚华人史新编第二册 [History of Malaysian Chinese new edition 2], edited by Lin Chooi Kwa 林水濠, Ho Khai Leong 何启良, Hou Kok Chung 何国忠, and Lai Kuan Fook 赖观福. Kuala Lumpur: Federation of Chinese Associations Malaysia 马来西亚中华大会堂总会, 1998*a*.

———. *Malaixiya Huawen Jiaoyu Fazhanshi* 马来西亚华文教育发展史 [History of Chinese education in Malaysia] 1. Kuala Lumpur: United Chinese Schoolteachers' Association of Malaysia, 1998*b*.

———. *Malaixiya Huawen Jiaoyu Fazhanshi* 马来西亚华文教育发展史 [History of Chinese education in Malaysia] 2. Kuala Lumpur: United Chinese Schoolteachers' Association of Malaysia, 1998*c*.

———. *Malaixiya Huashe Wenshi Lunji* 马来西亚华社文史论集 [History of Chinese community in Malaysia]. Johore: Southern College 南方学院, 1999.

———. *Malaixiya Huawen Jiaoyu Fazhanshi* 马来西亚华文教育发展史 [History of Chinese education in Malaysia] 3. Kuala Lumpur: United Chinese Schoolteachers' Association of Malaysia, 2001.

———. *Malaixiya Huawen Jiaoyu Fazhanshi* 马来西亚华文教育发展史 [History of Chinese education in Malaysia] 4. Kuala Lumpur: United Chinese Schoolteachers' Association of Malaysia, 2003.

———. *Malaixiya Huawen Jiaoyu Fazhan Jianshi* 马来西亚华文教育发展简史 [Simplified history of Chinese education development in Malaysia]. Johore: Southern College 南方学院, 2005.

Teoh, Ai Ling. "Pertubuhan Dong Zong: Struktur dan Fungsi" [Organization of Dong Zong: Structures and functions]. Master's thesis, Faculty of Social Sciences and Humanities, Universiti Kebangsaan Malaysia, 1999.

Thelen, Kathleen. "Historical Institutionalism in Comparative Politics". *The Annual Review of Political Science* 2 (1999): 381–99.

———. *How Institutions Evolve: The Political Economy of Skills in Germany, Britain, the United States and Japan*. Cambridge, New York: Cambridge University Press, 2004.

Thock, Kiah Wah 祝家华. "Cong Nahan, Panghuang Dao Fanpan: Pingdeng De Mengmo" 从呐喊, 彷徨到反叛: 平等的梦魇 [From frustration, hesitation to rebellion: The nightmares of just]. In *Dangdai Dama Huaren Zhengzhi Shengsi* 当代大马华人政治省思 [Contemporary political reflections of Chinese in

Malaysia], edited by Ho Khai Leong 何启良. Kuala Lumpur: Huazi Resource and Research Centre, 1994*a*.

———. *Jiegou Zhengzhi Shenhua Dama Liangxian Zhengzhi De Pingxi 1985–1992* 解构政治神话: 大马两线政治的评析 1985–1992 [Analysis of the dual political alliance in Malaysia 1985–1992]. Kuala Lumpur: Huazi Resource and Research Centre, 1994*b*.

Thomas, Clive, ed. *Political Parties and Interest Groups: Shaping Democratic Governance*. Boulder: L. Rienner, 2001.

Tilly, Charles. *From Mobilization to Revolution*. New York: Addison-Wesley, 1978.

———. *The Contentious French: Four Centuries of Popular Struggle*. Cambridge: Harvard University Press, 1986.

———. *Popular Contention in Great Britain 1785–1834*. Cambridge: Harvard University Press, 1995.

———. *Social Movements 1768–2004*. Boulder: Paradigm, 2004.

Tongbao 通报. "Zhiyou Tuanjie, Huaren Cai Youdejiu, Shenmuyu Canjia Dahui Yuanyou Ji Yanjiang" 只有团结, 华人才有得救, 沈慕羽参加大会缘由及演讲 [Chinese can survive if they are united, the reason for Sim Mow Yu to speak and participate in the convention]. 9 February 1971.

———. "Zhuangdijun Tan Huajiao Renshi Canzheng, Xubanyan Jiding Juese, Dongjiaozong Buyi Chanzheng" 庄迪君谈华教人士参政, 须扮演既定角色, 董教总不宜参政 [Thuang Pik King: United Chinese School Committees' Association of Malaysia needs to perform its established role and therefore is not suited to participate in politics]. 7 August 1990.

Torii, Takashi. "The Mechanism for State-led Creation of Malaysia's Middle Classes". *The Developing Economies* XLI, no. 2 (June 2003): 221–42.

Touraine, Alaine. *The Return of the Actor*. Minneapolis: University of Minnesota Press, 1988.

Truman, David. *The Governmental Process: Political Interests and Public Opinion*. New York: Alfred A. Knopf, 1951.

UCSCAM (United Chinese School Committees' Association of Malaysia 马来西亚华校董事联合会总会). *Dongzong Huixun* 董总会讯 [United Chinese School Committees' Association of Malaysia Newsletter]. 15 March 1987*a* <http://www.djz.edu.my/v2/daobao/hui%20xun%20(1987-03-15).pdf> (accessed 8 September 2013).

———. *Dongzong Sanshinian* 董总卅年 [United Chinese School Committees' Association of Malaysia's thirtieth anniversary magazine] 1. Kuala Lumpur: United Chinese School Committees' Association of Malaysia, 1987*b*.

———. *Dongzong Sanshinian* 董总卅年 [United Chinese School Committees' Association of Malaysia's thirtieth anniversary magazine] 2. Kuala Lumpur: United Chinese School Committees' Association of Malaysia, 1987*c*.

———. *Dongzong Sanshinian* 董总卅年 [United Chinese School Committees' Association of Malaysia's thirtieth anniversary magazine] 3. Kuala Lumpur: United Chinese School Committees' Association of Malaysia, 1987*d*.

————. *Malaixiya Huaxiao Dongshihui Zonghui Dongjiaozong Huawen Duzhong Fazhan Gongzuo Weiyuanhui 1987 Nian Gongzuo Baogaoshu* 马来西亚华校董事会总会 董教总华文独中发展工作委员会1987年工作报告书 [United Chinese School Committees' Association of Malaysia and *Dongjiaozong* Independent Chinese Secondary Schools Working Committee 1987 working report]. Kuala Lumpur: United Chinese School Committees' Association of Malaysia, 1988.

————. *Malaixiya Huaxiao Dongshihui Zonghui Dongjiaozong Huawen Duzhong Fazhan Gongzuo Weiyuanhui 1988 Nian Gongzuo Baogaoshu* 马来西亚华校董事会总会 董教总华文独中发展工作委员会1988年工作报告书 [United Chinese School Committees' Association of Malaysia and *Dongjiaozong* Independent Chinese Secondary Schools Working Committee 1988 working report]. Kuala Lumpur: United Chinese School Committees' Association of Malaysia, 1989.

————. *Malaixiya Huaxiao Dongshihui Zonghui Dongjiaozong Huawen Duzhong Fazhan Gongzuo Weiyuanhui 1989 Nian Gongzuo Baogaoshu* 马来西亚华校董事会总会 董教总华文独中发展工作委员会1989年工作报告书 [United Chinese School Committees' Association of Malaysia and *Dongjiaozong* Independent Chinese Secondary Schools Working Committee 1989 working report]. Kuala Lumpur: United Chinese School Committees' Association of Malaysia, 1990.

————. *Malaixiya Huaxiao Dongshihui Zonghui Dongjiaozong Huawen Duzhong Fazhan Gongzuo Weiyuanhui 1990 Nian Gongzuo Baogaoshu* 马来西亚华校董事会总会 董教总华文独中发展工作委员会1990年工作报告书 [United Chinese School Committees' Association of Malaysia and *Dongjiaozong* Independent Chinese Secondary Schools Working Committee 1990 working report]. Kuala Lumpur: United Chinese School Committees' Association of Malaysia, 1991.

————. *Malaixiya De Huawen Jiaoyu Diyiqi Zhi Dibaqi Hedingben* 马来西亚的华文教育第一期至第八期合订本 [Bound edition of Chinese education in Malaysia 8 vols.]. Kuala Lumpur: United Chinese School Committees' Association of Malaysia, 1992*a*–2008.

————. *Malaixiya Huawen Duli Zhongxue Ziliao Diaocha Baogaoshu* 马来西亚华文独立中学资料调查报告书 [Survey report on independent Chinese secondary schools in Malaysia]. Kuala Lumpur: United Chinese School Committees' Association of Malaysia, 1992*b*.

————. *Malaixiya Huaxiao Dongshihui Zonghui Dongjiaozong Huawen Duzhong Fazhan Gongzuo Weiyuanhui 1991 Nian Gongzuo Baogaoshu* 马来西亚华校董事会总会 董教总华文独中发展工作委员会1991年工作报告书 [United Chinese School Committees' Association of Malaysia and *Dongjiaozong* Independent Chinese Secondary Schools Working Committee 1991 working report]. Kuala Lumpur: United Chinese School Committees' Association of Malaysia, 1992*c*.

————. *Malaixiya Huaxiao Dongshihui Zonghui Dongjiaozong Huawen Duzhong Fazhan Gongzuo Weiyuanhui 1992 Nian Gongzuo Baogaoshu* 马来西亚华校董事会总会 董教总华文独中发展工作委员会1992年工作报告书 [United Chinese School Committees' Association of Malaysia and *Dongjiaozong* Independent Chinese Secondary Schools Working Committee 1992 working report]. Kuala Lumpur: United Chinese School Committees' Association of Malaysia, 1993.

————. *Malaixiya Huaxiao Dongshihui Zonghui Dongjiaozong Huawen Duzhong Fazhan Gongzuo Weiyuanhui 1993 Nian Gongzuo Baogaoshu* 马来西亚华校董事会总会 董教总华文独中发展工作委员会1993年工作报告书 [United Chinese School Committees' Association of Malaysia and *Dongjiaozong* Independent Chinese Secondary Schools Working Committee 1993 working report]. Selangor: United Chinese School Committees' Association of Malaysia, 1994.

————. *Malaixiya Huaxiao Dongshihui Zonghui Dongjiaozong Huawen Duzhong Fazhan Gongzuo Weiyuanhui 1994 Nian Gongzuo Baogaoshu* 马来西亚华校董事会总会 董教总华文独中发展工作委员会1994年工作报告书 [United Chinese School Committees' Association of Malaysia and *Dongjiaozong* Independent Chinese Secondary Schools Working Committee 1994 working report]. Selangor: United Chinese School Committees' Association of Malaysia, 1995.

————. *Malaixiya Huaxiao Dongshihui Zonghui Dongjiaozong Huawen Duzhong Fazhan Gongzuo Weiyuanhui 1995 Nian Gongzuo Baogaoshu* 马来西亚华校董事会总会 董教总华文独中发展工作委员会1995年工作报告书 [United Chinese School Committees' Association of Malaysia and *Dongjiaozong* Independent Chinese Secondary Schools Working Committee 1995 working report]. Selangor: United Chinese School Committees' Association of Malaysia, 1996.

————. *Malaixiya Huaxiao Dongshihui Zonghui Dongjiaozong Huawen Duzhong Fazhan Gongzuo Weiyuanhui 1996 Nian Gongzuo Baogaoshu* 马来西亚华校董事会总会董教总华文独中发展工作委员会1996年工作报告书 [United Chinese School Committees' Association of Malaysia and *Dongjiaozong* Independent Chinese Secondary Schools Working Committee 1996 working report]. Selangor: United Chinese School Committees' Association of Malaysia, 1997.

————. *Malaixiya Huaxiao Dongshihui Zonghui Dongjiaozong Huawen Duzhong Fazhan Gongzuo Weiyuanhui 1997 Nian Gongzuo Baogaoshu* 马来西亚华校董事会总会 董教总华文独中发展工作委员会1997年工作报告书 [United Chinese School Committees' Association of Malaysia and *Dongjiaozong* Independent Chinese Secondary Schools Working Committee 1997 working report]. Selangor: United Chinese School Committees' Association of Malaysia, 1998.

———. *Malaixiya Huaxiao Dongshihui Zonghui Dongjiaozong Huawen Duzhong Fazhan Gongzuo Weiyuanhui 1998 Nian Gongzuo Baogaoshu* 马来西亚华校董事会总会董教总 华文独中发展工作委员会1998年工作报告书 [United Chinese School Committees' Association of Malaysia and *Dongjiaozong* Independent Chinese Secondary Schools Working Committee 1998 working report]. Selangor: United Chinese School Committees' Association of Malaysia, 1999.

———. *Jianjue Fandui Hongyuan Xuexiao Jihua* 坚决反对宏愿学校计划 [Determined opposition on the Vision Schools Program]. Selangor: United Chinese School Committees' Association of Malaysia, 2000*a*.

———. *Malaixiya Huaxiao Dongshihui Zonghui Dongjiaozong Huawen Duzhong Fazhan Gongzuo Weiyuanhui 1999 Nian Gongzuo Baogaoshu* 马来西亚华校董事会总会 董教总华文独中发展工作委员会1999年工作报告书 [United Chinese School Committees' Association of Malaysia and *Dongjiaozong* Independent Chinese Secondary Schools Working Committee 1999 working report]. Selangor: United Chinese School Committees' Association of Malaysia, 2000*b*.

———. *Fengyun Jidang Yibaibashinian: Malaixiya Huawen Jiaoyu Tupianji* 风云激荡一百八十年: 马来西亚华文教育图片集 [180 years of history: Pictorial collection of Chinese education in Malaysia]. Selangor: United Chinese School Committees' Association of Malaysia, 2001*a*.

———. *Malaixiya Huaxiao Dongshihui Zonghui Dongjiaozong Huawen Duzhong Fazhan Gongzuo Weiyuanhui 2000 Nian Gongzuo Baogaoshu* 马来西亚华校董事会总会 董教总华文独中发展工作委员会2000年工作报告书 [United Chinese School Committees' Association of Malaysia and *Dongjiaozong* Independent Chinese Secondary Schools Working Committee 2000 working report]. Selangor: United Chinese School Committees' Association of Malaysia, 2001*b*.

———. *Malaixiya Huaxiao Dongshihui Zonghui Dongjiaozong Huawen Duzhong Fazhan Gongzuo Weiyuanhui 2001 Nian Gongzuo Baogaoshu* 马来西亚华校董事会总会 董教总华文独中发展工作委员会2001年工作报告书 [United Chinese School Committees' Association of Malaysia and *Dongjiaozong* Independent Chinese Secondary Schools Working Committee 2001 working report]. Selangor: United Chinese School Committees' Association of Malaysia, 2002*a*.

———. *Shinian Huajiao Qingyuan, 1991–2001 Shinian Juanxian Dongjiaozong Jiaoyu Zhongxin Jijin Xinjiyuan Jianshe Yufazhan Jijin Zhengxinlu* 十年华教情缘, 1991–2001十年捐献董教总教育中心基金新纪元建设与发展基金征信录 [List of donors who donated to *Dongjiaozong* Higher Learning Center and New Era College Development Fund from 1991 to 2001]. Selangor: United Chinese School Committees' Association of Malaysia, 2002*b*.

———. *Malaixiya De Huawen Jiaoyu Yundong: Malaixiya Huawen Jiaoyu 184 Nian Jianshi 1819–2003* 马来西亚的华文教育运动: 马来西亚华文教育184年

简史 1819–2003 [Simplified history of Chinese education movement in Malaysia 1819–2003]. Selangor: United Chinese School Committees' Association of Malaysia, 2003*a*.

———. *Malaixiya Huaxiao Dongshihui Zonghui Dongjiaozong Huawen Duzhong Fazhan Gongzuo Weiyuanhui 2002 Nian Gongzuo Baogaoshu* 马来西亚华校董事会总会 董教总华文独中发展工作委员会2002年工作报告书 [United Chinese School Committees' Association of Malaysia and *Dongjiaozong* Independent Chinese Secondary Schools Working Committee 2002 working report]. Selangor: United Chinese School Committees' Association of Malaysia, 2003*b*.

———. *Dongzong 50 Nian Tekan: 1954–2004* 董总50年特刊: 1954–2004 [Commemoration magazine of United Chinese School Committees' Association of Malaysia's fiftieth anniversary: 1954–2004]. Selangor: United Chinese School Committees' Association of Malaysia, 2004*a*.

———. *Malaixiya Huawen Jiaoyu* 马来西亚华文教育 [Chinese education in Malaysia]. Selangor: United Chinese School Committees' Association of Malaysia, 2004*b*.

———. *Malaixiya Huawen Jiaoyu* 马来西亚华文教育 [Malaysia Chinese education] 1 (June 2004*c*).

———. *Malaixiya Huaxiao Dongshihui Zonghui Dongjiaozong Huawen Duzhong Fazhan Gongzuo Weiyuanhui 2003 Nian Gongzuo Baogaoshu* 马来西亚华校董事会总会 董教总华文独中发展工作委员会2003年工作报告书 [United Chinese School Committees' Association of Malaysia and *Dongjiaozong* Independent Chinese Secondary Schools Working Committee 2003 working report]. Selangor: United Chinese School Committees' Association of Malaysia, 2004*d*.

———. *Malaixiya Huaxiao Dongshihui Zonghui Dongjiaozong Huawen Duzhong Fazhan Gongzuo Weiyuanhui 2004 Nian Gongzuo Baogaoshu* 马来西亚华校董事会总会 董教总华文独中发展工作委员会2004年工作报告书 [United Chinese School Committees' Association of Malaysia and *Dongjiaozong* Independent Chinese Secondary Schools Working Committee 2004 working report]. Selangor: United Chinese School Committees' Association of Malaysia, 2005.

———. *Malaixiya Huaxiao Dongshihui Zonghui Dongjiaozong Huawen Duzhong Fazhan Gongzuo Weiyuanhui 2005 Nian Gongzuo Baogaoshu* 马来西亚华校董事会总会 董教总华文独中发展工作委员会2005年工作报告书 [United Chinese School Committees' Association of Malaysia and *Dongjiaozong* Independent Chinese Secondary Schools Working Committee 2005 annual working report]. Selangor: United Chinese School Committees' Association of Malaysia, 2006*a*.

———. "Zhendui Meiti Baodao Quanguo Xiaozhang Zhigonghui Maliujia Fenhui Zhuxi Yangqingliang Xiaozhang Biaoshi 'Yuqing Dongzong Tingzhi Zaixuexiao Shitang Zhaobiao Yishishang, Daya He Weinan Xiaozhang' De Tanhua Fabiao

Wengao" 针对媒体报导全国校长职工会马六甲分会主席杨清亮校长表示
'吁请董总停止在学校食堂招标一事上, 打压和为难校长' 的谈话发表文告
[Press statement in response to National Union of Heads of Schools Malacca
Branch's Deputy Chairman Yang Qing Liang's comments on 'United Chinese
School Committees' Association of Malaysia should stop oppressing school
principals and deliberately making things difficult for school principals on the
issue of the rental rights of school canteens']. 19 February 2006*b*.

———. "Youguan Dongzong Yu Jiaozong Guanxi De Wengao" 有关董总与教总
关系的文告 [Press statement on the relationship between United Chinese
School Committees' Association of Malaysia and United Chinese Schoolteachers'
Association of Malaysia]. 14 October 2006*c*.

———. *Malaixiya Huaxiao Dongshihui Zonghui Dongjiaozong Huawen Duzhong
Fazhan Gongzuo Weiyuanhui 2006 Nian Gongzuo Baogaoshu* 马来西亚华校
董事会总会 董教总华文独中发展工作委员会2006年工作报告书 [United
Chinese School Committees' Association of Malaysia and *Dongjiaozong*
Independent Chinese Secondary Schools Working Committee 2006 working
report]. Selangor: United Chinese School Committees' Association of Malaysia,
2007.

———. *Malaixiya Huaxiao Dongshihui Zonghui Dongjiaozong Huawen Duzhong
Fazhan Gongzuo Weiyuanhui 2007 Nian Gongzuo Baogaoshu* 马来西亚华校
董事会总会 董教总华文独中发展工作委员会2007年工作报告书 [United
Chinese School Committees' Association of Malaysia and *Dongjiaozong*
Independent Chinese Secondary Schools Working Committee 2007 working
report]. Selangor: United Chinese School Committees' Association of Malaysia,
2008*a*.

———. "United Chinese School Committees' Association of Malaysia Statement
of Income and Expenditure for the Year Ended 31 December 2008". Office
document. Selangor: United Chinese School Committees' Association of
Malaysia, 2008*b*.

———. *Malaixiya Huaxiao Dongshihui Zonghui Dongjiaozong Huawen Duzhong
Fazhan Gongzuo Weiyuanhui 2008 Nian Gongzuo Baogaoshu* 马来西亚华校
董事会总会 董教总华文独中发展工作委员会2008年工作报告书 [United
Chinese School Committees' Association of Malaysia and *Dongjiaozong*
Independent Chinese Secondary Schools Working Committee 2008 working
report]. Selangor: United Chinese School Committees' Association of Malaysia,
2009.

———. *Malaixiya Huaxiao Dongshihui Zonghui Dongjiaozong Huawen Duzhong
Fazhan Gongzuo Weiyuanhui 2009 Nian Gongzuo Baogaoshu* 马来西亚华校
董事会总会 董教总华文独中发展工作委员会2009年工作报告书 [United
Chinese School Committees' Association of Malaysia and *Dongjiaozong*
Independent Chinese Secondary Schools Working Committee 2009 working
report]. Selangor: United Chinese School Committees' Association of Malaysia,
2010.

———. *Malaixiya Huaxiao Dongshihui Zonghui Dongjiaozong Huawen Duzhong Fazhan Gongzuo Weiyuanhui 2010 Nian Gongzuo Baogaoshu* 马来西亚华校董事会总会 董教总华文独中发展工作委员会2010年工作报告书 [United Chinese School Committees' Association of Malaysia and *Dongjiaozong* Independent Chinese Secondary Schools Working Committee 2010 working report]. Selangor: United Chinese School Committees' Association of Malaysia, 2011.

———. *Malaixiya Huaxiao Dongshihui Zonghui Dongjiaozong Huawen Duzhong Fazhan Gongzuo Weiyuanhui 2011 Nian Gongzuo Baogaoshu* 马来西亚华校董事会总会 董教总华文独中发展工作委员会2011年工作报告书 [United Chinese School Committees' Association of Malaysia and *Dongjiaozong* Independent Chinese Secondary Schools Working Committee 2011 working report]. Selangor: United Chinese School Committees' Association of Malaysia, 2012.

UCSCAM et al. (United Chinese School Committees' Association of Malaysia 马来西亚华校董事联合会总会, United Chinese Schoolteachers' Association of Malaysia 马来西亚华校教师会总会, Federation of Alumni Associations of Taiwan Universities of Malaysia 马来西亚留台校友会联会总会, Nanyang University Alumni Association of Malaya 马来亚南大校友会, United Chinese School Alumni Association 华校校友会联合会总会, Malaysian Seven Major Clans Associations 七大乡团协调委员会, and Federation of Chinese Associations Malaysia 马来西亚中华大会堂总会). "Huifu Yi Muyu Zuowei Xiaoxue Shulike Jiaoxue Meijieyu Beiwanglu" 恢复以母语作为小学数理科教学媒介语备忘录 [Memorandum to revert the teaching of Mathematics and Science subjects at primary schools using mother tongue]. Memorandum submitted to the Deputy Prime Minister cum Minister of Education. 26 May 2009.

UCSCAM et al. (United Chinese School Committees' Association of Malaysia 马来西亚华校董事联合会总会, United Chinese Schoolteachers' Association of Malaysia 马来西亚华校教师会总会, Selangor Chinese Assembly Hall 雪兰莪中华大会堂, Nanyang University Alumni Association of Malaya 马来亚南大校友会, and Federation of Alumni Associations of Taiwan Universities of Malaysia 马来西亚留台校友会联会总会). "Dui 1990 Nian Jiaoyu Faling Caoan De Xiugai Jianyi" 对1990年教育法令草案的修改建议 [Proposals on the Draft of 1990 Education Act]. Proposal submitted to Education Act Advisory Council. 7 March 1991.

UCSTAM (United Chinese Schoolteachers' Association of Malaya/Malaysia 马来(西)亚华校教师会总会). "Lianhebang Huaxiao Jiaoshi Zonghui Xuanyan" 联合邦华校教师总会宣言 [Declaration of United Chinese Schoolteachers' Association of Malaya]. Unpublished document. 3 February 1952*a*.

———. "Quanma Huaxiao Dongjiao Ji Mahua Daibiao Dierci Lianxi Huiyi Jilu 1952" 全马华校董教及马华代表第二次联席会议记录 1952 [Meeting minutes of the Second Joint Conference of Chinese School Committees and

Chinese Schoolteachers Representatives with Malayan Chinese Association Representatives 1952]. Kuala Lumpur: United Chinese Schoolteachers' Association of Malaya, 1952*b*.

———. "Jiaozong Fandui Gai Fangyuan Xuexiao Wei Guomin Xuexiao Xuanyan" 教总反对改方言学校为国民学校宣言 [Memorandum submitted by the United Chinese Schoolteachers' Association of Malaya in opposition of the conversion of vernacular schools into national schools]. Unpublished document. 18 October 1954.

———. *Jiaoshi Zazhi Duli Daxue Zhuanhao* 教师杂志独立大学专号 [Teacher's Journal Special edition on Merdeka University] (1968).

———. *Jiaoshi Zazhi* 教师杂志 [Teacher's Journal] 10, no. 1 (1975).

———. *Jiaoshi Zazhi* 教师杂志 [Teacher's Journal] 11, no. 2 (1976).

———. *Jiaozong Chengli Sanshisan Nian Huawen Jiaoyu Shiliao* 教总成立三十三年: 华文教育史料 [United Chinese Schoolteachers' Association of Malaysia's thirty-third anniversary: Collection of materials on Chinese education] 1. Kuala Lumpur: United Chinese Schoolteachers' Association of Malaysia, 1983*a*.

———. *Jiaozong Chengli Sanshisan Nian Huawen Jiaoyu Shiliao* 教总成立三十三年: 华文教育史料 [United Chinese Schoolteachers' Association of Malaysia's thirty-third anniversary: Collection of materials on Chinese education] 2. Kuala Lumpur: United Chinese Schoolteachers' Association of Malaysia, 1983*b*.

———. *Jiaozong Chengli Sanshisan Nian Huawen Jiaoyu Shiliao* 教总成立三十三年: 华文教育史料 [United Chinese Schoolteachers' Association of Malaysia's thirty-third anniversary: Collection of materials on Chinese education] 3. Kuala Lumpur: United Chinese Schoolteachers' Association of Malaysia, 1983*c*.

———. *Malaixiya Huaxiao Jiaoshihui Zonghui Dongjiaozong Quanguo Fazhan Huaxiao Gongweihui 1986 Nian Gongzuo Baogaoshu* 马来西亚华校教师会总会董教总全国发展华小工委会1986年工作报告书 [United Chinese Schoolteachers' Association of Malaysia and *Dongjiaozong* Chinese Primary Schools Working Committee 1986 working report]. Kuala Lumpur: United Chinese Schoolteachers' Association of Malaysia, 1987*a*.

———. *Malaixiya Huaxiao Jiaoshihui Zonghui Qingzhu 33 Zhounian Jinian Tekan* 马来西亚华校教师会总会庆祝33周年纪念特刊 [Commemoration magazine of United Chinese Schoolteachers' Association of Malaysia's thirty-third anniversary]. Kuala Lumpur: United Chinese Schoolteachers' Association of Malaya, 1987*b*.

———. *Malaixiya Huaxiao Jiaoshihui Zonghui 1987 Nian Gongzuo Baogaoshu* 马来西亚华校教师会总会1987年工作报告书 [United Chinese Schoolteachers' Association of Malaysia 1987 working report]. Kuala Lumpur: United Chinese Schoolteachers' Association of Malaysia, 1988.

————. *Malaixiya Huaxiao Jiaoshihui Zonghui 1988 Nian Gongzuo Baogaoshu* 马来西亚华校教师会总会1988年工作报告书 [United Chinese Schoolteachers' Association of Malaysia 1988 working report]. Kuala Lumpur: United Chinese Schoolteachers' Association of Malaysia, 1989.

————. *Malaixiya Huaxiao Jiaoshihui Zonghui 1989 Nian Gongzuo Baogaoshu* 马来西亚华校教师会总会1989年工作报告书 [United Chinese Schoolteachers' Association of Malaysia 1989 working report]. Kuala Lumpur: United Chinese Schoolteachers' Association of Malaysia, 1990.

————. *Malaixiya Huaxiao Jiaoshihui Zonghui 1990 Nian Gongzuo Baogaoshu* 马来西亚华校教师会总会1990年工作报告书 [United Chinese Schoolteachers' Association of Malaysia 1990 working report]. Kuala Lumpur: United Chinese Schoolteachers' Association of Malaysia, 1991.

————. *Malaixiya Huaxiao Jiaoshihui Zonghui 1991 Nian Gongzuo Baogaoshu* 马来西亚华校教师会总会1991年工作报告书 [United Chinese Schoolteachers' Association of Malaysia 1991 working report]. Kuala Lumpur: United Chinese Schoolteachers' Association of Malaysia, 1992.

————. *Malaixiya Huaxiao Jiaoshihui Zonghui 1992 Nian Gongzuo Baogaoshu* 马来西亚华校教师会总会1992年工作报告书 [United Chinese Schoolteachers' Association of Malaysia 1992 working report]. Kuala Lumpur: United Chinese Schoolteachers' Association of Malaysia, 1993.

————. *Malaixiya Huaxiao Jiaoshihui Zonghui Dongjiaozong Quanguo Fazhan Huaxiao Gongweihui 1993 Nian Gongzuo Baogaoshu* 马来西亚华校教师会总会董教总全国发展华小工委会1993年工作报告书 [United Chinese Schoolteachers' Association of Malaysia and *Dongjiaozong* Chinese Primary Schools Working Committee 1993 working report]. Kuala Lumpur: United Chinese Schoolteachers' Association of Malaysia, 1994.

————. *Malaixiya Huaxiao Jiaoshihui Zonghui Dongjiaozong Quanguo Fazhan Huaxiao Gongweihui 1994 Nian Gongzuo Baogaoshu* 马来西亚华校教师会总会 董教总全国发展华小工委会1994年工作报告书 [United Chinese Schoolteachers' Association of Malaysia and *Dongjiaozong* Chinese Primary Schools Working Committee 1994 working report]. Selangor: United Chinese Schoolteachers' Association of Malaysia, 1995.

————. *Malaixiya Huaxiao Jiaoshihui Zonghui Dongjiaozong Quanguo Fazhan Huaxiao Gongweihui 1995 Nian Gongzuo Baogaoshu* 马来西亚华校教师会总会董教总全国发展华小工委会1995年工作报告书 [United Chinese Schoolteachers' Association of Malaysia and *Dongjiaozong* Chinese Primary Schools Working Committee 1995 working report]. Selangor: United Chinese Schoolteachers' Association of Malaysia, 1996.

————. *Malaixiya Huaxiao Jiaoshihui Zonghui Dongjiaozong Quanguo Fazhan Huaxiao Gongweihui 1996 Nian Gongzuo Baogaoshu* 马来西亚华校教师会总会 董教总全国发展华小工委会1996年工作报告书 [United Chinese Schoolteachers' Association of Malaysia and *Dongjiaozong* Chinese Primary Schools Working Committee 1996 working report]. Selangor: United Chinese Schoolteachers' Association of Malaysia, 1997.

————. *Malaixiya Huaxiao Jiaoshihui Zonghui Dongjiaozong Quanguo Fazhan Huaxiao Gongweihui 1997 Nian Gongzuo Baogaoshu* 马来西亚华校教师会总会 董教总全国发展华小工委会1997年工作报告书 [United Chinese Schoolteachers' Association of Malaysia and *Dongjiaozong* Chinese Primary Schools Working Committee 1997 working report]. Selangor: United Chinese Schoolteachers' Association of Malaysia, 1998.

————. *Malaixiya Huaxiao Jiaoshihui Zonghui Dongjiaozong Quanguo Fazhan Huaxiao Gongweihui 1998 Nian Gongzuo Baogaoshu* 马来西亚华校教师会总会 董教总全国发展华小工委会1998年工作报告书 [United Chinese Schoolteachers' Association of Malaysia and *Dongjiaozong* Chinese Primary Schools Working Committee 1998 working report]. Selangor: United Chinese Schoolteachers' Association of Malaysia, 1999.

————. *Malaixiya Huaxiao Jiaoshihui Zonghui Dongjiaozong Quanguo Fazhan Huaxiao Gongweihui 1999 Nian Gongzuo Baogaoshu* 马来西亚华校教师会总会 董教总全国发展华小工委会1999年工作报告书 [United Chinese Schoolteachers' Association of Malaysia and *Dongjiaozong* Chinese Primary Schools Working Committee 1999 working report]. Selangor: United Chinese Schoolteachers' Association of Malaysia, 2000.

————. *Malaixiya Huaxiao Jiaoshihui Zonghui Dongjiaozong Quanguo Fazhan Huaxiao Gongweihui 2000 Nian Gongzuo Baogaoshu* 马来西亚华校教师会总会 董教总全国发展华小工委会2000年工作报告书 [United Chinese Schoolteachers' Association of Malaysia and *Dongjiaozong* Chinese Primary Schools Working Committee 2000 working report]. Selangor: United Chinese Schoolteachers' Association of Malaysia, 2001.

————. *Malaixiya Huaxiao Jiaoshihui Zonghui Dongjiaozong Quanguo Fazhan Huaxiao Gongweihui 2001 Nian Gongzuo Baogaoshu* 马来西亚华校教师会总会 董教总全国发展华小工委会2001年工作报告书 [United Chinese Schoolteachers' Association of Malaysia and *Dongjiaozong* Chinese Primary Schools Working Committee 2001 working report]. Selangor: United Chinese Schoolteachers' Association of Malaysia, 2002.

————. *Malaixiya Huaxiao Jiaoshihui Zonghui Dongjiaozong Quanguo Fazhan Huaxiao Gongweihui 2002 Nian Gongzuo Baogaoshu* 马来西亚华校教师会总会 董教总全国发展华小工委会2002年工作报告书 [United Chinese Schoolteachers' Association of Malaysia and *Dongjiaozong* Chinese Primary Schools Working Committee 2002 working report]. Selangor: United Chinese Schoolteachers' Association of Malaysia, 2003.

————. *Malaixiya Huaxiao Jiaoshihui Zonghui Dongjiaozong Quanguo Fazhan Huaxiao Gongweihui 2003 Nian Gongzuo Baogaoshu* 马来西亚华校教师会总会 董教总全国发展华小工委会2003年工作报告书 [United Chinese Schoolteachers' Association of Malaysia and *Dongjiaozong* Chinese Primary Schools Working Committee 2003 working report]. Selangor: United Chinese Schoolteachers' Association of Malaysia, 2004.

———. *Malaixiya Huaxiao Jiaoshihui Zonghui Dongjiaozong Quanguo Fazhan Huaxiao Gongweihui 2004 Nian Gongzuo Baogaoshu* 马来西亚华校教师会总会 董教总全国发展华小工委会2004年工作报告书 [United Chinese Schoolteachers' Association of Malaysia and *Dongjiaozong* Chinese Primary Schools Working Committee 2004 working report]. Selangor: United Chinese Schoolteachers' Association of Malaysia, 2005.

———. *Malaixiya Huaxiao Jiaoshihui Zonghui Dongjiaozong Quanguo Fazhan Huaxiao Gongweihui 2005 Nian Gongzuo Baogaoshu* 马来西亚华校教师会总会 董教总全国发展华小工委会2005年工作报告书 [United Chinese Schoolteachers' Association of Malaysia and *Dongjiaozong* Chinese Primary Schools Working Committee 2005 working report]. Selangor: United Chinese Schoolteachers' Association of Malaysia, 2006.

———. "30 Ren Huo Yixia De Weixing Huaxiao Diaocha Baogao" 30人或以下的微型华小调查报告 [Survey report on Chinese schools with less than thirty students]. Office document. Selangor: United Chinese Schoolteachers' Association of Malaysia, 2007*a*.

———. "Huaxiao Jianxiao, Qianxiao He Weixing Huaxiao Ziliaoji" 华小建校、迁校和微型华小资料集 [Collection of information on constructions and relocations of Chinese primary schools and schools with less than thirty students]. Office document. Selangor: United Chinese Schoolteachers' Association of Malaysia, 2007*b*.

———. *Malaixiya Huaxiao Jiaoshihui Zonghui Dongjiaozong Quanguo Fazhan Huaxiao Gongweihui 2006 Nian Gongzuo Baogaoshu* 马来西亚华校教师会总会 董教总全国发展华小工委会2006年工作报告书 [United Chinese Schoolteachers' Association of Malaysia and *Dongjiaozong* Chinese Primary Schools Development Working Committee 2006 working report]. Selangor: United Chinese Schoolteachers' Association of Malaysia, 2007*c*.

———. "Dongjiaozong Quanguo Fazhan Huawen Xiaoxue Gongzuo Weiyuanhui Jianzhang" 董教总全国发展华文小学工作委员会简章 [Simplified constitution of *Dongjiaozong* National Chinese Primary Schools Development Working Committee]. Office document. Selangor: United Chinese Schoolteachers' Association of Malaysia, 2008*a*.

———. *Malaixiya Huaxiao Jiaoshihui Zonghui Dongjiaozong Quanguo Fazhan Huaxiao Gongweihui 2007 Nian Gongzuo Baogaoshu* 马来西亚华校教师会总会 董教总全国发展华小工委会2007年工作报告书 [United Chinese Schoolteachers' Association of Malaysia and *Dongjiaozong* Chinese Primary Schools Working Committee 2007 working report]. Selangor: United Chinese Schoolteachers' Association of Malaysia, 2008*b*.

———. *Malaixiya Huaxiao Jiaoshihui Zonghui Dongjiaozong Quanguo Fazhan Huaxiao Gongweihui 2008 Nian Gongzuo Baogaoshu* 马来西亚华校教师会总会 董教总全国发展华小工委会2008年工作报告书 [United Chinese Schoolteachers' Association of Malaysia and *Dongjiaozong* Chinese Primary Schools Working Committee 2008 working report]. Selangor: United Chinese Schoolteachers' Association of Malaysia, 2009.

———. *Malaixiya Huaxiao Jiaoshihui Zonghui Dongjiaozong Quanguo Fazhan Huaxiao Gongweihui 2009 Nian Gongzuo Baogaoshu* 马来西亚华校教师会总会 董教总全国发展华小工委会2009年工作报告书 [United Chinese Schoolteachers' Association of Malaysia and *Dongjiaozong* Chinese Primary Schools Working Committee 2009 working report]. Selangor: United Chinese Schoolteachers' Association of Malaysia, 2010.

———. *Malaixiya Huaxiao Jiaoshihui Zonghui Dongjiaozong Quanguo Fazhan Huaxiao Gongweihui 2010 Nian Gongzuo Baogaoshu* 马来西亚华校教师会总会 董教总全国发展华小工委会2010年工作报告书 [United Chinese Schoolteachers' Association of Malaysia and *Dongjiaozong* Chinese Primary Schools Working Committee 2010 working report]. Selangor: United Chinese Schoolteachers' Association of Malaysia, 2011.

———. *Malaixiya Huaxiao Jiaoshihui Zonghui Dongjiaozong Quanguo Fazhan Huaxiao Gongweihui 2011 Nian Gongzuo Baogaoshu* 马来西亚华校教师会总会 董教总全国发展华小工委会2011年工作报告书 [United Chinese Schoolteachers' Association of Malaysia and *Dongjiaozong* Chinese Primary Schools Working Committee 2011 working report]. Selangor: United Chinese Schoolteachers' Association of Malaysia, 2012.

Utusan Malaysia, "Program Sekolah Integrasi" [Integration school program]. 7 August 1985.

———. "Jangan Personal Hak Istimewa Melayu-Aziz" [Aziz: Do not question the special rights of the Malay]. 18 August 2000*a*.

———. "Kerajaan Tidak Akan Berundur Walau Satu Langkah Pun, PM: Hak Melayu Dipertahan" [Prime Minister: The government will defend the Malay rights]. 18 August 2000*b*.

———. "Mencabar Kewibawaan Melayu" [Challenging the Malay authority]. 18 August 2000*c*.

———. "Najib: Jangan Bermain Api Perkauman" [Najib: Do not play with fire on ethnic related issues]. 18 August 2000*d*.

———. "Rakyat Berhak Membuat Tuntutan-Hadi" [Hadi: The people have the right to make claims]. 18 August 2000*e*.

———. "Hak Melayu: Usah Lupa Sejarah" [Malay rights: Do not forget the past]. Headlines. 19 August 2000*a*.

———. "Hentikan Kenyataan Jejas Keharmonian" [Stop all statements that will disrupt harmony]. 19 August 2000*b*.

———. "Pelbagai Pihak Mahu Kerajaan Mempertahankan Hak Melayu" [Multiple parties requested the government to defend the Malay rights]. 19 August 2000*c*.

———. "Rafidah: Jangan Lagi Persoalkan Isu Perkauman" [Rafidah: Stop questioning ethnic related issues]. 19 August 2000*d*.

———. "Gerakan Sokong Hak Keistimewaan Orang Melayu" [Movement to support Malay special rights]. 20 August 2000*a*.

———. "PM: Hak Melayu Ditahan" [Prime Minister: Malay rights are being held hostage]. 20 August 2000*b*.

————. "Hak Melayu Tetap Dipertahan Selagi UMNO Berkuasa" [Malay rights will be defended as long as United Malays National Organisation remains in power]. 21 August 2000*a*.

————. "Melayu Kini Dianggap Lemah" [Malays are perceived as weak]. 21 August 2000*b*.

————. "Melayu Rasa Terancam" [Malays feel threatened]. 21 August 2000*c*.

————. "Pertahankan Kuota Kemasukan Ke University" [Defending the quota for university enrolment]. 21 August 2000*d*.

————. "Tuntutan 17 Perkara Melampaui Batas" [The seventeen appeals exceeded boundaries]. 22 August 2000.

————. "PAS Tuduh Isu Hak Istimewa Melayu Lakonan" [PAS accused the Malay special rights issues as a performance]. 23 August 2000.

Veltmeyer, Henry. *Civil Society and Social Movement: The Dynamics of Intersectoral Alliances and Urban-Rural Linkages in Latin America.* Geneva: United Nations Research Institute for Social Development, 2004.

Vlieland, C.A. *British Malaya: A Report on the 1931 Census and on Certain Problems of Vital Statistics.* England and Malaya: Office of the Crown Agents for the Colonies and Malayan Information Agency, 1932.

von Vorys, Karl. *Democracy without Consensus: Communalism and Political Stability in Malaysia.* Princeton: Princeton University Press, 1975.

Walker, Jack Jr. *Mobilizing Interest Groups in America: Patrons, Professions and Social Movements.* Ann Arbor: University of Michigan Press, 1991.

Wang, Shiow Nan 王秀南. *Xingma Jiaoyu Fanlun* 星马教育泛论 [On education in Malaysia and Singapore]. Singapore: Union Book 友联书局, 1970.

Wazir Jahan Karim. *Women and Culture: Between Malay Adat and Islam.* San Francisco and Oxford: Westview, 1992.

Weiss, Meredith. *Protest and Possibilities.* California: Stanford University Press, 2006.

Weiss, Meredith and Saliha Hassan, eds. *Social Movements in Malaysia.* New York: Taylor and Francis, 2003.

Wilkinson, Paul. *Social Movement.* London: Paul Mall, 1971.

Willford, Andrew. *Cage of Freedom: Tamil Identity and the Ethnic Fetish in Malaysia.* Ann Arbor: University of Michigan Press, 2006.

Wilson, John. *Introduction to Social Movement.* New York: Basic Books, 1973.

Wong, James Wing On. "Language Switch: Imminent UMNO and MCA-Gerakan Showdown". *Malaysiakini*, 21 October 2002 <http://www.malaysiakini.com/opinions/21904> (accessed 9 September 2013).

Wong, Loon. "The State and Organised Labour in West Malaysia". *Journal of Contemporary Asia* 23, no. 2 (1993): 214–37.

Xie, Jing Jing 谢晶晶. "Yi Ganrao Gongzhong Dichu Yinshuafa Weiyou Jingfang Zutuijie Huangse Xingqiliu" 以干扰公众抵触印刷法为由警方阻推介黄色星期六 [Police stopped the launch of Yellow Saturday Campaign on the basis that it will cause public disturbance and it has violated the Printing Act]. *Merdeka Review*, 17 November 2007 <http://www.merdekareview.com/print_news.php?n=5388> (accessed 2 September 2013).

Xinwanbao 新晚报. "Quanguo Huaxiao Yaobake, Xian Anhua 14 Tian Nei Jiejue" 全国华小要罢课, 限安华14天内解决 [All Chinese primary schools in Malaysia will participate in the strike, Anwar is given fourteen days to solve the problem]. 4 October 1987.

Yau, Teck Kong 姚迪刚, ed. *Liutailianzong Tongxunlu 2008–2010* 留台联总通讯录 2008–2010 [Contacts directory of the Federation of Alumni Associations of Taiwan Universities of Malaysia 2008–2010]. Selangor: Federation of Alumni Associations of Taiwan Universities of Malaysia 马来西亚留台校友会联会总会, 2008.

YCSHEC (Yuk Choy School History Editorial Committee 百年育才校史编委会), ed. *Bainian Fengyun: Bainian Yucai Juaner* 百年风云: 百年育才卷二 [Challenges faced: History of Yuk Choy School 2]. Perak: School Committee of Yuk Choy High School 吡叻育才中学独立董事部, 2008.

Yen, Ching Hwang. "Early Chinese Clan Organizations in Singapore and Malaya, 1819–1911". *Journal of Southeast Asian Studies* 12, issue 1 (March 1981): 62–91.

———. "Historical Background". In *The Chinese in Malaysia*, edited by Lee Kam Hing and Tan Chee Beng. New York: Oxford University Press, 2000.

Yeok, Kim Yew. "Education, National Identity and National Integration: A Survey of Secondary School Students of Chinese Origin in Urban Peninsular Malaysia". Ph.D. dissertation, California Stanford University, 1982.

Zainal Abidin Ahmad. "Educational Reform and Ethnic Response: A Historical Study of the Development of a National System of Education in West Malaysia". Ph.D. dissertation, Los Angeles University of California, 1980.

Zakaria Ahmad. "Malaysia: Quasi Democracy in a Divided Society". In *Democracy in Developing Countries: Asia* 3, edited by Larry Diamond, Juan J. Linz, and Seymour Martin Lipset. Boulder: Lynne Rienner, 1989.

Zald, Mayer. "Looking Backward to Look Forward: Reflections on the Past and Future of the Resource Mobilization Research Program". In *Frontiers in Social Movement Theory*, edited by Carol Mueller and Aldon Morris. New Haven: Yale University Press, 1992.

Zald, Mayer and Roberta Ash. "Social Movement Organizations: Growth, Decay and Change". In *Studies in Social Movements: A Social Psychological Perspectives*, edited by Barry McLaughlin. New York: Free Press, 1969.

Zeng, Rong Cheng 曾荣盛 et al. *Malaixiya Fujianren Xingxue Banxiao Shiliaoji* 马来西亚福建人兴学办教史料集 [Collection of materials on the founding and maintaining of Chinese schools by Hokkien Chinese in Malaysia]. Kuala Lumpur: Federation of Hokkien Associations Malaysia 马来西亚福建社团联合会, 1993.

Zhan, Yuan Duan 詹缘端. "Linhuangsheng, Malaixiya Huawen Jiaoyu De Wuming Yingxiong" 林晃升, 马来西亚华文教育的无名英雄 [Lim Fong Seng, the unknown hero of Chinese education movement]. In *Chuangye Yu Hugen:*

Malaixiya Huaren Lishi Renwu Rushangpian 创业与护根: 马来西亚华人历史与人物儒商篇 [Malaysian Chinese history and personalities: The entrepreneurial elites], edited by Lim Chooi Kwa 林水濠. Kuala Lumpur: Centre for Malaysian Chinese Studies, 2003.

Zhang, Guo Hao 张国豪. "Yixiaocuo Xiaozhang Jiegu Xiang Dongzong Kaihuo De Muhou Yuanyin" 一小撮校长借故向董总'开火'的幕后原因 [Hidden factors that prompt some school principals to attack the United Chinese School Committees' Association of Malaysia]. *Merdeka Review*, 27 February 2006 <http://www.merdekareview.com/print_news.php?n=1260> (accessed 4 September 2013).

Zhang, Jing Liang 张景良, ed. *Memorandum Kebudayaan Kebangsaan Keluaran Khas (Bahasa Cina, Bahasa Inggeris dan Bahasa Malaysia)* 国家文化备忘录特辑: 华文、英文及国文 [Special edition on Memorandum on National Cultural Policy in Chinese, English, and Malay]. Kuala Lumpur: Fifteen Leading Chinese Guilds and Associations of Malaysia, 1983.

Zhen, Gong 甄供, *Boxia Chunfeng Wanli: Bilizhou Huawen Duzhong Fuxingyundong Jishi* 播下春风万里: 吡叻州华文独中复兴运动纪实 [Documentary of Perak independent Chinese secondary schools revival movement]. Selangor: United Chinese School Committees' Association of Malaysia, 1996.

———. *Huajiao Chunlei Linhuangsheng* 华教春雷林晃升 [Lim Fong Seng: The exceptional leader of Chinese education movement]. Selangor: United Chinese School Committees' Association of Malaysia, 2006.

Zhuan, Zhao Sheng 庄兆声. *Malaixiya Jichu Jiaoyu* 马来西亚基础教育 [The fundamental education in Malaysia]. Guangzhou: Guangdong Jiaoyu 广东教育, 2004.

Zirakzadeh, Cyrus. *Social Movements in Politics: A Comparative Study*. London: Longman, 1997.

Zurcher, Louis and Russell Curtis. "A Comparative Analysis of Propositions Describing Social Movement Organizations". *The Sociological Quarterly* 14, no. 2 (Spring 1973): 175–88.

GLOSSARY OF NON-ENGLISH TEXT

affiliated independent Chinese secondary schools
(国民型华文中学董事部兼办独立中学)

Alliance of Fifteen Leading Chinese Guilds and Associations
(全国十五华团领导机构)

Alliance of Seven Chinese Education-Related Guilds and Associations
(华教界七华团)

Alliance of Three campaign (三结合)

appointed standing committee members (委任委员务)

Association of Chinese Chambers of Commerce and Industry of Malaysia
(马来西亚中华总商会)

Awareness Campaign for Chinese Primary Schools' School Committees
(华小董事觉醒运动)

Beijing Normal University (北京师范大学)

Bock Tai Hee (莫泰熙)

Campaign to Strengthen the Role of School Committees in Chinese
Primary Schools (强化华小董事会运动)

Cantonese (广东话)

Centre for Malaysian Chinese Studies (华社研究中心)

Chai Yah Han (蔡亚汉)

Chairman (主席/董事长)

Chairmen Group (主席团)

Chen Li Qun (陈利群)

Chen Wing Sum (曾永森)

Cheng Ho University (郑和大学)

Cheng Ji Mou (陈济谋)

Chew Saw Eng (周素英)

Chian Heng Kai (陈庆佳)

Chiew Swee Peow Chinese Education Trust Fund (周瑞标教育基金)

Chin Choong Sang (陈松生)

Chin Peng (陈平)

Chinese (华文)

Chinese Cultural Congress (全国华人文化节)

Chinese Education Card (华教卡)

Chinese Education Festival (华教节)

Chinese Education Torch Relay (华教火炬行)

Chinese Education Working Committee (华教工作委员会)

Chinese guilds and associations (华人社团)

Chinese new villages (新村)

Chinese primary schools (华文小学)

Chinese Resource and Research Centre (华社资料研究中心)

Chinese schoolteachers' associations (华人教师公会)

Chinese secondary schools (华文中学)

Chinese Solidarity Conventions (全国华人团结大会)

Chong Chin Shoong (张征雄)

Chong Joon Kin (张永庆)

Chong Khoon Lin (张崑灵)

Chong King Liong (张景良)

Chong Min Chang (钟敏章)

Choong Ee Hoong (钟一泓)

Choong Pai Chee (庄白绮)

Choong Wei Chuan (钟伟前)

Chung Hwa Confucian High School (孔圣庙中华中学)

Chung Ling High School (钟灵中学)

Civilisational Islam (*Islam hadhari*)

Coalition for Clean and Fair Election (*Gabungan Pilihanraya Bersih dan Adil*)

Confucian Secondary School (尊孔中学)

Convention of Chinese Guilds and Associations Against the Invasion of Rights (华团反侵略大会)

Converted Chinese School Principals' Association (国民型中学校长理事会)

converted Chinese secondary schools (国民型华文中学)

Council of Perak Chinese School Committees (吡叻华校董事会联合会)

David Chen (陈充恩)

death is better than life with humiliation (士可杀不可辱)

Department of Curriculum (课程局)

Department of Publication (出版局)

Ding Pin Song (丁品松)

Dongjiaozong (董教总)

Dongjiaozong Chinese Primary Schools Working Committee (董教总全国发展华小工作委员会)

Dongjiaozong Converted Chinese Secondary Schools Working Committee (董教总全国国民型中学工作委员会)

Dongjiaozong Higher Learning Centre (董教总教育中心)

Dongjiaozong Higher Learning Centre and New Era College Development Fund (董教总教育中心基金, 新纪元学院建设及发展基金)

Dongjiaozong's opinion on the Malaysia Education Blueprint 2006–2010 (董教总对2006至2010年教育发展大蓝图总体意见书)

Dongjiaozong's overall opinion on the Malaysia Education Blueprint 2001–2010 (董教总对2001至2010年教育发展大蓝图总体意见书)

Dongzong (马来西亚华校董事联合会总会)

Education Act Advisory Council (*Majlis Perundangan Akta Pendidikan*)

Education Research Center (教育研究中心)

Eng Ling Chinese Primary School (永宁华文小学)

Er Joo Tiong (余裕忠)

Federation of Alumni Associations of Taiwan Universities of Malaysia (马来西亚留台校友会联会总会)

Federation of Chinese Associations Malaysia (马来西亚中华大会堂总会)

Federation of Hainan Association Malaysia (马来西亚海南公会联合会)

Federation of Hakka Association Malaysia (马来西亚客家公会联合会)

Federation of Hokkien Association Malaysia (马来西亚福建社团联合会)

Federation of Kwangtung Association Malaysia (马来西亚广东会馆联合会)

Federation of Malaya Chinese Guilds Association
(马来亚华人行业社团总会)

Federation of Malaya Chinese Senior Normal Graduate Teachers' Union
(高师职总)

Federation of Teochew Association Malaysia (马来西亚潮州公会联合会)

financial management committee (*lembaga pengurus kewangan*)

Fong Chan Onn (冯镇安)

Foo Wan Thot (胡万铎)

Foon Yew High School (宽柔中学)

general officer (座办)

general secretary (总务)

Goh Chee Yan (吴志渊)

going beyond political party but not beyond politics
(超越政党, 不超越政治)

Grand Three Associations of Chinese Education
(三大机构华文教育中央委员会)

Grand Three Associations of Chinese Education's National Convention
of Chinese Education in Malaya (三大机构华文教育中央委员会全国
华文教育大会)

Gu Hsing Kuang (顾兴光)

Guangxi Association Malaysia (马来西亚广西公会总会)

*Guiding Principles of Educational Reform of Malaysian Independent Chinese
Secondary Schools* (独中教育改革纲领)

Guiding Principles of Malaysian Independent Chinese Secondary Schools
(华文独立中学建议书)

Hainanese (海南)

Hakka (客家)

Han Chiang High School (韩江中学)

Handbook for Chinese Education Workers (华教工作者手册)

hanyupinyin (汉语拼音)

Harmony and Union University (协和大学)

Higher Education in China Exhibition (中国高等教育展)

Hokkien (福建话)

Hon Choon Kim (韩春锦)

Hong Leong Group (丰隆集团)

Hong Woan Ying (孔婉莹)

Hoo Huo Shan (胡火山)

Hou Heng Hua (侯亨桦)

Hou Kok Chung (何国忠)

Hua Lian High School (太平华联中学)

Huang Guan Qin (黄冠钦)

Huang Yun Yue (黄润岳)

Huang Zhao Fa (黄招发)

Huang Zhen Bu (黄振部)

Independent Chinese secondary schools (华文独立中学)

Independent Chinese Secondary Schools Education Alliance
(独中教育联盟)

Independent Chinese Secondary Schools Development Committee
(独中发展小组)

Independent Chinese Secondary Schools Development Sponsorship Program
(全国华文独中发展基金常年赞助人)

Independent Chinese Secondary Schools Principal' Association
(独中校长理事会)

Integrated Schools Project (*Rancangan Sekolah Integrasi*)

Jiaozong (马来西亚华校教师会总会)

Join BN, Rectify BN (打进国阵, 纠正国阵)

Joint Conference of Chinese School Committees and Schoolteachers'
Representatives in Federation of Malaya with MCA Representatives
(联合邦华校董教代表及马华公会代表联席会议)

Joint Declaration of National Chinese Guilds and Associations
(全国华团联合宣言)

Kajang Fah Kiew Chinese School (加影华侨学校产业受托会)

Kakyo Shukusei (purge through purification)

Kang Chin Seng (江真诚)

Kang Siew Khoon (江秀坤)

Kelantan Chung Wah Independent High School (吉兰丹中华独立中学)

Kerk Choo Ting (郭洙镇)

Khew Khing Ling (丘琼润)

Khing Ming Chinese Primary School (竞明华文小学)

Khoo Kay Peng (邱继炳)

Khoo Seong Chi (邱祥炽)

Kluang Chong Hwa High School (居銮中华中学)

Koh Tsu Koon (许子根)

Ku Hung Ting (古鸿廷)

Kua Kia Soong (柯嘉逊)

Kuala Lumpur and Selangor Chinese Assembly Hall
(吉隆坡暨雪兰莪中华大会堂)

Kuala Lumpur Chen Moh Chinese Primary School (吉隆坡精武华文小学)

Kuala Lumpur University (吉隆坡大学)

Kuang Hee Pang (邝其芳)

Kuen Cheng High School (坤成中学)

Kuomintang (国民党)

Kwongwahyitpoh (光华日报)

Ladang Hillside Chinese Primary School (丘晒园华文小学)

Lau Pak Kuan (刘伯群)

Lee Ban Chen (李万千)

Lee Chang Jing (李长景)

Lee Foundation (李氏基金)

Lee Hau Shik (李孝式)

Lee Hing (吕兴)

Lee Kim Sai (李金狮)

Lee Leong Sze (利亮时)

Lee San Choon (李三春)

Lee Thean Hin (李天兴)

Leong Tzi Liang (林子量)

Leong Yew Koh (梁宇皋)

Leung Cheung Ling (梁长龄)

Lew Bon Hoi (廖文辉)

Li Da Ting (李达庭)

Li Hui Jin (李惠衿)

Li Yi Qiang (李毅强)

Li Yue Tong (李岳通)

Liang Sheng Yi (梁胜义)

Lick Hung Chinese Primary School (力行华文小学)

Liew Kan Ba (刘崇汉)

Lim Chong Eu (林苍佑)

Lim Fong Seng (林晃升)

Lim Geok Chan (林玉静)

Lim Keng Yaik (林敬益)

Lim Kit Siang (林吉祥)

Lim Lian Geok (林连玉)

Lim Lian Geok Award (林连玉精神奖)

Lim Lian Geok Cultural Development Center (林连玉基金会)

Lim Ming King (林明镜)

Lin Mei Yan (林美燕)

Lin Wu Cong (林武聪)

Lin Yu Lian (林玉莲)

Ling Liong Sik (林良实)

Liu Bo Kui (刘伯奎)

Liu Huai Gu (刘怀谷)

Loot Ting Yee (陆庭瑜)

Low Sik Thong (刘锡通)

Mah Cheok Tat (马卓达)

Malacca Chinese Education and Progressive Association
(马六甲华校董事会联合会)

Malacca Chinese Schoolteachers' Association (马六甲华校教师公会)

Malaya Chinese Senior Normal Graduate Teachers' Union
(马来亚联合邦华文高级师范)

Malaya in Oppose on the Conversion of Vernacular Schools into
National Schools (教总反对改方言学校为国民学校宣言)

Malaysian Chinese Association (马来西亚华人公会)

Malaysian Chinese Organisations' Election Appeals Committee
(马来西亚华人社团大选诉求委员会)

Malaysian Federated San Kiang Association (马来西亚三江总会)

Malaysian Independent Chinese Secondary Schools Working Committee
(董教总全国发展华文独立中学工作委员会)

Malaysian National Primary Syllabus (*Kurikulum Bersepadu Sekolah Rendah*)

Malaysian People's Movement Party (*Parti Gerakan Rakyat Malaysia*)

Malaysian Qualifications Agency (*Agensi Kelayakan Malaysia*)

Malaysian Seven Major Clans Associations (七大乡团协调委员会)

Management Handbook for Chinese Primary Schools (华小管理机制指南)

MCA Central Working Committee (马华中央工作委员会)

Memorandum for the Return of Vernacular Education
(还我母语教育各忘录)

Memorandum of Demands on Chinese Education by Chinese Citizens
in the Federation (本邦华人对教育总要求)

Memorandum of Joint Declaration of National Chinese Guilds and
Associations (贯彻华团联合宣言)

Memorandum on National Cultural Policy (国家文化备忘录)

Memorandum Submitted by the United Chinese Schoolteachers'
Association of Malaya in Opposition of the Conversion of Vernacular
Schools into National Schools (教总反对改方言学校为国民学校宣言)

Memorandum Submitted by the United Chinese Schoolteachers'
Association of Malaysian Higher School Certificate
(*Sijil Tinggi Persekolahan Malaysia*)

Memorandum to Acquire for Citizenship by Representatives of
Chinese Associations and Guilds in The Federation of Malaya
(马来亚联合邦华人社团代表争取公民权宣言)

Memorandum to the Prime Minister for a Rightful Place of the
Chinese Language (为争取华文地位向首相东姑阿都拉曼呈送备忘录)

Merdeka College (独立学院)

Merdeka University (独立大学)

Merdeka University Formation Working Committee
(马来西亚独立大学筹备工作委员会)

Merdeka University Founders' Assembly (马来亚独立大学发起人大会)

Merdeka University (Limited) Company (独立大学有限公司)

Movement to Eliminate Teaching and Learning Science and Mathematics in English Program (*Gerakan Mansuhkan Pengakaran dan Pembelajaran Sains dan Metematik dalam Bahasa Inggeris*)

Muslim Youth Movement of Malaysia (*Angkatan Belia Islam Malaysia*)

Nanyang University (南洋大学)

Nanyang University Alumni Association of Malaya (马来亚南大校友会)

Nanyangshangpao (南洋商报)

National Accreditation Board (*Lembaga Akreditasi Negara*)

National Chinese Civic Rights Committee (全国华团民权委员会)

National Chinese Guilds and Associations Cultural Program (全国华团文化工作总纲领)

National Chinese Guilds and Associations Cultural Working Committee (全国华团文化工作委员会)

National Conference for Independent Chinese Secondary Schools Development (全国发展华文独中运动大会)

National Convention of Chinese Schoolteachers' Associations in Malaya (全马教师公会代表大会)

National Convention of Chinese School Committees and Schoolteachers (全国华校董教大会)

National Convention on Expansion of Chinese Education (全马华文教育扩大会议)

National Cultural Policy (*Dasar Kebudayaan Negara*)

National Economic Advisory Council (*Majlis Perundingan Ekonomi Negara*)

National Front coalition (*Barisan Nasional*)

National Independent Chinese Secondary Schools Development Fund (全国华文独中发展基金)

National Seminar for Converted Chinese Secondary Schools' School Committees (全国国民型中学董事交流会)

National Union of Heads of Schools (全国校长职工会)

national-type primary schools (国民型小学)

Negeri Sembilan Chinese School Committees Council (森美兰华校董事会联合会)

Negeri Sembilan Chinese Schoolteachers' Association (森美兰华校教师公会)

New Era College (新纪元学院)

New Era College Sponsorship Program (新纪元学院发展基金赞助人)

Newsletter on Chinese education (华教导报)

Ng Wei Siong (吴维湘)

Ngan Ching Wen (颜清文)

Ngeow Yin Ngee (饶仁毅)

Ong Ka Ting (黄家定)

Ong Keng Seng (王景成)

Ong Kow Ee (王超群)

Ong Tin Kim (王添庆)

One-Person, One-Dollar for Merdeka University Legal Fee
(一人一元独大法律基金)

Organizational Rules and Regulations of the Malaysian Independent Chinese Secondary Schools Working Committee
(董教总全国发展华文独立中学运动工作委员会组织规章)

Pan-Malaysian Islamic Party (*Parti Islam Semalaysia*)

Pang Chong Leong (彭忠良)

Pang Siew Fian (冯秋萍)

Penang and Province Wellesley United Chinese School Management Association (槟威华校董事会联合会)

Penang Chinese Education Working Committee
(槟城州华文教育工作委员会)

Penang Chinese Girls' High School (槟华女中)

Penang Chinese School Alumni Association (槟州华校校友会联合会)

Penang Chinese Schoolteachers' Association (槟城华校教师会)

People's Alliance (*Pakatan Rakyat*)

People's Coalition (*Gagasan Rakyat*)

People's Justice Party (*Parti Keadilan Rakyat*)

Perak Independent Chinese Secondary Schools Development Working Committee (吡叻州发展华文独中工作委员会)

Perak United State-Level Chinese Schoolteachers' Association
(吡叻州华校教师会联合会)

Petition for Incorporation Order for the Establishment of Merdeka University (呈最高元首请求恩准创办独立大学请愿书)

pine tree-planting ceremony (百万松柏献华教)

Poi Lam High School (培南独中)

presidential association (主席区)

Professional Teaching Program (教育专业系)

promotion of the dual coalition system (两线制)

Proposals on the Draft of the 1990 Education Act
(对1990年教育法令草案的修改建议)

Protest Assembly of National Chinese Guilds and Associations and
Political Parties (全国华团政党抗议大会议)

Pua Eng Chong (潘永忠)

Quek Leng Chan (郭令灿)

Quek Suan Hiang (郭全强)

Red Bands of the Holy War (*Sabillah*)

Reform (*reformasi*)

*Sample of Working Guidelines for Malaysia Chinese Primary School
Committee* (马来西亚华文小学董事会工作手册样本)

Second Conference of the Pan-Malayan Chinese Schoolteachers'
Association (全马教师公会第二次代表大会)

Second Joint Conference of Chinese School Committees and
Schoolteachers' Representatives in Federation of Malaya with MCA
Representatives (联合邦华校董教代表及马华公会代表第二次联席会议)

Segamat Central Site Chinese Primary School (中央华文小学)

Sekolah Menengah Pei Yuan (Private) KPR (培元独中)

Sekolah Menengah San Min (Suwa) (安顺三民独中)

Sekolah Menengah Yik Ching Yik Ching (育青中学)

Sekolah Tinggi Nan Hwa Ayer Tawar (南华独中)

Selangor Chinese Assembly Hall (雪兰莪中华大会堂)

Selangor Development Corporation (*Perbadanan Kemajuan Negeri Selangor*)

Selangor Hokkien Association (雪兰莪福建会馆)

Selangor Petaling Jaya District Chinese Primary Schools Parents
Association (八打灵县华小家长会)

Seminar of National Chinese Leaders in Malaya (全马华人领袖座谈会)

Seminar on Independent Chinese Secondary Schools (华文独中研讨会)

senior normal graduate schoolteachers (华文高级师范毕业教师)

Sha Yun Yeo (沙渊如)

Shen Jai High School (深斋中学)

Shen Ting (沈亭)

Shum Thin Khee (沈天奇)

Sinchew Daily (星洲日报)

social organization (社团)

Sons of the earth (*bumiputeras*)

Soo Thien Ming (苏天明)

Soon Jian Chinese Primary School (循然华文小学)

South China Normal University (华南师范大学)

Southeast Asia Chinese Education Bulletin (东南亚华文教育通讯)

Southeast Asian Chinese Language Teaching Convention
(东南亚华文教学研讨会)

Southern College (南方学院)

Sponsorship Program for Chinese Primary Schools Development
(全国华文小学发展基金常年赞助人)

state level Chinese assembly halls (华人大会堂)

state level Chinese school committees' associations (董事联合会)

State of Johore Chinese School Managers and Teachers' Association
(柔佛州华校董教联合会)

Suggestions on the Ninth Malaysia Plan (第九大马计划的建议书)

Tan Ai Mei (陈爱梅)

Tan Cheng Lock (陈祯禄)

Tan Cheng Lock University (陈祯禄大学)

Tan Kah Kee (陈嘉庚)

Tan Seng Giaw (陈胜尧)

Tan Siew Sin (陈修信)

Tan Tai Kim (陈大锦)

Tan Tiong Hai (陈东海)

Tan Yew Sing (陈友信)

Tang Ah Chai (陈亚才)

Tang Tze Ying (陈子鹦)

Tay Lian Soo (郑良树)

Teachers' Journal (教师杂志)

Teaching and Learning Science and Mathematics in English Program
(*Pengajaran dan Pembelajaran Sains dan Matematik dalam Bahasa Inggeris*)

Teaching of Chinese Language to Non-Chinese Teachers (对外汉语教学)

Teh Hon Seng (郑云城)

Teng Chang Khim (邓章钦)

Teochew (潮州)

Tew Say Kop (张志开)

Thousand Men Fundraising Dinner in December 1996 (1214千万心宴)

Thuang Pik King (庄迪君)

Tiananmen Square (天安门广场)

Tianhou Temple (天后宫)

Toh Kin Woon (杜乾焕)

Too Joon Hing (朱运兴)

Torch Movement (火炬运动)

Treasurer (财政)

Tsun Jin High School (循人中学)

Tsung Wah Private Secondary School (崇华中学)

Tun Tan Cheng Lock Chinese Primary School (陈祯禄华文小学)

Tunku Abdul Rahman College (拉曼学院)

Tunku Abdul Rahman University (拉曼大学)

Unified Curriculum Subcommittee (独中统一课程编委会)

Unified Examination Certificate (华文独中高初中统一考试)

Unified Examination Subcommittee (独中统一考试委员会)

Unified Federation of Malaysian Chinese Assembly Hall
(马来西亚中华大会堂联合会)

United Chinese School Alumni Association (华校校友会联合会总会)

United Chinese School Committees' Association of Malaysia
(马来西亚华校董事联合会总会)

United Chinese School Committees' Association of Selangor and Kuala
Lumpur (雪兰莪暨吉隆坡联邦直辖区华校董事会联合会)

United Chinese Schoolteachers' Association of Malaysia
(马来西亚华校教师会总会)

United Malays National Organisation (*Pertubuhan Kebangsaan Melayu Bersatu*)

Vision Schools Project (*Rancangan Sekolah Wawasan*)

Wai Sin Chinese Primary School in Perak (维新华文小学)

Wang Guo Feng (王国丰)

Wang Siow Nan (王秀南)

Wang Wen Han (王文汉)

Wang Yoon Nien (汪永年)

Weeding Operation (*Operasi Lalang*)

Wen Tien Kuang (温典光)

Wong Wai Keat (黄伟豪)

Wu Teh Yao (吴德耀)

Xiamen University Nanyang Research Institute Project (厦门大学南洋研究院研究计划案)

Xu Min Yan (余明炎)

Yan Yuan Zhang (严元章)

Yang Pei Keng (杨培根)

Yang Qing Liang (杨清亮)

Yang Ya Ling (杨雅灵)

Yang Yin Chong (杨应俊)

Yap Hon Kiat (叶翰杰)

Yap Sin Tian (叶新田)

Ye Hong En (叶鸿恩)

Ye Xia Guang (叶夏光)

Yeoh Ban Eng (杨万荣)

yi (义)

Yong Xu Ling (杨旭龄)

Yoong Suan (杨泉)

Yow Lee Fung (姚丽芳)

Yuk Choy High School (Private) (育才独立中学)

Zeng Dun Hua (曾敦化)

Zhang Xi Chong (张喜崇)

INDEX

F

Federation of Alumni Associations of Taiwan Universities of Malaysia (马来西亚留台校友会联会总会), 113, 121–22

Federation of Chinese Associations Malaysia (马来西亚中华大会堂总会), 116, 120–22

Federation of Malaya Chinese Guilds Association (马来亚华人行业社团总会), 50–51, 54, 58

Federation of Malaysia (1963), 21, 57

Fenn-Wu Report (*Chinese Schools and the Education of Chinese Malayans*), 43

Fong Chan Onn (冯镇安), 91

Foo Wan Thot (胡万铎), 114–16, 126, 144, 157, 168

fundraising campaigns, 80–81, 118, 172–73

G

General Ne Win's military regime (Burma), 21

Gerakan, 22, 30, 61, 92, 106–107, 115, 118, 120, 175–76

Goh Chee Yan (吴志渊), 48

going beyond political party but not beyond politics (超越政党, 不超越政治), 110

Grand Three Associations of Chinese Education (三大机构华文教育中央委员会), 4, 45–49, 52, 54, 59, 62, 71, 135, 167

Grand Three Associations of Chinese Education's National Convention of Chinese Education in Malaya (三大机构华文教育中央委员会全国华文教育大会), 53

grassroots movement (Thailand), 14–15

Gu Hsing Kuang (顾兴光), 62

Guiding Principles of Educational Reform of Malaysian Independent Chinese Secondary Schools (独中教育改革纲领), 141

Guiding Principles of Malaysian Independent Chinese Secondary Schools (华文独立中学建议书), 136

GuocoLand Industries, 156

H

Han Chiang High School (韩江中学), 52

Handbook for Chinese Education Workers (华教工作者手册), 88

hanyupinyin (汉语拼音), 33

Higher Education in China Exhibition (中国高等教育展), 152

Hindu Rights Action Force, 26, 124

Hokkien (福建话), 31, 44

Hon Choon Kim (韩春锦), 123

Hong Leong Group, 156

Hoo Huo Shan (胡火山), 88

Hope Foundation, 118

Hou Kok Chung (何国忠), 157

Huang Guan Qin (黄冠钦), 29

Huang Yun Yue (黄润岳), 56

Huang Zhao Fa (黄招发), 27

Hume Industries, 156

hybrid regimes, 12–13

I

inclusive-based social movements, 23–24

independent Chinese secondary schools (华文独立中学), 56, 134–42

achievements and operation, 141

organizational chart, 137

student distribution in Malaysia, 140

three levels of schoolteachers, 139

ABOUT THE AUTHOR

Ang, Ming Chee wrote *Institutions and Social Mobilization: The Chinese Education Movement in Malaysia, 1951–2011* as her doctoral dissertation at the National University of Singapore. She is now a postdoctoral fellow at Lund University, Sweden and continues researching on politics, people, and protests in Southeast Asia. Her works consists of rich indigenous and important bottom-up empirical evidence, with a special focus on collective identity based on ethnicity, culture, and religion. Her other works include "Social Mobilization of the Underdogs: The Damansara Save Our School Movement in Malaysia", *Pacific Affairs* 85, no. 2 (June 2012): 313–33. She can be contacted at angmingchee@gmail.com.